# Dynamic Analysis
# of Open Economies

# Dynamic Analysis of Open Economies

**MASANAO AOKI**
*Department of System Science*
*School of Engineering and Applied Science*
*University of California, Los Angeles*
*Los Angeles, California*

 1981

**ACADEMIC PRESS**
A Subsidiary of Harcourt Brace Jovanovich, Publishers
New York   London   Toronto   Sydney   San Francisco

COPYRIGHT © 1981, BY ACADEMIC PRESS, INC.
ALL RIGHTS RESERVED.
NO PART OF THIS PUBLICATION MAY BE REPRODUCED OR
TRANSMITTED IN ANY FORM OR BY ANY MEANS, ELECTRONIC
OR MECHANICAL, INCLUDING PHOTOCOPY, RECORDING, OR ANY
INFORMATION STORAGE AND RETRIEVAL SYSTEM, WITHOUT
PERMISSION IN WRITING FROM THE PUBLISHER.

ACADEMIC PRESS, INC.
111 Fifth Avenue, New York, New York 10003

*United Kingdom Edition published by*
ACADEMIC PRESS, INC. (LONDON) LTD.
24/28 Oval Road, London NW1 7DX

```
Library of Congress Cataloging in Publication Data

Aoki, Masanao.
   Dynamic analysis of open economies.

   Bibliography:  p.
   Includes index.
   1. Statics and dynamics (Social sciences)  2. Economic
policy--Mathematical models.  3. International economic
relations--Mathematical models.  4. Foreign exchange--
Mathematical models.  I. Title.
   HB145.A58           339.5         80-2763
ISBN  0-12-058940-0                  AACR2
```

PRINTED IN THE UNITED STATES OF AMERICA

81 82 83 84    9 8 7 6 5 4 3 2 1

*To the Memory of My Father*

# Contents

*Preface* xiii
*Scope of the Investigation* xvii
*Notation* xxi
*List of Symbols* xxv

### Part One ANALYTICAL CONCEPTS AND TOOLS OF COMPARATIVE DYNAMIC ANALYSIS

### 1 State-Space Representation of Dynamic Models

| | | |
|---|---|---|
| 1.1 | Analytical Models | 3 |
| 1.2 | State-Space Representation | 5 |
| 1.3 | Notion of Equilibrium and Long-Run Policy Implications | 7 |
| 1.4 | Example: A Balanced Growth Path of a Small Open Economy | 9 |

### 2 Variational Methods in Comparative Dynamic Analysis

| | | |
|---|---|---|
| 2.1 | Introduction | 12 |
| 2.2 | Reference Time Paths | 14 |
| 2.3 | Variational Equations | 15 |
| 2.4 | Sensitivity Analysis | 23 |

### 3 Variational Dynamic Equation: An Example of Fiscal Policy in a Macroeconomic Model

| | | |
|---|---|---|
| 3.1 | Model | 31 |
| 3.2 | Momentary Equilibrium | 32 |
| 3.3 | Dynamics | 33 |
| 3.4 | Long-Run Equilibrium | 33 |

vii

|     |                                                                 |    |
| --- | --------------------------------------------------------------- | -- |
| 3.5 | Variational Relations: Shifting Momentary Equilibrium           | 34 |
| 3.6 | Variational Dynamics                                            | 37 |
|     | Appendix                                                        | 40 |

## 4 Dynamic Policy Multipliers (Impulse Response Functions)

|     |                                                |    |
| --- | ---------------------------------------------- | -- |
| 4.1 | Dynamic Multipliers of Continuous Time Models  | 41 |
| 4.2 | Discrete-Time Policy Multiplier                | 45 |
| 4.3 | Multiplier in a Small Open Economy: An Example | 45 |

## 5 How to Evaluate Structural Differences: Application of Perturbation Theory

|     |                                                             |    |
| --- | ----------------------------------------------------------- | -- |
| 5.1 | Basic Procedure                                             | 52 |
| 5.2 | Structural Perturbation Method                              | 55 |
| 5.3 | Choice of State Vectors in Models of Interdependent Economies | 58 |
| 5.4 | Example: Effects of Trade on National Incomes               | 59 |

## 6 Controllability and Theory of Economic Policy

|     |                                     |    |
| --- | ----------------------------------- | -- |
| 6.1 | Controllability                     | 65 |
| 6.2 | Path Controllability                | 67 |
| 6.3 | Policies with No Spill-Over Effects | 69 |
| 6.4 | Stabilizability                     | 69 |
| 6.5 | Example                             | 71 |

## 7 Linkages of National Economies

|     |                       |    |
| --- | --------------------- | -- |
| 7.1 | Introduction          | 73 |
| 7.2 | Interest Rate Linkage | 74 |
| 7.3 | Price Linkages        | 74 |
| 7.4 | Terms-of-Trade Linkage | 76 |
| 7.5 | Expectations          | 77 |

## 8 Sources of Dynamics and Their Interactions

|     |                                                                                          |    |
| --- | ---------------------------------------------------------------------------------------- | -- |
| 8.1 | Variational Dynamic Equations                                                            | 80 |
| 8.2 | Example 1: A Small Open Economy with Full Employment and Purchasing Power Parity         | 84 |
| 8.3 | Regressive Expectations and Consistency cum Stability                                    | 93 |
| 8.4 | Example 2: Effects of Bond-Financed Budget Deficit on Short-Run Stability                | 97 |

Contents

## Part Two  SMALL OPEN ECONOMIES

### 9 A Growing Economy: Influences of Capital Growth on the Dynamic Multiplier

| | | |
|---|---|---|
| 9.1 | The Model | 107 |
| 9.2 | Fiscal Multipliers | 115 |
| 9.3 | Numerical Example | 117 |
| 9.4 | Discussions and Summaries | 118 |

### 10 Stabilization Policies in a Small Open Economy

| | | |
|---|---|---|
| 10.1 | The Model | 121 |
| 10.2 | Long-Run Equilibrium | 122 |
| 10.3 | Variational Differential Equations | 124 |
| 10.4 | Short-Run Stability of the Variational Dynamics | 128 |
| 10.5 | Policy Reaction Functions | 130 |
| | Appendix 1  Deviation of the Expression for $e$ | 131 |
| | Appendix 2  Variational IS Curve | 132 |

### 11 Short-Run Comparative Dynamic Analysis of a Small Open Economy with Variable Wage Rates

| | | |
|---|---|---|
| 11.1 | The Model | 137 |
| 11.2 | Long-Run Equilibrium | 141 |
| 11.3 | Short-Run Analysis | 142 |
| 11.4 | Are Variable Wage Rates More Inflationary? An Example of Structural Perturbation Analysis | 159 |
| 11.5 | Numerical Examples | 163 |
| 11.6 | Elaborations | 166 |
| | Appendix  The Variational Disposable Income Expression | 169 |

## Part Three  MULTIPLE-COUNTRY MODELS OF THE WORLD

### 12 Two-Country Model: A Preliminary Analysis

| | | |
|---|---|---|
| 12.1 | Implications of Structural Differences | 177 |
| 12.2 | Distributional Effects of Monetary Policies | 185 |

### 13 Monetary Policies in a Two-Country Model of the World

| | | |
|---|---|---|
| 13.1 | Introduction | 188 |
| 13.2 | Structural Perturbation Analysis | 192 |

|       |                                                                                  |     |
| ----- | -------------------------------------------------------------------------------- | --- |
| 13.3  | Policy Sensitivity and Distributional Effects                                    | 194 |
| 13.4  | The Model                                                                        | 200 |
| 13.5  | Reduced Form Equations of the Reference Variational Model $\mathscr{VM}_0$       | 203 |
| 13.6  | Dynamics of the Reference Model                                                  | 208 |
| 13.7  | Dynamics of $\mathscr{VM}$                                                       | 211 |
| 13.8  | Policy Effects                                                                   | 215 |
| 13.9  | Elaborations on the Basic Model                                                  | 221 |
| 13.10 | Numerical Examples                                                               | 223 |
|       | Appendix  Calculation of the Averages and the Differences                        | 240 |

## 14 Two-Country Model of the World under Key Currency Regime

|      |                                                                |     |
| ---- | -------------------------------------------------------------- | --- |
| 14.1 | Introduction                                                   | 241 |
| 14.2 | The Model                                                      | 243 |
| 14.3 | Variational Dynamics                                           | 247 |
| 14.4 | Stability Analysis under Rigid Wage Rates                      | 252 |
| 14.5 | Stability: Flexible Wage Rates                                 | 255 |
| 14.6 | Elaborations on the Basic Model                                | 261 |
|      | Appendix 1  Derivation of Variational Reduced Form Equation (6) | 264 |
|      | Appendix 2  Characteristic Equation of $\Phi$                   | 265 |
|      | Appendix 3  Wage Rate Dynamics                                  | 269 |

## 15 Interdependence in a Three-Country Model

|      |                                                                    |     |
| ---- | ------------------------------------------------------------------ | --- |
| 15.1 | Introduction                                                       | 272 |
| 15.2 | The Model                                                          | 273 |
| 15.3 | Benchmark Model                                                    | 277 |
| 15.4 | Nonsymmetrical Model: Distributional Effects of Instruments        | 281 |
| 15.5 | Nonsymmetrical Model: Monetary Union                               | 290 |

## APPENDIXES

**A  Dynamic Multipliers of ARMA Model**  299

**B  Disposable Income Calculation**  302

**C  Regressive Expectations and Perfect Foresight Assumption**  304

**D  Short-Run Stability of Variational Equations**  315

| E | Calculation of the Transition Matrix | 319 |
|---|---|---|
| F | Perturbation Analysis of Matrix Exponential Functions | 320 |

**References** 327

*Index* 335

# Preface

Most economic systems are dynamically coupled to one another. Although systems may sometimes be examined in "isolation" on the assumption that interactions among them and with the environments in which they function can be ignored, such analysis can be only approximate. The interactions exist, of course. Because our knowledge of an economy is only approximate, and because the models we employ only dimly reflect very complex economic reality, such approximate analysis is sometimes justified. We cannot, however, neglect interdependence between the object of our examination and the rest of the world entirely. The study of open economies is a case in point.

While some economies may be analyzed as "small open economies" in which the rest of the world is treated as exogenous, not all economies may be analyzed this way; and not all questions can be analyzed this way either. Influences that some economies exert internationally and the feedback effects or repercussions must be explicitly considered in the analysis.

Because models of open economies provide very important and interesting examples of interconnected macroeconomic systems, I have for some time now been interested in the dynamic behavior of open economies in general, and dynamic interactions among several interconnected economies in particular. This has led me to examine related questions of how economies with different structures are affected by common exogenous disturbances and how these disturbances spread throughout the world as well as questions of policy coordination among nations and of how decisions made in one country affect other economies, when each country's policy maker acts more or less independently of policy makers elsewhere.

The emphasis here is on dynamic responses of models of open economies. I find that most results on open economies available in economic literature refer either to impact or to comparative static analysis. I have therefore found it necessary to conduct most of the dynamic analysis myself.

I record here both the results of my examination of the dynamic behavior of models of open economies and an exposition of the techniques of dynamic analysis that I used, since these techniques are not standard and merit wider use.

Both simple and relatively more fully specified models are used to illustrate my procedures. The latter models reflect recent developments in models of deterministic macroeconomic open economies. Although various behavioral relations in the models of this book are not explicitly derived by intertemporal optimizations by economic agents as in some more recent and simple models, this fact does not preclude a possibility that some of the behavioral relations may be derivable or be suggested by these optimization procedures.

I have confined this book to deterministic models partly because stochastic models require additional tools that are best discussed separately, and partly because what I discuss here serves as a basis to develop my treatment of stochastic models. Deterministic models can also serve as a certainty equivalent version of stochastic models. Most of the important concepts and techniques, such as the variational analysis and structural perturbation examination, apply to stochastic systems as well. Since some of the economic applications of the techniques I describe here are new, I feel that it is best to avoid in this book the additional complications associated with stochastic models.

Before we begin, let me add a word about the use of algebra and elementary differential or difference equations as analytical tools. The effects of open market operations are customarily evaluated by using graphs that draw (straight) lines to represent various asset equilibrium conditions in a plane, typically with an interest rate and the exchange rate as coordinates. (See Girton and Henderson (1973) as a representative of such analysis.) The graphical approach works well when there is a small number of variables to keep track of, as in the case of impact analysis of open market operations or of intervention into the exchange market of the asset sector composed of a few financial assets. However, when the goods sector is included in the analysis in order to consider the influences of changes in the output or its price level, when wage rates are variable, or when effects of fiscal expansion not matched by real tax increase (unbalanced budget fiscal expansion) are to be examined, the graphical approach becomes a messy way to keep track of variables.

In writing this book, I have benefited from comments by and discussions with my colleagues and students. My special thanks go to Professor W. H. Branson, who has been very helpful in many ways. Professor S. Kamiyama, Messrs. K. Mashiyama and B. A. Jensen read an early version of the manuscript. I have benefited from comments and discussion with Professors R. C. Marston, Y. Shinkai, Y. Murata, A. Takayama, D. Freedman, J. Frankel, J. B. deMacedo, and Dr. M. Canzoneri.

*Preface*

A grant from the National Science Foundation enabled me to pursue a research program, some results of which are included in this book, for which I am grateful.

The manuscript has been typed expertly by Gloria (Ginger) Nystrom with some assistance from Faith Flagg and Diane Lueddemann.

*Institute of Social and Economic Research*　　　　　　Masanao Aoki
*Osaka University*
*Osaka, Japan*

# Scope of the Investigation

We study how macroeconomic policy instruments affect open economies under flexible exchange rate regimes and examine the extent to which interdependence of national economies affects assessment of national policy effectiveness in a dynamic context. Traditionally, questions related to policy effectiveness have been examined only at impacts and at steady-state (long-run) equilibria. In this study we evaluate behavior of open economies not only at the instant of exogenous shocks or changes in instruments, but also after some time has elapsed since the last impacts. We answer the question, How much do dynamics matter? by examining behavior of a wide range of models and drawing general conclusions. To carry out this study, we develop a set of techniques associated with variational analysis and theory of perturbation. These methods, ideally suited for conducting comparative dynamic analysis of economic models, are systematically applied to the models of the open economies we consider.

The study reported here is theoretical, dealing with analytical rather than econometric models. We do not study nor do we draw policy implications for any particular country, although assumptions embedded in the models may reflect some of the structural, institutional constraints or special circumstances in some countries.

Much literature exists on exchange rate dynamics, internal and external balances, transmissions of inflation, effects of wage indexation, and the like. These topics also interest us. We attempt to examine these problems more systematically by constructing our basic analytical general equilibrium models more explicitly and by paying closer attention to various sources of dynamics. The novel methods we employ to compare consequences of alternative policies are also more powerful, having been designed particularly for comparative dynamic studies.

The emphasis on dynamic analysis distinguishes this book from several others with similar objectives. We approach dynamics via equilibrium dynamics, i.e., dynamics that describe how momentary equilibrium states shift over time because of changing stocks of assets and changing expectations. More specifically, by systematic applications of variational analysis, we examine how endogenous variables deviate from a trend or from other reference time paths because of changes in instruments or exogenous disturbances. Various studies suggest rudiments of this procedure, where "detrended" log-linear specifications of models are frequently used to compare consequences of alternative policy regimes, or of exogenous shocks. Econometricians employ a similar procedure, comparing a "control" simulation run to other simulation runs on digital computers. We make systematic and explicit comparisons for the analytical models of the open economies constructed in this book.

Certain simple models are examined as benchmark cases. Dynamic behaviors of models that are elaborations on the simple models are then analyzed by treating the elaborations as perturbations on the original models. These two methods, variational dynamic analysis and analysis by theory of perturbation, enable us to get some insight into the nature of the dynamic interdependence of macroeconomic policies. Loosely speaking, we use variational analysis to examine dynamic behavior of a model near a reference time path and to apply perturbation theory to compare the dynamic behaviors of models that are similar in structure.

Besides systematically applying variational and perturbation techniques to obtain comparative dynamic results, we offer an analytical innovation for dealing with models of the world that are composed of several countries and show the usefulness of path controllability. We find that several other concepts from system theory are particularly well qualified to assess the interdependence of national economies and, more specifically, to investigate how the influences of instruments of national policies spread internationally. These concepts, together with analytical tools, are developed in the first part of the book and then applied to models of a small open economy, to two-country models of the world, and to a three-country world model.

The dynamic analysis proper of open economies begins in Part Two, which is devoted to models of small open economies. Two- and multiple-country models of the world are considered in Part Three.

The models analyzed incorporate the more recent portfolio balance approach to the asset sectors. In each case, the dynamics of the basic model are analyzed first and then various elaborations are discussed. Our models consistently observe stock-flow relationships. The influence of government budget imbalances and current account on stocks of domestic and foreign financial assets are modeled explicitly. The effects of wealth and interest earnings on domestic government bonds and foreign financial assets are included whenever practical.

## Scope of the Investigation

This classification of models into the so-called small-country model and multiple-country model of the world notwithstanding, we recognize that there are several other possible groupings. Helliwell (1979), for example, makes these divisions: (i) models that impose the purchasing-power parity condition, (ii) those with the interest-rate parity condition, and (iii) those in which neither condition is imposed. We can superimpose onto our basic classification of open economies into small open and multiple-country models a dichotomy with and without wage indexation, with and without imported intermediate goods, or the distinction of the level of disaggregation of outputs by traded or nontraded goods.

The most complete model of a small open economy that we discuss in Part Two has domestic money, domestic bonds, and foreign bonds as the financial assets available to domestic residents. In the real sector, the goods produced in the economy are assumed to be an imperfect substitute for the world goods. We impose neither the purchasing-power parity condition, nor the (covered) interest-rate parity condition. Although we do not wish to be exhaustively taxonomic in our dealings, we proceed from a simple model and deal with progressively complex models. Basic models for a small open economy, two- and three-country models of the world, are later elaborated by adding further refinements in the course of our discussions of them.

How do symmetric specifications of individual countries modify dynamic behavior of the world models? Do national disturbances become synchronized? How? What are the distributional effects of exogenous shocks and policy instrument changes in the world models? We address these and other related questions in Part Three.

Long-run comparative static properties of models are well documented and have not therefore been emphasized here. Long-run equilibrium is examined only as necessary to assure that the models have not been improperly specified as far as their long-run behavior goes, that the models do not exhibit pathological properties, and to determine long-run equilibrium states or paths that can serve as reference states or reference paths in our variational analysis.

Although the basic notions of variational dynamics and the structural perturbation method are also applicable to stochastic models, we do not cover stochastic models of open economies. This topic has been reserved for a separate work in order to keep our treatment of the dynamics of deterministic open economies reasonably self-contained without being encumbered by technicalities of stochastic dynamic analysis. This is not to deny the importance of stochastic considerations in open economies. Stochastic considerations should be paramount in stabilization discussions and in discussions of choices of regimes since any proposed schemes must be evaluated for possible performance in random environments. We point out that the procedures developed in this book can be interpreted as "certainty equivalent" approaches to stochastic systems. Furthermore, the ideas of comparative dynamics and sensitivity analysis are valid for stochastic systems and will be important in assessing stochastic system dynamic behavior and policy effects, especially in conjunction with Ito's lemma.

Summaries of individual chapters can be found at the beginning of each part.

# Notation

To distinguish impact analysis, which analyzes changes induced on endogenous variables at the same instant that instrument changes take place, from short-run analysis, which investigates changes of endogenous variables some time after such instrument changes occur, we use the notation $\Delta$ and $\delta$ to indicate variation of variables in impact analysis and short-run analysis, respectively. For example, $\delta i(t)$ is defined by

$$i(t) = i^0(t) + \delta i(t), \quad t \geq t_0,$$

where $i$ and $i^0$ are the respective perturbed and reference time paths of the interest rate; i.e., $\delta i(t)$ is the difference between the perturbed path and a reference time path of $i$. We generally use superscript 0 to refer to a value on the reference path. See Chapter 1 for the notion of reference paths. If an open market operation is conducted at time $t_0$, then $\delta i(t_0) = \Delta i(t_0)$ is the discontinuous (instantaneous) change in $i$ at the time of the open market operation conducted at $t_0$, but $\delta i(t_0 + \delta t) \neq \Delta i(t_0)$, generally, where $\delta t > 0$ denotes a small time interval. Here we note that variables governed by differential equations do not change discontinuously.

Except for the interest rate, we use lowercase letters to denote relative deviations. For example,

$$M(t) = M^0(t)(1 + m(t)) + o(t),$$

where $M$ denotes money stock, $o(t)$ higher order of smallness, and where we shall denote proportional changes by lowercase letters, e.g., $m(t) = \delta M(t)/M^0(t)$, where $\delta M(t) = M(t) - M^0(t)$.

The initial condition for $m$ is given by

$$m(t_0) = \delta M(t_0)/M^0(t_0) = \Delta M(t_0)/M^0(t_0),$$

where $\Delta M$ is subject to stock constraints and is nonzero only if an open market operation is conducted at time $t_0$. See Section 2.3 for a more complete explanation.

In our notation, a dot over a variable denotes differentiation with respect to time, i.e., $\dot{x} = dx/dt$, $\dot{B} = dB/dt$, etc. [not to be confused with rates of change $(dx/dt)/x$ or $(dB/dt)/B$].

An overbar denotes either an exogenously fixed constant or a long-run equilibrium value or a constant value along the reference path of a variable. The caret symbol ^ over a variable indicates expected values, not rates of changes. The caret is also used to denote Laplace transforms.

In addition, a numerical subscript on a function usually refers to the partial derivative with respect to one of the arguments. For example, the derivative with respect to the first argument is represented by the subscript one. The total derivative of a function with respect to its argument is denoted by a prime. For example, the second derivative of $f(x)$ is written as $f''(x)$. Also ( ) is used to denote arguments of functions. Finally, it is assumed that the derivatives of the functions postulated exist.

To avoid repetitious writings of integral signs in expressing solutions of differential equations, we use the following shorthand notation: We write the solution of a linear differential equation

$$\dot{z}(t) = A(t)z(t) + B(t)x(t)$$

as

$$z(t) = Z(t, 0)z(0) + (Z, Bx)(t, 0),$$

where the matrix $Z(t, s)$ is the transition matrix (fundamental solution matrix) of the differential equation. When the matrix $A$ is constant, then the transition matrix $Z(t, s)$ equals $\exp(A(t - s))$. The second term of the solution expresses the effect of the instrument $\mathbf{x}$ on the solution and is given in our shorthand notation. It stands for the integral

$$(Z, Bx)(t, 0) = \int_0^t Z(t, s)B(s)x(s) \, ds.$$

We also write this as $(ZB, \mathbf{x})$.

Because of linearity of integration, the following relations are valid for our notation:

(P1) $\qquad (Z, aBx) = a(Z, Bx) \qquad$ for any scalar $a$,

(P2) $\qquad (Z, Bx + Dv) = (Z, Bx) + (Z, Dv),$

(P3) $\qquad F(Z, Bx) = (FZ, Bx)$

for a constant matrix $F$ which is compatible with $Z$, i.e., for which $FZ$ is defined.

To illustrate the use of this notation, we write the solutions of the next set of two coupled differential equations in our notation. Given

$$\dot{z} = Az + Bw + Cx, \qquad \dot{w} = Dw + Ev,$$

## Notation

where **x** and **v** are the exogenous inputs (instruments), the solution of the second differential equation is, in our notation,

$$\mathbf{w}(t) = W(t, 0)\mathbf{w}(0) + (W, E\mathbf{v}),$$

where $W(t, s)$ is the transition matrix of the second equation. The first differential equation has the solution of the form

$$\mathbf{z}(t) = Z(t, 0)\mathbf{z}(0) + (Z, B\mathbf{w} + C\mathbf{x}) = Z(t, 0)\mathbf{z}(0) + (Z, B\mathbf{w}) + (Z, C\mathbf{x}),$$

where (P2) is used and $Z(t, s)$ is the transition matrix of the first equation. The term $(Z, B\mathbf{w})$ can further be written by substituting the solution for **w** as

$$(Z, B\mathbf{w}) = (Z, BW)\mathbf{w}(0) + (Z, B(W, E\mathbf{v})),$$

where the first term stands for $[\int_0^t Z(t, s)B(s)W(s, 0)\, ds]\mathbf{w}(0)$.

We introduce another notational convention to express the last term of the above equation so that the effect of the instrument **v** is more directly exhibited. This can be done by changing the order of integration for which this shorthand notation stands:

$$\int_0^t Z(t, \tau)B\left[\int_0^t W(\tau, s)E\mathbf{v}(s)\, ds\right]\, d\tau = \int_0^t \left[\int_s^t Z(t, \tau)BW(\tau, s)\, d\tau\right]E\mathbf{v}(s)\, ds.$$

Thus we define

$$(BW)*Z(t, s) = \int_s^t Z(t, \tau)BW(\tau, s)\, d\tau.$$

With a constant $B$, $(Z, B\mathbf{w})$ equals $(ZB, \mathbf{w})$. Hence we have the equality $(BW)*Z = W*(ZB)$. We can write for a constant $E$[1]

(P4) $\quad (Z, B(W, E\mathbf{v})) = (ZB, (W, E\mathbf{v})) = (W*ZB, E\mathbf{v})$

$$= (W*ZBE, \mathbf{v}) = \int_0^t (W*ZB)(t, s)E\mathbf{v}(s)\, ds,$$

where

$$(W*ZB)(t, s) = \int_s^t Z(t, \tau)B(\tau)W(\tau, s)\, d\tau.$$

---

[1] If we strictly follow our notational convention, $(Z, B\mathbf{w}) = (B*Z, \mathbf{w}) = (B*Z, (W, E\mathbf{v})) = (W*(B*Z), E\mathbf{v}) = (E*(W*(B*Z)), \mathbf{v})$. However, only for a transition matrix is the operation * crucial. We can always resolve any doubt by returning to the original integral expressions, e.g.,

$$(E*(W*(B*Z)), \mathbf{v}) = \int_0^t \left\{\int_s^t Z(t, \tau)B(\tau)W(\tau, s)E(s)\mathbf{v}(s)\, d\tau\right\} ds.$$

# List of Symbols

*Asset sector variables*

| | |
|---|---|
| $A$ | Nominal wealth of the private sector |
| $B$ | Stock of domestic bonds held by domestic private sector[1] |
| $B_g$ | Stock of government bonds held by the domestic private sector[2] |
| $D$ | Domestic component of domestic money stock (domestic credit) |
| $E$ | Exchange rate (domestic currency price of a unit of foreign currency) |
| $F$ | Stock of international bonds domestically held, i.e., either by the domestic government and the private sector or by the private sector alone[3] |
| $R$ | Foreign exchange (international reserve) held by the domestic government (central bank) |
| $V$ | $B + B_g$ when private and government bonds are assumed to be perfect substitutes |
| $i$ | Domestic interest rate |
| $\pi$ | Expected domestic output price inflation |
| $\varepsilon$ | Expected rate of depreciation of the exchange rate |

*Real sector variables*

| | |
|---|---|
| $B_T$ | Balance of trade in foreign exchange, i.e., $PX/E - P^*I_m$ |

[1] Bonds are sometimes treated as consols and at other times as fixed in nominal value with variable rate of return. In the former, the symbol $B$ stands for the number of consols so that $B/i$ is the market value in domestic currency.

[2] This distinction between $B$ and $B_g$ is not always made for simple models.

[3] $B^*$ is sometimes used to denote stock of international bonds held by the domestic private sector.

*Real sector variables*

| | |
|---|---|
| $C$ | Real consumption demand for domestic goods by domestic residents |
| $D_f$ | Domestic government budget deficit |
| $F(\ )$ | Production function |
| $G$ | Government expenditure on current goods and services |
| $I$ | Real investment |
| $I_m$ | Real imports demand |
| $K$ | Capital stock |
| $qK$ | Real value of the stock of equity capital |
| $P$ | Output good price |
| $P_I$ | Consumer price index |
| $T$ | Real tax receipts |
| $X$ | Real export demand |
| $W$ | Money wage rate (except in Chapter 3, where $W$ is used to denote real private wealth) |
| $l$ | Coefficients in variational real demand equations |
| $\Omega$ | Coefficients in variational expressions for balance of trade |

Various Greek letters are used to indicate exogenous parameters such as adjustment speeds.

*Dynamics*

| | |
|---|---|
| $\Phi, \Psi, A$ | Usually denote dynamic matrices in state-space representation of variational dynamics |
| $z$ | State vector (except in Chapter 14) |
| $\mu_i$ or $m_i$ | Coefficients in the variational government budget constraint equation |
| $\tau = (\partial T/\partial Y)(Y/T)$ | |

# Part One | Analytical Concepts and Tools of Comparative Dynamic Analysis

In the eight chapters of Part One, we collect concepts and tools we find useful in conducting comparative dynamic analysis of models of open economies. Their usefulness will be illustrated in Parts Two and Three. After a brief statement on state-space representation of dynamic systems, Chapter 2 describes two of the basic techniques used throughout this book: variational dynamic analysis and sensitivity analysis. One is based on the notion of comparing time paths of the economy that lie near some reference paths or states by variational dynamics which describe short-run deviations of model time paths from the reference time paths. Variational dynamics thus describe neighboring time paths of the reference time paths, i.e., how models behave near their "control" solution time paths. Consequences of changes of macroeconomic policy instruments as well as changes of exogenous circumstance are evaluated by this method. Note that we are not comparing alternative long-run equilibrium or growth paths. Our emphasis is on assessing consequences of policy instrument changes or exogenous shocks by comparing the induced changes of time paths of some endogenous variables. We show that "detrended" log-linear models are nothing but variational dynamic models of the economy about some trend or reference time paths. The other method is based on the notion of structural variation, i.e., on comparing time paths of economies with different structural characteristics (when they are subjected to a common disturbance) and is introduced as a systematic way of conducting sensitivity analysis of model structure variations, in order to compare models with different structural characteristics. This notion is later elaborated on in Chapter 5.

Chapter 3 illustrates variational dynamic analysis procedure on a closed economy model. Dynamical policy multipliers are discussed in Chapter 4. Chapter 6 collects system theoretic results on instruments' ability to stabilize economy or modify time paths of selected target variables. Chapter 7 briefly enumerates several linkages of national economies. In Chapter 8 several sources of dynamics in open economies and their interactions are discussed and illustrated by two examples of small open economies. In Sections 8.2 and 8.3 we analyze the same example under alternative assumptions of regressive and perfect foresight expectations on the exchange rate and demonstrate the equivalence of (conditionally) stable perfect foresight expectations with stable consistent regressive expectations on a two-dimensional dynamics. The example in Section 8.4 evaluates dynamic effects of bond financing of the government budget deficit.

# 1 | State-Space Representation of Dynamic Models

## 1.1 Analytical Models

There are two classes of macroeconomic models: analytical and econometric. The latter can generally embody higher levels of disaggregation than the former and usually incorporates more detailed behavioral relations than the former. Econometric models, however, require specific sets of numerical values to generate specific sets of time paths, while analytical models need no such specific numbers to generate qualitatively useful results. The two classes of models are complementary because analytical models can serve, for example, as a guide to design numerical experiments to be run on econometric models, while simulation results obtained from econometric models may suggest certain modifications to be made on analytical models. This book deals exclusively with analytical models of open economies, even though we resort from time to time to numerical examples of hypothetical economies to illustrate certain points.[1]

Analytical models are made up of a set of definitional identities, a set of algebraic behavioral relations, and a system of differential or difference equations representing dynamic adjustment processes in financial markets, goods markets, labor markets, and so on. The number of markets incorporated in models depends on disaggregation of the models.

---

[1] Analytical dynamic models in the economic literature tend to be at most two-dimensional. Two (stock) variables are allowed to change with time. Low dimensionality may have caused some economists to dismiss analytical models as being artificial and useless. In this book we routinely discuss three-dimensional dynamics and sometimes four-dimensional dynamics as well. More important than these specific examples in this book is our view that these relatively low-dimensional analytical dynamic models are useful and that one need not jump from second-order dynamic models directly to large-scale econometric models to gain useful insights into the workings of economies.

If we pursue a high degree of disaggregation to describe markets in economy, then models become too complex to be examined analytically. Therefore, several assumptions or approximations are routinely adopted to reduce the dimension of dynamics and the complexity of models. One is to assume instantaneous adjustment of certain variables to achieve continuous market clearing. Commonly, asset prices (yields) are regarded as such variables. They can change discontinuously to ensure continuous market clearing. Relative prices sometimes are also assumed to adjust instantly to clear markets. A second simplifying assumption is to fix stocks of assets by assumption or to regard some variables as adjusting so slowly that we can assume them to be constant for the purpose of analysis. This frequently occurs in short-run analysis.[2] For example, even in the presence of nonzero savings or investment, asset or capital stocks are regarded as constant in this approximation; similarly, wages and prices are treated as fixed in some "Keynesian" analyses of output and employment adjustment. Balanced budget expansion of fiscal expenditure is an example well known in the literature of policy analysis, which is designed to keep stocks of government debt constant. We dispense with this assumption in some of our analyses and can analyze resulting changes of stocks of government debt that are not exactly matched by tax increase.

Some variables are assumed to be tied to exogenous variables which are assumed to be constant. This is a third simplifying assumption. In a small open economy, the interest rate or the price level is often assumed to be tied to the exogenously fixed world rates of interest or the world price level. We return to this kind of approximation in Part Two of this book. Finally, some variables are simply assumed to be constant without good justification. This is an implication of some partial equilibrium analysis. We avoid partial equilibrium analysis because substantial error in analyzing interactions among some endogenous variables may result from such partial equilibrium analysis assumptions.

All of these assumptions or approximation schemes help to reduce the dynamic dimension of the models. With sufficient number of assumptions, models are sometimes reduced to a simple dynamic adjustment process described by a single differential (or difference) equation, or at most to a two-dimensional dynamic equation, whose properties are well enough understood to yield qualitative predictions. However, this practice involves too extreme a reduction of dynamics to be useful in many applications. We shall pursue an intermediate degree of aggregation in this book and deal with three- or more dimensional dynamic equations when necessary. With simple models, signs of coefficients in dynamic equations can be assigned often from

---

[2] Short-run analysis in literature, however, is what we call the impact analysis and does not involve dynamics.

signs of more basic coefficients in the model. As models become more complex, such a procedure becomes less feasible. The degree of ambiguity of the theoretical prediction increases with the model's complexity and generality. To resolve ambiguities, we sometimes assign plausible values to relevant parameters in models and use the models as hypothetical numerical examples.[3]

## 1.2 State-Space Representation

We put analytical models into "state-space" representation. Loosely speaking, given the future time paths of policy instruments or policy reaction functions and exogenous disturbance terms, knowledge of present values of state variables of the model suffices to determine uniquely all future time paths of the state variables of the models, as well as other endogenous variables of the model.[4] This is a convenient form to analyze dynamics since techniques and concepts associated with dynamic models are available mostly for models in state-space representation. We shall return to this point when discussing policy multipliers. For the moment, we outline what a "dynamic model" represents.

Let $Z$ be a state vector, i.e., a (minimal) collection of endogenous variables which uniquely determines the future time paths of all endogenous variables in economy, once future time paths of the instruments or decision variables and exogenous variables are specified. For example, for continuous time models, if $Z$ is governed by a (vector) differential equation

(1) $$\dot{Z} = f(Z, X; t, \xi),$$

where $X$ is the instrument vector and where $\xi$ is a vector of exogenous variables, then $Z$ is a state vector under a suitable regularity condition which ensures the existence and uniqueness of solutions of (1) because all future values of $Z$ are uniquely determined by its initial condition and the future time paths of the instrument vector and the exogenous vector. The time variable $t$ is included in the arguments of $f(\cdot)$ to indicate a possibility that the dynamics may vary with time. When $\xi$ is random, we have a stochastic system. We do not go into the detailed specification of stochastic models.[5] All endogenous variables of a model not represented in $Z$, denoted by $Q$,

---

[3] This procedure is more satisfactory than it may first appear because sensitivity analysis can be employed to assess consequences of (small) model parameter changes.

[4] A state space equation thus admits a unique solution. This uniqueness is the deterministic counterpart of the Markovian property of Markov processes.

[5] We may employ discrete-time models. The state vector $Z_k$ is then governed by a (vector) difference equation $Z_{k+1} = f_k(Z_k, X_k, \xi_k)$, where the subscript $k$ refers to the $k$th period. More will be said about discrete-time models later.

must be expressible as functions of Z, X, and possibly some exogenous variables $\zeta$ as

(1')
$$Q = g(Z, X, t; \zeta)$$

for Z to serve as a state vector of the economy.

We note that choice of a state vector is by no means unique.

The dynamic equation (1) is derived from the structural form specification of a model. Some of the structural equations are dynamic equations representing stock-flow relations in the economic models, while the others are purely algebraic equations relating some of Z and X as accounting identities.[6] Other equations describe dynamic changes in expectations, wage rates, and such that are not of stock-flow variety.

The stock-flow relations are of the form $\dot{Z} = F(Z, V, X, t)$, while the algebraic relations are expressed as

$$G(X, Z, V, X, t) = 0,$$

where Z and V are some endogenous variables and X is a vector of policy instruments. If $G(\cdot)$ can be solved for V in terms of Z (at least locally), then a vector differential equation for Z of the form (1) results by substituting V out from the differential equation for Z.

Referring back to (1), we note that some of the components of the vector Z are not necessarily available for direct measurement. In such situations an "observation" equation explicitly specifies what is being observed, i.e., available for measurement,

(2)
$$U = g(Z, X, t; \eta),$$

where $\eta$ is the exogenous disturbance vector representing measurement inaccuracy. Equation (2) specifies that the vector U is the information added to the information set at time $t$. We cannot go into the subtle question of who acquires this piece of new information here. Some cases may quite conceivably show two or more groups of economic agents with different information sets, i.e., a group may have its own observation equation. Here we assume that (2) represents the information acquisition program of a policy maker.

What a policy maker observes need not be the same as the set of endogenous variables that he seeks to control or influence. In general he may

---

[6] Algebraic relations other than (accounting) identities are usually associated with financial variables and represent an extreme or a limiting form of dynamic equation with very quick responses. For example, a differential equation $\mu \, dU/dt = H(S, U, V, X, t)$, where $\mu$ is a very small positive number, is often approximated by an algebraic equation which is the limit of the differential equation by letting $\mu$ go to zero, i.e., $0 = H(S, U, V, X, t)$. Noninstantaneous portfolio adjustment may be modeled as $\mu \, dM/dt = F(M^d - M)$ or $\mu \, dE/dt = G(M^d - M)$ for some function $F(\cdot)$ and $G(\cdot)$. With small positive $\mu$, the differential equations must be analyzed by the singular perturbation method [see Bender and Orszag (1978)].

observe more variables than he is interested in controlling. A vector of endogenous variables that a policy maker is interested in controlling is often called the target vector $V$, which may be a subset of $Q$ or $Z$ and is related to $Z$ and $X$ by

(3) $$V = h(Z, X, t; \zeta).$$

Here the vector $\zeta$ represents random slippage (disturbances) between the targets and the instruments.

We shall adopt this general framework for representing a dynamic model by (1), (2), and (3) in this book. Concrete application will provide the ultimate test of this framework's usefulness in representing dynamics. Because we deal only with deterministic models in this book, we drop stochastic disturbance terms from (1), (1'), (2), and (3) and regard $X$ to include instrument variables, which are not explicitly endogenized by reaction functions, and all exogenous variables in the model as well.

See appendix A at the end of the book for a procedure of converting autoregressive moving average (ARMA) models to state-space representation. See Aoki (1976) for more detailed discussion on equivalence of models in ARMA and state-space forms.

## 1.3 Notion of Equilibrium and Long-Run Policy Implications

When the dynamic behavior of an economic system is modeled mathematically by the solution curves of a differential equation (or a difference equation)

(4) $$\dot{Z} = f(Z; X),$$

where $Z$ is the state vector and $X$ is the vector of instruments or some exogenous variables, we define an equilibrium of (4) with $X$ fixed at $\bar{X}$ to be $\bar{Z}$ such that $f(\bar{Z}; \bar{X}) = 0$; i.e., $\bar{Z}$ does not change with time.[7] This is the usual mathematical definition of the equilibrium state [see, for example, Hirsch and Smale (1974)]. The time variable $t$ will also appear in differential equation (4) explicitly if some characteristics or structure of the economy changes with time. In this case we define $\bar{Z}$ to be the state such that $f(\bar{Z}; \bar{X}, t) = 0$ for all $t \geq 0$.

Equilibrium states are thus states that do not change with time. Equilibrium states are important because we are interested in learning how models will

---

[7] With a difference equation analog of (4), $Z_{k+1} = f_k(Z_k, X_k)$, its equilibrium corresponding to $X_k = \bar{X}$ for all $k$ is given by $\bar{Z} = f_k(\bar{Z}, \bar{X})$ for all $k$.

behave in the long run. For example, Rutledge states that "Fisher felt that steady-state—or full equilibrium—properties were of great interest. Long-run conditions provide us with information about where a given system would come to rest if all exogenous variables were to remain fixed; hence they help us to identify the major directions of adjustment in endogenous variables to expect which may ultimately aid us in formulating policies (Rutledge, 1977, p. 202)." The mathematical notion of equilibrium does not, by itself, correspond to any specific economic notion of equilibrium. By a change of variables, the differential equation can be modified so that equilibrium in the mathematical sense can be made to correspond to different economic notions of equilibrium such as steady-state or long-run equilibrium. The next example clarifies this point.

Consider the scalar differential equation

$$\dot{Z} = aZ.$$

The mathematical equilibrium state is $Z = 0$. The solution of this differential equation is $Z = Z_0 e^{at}$ for some initial condition $Z_0$. Change the variable to $W = Z - Z_0 e^{at}$. In other words, we measure deviation from $Z_0 e^{at}$ as $W$. This new variable $W$ also satisfies a differential equation of the same type:

$$\dot{W} = aW$$

since $\dot{W} = \dot{Z} - aZ_0 e^{at} = a(Z - Z_0 e^{at})$. The equilibrium of this transformed differential equation is $W = 0$. This equilibrium state, however, is $Z_0 e^{at}$ in the original variable $Z$. The equilibrium for the variable $W$, therefore, is an exponential growth path in the variable $Z$. This latter could be a steady-state growth path of a growth model, for example.[8]

We can often deduce relations that must hold among trend rates of several endogenous variables without specifying an explicit (growth) model. These relations may frequently be derived by logarithmic differentiation of behavioral equations. Here we give some indications of the nature of constraints imposed by long-run equilibrium conditions by considering a simple demand for real balances in the long-run or steady-state equilibrium.

Take the usual demand function for money $M/P = L(Y, i)$, where $M$ is the stock of money, $P$ the price level, $Y$ real output, and $i$ the interest rate, all evaluated in the steady-state equilibrium. Differentiate this equation logarithmically to derive a relation among the rates of changes $\dot{M}/M - \dot{P}/P = (L_1 Y/L)\dot{y} + (L_2 i/L)\dot{i}/i$. The rate of growth of money is divided into three

---

[8] In general, any pair of time functions $Z(t)$ and $X(t)$ that satisfy (4) describes dynamic behavior of the economy. Of particular interest are the pairs with special properties such as the exponential growth where components of $Z$ and/or $X$ grow at (not necessarily the same) constant rates. These paths may define long-run growth paths of the economy or may be used as reference paths in the sense to be described in Section 2.2.

effects: increases in price, output, and interest rate. If the interest rate is exogenously held fixed and $Y$ is at full employment level, then $\dot{i} = 0$ and $\dot{Y}/Y = 0$, leaving $\dot{M}/M = \dot{P}/P$. Growth in the money stock is fully reflected as a price increase. In a more general case, model specifications will determine the portion of the money stock growth rate which is reflected in price increases, output increases, and increases in the interest rate. If output is growing at an exogenous rate $n$ due to the exponential growth in capital and labor, then the inflation rate in the reference path must be $\dot{P}/P + an = \dot{M}/M$, where $a$ is the output elasticity of demand for real balances evaluated along the trend path. As another example, consider portfolio balance asset demand equations

$$M/E = \alpha(i^*)A \quad \text{and} \quad F = (1 - \alpha(i^*))A.$$

These equations show how wealth $A$, denominated in foreign currency, is to be divided between domestic money stock $M$ and foreign bond stock $F$. $E$ is the exchange rate (domestic currency price of a unit of foreign currency). Assume that the foreign interest rate $i^*$ is exogenously held constant. Logarithmic differentiation of the ratio $M/EF = $ const yields $\dot{M}/M = \dot{E}/E + \dot{F}/F$. Therefore, any time path along which the asset demands are continuously met must be such that the rates of changes of $M$, $F$, and $E$ satisfy this constraint. This relation thus illustrates the constraint imposed on long-run policy choices. To see this simply, assume that $\dot{F}/F$ is exogenously determined (from requirements on a long-run current account, for example). Then the rate of domestic money stock growth and that of changes of the exchange rate are related; these rates cannot be assigned independently. For example, if $E$ is to be held at a constant level along the long run, i.e., reference path, then the rate of the money stock growth must be chosen to equal $\dot{F}/F$. If the rate of money stock growth is chosen as a policy variable, then the rate of the exchange rate depreciation necessarily equals $\dot{M}/M$ minus $\dot{F}/F$. In this way, long-run policy choices are constrained by long-run equilibrium conditions. We return to this point in Parts Two and Three of this book. Porter (1976) makes a similar point.

## 1.4 Example: A Balanced Growth Path of a Small Open Economy

Later we mention a balanced-growth path as a possible reference-time path in performing comparative dynamic analysis. Here we describe a very simple growth model of a small open economy in which the output price, exchange rate, and interest rate all remain constant along the growth path. A long-run equilibrium state of this model is this balanced growth path.

This is a slightly modified Dornbusch model (Dornbusch, 1971). The output good, which is a perfect substitute for the world good, is produced by a linear homogeneous production function. With the purchasing power parity condition imposed, we assume that $P = E$ setting the world price to one without loss of generality. The growth rate of population $n$ is exogenous. The model has two financial assets: money, which is nontraded, and international bonds. Domestic bonds and the international bonds are perfect substitutes and are not distinguished. In view of the fact that the exchange rate (and the price level) are constant along the growth path, we can assume that expectations on the exchange rate changes and on inflation are all static and equal zero. Denoting the "world" interest rate by $i^*$, the asset demands functions are specified by

$$L = \alpha(i^*)a \quad \text{and} \quad B = \beta(i^*)a,$$

where $a$ is the real wealth,[9] $L$ represents real balances, and $B$ is the real stock of international bonds in the private sector. The output is given by

$$Y = F(K, N), \quad \text{where} \quad \dot{N}/N = n.$$

We assume that $i^*$ is constant. Then $L/B$ is a constant; the logarithmic differentiation of this ratio shows that $\dot{L}/L = \dot{B}/B$ along the growth path. We logarithmically differentiate the production function $Y = F(K, N)$ to show that

$$\dot{Y}/Y = (F_K K/F)(\dot{K}/K) + (F_N N/F)(\dot{N}/N).$$

By linear homogeneity of $F$, we know that $(F_K K + F_N N)/F = 1$; hence the rates $n = \dot{N}/N = \dot{K}/K = \dot{Y}/Y$ are compatible with the balanced growth path.

Because $\dot{K}/K = n$, net investment $I$ is $nK$ on the growth path or, letting $\phi$ denote the output–capital ratio, we can write it as

$$\dot{K} = I = bY,$$

where $b = n/\phi$. The government budget deficit is assumed to be financed 100% by new money issue. The supply of money increases according to

(5) $$\dot{M}/P = G - T = gY,$$

where the deficit is assumed to be $g\%$ of the real output $Y$.[10]

---

[9] Dornbusch uses income instead of $a$. We can think of $a$ as a multiple (possibly depending on $i^*$) of income.

[10] If we adopt $\dot{M}/M = \mu$ instead of the money supply process of (5), then $\dot{M}/M = \dot{P}/P = \dot{E}/E = \mu$. The asset demand function remains the same since the difference of the yields of holding $L$ and $B$ is still $i^*$.

## 1.4 Example: A Balanced Growth Path of a Small Open Economy

Balance of trade $B_T$ can be written as the excess of output over absorption

$$B_T = Y - C - G - I = Y - T - C - (G - T) - I$$
$$= (Y - T + i^*B) - C - (G - T) - I - i^*B,$$

where $Y - T + i^*B$ is disposable income because of the zero inflation rate. Hence $Y - T + i^*B - C$ is the saving or the increase in wealth $\dot{a} = na$. Therefore, the trade balance is also growing at the rate $n$

$$B_T = na - (G - T) - I - i^*B = \{n - i^*\beta(i^*)\}a - (b + g)Y.$$

The stock demand for bonds grows according to $\dot{B}$, a part of which is satisfied domestically by $I$ and the remainder is satisfied by increased holdings of the international bonds, i.e., the capital outflow $\dot{F}$ is expressible as[11]

$$\dot{F} = \dot{B} - I = nB - bY = n\beta(i^*)a - bY.$$

Note that a part of the flow demand for real balances is met by the domestic money increase $gY$ and the remainder comes from the balance-of-payment surplus BOP, where

$$\text{BOP} = B_T + i^*B - \dot{F} = n\alpha(i^*)a - gY.$$

The current account is expressible as

$$B_T + i^*B = na - (b + g)Y.$$

Neither need be zero since the exchange rate remains constant along the growth path. The consumption is also growing with the rate $n$ since it is given by

$$C = Y' - na \quad \text{or} \quad C = Y + \{i^*\beta(i^*) - n\}a.$$

In this model, the exchange rate remained constant. Later we discuss several models in which the exchange rate does not remain constant in the long run but shows a constant rate of depreciation.

---

[11] Alternatively, the trade balance can be expressed as a residual in the balance of payments, $B_T = \text{BOP} - i^*B + \dot{F}$.

# 2 | Variational Methods in Comparative Dynamic Analysis

## 2.1 Introduction

We introduce one of the two basic concepts for conducting comparative dynamic analysis in this chapter. The other is introduced in Chapter 5.

In order to learn how economies behave over time in response to alternate shocks and alternate policy regimes, we must pose a very general question: Is there a systematic procedure for conducting comparative dynamic analysis of a nonlinear macroeconomic model? More specifically, we inquire, how can dynamic effects of different policy regimes or exogenous disturbances on a nonlinear macroeconomic model be evaluated? The key word here is dynamic. We realize that impact effects and long-run (steady-state or stationary state) effects of a given disturbance or a change in instrument are frequently evaluated. But most analysis leaves inter-run, or finite-time effects untouched.

Take policy multipliers, for example. Policy multipliers carry important pieces of information about the magnitudes and time pattern of the effect of macroeconomic policy instruments. In practice, an explicit analytical solution of the multipliers of a nonlinear dynamic economic model is difficult to obtain. Therefore, we find that studies generally evaluate multipliers at only two points in time, namely, at a point of impact of policy changes (impact multipliers) and at a steady state or at an equilibrium (long-run multipliers). The latter shows the asymptotic effects of policy changes as time approaches infinity since the last policy changes. Sometimes simulation is used to obtain information on how the multipliers vary over time. This is especially true in the case of large econometric models. In small analytical macroeconomic models, however, no attempts are usually made to evaluate how the multipliers behave over time, even though such information is no doubt extremely valuable in assessing the effectiveness of policy instruments. We return to policy multipliers in Chapter 4.

## 2.1 Introduction

In attempting to answer the question, we recognize that while a well-developed theory exists for dealing with linear dynamic systems, it does not cover nonlinear systems at all. This prompts the second question: Since most economic models are nonlinear, how can the linear system theory be applied to comparative dynamic analysis of them?

In this chapter we shall outline a procedure for examining dynamic behavior of a nonlinear economic model near some specified trend or "reference" time path. The circumstances or the context in which the comparative dynamic analysis is to be conducted largely determines the choice of the reference path. Let us return to this point later, after establishing a standard framework for conducting comparative dynamic analysis for nonlinear economic dynamic models.

We first show that a technique analogous to that used for deriving long-run multipliers can be employed to derive inter-run policy multipliers, and also to call attention to an often neglected distinction between the linearization of nonlinear models at a point and that about a time path.

The procedure generally utilized for deriving long-run multipliers follows these lines: The long-run equilibrium state of the model is obtained first. The stability in the neighborhood of the equilibrium point is then examined by expanding the original equations into the Taylor series about the equilibrium point, retaining only the first-order terms and examining the stability of the linearized system. Being assured of at least local stability, the long-run multipliers are then calculated about the equilibrium point. This analysis, however, does not capture a well-known phenomenon that if the economy is not sufficiently close to the equilibrium, then the same dosage of the macroeconomic policy instruments would affect the economy differently depending on the time path it is following on its way to the equilibrium state, and hence the policy multipliers would behave differently. None of this should be surprising because the model is nonlinear.

In addition, we argue that finite-time policy multipliers convey useful information on how the economy is affected by the instruments. This is so because policy makers may wish to deviate temporarily from these time paths determined by their long-run choices ("reference time paths") and to evaluate their immediate or later effects. These effects are captured by impact and finite-time multipliers evaluated not at equilibrium but along the reference.

Our analysis in Parts Two and Three of time paths shows that they can indeed be quite different. Also see Aoki (1980a) for a simple numerical illustration of these differences. In short, interactions between the long-run and short-run policies can be examined effectively by deriving finite-time policy multipliers.

Readers who are accustomed to seeing simple analyses in the literature may feel that analyses reported in these two parts of the book are overly and unnecessarily complicated. We cannot largely avoid these complications for two reasons. First, models in Parts Two and Three are not partial equilibrium models. Interactions between the asset sectors and real sectors are explicitly and dynamically treated on an equal footing. When one sector is emphasized over others, analyses simplify, often considerably. Dornbusch (1976b) and Frankel (1979) illustrate this observation. Their analyses are simpler because they focus on the exchange rate using very abbreviated description of real sector (by not including the labor sector or government budget constraints in their analyses), for example.[1] Second, not only we treat stationary or steady states of the models but also, and more importantly, analyze deviations of endogenous variables from their respective reference path values, i.e., we conduct comparative dynamic analyses.

From time to time we illustrate how our analyses simplify by reverting to partial equilibrium analyses.

## 2.2 Reference Time Paths

For comparison, we must have a standard or a basis against which to compare. Therefore, the notion of a "control experiment" or a "control solution" as the standard of comparison crops up invariably in diverse fields such as chemistry, medicine, or psychology. In econometrics, the notion of a "control solution" of a large econometric model is well known. This is the time path of the economy against which alternate time paths of the economy, resulting from changes in some policy variables or exogenous shocks, are to be compared.

This notion is an element of our analytical framework for comparative dynamics. First, a standard or reference time history of the model is chosen. (This requires that some time paths of the policy instruments be accepted as standard time paths.) This is our control solution. Since the word "control" may be confused with the control variables which are sometimes used to denote instruments, we adopt the term "reference solution" (or "reference" for short) to denote the standard set of time paths of the model's endogenous variables. For models where growth is unimportant, the reference solution may be not a time path but rather a point in the state space (i.e., long-run stationary equilibrium state). In other models, the reference may represent a trend or steady-state (or balanced) growth path. The purpose of the analysis largely dictates our choice of reference. Often deviations from a trend time path are considered in response to an exogenous shock in the literature.

---

[1] Compare our two-country model of Chapter 13, Part Two, with the two-country model in Frankel (1979).

## 2.3 Variational Equations

In such cases a trend path serves as the reference time path. Detrending economic variables implicitly select the trend path as the reference path. For an example of macroeconomic models, which are specified following logarithmic transformations and removals of linear trends (in logarithmic variables), see Taylor (1979, p. 3). His model describes the deviations of the endogenous variables from secular trends, i.e., his model is in variational equation form to which we turn in Section 2.3.

A reference path cannot be a total fiction but must be a time path which the model can actually exhibit under some circumstances, i.e., given some time paths of instruments and exogenous variables. For example, in discussing several models of open economies in Parts Two and Three of this book, we examine their long-run equilibrium solutions. Suppose that residents of an economy hold two financial assets, domestic money $M$ and foreign bonds $F$, in proportion as determined exogenously, i.e., $M/EF = \text{const}$, where $E$ is the exchange rate. Such a relation is a condition of the asset sector equilibrium. Because we assume that the asset sector is continuously in equilibrium, the rates of changes of $M$, $E$, and $F$ must bear a relation; i.e., $\dot{M}/M = \dot{E}/E + \dot{F}/F$. Any reference time path to be used for this model must consequently be such that this relation about the rates of changes of these variables must be satisfied along the reference time path.

### 2.3 Variational Equations

We start by recalling the procedure for obtaining linear approximations to a nonlinear dynamic model about a point and about a time path, in order to emphasize the differences of the resulting variational equations. Section 2.3.1 describes the former and Section 2.3.2 the latter.

Many studies specify models in log-linear forms, i.e., models are linear in logarithms of variables. The reader should note that variational equations of nonlinear models are essentially log-linear specifications of the models.

#### 2.3.1 Log-Linear Forms

Log-linear relations are often employed in econometric works and in some analytical works. Wan and Majumdar (1980) base their choice of log-linear functional forms on analytic convenience. Actually, log-linear functional forms naturally arise as variational models. Variational equations of percentage deviational variables of algebraic equations are nothing but the familiar log-linear relations. Later we also show that detrended variational equations are log linear. To illustrate the former, let the relations among the variables $X$, $Y$, and $Z$ be specified by $Z = F(X, Y)$. The relative deviations of these variables from stationary or constant values $\bar{X}$, $\bar{Y}$, and $\bar{Z}$ where $\bar{Z} = F(\bar{X}, \bar{Y})$ are denoted by $x = (X - \bar{X})/\bar{X}$, $y = (Y - \bar{Y})/\bar{Y}$, and $z = (Z - \bar{Z})/\bar{Z}$ if $\bar{X}$, $\bar{Y}$, and $\bar{Z}$ are nonzero. Taking the variation of $Z$, we derive $\delta Z = F_1(\bar{X}, \bar{Y})\delta X + F_2(\bar{X}, \bar{Y})\delta Y$, where $\delta X = X - \bar{X}$, $\delta Y = Y - \bar{Y}$, and $\delta Z = Z - \bar{Z}$. We can then derive the relation among $x$, $y$, and $z$ as

$$z = ax + by,$$

where

$$a = F_1(\bar{X}, \bar{Y})\bar{X}/F(\bar{X}, \bar{Y}) \quad \text{and} \quad b = F_2(\bar{X}, \bar{Y})\bar{Y}/F(\bar{X}, \bar{Y}),$$

which is the relation among variations of the logarithms of $X$, $Y$, and $Z$, i.e., $\ln X$, $\ln Y$, and $\ln Z$. Two of the most common cases illustrate this expression. From the algebraic relation $\delta(X + Y) = \delta X + \delta Y$, the relative deviational variables $x$ and $y$ are related by $\delta(X + Y)/(\bar{X} + \bar{Y}) = \bar{X}(\bar{X} + \bar{Y})^{-1}x + \bar{Y}(\bar{X} + \bar{Y})^{-1}y$. Similarly, $\delta(XY)$ in relative deviational variables becomes $x + y$.

When some of $\bar{X}$, $\bar{Y}$, and $\bar{Z}$ are zero, then the corresponding variables are deviations of these variables. We use the usual Taylor series expansion for these variables. For example, suppose $\bar{X}$ is zero. Then we have

$$z = aX + by,$$

where

$$a = F_1(0, \bar{Y})/F(0, \bar{Y})$$

and $b$ is as defined above.

As an example, consider the following: In the portfolio balance approach, a desired holding of a financial asset, say government bonds, is expressed as

$$B = \beta(\mathbf{i}, A),$$

where $\mathbf{i}$ is a vector of relative yields of different financial assets and $A$ is a measure of portfolio size. Taking the variation of the above, the change in the desired holding can be expressed as the sum of two parts

$$\delta B = \beta_1 \, \delta\mathbf{i} + \beta_2 \, \delta A,$$

where the first term represents that part of changes in desired asset holdings due to changes in one or more interest rates with the size of the portfolio held constant, and the second term represents the part of changes in the asset demand due to growth in the size of the portfolio with other variables held constant. In studies of the portfolio balance approach to the analysis of

## 2.3 Variational Equations

capital flows, the former is called the stock-shift effect, and the latter is called the continuing-flow effect. We can render this in log-linear form as

$$\delta B/B = (\beta_1/\beta)\, \delta \mathbf{i} + (\beta_2 A/\beta)(\delta A/A).$$

In the impact analysis, the size of the portfolio does not change except for the valuation effects which we shall discuss later. In the interim run, the size of the portfolio does change because of capital gains and losses caused by changes in the yields and because of nonzero flows of savings, investments, unbalanced government budget, and so forth.

As an additional illustration, consider a simple equation for real balances given by $M/P = e^{-\alpha i} Y^\beta$. Denoting reference path values by overbars, this equation can be equivalently written as

$$(1 + m)/(1 + p) = e^{-\alpha\, \delta i}(1 + y)^\beta,$$

because $\overline{M}/\overline{P} = e^{-\alpha \bar{i}} \overline{Y}^\beta$ obtains at equilibrium.

Treating the lowercase variables as small, this relation is the same as $m - p = -\alpha\, \delta i + \beta y$, a log-linear specification for money demand often found in the literature. The reference path can be a stationary state, i.e., $\overline{M}, \overline{P}, \bar{i},$ and $\overline{Y}$ can be constant, or a steady state in which $\overline{M}$ and $\overline{P}$ are growing at the same rate and where $\bar{i}$ and $\bar{y}$ remain constant, for example. Other steady states are also possible.

Our convention for deviational notations focuses directly on relations among deviational variables and allows us to describe compactly relations among relative deviations. To illustrate, let us describe the relation between the exchange rates on and off an equilibrium state, $\overline{E}$ and $E$, in a two-country model of the world. Suppose the rates of interest $i$ and $i^*$ in the two countries are related by $\varepsilon = i - i^*$, where the expected rate of depreciation of the exchange rate $\varepsilon$ is posited to depend on $E/\overline{E}$ and $\pi - \pi^*$ by

(∗) $$\varepsilon = -\theta \ln(E/\overline{E}) + \pi - \pi^*,$$

where $\pi - \pi^*$ is the long-run inflation rate differential between the two countries.[2]

When these two equations are solved for $E$ as

$$\ln E = \ln \overline{E} - \{i - \pi - (i^* - \pi^*)\}/\theta,$$

we obtain the relation we seek.

In our notation this is simple

$$e = -(\delta i - \delta i^*)/\theta,$$

---

[2] These two equations which formed the basis of our little illustration often appear in the literature, e.g., Frankel (1979). The first reflects the assumption of uncovered interest rate parity. In a perfect foresight economy, it follows directly. The second states an assumption.

where we note that $\ln(1 + e)$ approximately equals $e$ for $|e|$ small, and we write $\delta i$ for $i - \bar{i}$. Then we can write $i - \pi - (i^* - \pi^*) = i - \bar{i} + \bar{i} - \pi - (i^* - \bar{i}^* + \bar{i}^* - \pi^*) = \delta i - \delta i^*$ since $i - i^* = \pi - \pi^*$, which follows by setting $E$ to $\bar{E}$ in the above.

Note that in writing the deviational relation (∗), we need not explicitly derive $\bar{E}$ or $\bar{\pi}$.[3]

### 2.3.2 Detrended Log-Linear Equations

Referring back to (1) of Section 1.2, let us denote reference path values by superscript zero. The instruments associated with the reference solution is then denoted by $X^0(t)$ at time $t$. The corresponding state vector is $Z^0(t)$. (It is easier to consider them for deterministic models. We therefore abstract from stochastic disturbances, i.e., zero random disturbances are associated with reference time paths.) The time paths from some initial time $t_0$ are $X^0(t)$ and $Z^0(t)$, $t \geq t_0$. The time paths for the instruments and the state vector are mutually compatible, or consistent with the model of the economy in that they are generated as the solution of the (nonlinear) model, i.e.,

$$(1) \qquad \dot{Z}^0(t) = f(Z^0(t), X^0(t), t), \qquad t \geq t_0,$$

where $t$ and all its first-order partial derivatives are continuous in some domain containing the solution curve $Z^0(t)$.

When the instrument time paths are modified from those associated with the reference solution, new instrument time paths $X(t)$, $t \geq t_0$, generate a different set of time paths for the endogenous variables. Thus, the state vector time path $Z(t)$, $t \geq t_0$, generally is different from the reference time path $Z^0(t), t \geq t_0$. The time paths $Z(t)$ and $X(t), t \geq t_0$, are called perturbed time paths, as they are perturbed off the reference time paths. We denote the differences by

$$\delta Z(t) = Z(t) - Z^0(t), \quad t \geq t_0 \qquad \text{and} \qquad \delta X(t) = X(t) - X^0(t), \quad t \geq t_0.$$

They are called variation or perturbation of $Z^0(t)$ and $X^0(t)$, respectively. When $Z(t) = Z^0(t) + \delta Z(t)$ and $X(t) = X^0(t) + \delta X(t)$ are substituted into

---

[3] If these equilibrium values are also desired, we must augment the original two equations, for example, by a conventional money demand function $\bar{M}/\bar{P} = e_{\bar{i}}^{-\alpha \bar{i}} \bar{Y}^{\beta}$ and an assumed relation among $\bar{E}$, $\bar{P}$, and $\bar{P}^*$, the purchasing power parity $\bar{P} = \bar{E}\bar{P}^*$, for example. Then $\bar{E} = \bar{P}/\bar{P}^* = (\bar{M}/\bar{M}^*)e^{\alpha(\bar{\pi} - \bar{\pi}^*)}(\bar{Y}/\bar{Y}^*)^{-\beta}$, where $\alpha$ and $\beta$ are assumed to be the same in the two countries and the equality of $\bar{i} - \bar{i}^*$ with $\pi - \pi^*$ is used. The expression for $\pi$ can also be obtained from the money demand equation. For example, on the assumption that $\bar{i}$ is constant and $\bar{Y}$ is growing at the rate $\gamma$ on the reference (growth) path, differentiate the money demand equation logarithmically with respect to time to derive

$$\pi = \mu - \beta\gamma,$$

here $\mu$ is the equilibrium rate of money stock growth.

## 2.3 Variational Equations

(1), and (1) is expanded into a Taylor series about the reference time path, the linear approximation becomes

(2) $\quad \delta \dot{Z}(t) = f_z(Z^0(t), X^0(t), t)\, \delta Z(t) + f_x(Z^0(t), X^0(t), t)\, \delta X(t).$

This equation, in which higher order terms in $\delta Z$ and $\delta X$ are ignored (by implicitly treating variation as small), is known as the variational equation of (1).

Note that the variational equation is *linear* in the perturbed variables even when the original Eq. (1) is nonlinear.

The variational equation is useful to examine alternate time paths of the economy in a "neighborhood" of the reference time path, resulting from "small" variation of the reference time paths of instruments.[4] Analysis of the $\delta Z$-time path in response to alternate $\delta X$-time paths is exactly what we mean by comparative dynamics of the original model (1).

To express deviations in percentage terms, define $\mathbf{z}(t) = \delta Z(t)/Z^0(t)$ and $\mathbf{x}(t) = \delta X(t)/X^0(t)$.[5]

Differentiate $z(t)$ with respect to time to see that

$$\dot{z}(t) = \delta \dot{Z}/Z^0 - l_z(t) z(t),$$

where the second term $l_z(t)$ is defined to be $\dot{Z}^0/Z^0$ which is the rate of change of $Z$ along the reference path, i.e., $l_z(t)$ is the trend rate of change. To emphasize the fact that it may be changing with time along the trend path, we show $l_z$ as a function of time. Thus the variational equation of (1) in percentage deviation terms becomes[6]

(3) $\quad \dot{\mathbf{z}}(t) = A(t)\mathbf{z}(t) + B(t)\mathbf{x}(t),$

where the $(i, j)$th component of the matrix $A$ is

$$A_{ij}(t) = \frac{\partial f_i}{\partial Z_j}(Z^0(t), X^0(t), t) \frac{Z_j^0(t)}{Z_i^0(t)} - \frac{f_i}{Z_i^0(t)}(Z^0(t), X^0(t), t) \Delta_{ij}$$

and

$$B_{ij}(t) = \frac{\partial f_i}{\partial X_j}(Z^0(t), X^0(t), t) \frac{X_j^0(t)}{Z_i^0(t)},$$

where $\Delta_{ij}$ is zero for $i \neq j$ and one otherwise.

Equation (3) is the variational equation of (1) in relative deviation terms.[7] Even when the original Eq. (1) does not depend explicitly on $t$, the matrix $A$

---

[4] By a neighborhood of a time path we mean a tube containing the time path, and not a disk or sphere about a point in an Euclidean space.

[5] When $Z$ and $X$ are vectors, we denote this by componentwise division, e.g., $z_i(t) = \delta Z_i(t)/Z_i^0(t)$ for the $i$th component.

[6] When $Z$ is an $n$-dimensional vector and $X$ is a $k$-dimensional vector, $A$ is the $n \times n$ matrix and $B$ is the $n \times k$ matrix.

[7] Variational equations of difference equations are also linear in variational state and instrument variables.

and $B$ are generally functions of time since $Z^0(t)$ and $X^0(t)$ are functions of time. Hence (3) is a time-varying linear differential equation. For some special but important class of reference time paths, the variational differential equations turn out to have constant coefficients.

If we take the reference path to be a trend or a growth path of the economy, then the variational vector $\delta Z(t)$ represents "detrended" variables of the economy. The equation for the relative deviational variables $z(t)$ then represents a detrended log-linear model of the economy.

Before we leave this section on linearization, a final word is offered to avoid possible confusion about our linearization procedure. Linearization of a nonlinear (algebraic or differential equation) relation about its equilibrium value or state is a common practice in economics. Examining shifts in equilibrium values or states in response to changes in exogenous conditions or instruments is also commonly practised, it being basic to comparative static analysis. How the transition is made between the two equilibria corresponding to "before" and "after" the changes is sometimes not made explicit in the economic literature. Our perturbation procedure does not relate linear approximations of nonlinear models about these two equilibria, i.e., about the old equilibrium before the shock and about the new equilibrium after the shock, because the two linear approximations refer to two *different* reference states. Only when a transition path between the two equilibria is given (or at least can be solved out "in principle"), then that path can be chosen as our reference path, and the variational equation describes behavior of the model near this transition path. See Aoki (1980a) for numerical illustrations of these three types of approximations. In this book we usually do not deal with two equilibrium states or two reference time paths. We choose a single "control" solution state or time path as the reference, and examine its neighborhood. The context of analysis determines the nature of the reference. Hence we do not discuss transition from one reference path to another in a same problem. Rather, we examine how our models deviate from the chosen reference path in response to "small" changes in exogenous circumstances or instruments.

### 2.3.3 Superposition Principle

Because (3) is linear, its solution is expressible as

(4) $$z(t) = \phi(t, t_0)z(t_0) + \int_{t_0}^{t} \phi(t, \tau)B(\tau)x(\tau)\,d\tau,$$

where $\phi(t, t_0)$ is the fundamental matrix of solutions (Coddington and Levinson, 1955, p. 69). This matrix is also known as the transition matrix

## 2.3 Variational Equations

in system literature. It satisfies the same differential equation as the homogenous part of (3).[8]

$$d\phi(t, t_0)/dt = A(t)\phi(t, t_0), \quad \phi(t_0, t_0) = I.$$

Its column vectors are the $n$ linearly independent solutions of the homogeneous part of (3).

The solution (4) is composed of two parts; the first term represents the effects of nonzero initial condition $z(t_0) \neq 0$, and the second term is due to the cumulative effects of past instrument values. The second term can be further decomposed as

$$\sum_{i=1}^{r} \int_{t_0}^{t} \phi(t, \tau) b_i(\tau) x_i(\tau) \, d\tau$$

by writing $B(\tau)x(\tau)$ as $\sum_{i=1}^{r} b_i(\tau)x_i(\tau)$, where $b_i(\tau)$ is the $i$th column vector of the matrix $B(\tau)$ and $x_i(\tau)$ is the $i$th component of the $r$-dimensional instrument vector, i.e., $i$th instrument. The effects of the initial condition and the instruments linearly add up, i.e., superimpose on each other. The effects of each instrument also superimpose to produce the total effects of all the instruments on the state vector. The fact that effects due to different causes add up for linear dynamics is known as *superposition principle* in linear system theory.

In economic analysis various (thought) experiments are usually run by keeping all but one (causal) factor fixed, or models are so constructed that only one factor plays a major role in model dynamic behavior. For example, an open market operation is often examined under the balanced budget condition to "avoid" mixing the effects of an open market operation with the government budget policies, i.e., (discontinuous) changes in the stock of the government bonds held by the central bank are introduced while the total stock of government bonds in the economy remains constant [see Takayama (1978, footnote 45) and Rodriguez (1977)]. Brock provides another example in Brock (1975, p. 134) when he states "... the welfare effects of errors of expectations are to be separated from the welfare effects of a correctly anticipated inflation."

Some economic analysis fails to recognize that effects of initial conditions and instruments cannot be separately examined and that different causal factors cannot be separately examined in nonlinear models. Only with linear (variational) models such as log-linear detrended models are such separate investigations fully justified.

---

[8] When the matrix $A$ is constant, $\phi(t, t_0) = \exp A(t - t_0)$. Appendix E explicitly carries out the expression for a $2 \times 2$ matrix $A$.

### 2.3.4 Dynamic Policy Multiplier

We can use (4) to derive the dynamic policy multiplier of the variational equation (3), i.e., the effects of $x(s)$ on $z(t)$, $s \leq t$, which may be expressed as the matrix $\partial z(t)/\partial x(s)$. For this purpose, consider an impulse as $x$, i.e.,

$$x(\tau) = \begin{cases} \bar{x}, & s \leq \tau \leq s + h, \\ 0, & \text{otherwise} \end{cases}$$

for a small positive $h$. Then the integral in (4) becomes approximately $\{\phi(t, s)B(s)\}\bar{x}h$, showing that $\phi(t, s)B(s)$ is the expression for the dynamic policy multiplier associated with the variational dynamic equation (3). We return to this point later in Chapter 4.

### 2.3.5 Perfect Foresight Model

Sometimes (3) is more conveniently solved with a terminal condition rather than an initial condition specified. In that case we write the solution of (3) as

$$z(t) = \phi(t, T)z(T) + \int_T^t \phi(t, \tau)B(\tau)x(\tau)\, d\tau.$$

This replaces (4).

That this satisfies (3) can be verified by direct differentiation noting that $\partial \phi(t, T)/\partial t = A(t)\phi(t, T)$. When $T$ approaches infinity, we must impose a terminal condition

$$\lim_{T \to \infty} \phi(t, T)z(T) = 0$$

to have a well-defined $z(t)$. Then

$$z(t) = -\int_t^\infty \phi(t, \tau)B(\tau)x(\tau)\, d\tau.$$

Sargent and Wallace (1973) uses this representation.

The discrete-time version of this is as follows: Given

$$z_t = \phi^t z_0 + \sum_{s=1}^t \phi^{t-s} b x_s,$$

which is a solution to

$$z_t = \phi z_{t-1} + b x_t,$$

## 2.4 Sensitivity Analysis

solve it for $z_0$ at $t = T$

$$z_0 = \phi^{-T} z_T - \sum_{s=1}^{T} \phi^{-s} b x_s.$$

Use this to express $z_t$ in terms of $z_T$ as

$$z_t = \phi^{t-T} z_T - \sum_{s=1}^{T} \phi^{t-s} b x_s + \sum_{s=1}^{t} \phi^{t-s} b x_\tau = \phi^{t-T} z_T - \sum_{s=t+1}^{T} \phi^{t-s} b x_s.$$

The transversality condition becomes

$$\lim_{T \to \infty} \phi^{t-T} z_T = 0 \quad \text{for any finite } t.$$

### 2.4 Sensitivity Analysis

Economies respond differently to the same exogenous shock or change of instrument because they differ in some essential economic structural characteristics. To complete the analysis of model behavior and macroeconomic policy effectiveness we must evaluate how changes in model parameters or specifications alter the results of analysis. Sensitivity study examines, among other things, dependence of (dynamic) policy multipliers on structural characteristics and parameters.[9] We can deduce the consequences of small parameter changes by extending the method of Section 2.3. Evaluating effects of large parameter variations generally requires a different method, unless the dynamics are linear, because the variational analysis works best for small changes. Yet another method may be needed to assess the implications of model structural change if it cannot conveniently be parametrized. In this section we shall address these questions of sensitivity by outlining three methods.[10]

### 2.4.1 Large Parameter Variations of a Linear Dynamic System

With linear dynamic equations we can explicitly treat effects of parameter variations, large or small. Take, for example, $A(\theta) = \theta A_1 + (1 - \theta) A_2$, $0 \leq \theta \leq 1$. Consider, then

$$\dot{Z} = A(\theta) Z + B(\theta) X, \quad \text{and} \quad \dot{Z}^0 = A(\theta^0) Z^0 + B(\theta^0) X.$$

---

[9] L. Katseli-Papaefstratiou and N. P. Marion (1980) study dependence of impact effects on some exogenous and structural parameters. Aoki (1980d) conducts sensitivity analysis of dynamic multipliers. See Cruz (1973) on methodology.

[10] Effects of large changes in parameters or exogenous variables can always be estimated by computer simulation. For example, Fair (1980) discusses a stochastic simulation procedure to estimate the uncertainty of policy effects in nonlinear models.

We wish to evaluate the effects of the parameter changes from $\theta^0$ to $\theta$ on $Z$, assuming that the same exogenous term $X$ is applied in both cases.

Let the change in the dynamic matrix be denoted by $C$, i.e., $C$ equals $A(\theta) - A(\theta^0)$. Let $\delta Z$ stand for $Z - Z^0$. It is governed by the differential equation

$$\delta \dot{Z} = A(\theta)\, \delta Z + C Z^0 + \{B(\theta) - B(\theta^0)\} X.$$

Note that this is an exact expression, involving no approximation, hence valid for any change in the parameter value. If the difference of the values $\theta$ and $\theta^0$ is small in some sense, then the matrix $A(\theta)$ multiplying $\delta Z$ may be replaced by $A(\theta^0)$ to save some calculations. This approximation is later used in Chapters 12 and 13 of Part Three.

### 2.4.2 Small Parameter Variations

The procedure of Section 2.3 can easily be adapted to examine effects of different parameter values in the model. Suppose we use $\theta$ to denote a vector composed of model parameters in the dynamic equation

$$\dot{Z} = f(Z, X; t, \theta), \tag{5}$$

and $Z^0$, $X^0$ correspond to the "nominal" vector $\theta^0$, where we now assume that $f, f_z,$ and $f_\theta$ are all continuous in some domain containing a reference solution path corresponding to $\theta = \theta^0$ and $X^0(t; \theta^0)$.

The reference time path $Z^0(t; \theta^0)$ is the solution of (5) with $\theta = \theta^0$ corresponding to a reference time path of the instrument $X^0(t; \theta^0)$. Then for the parameter value $\theta$ sufficiently close to $\theta^0$ a unique solution path $Z(t; \theta)$ of (5) exists for an instrument time path $X(t; \theta)$. The variation $\delta Z(t) = Z(t; \theta) - Z(t; \theta^0)$ is given by the solution of

$$\begin{aligned}\delta \dot{Z}(t) = &\; f_Z(Z^0(t; \theta^0), X^0(t; \theta^0), t; \theta^0)\, \delta Z(t) \\ &+ f_X(Z^0(t; \theta^0), X^0(t; \theta^0), t; \theta^0)\, \delta X(t) \\ &+ f_\theta(Z^0(t; \theta^0), X^0(t; \theta^0); t; \theta^0)\, \delta\theta,\end{aligned}$$

where

$$\delta\theta = \theta - \theta^0, \qquad \delta X(t) = X(t; \theta) - X^0(t; \theta^0).$$

Oniki (1973) uses this approach to perform comparative dynamics in optimal control.

When the sensitivity function (matrix) is defined by $U = (u_{ij})$, where $u_{ij}$ stands for $\partial Z_i / \partial \theta_j$ and $i$ and $j$ range over the dimensions of $Z$ and $\theta$, respectively, then the sensitivity function is governed by the differential

## 2.4 Sensitivity Analysis

equation: $\dot{U} = f_z U + f_x V + f_\theta$, where the matrix $V = (\partial X_i/\partial \theta_j)$ determines how $u_{ij}$ behaves with time. This equation is known as the sensitivity equation in the system literature. See papers collected in Cruz (1973) for further detail.

Sensitivity of performance index can analogously be analyzed in a context of optimal control. This topic, although important, is omitted because we do not discuss optimal control problems in this book.

### Example: Sensitivity of a Growth Path[11]

We compute growth paths of the capital stock of a simple growth economy governed by $\dot{k} = sf(k) - \lambda k$, where $k$ is the capital stock per capita, for a special case where $f(k)$ is proportional to $\sqrt{k}$, and consider the sensitivity of the growth path with respect to different $s$ values. In effect, we calculate the elasticity of the growth path with respect to the propensity to save $s$. We carry out the calculations in two ways: directly and via the variational equation.

Suppose the capital stock per capita is growing according to

$$\text{(6)} \qquad \dot{Z} = a\{\theta\sqrt{Z} - Z\}, \qquad 0 < Z(0) < 4, \quad a > 0,$$

where $\theta^0 = 2$.

The reference time path is given by the integral of this differential equation:

$$\sqrt{Z^0} = 2 - (2 - c)e^{-at/2},$$

where

$$c = \sqrt{Z(0)} \quad \text{or} \quad Z^0 = \{2(1 - e^{-at/2}) + ce^{-at/2}\}^2.$$

The solution of (6) with general $\theta$ is

$$\text{(6')} \qquad Z = \{\theta(1 - e^{-at/2}) + ce^{-at/2}\}^2.$$

Let $\theta = 2 + \delta\theta$ be the parameter that deviates from 2. Two is the value associated with the reference path. Let $z = \delta Z(t)/Z^0(t)$, where $\delta Z = Z(t) - Z^0(t)$ and where the superscript 0 is used to denote the reference time path. Then, to the first order of smallness in $\theta$,

$$\delta Z = Z - Z^0 = 2\{2(1 - e^{-at/2}) + ce^{-at/2}\}\{1 - e^{-at/2}\}\,\delta\theta.$$

---

[11] See Aoki (1980a) for another example. Another and more extensive example of small parameter variations is found in Chapter 11 where consequences of changes in the output supply responsiveness of a small open economy is studied as an example of structural characteristic differences of open economies.

Because of a simple dependence of the solutions of (6) on $\theta$, $\delta Z$ can be alternatively calculated directly from (6') as

$$\delta Z \simeq (\partial Z/\partial \theta)^0 \, \delta\theta;$$

therefore, the relative variation of $Z$ is given by

(7) $$z = \delta Z/Z^0 = \frac{2(1 - e^{-at/2}) \, \delta\theta}{2(1 - e^{-at/2}) + ce^{-at/2}}.$$

As time approaches infinity, the relative deviation approaches $\delta\theta$.

For this example, we calculated the solutions of (6) first and then derived the expression for the relative deviation from them. In general, we must solve the variational equation directly.

The variational equation of (6) is

$$\delta \dot{Z} = a\{(Z^{0-1/2} - 1)\, \delta Z + \sqrt{Z^0} \, \delta\theta\}.$$

Since $\dot{z} = \delta \dot{Z}/Z^0 - z\dot{Z}^0/Z^0$, the differential equation for $z$ is

(8) $$\dot{z} = -\frac{a}{\sqrt{Z^0}} z + \frac{a}{\sqrt{Z^0}} \, \delta\theta,$$

where

$$l_z = \frac{\dot{Z}^0}{Z^0} = \left(\frac{2}{\sqrt{Z^0}} - 1\right) a.$$

Equation (8) is a time-varying linear differential equation for $z$. Since

$$\int_\tau^t \frac{ds}{2 - (2 - c)e^{-as/2}} = \frac{t - \tau}{2} + \frac{1}{a} \ln\left\{\frac{2 - (2 - c)e^{-at/2}}{2 - (2 - c)e^{-a\tau/2}}\right\},$$

the transition matrix of (8) is given by

$$\phi(t, \tau) = \left\{\frac{2 - (2 - c)e^{-at/2}}{2 - (2 - c)e^{-a\tau/2}}\right\}^{-1} e^{-a(t - \tau)/2},$$

which appears in the solution of (8)

$$z(t) = \phi(t, 0)z(0) + \int_0^t \phi(t, \tau) \frac{a \, \delta\theta}{\sqrt{Z^0(\tau)}} \, d\tau.$$

With $z(0) = 0$, the solution of (8) is

$$z(t) = \left(\int_0^t \phi(t, \tau) \frac{a}{\sqrt{Z^0(\tau)}} \, d\tau\right) \delta\theta.$$

## 2.4 Sensitivity Analysis

This integral is straightforward to carry out and $z(t)$ thus obtained can be verified to be the same as (7).

### 2.4.3 Root-Locus Method

A method for evaluating effects of large changes in a single parameter is now described when the parameter enters linearly into the characteristic equation of linear dynamics. This method efficiently analyzes consequences of large changes in a single parameter value by a graphical method which displays parametrized loci of the eigenvalues of linear dynamic systems. This method was developed by Evans (1953) and is called the root-locus method.

We can use this method to examine sensitivity of dynamic responses with respect to a parameter by exhibiting how the eigenvalues vary with the parameter values. Write the characteristic equation by separating out terms depending on the parameter:

$$|xI - A| = D(x) + \theta N(x) = 0, \qquad (9)$$

where the matrix $A$ depends linearly on the parameter $\theta$, and $D(x)$ and $N(x)$ are polynomials in $x$. In (9) these polynomials do not contain $\theta$ and are assumed to be given in factored form as[12]

$$D(x) = \prod_{i=1}^{n}(x + p_i), \qquad N(x) = \prod_{j=1}^{m}(x + z_j), \qquad n \geq m.$$

Because the signs of $D$ and $N$ alternate between plus and minus as the argument $x$ traverses the real axis in any direction, we can straightforwardly determine intervals of $x$ values on which the roots of (9) cannot lie. For example, with a positive parameter $\theta$, those $x$ for which both $D$ and $N$ are positive cannot be the roots of (9). This consideration eliminates $x$ larger than $\max_{i,j}(p_i, z_j)$, for example. There are other simple rules which help draw the loci, such as a rule to determine asymptotes of the roots as the parameter values increase to infinity (there are $n - m$ asymptotes) and a rule to locate the points where the loci bifurcate, and so on. The reader is referred to Aoki (1976, Appendix D) or Takahashi et al. (1970) for a more systematic exposition of the method. Here we merely illustrate the method by applying it to a second- and a third-order polynomial.

First we analyze the characteristic polynomial of the dynamics describing the short-run adjustment of wage rates and domestic output prices in a small open economy with imported intermediate input good, after an exogenous

---
[12] Routh's test [see Takahashi et al. (1970)] can determine the number of roots with positive real parts.

shift in the price of the intermediate good. This example is taken from Aoki and Canzoneri (1979). Under passive monetary regime, the characteristic polynomial of the adjustment process is given by

(10) $$(x + \mu)(x + \phi_1) - (\mu - \pi)\phi_2 x = 0,$$

where $\pi$, $\mu$, $\phi_1$, and $\phi_2$ are all positive parameters. The parameter $\pi$ is the adjustment coefficient of the inflationary expectations on the consumer price index, and $\mu$ is the adjustment coefficient of the wage rate responses to a "gap" between the desired and actual real wage rates. The other parameters are treated as constants in this example and do not vary in our root-locus analysis. The dependence of the roots on the parameter $\pi$ and $\mu$ are next examined.

*$\pi$-sensitivity.* Rewrite (10) to put it in the form of (9) with $\pi$ as the parameter $\theta$

$$x^2 + \{\mu(1 - \phi_2) + \phi_1\}x + \mu\phi_1 = -\pi\phi_2 x.$$

On the assumption that $\phi_2$ is less than one, the quadratic polynomial on the left-hand side of the equality has two roots with negative real parts. With a zero value of $\pi$, they are the roots of (10). As $\pi$ becomes more positive, one of the roots approaches zero, and the other escapes to minus infinity. [Heuristically, we can see this by dividing both sides of (10) by $\pi$ and letting it approach infinity.]

Two patterns of loci (see Fig. 1) are possible depending on whether the roots of the quadratic polynomial on the left-hand side of (10) are real or complex. The loci are parametrized by $\pi$. One specifies a value for $\pi$, and two points on the loci are selected as the two roots of the characteristic equation (10). Quick-responding inflationary expectations correspond to a large positive value of $\pi$. We conclude that a large positive $\pi$ implies that wage

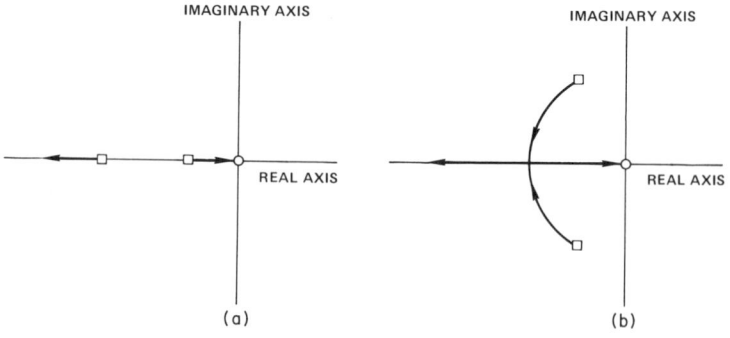

*Figure 1* Two possible patterns of root-locus plots as functions of parameter $\pi$.

## 2.4 Sensitivity Analysis

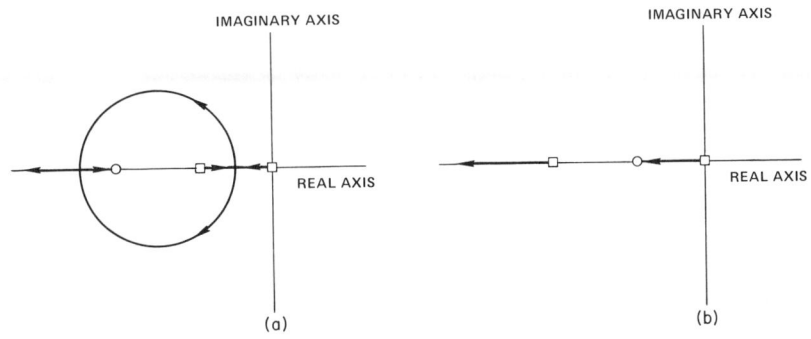

Figure 2   Two possible patterns of root-locus plots as functions of parameter $\mu$.

rates and the output prices respond sluggishly due to the presence of one root near zero, although the other root is of large negative value.

**$\mu$-sensitivity.** Next consider the roots of (10) as functions of $\mu$, the parameter representing the wage rate responsiveness in this economy. We separate $\mu$ terms out in (10) and rewrite the equation as

$$x(x + \phi_1 + \phi_2 \pi) = -\mu\{(1 - \phi_2)x + \phi_1\}.$$

When $\mu$ is zero, i.e., when the wage rate does not change, the roots are zero and $-\phi_1 - \phi_2 \pi$. As $\mu$ increases, either one of the two patterns of loci emerges, depending on the relative magnitude of $\phi_1(1 - \phi_2)^{-1}$ and $\phi_1 + \phi_2 \pi$.

In either case, as $\mu$ approaches infinity, one root approaches the zero of the right-hand side of (10), $-\phi_1(1 - \phi_2)^{-1}$ and the other escapes to minus infinity. The root-locus plot (see Fig. 2) indicates that the adjustment dynamics for the wage rates and output prices can oscillate for a range of $\mu$ values if $\phi_1 + \phi_2 \pi < \phi_1(1 - \phi_2)^{-1}$. Oscillations will eventually die out, however, because the real parts of the roots are all negative.

### 2.4.4  Structural Changes

Changes in model specifications modify model performances and effects of policy instruments. Analysis of these changes is probably the most important and difficult type of sensitivity analysis confronting us. Some results are robust, and remain valid even when some of the assumptions or model structures under which the results are obtained are (slightly) altered. Some other results become invalid as soon as a slightest departure is made from the set of assumptions or model structures.

Consider the following examples from the literature: Commenting on the model of Mundell (1968) and Johnson (1972), Myhrman (1976, p. 209) states: "The importance of really trying alternative specifications and investigating their effects on the results is often belittled as 'technicalities.' However, even small changes in the specification can result in important changes in the conclusions, as the treatment of capital mobility shows." Later, Tobin and de Macedo (1979), using a version of the Fleming–Mundell model, demonstrated that it is not so much degree of substitutability of domestic and foreign asset but rather inclusion or omission of the exchange rate variable from the asset demand functions that has the most sensitive implications on the relative effectiveness of monetary and fiscal policies. Branson (1980) also showed that the specification of real balances in the asset demand equations matters. It is the absence of the exchange rate in the demand for real balances that yields the Mundellian result that the fiscal instrument is impotent in a small open economy under a floating exchange rate regime. This famous result is a prime example of nonrobust results in open economy macroeconomics.

Clearly, even small changes in the model specifications sometimes produce qualitatively important differences in the model behavior. No systematic procedure can deal with all possible specification changes. Some structural changes can be analyzed by applying the theory of perturbation, which we introduce in Chapter 5, where we discuss a general procedure for assessing the effects of various structural changes introduced to variational dynamic equations. Examples are found in Chapters 12–15.

# 3 | Variational Dynamic Equation: An Example of Fiscal Policy in a Macroeconomic Model[1]

Comparing dynamic effects of policy instruments by calculating their variational dynamic multipliers requires variational dynamic equations. Here we illustrate our procedure for deriving variational dynamic equations on a familiar model of a closed economy, without the complications which are introduced by opening it to trade in goods and assets with the outside world. Policy multipliers are taken up in Chapter 4. We choose a somewhat simplified version of the macroeconomic model discussed by Cohen and McMenamin (1978). We use this model because it has a disaggregated financial sector with a simplified real sector which suits out illustrative purpose.

## 3.1 Model

There are three financial assets in this model: money, government bonds, and equity. Their demand functions are specified as follows:[2]

(1) $M/P = \alpha(\bar{r}, \bar{\rho}, \overset{+}{Y})W = $ real balances,

(2) $qK = \beta(\bar{r}, \overset{+}{\rho}, Y)W = $ real values of the stock of equity capital,

---

[1] This chapter applies the variational procedures of Chapter 2 to a closed economy model. The reader who prefers illustrations of our procedures on open economy models may skip this chapter without loss of continuity. Variational dynamic analysis of open economy models is first found in Chapter 8, where a simple model with two financial assests is discussed.

[2] Analysis slightly simplifies if the demand for real balances is respecified as $M/P = \alpha(r, \rho, Y)$. The two remaining asset demand functions must then be modified to reflect this change as $qK = \beta(r, \rho, Y)(W - M/P)$ and $B/rP = \gamma(r, \rho, Y)(W - M/P)$, indicating that the rest of the wealth consists of equity and bonds, i.e., $\beta$ and $\gamma$ sum to one. Redefining $L$ and $Z$ in Section 3.2 as $\alpha - M/P$ and $\beta(B/r + RK/\rho)$, respectively, this version of the model can be analyzed paralleling the developments of the main body of this chapter. We gain some simplifications in some of the expressions. For example, $L_B$, $L_K$, and $Z_M$ in (13′) now vanish in this version of the asset specification. Consequently, the parameter $\phi_2$ in (13′) is unambiguously negative. An increase in $B$ implies a drop in the rate of return on equity capital in this version. The expressions for $U_M$ and $U_B$ in the variational differential equations (18) and (19) also simplify somewhat.

where

(3)   $W = M/P + B/(rP) + qK =$ real private wealth

and where

$$q = R(\overset{+}{Y}, \overset{-}{K})/\rho \qquad = \text{capital stock valuation ratio,}$$

where the signs of functional dependence are recorded above the arguments of the functions. The demand for bonds is residually determined from (1), (2), and (3).[3] Here $B$ is the flow of nominal interest payments on government bonds, $r$ is the government bond interest rate, and $\rho$ is the rate of return on equity capital (cost of capital). The aggregate price level is assumed to hold at one from now on, for simplicity of analysis.

The disposable income $Y'$ is defined by $Y' = Y + B - T$. (Recall that the price level is held at one in this example.) By definition, $C = Y' - S$. Since $Y = C + I + G$, the equilibrium in the goods market is defined by

(4) $\qquad S(Y', W) + T(Y + B) = G + B + I(\rho, Y, K),$

where $S(\cdot)$ is the net saving, $T(\cdot)$ tax, $I(\cdot)$ the net investment, and where we assume $0 < T' < 1$.

## 3.2 Momentary Equilibrium

Before discussing the dynamics coming from the net investment changing capital stock and from the unbalanced government budget changing the stocks of money and bonds, we shall describe the momentary or temporary equilibrium of the economy for fixed stocks of financial assets.

The financial market equilibrium is defined by a pair of algebraic equations:

$$L(r, \rho, Y; M, B, K) = 0,$$

where

(5) $\qquad L(\cdot) = \alpha(r, \rho, Y)(M + B/r + RK/\rho) - M,$

and

(6) $\qquad Z(r, \rho, Y; M, B, K) = 0,$

where

$$Z(\cdot) = \beta(r, \rho, Y)(M + B/r + RK/\rho) - RK/\rho.$$

The variables $M$, $B$, and $K$ are predetermined variables. These two equations implicity determine $r$ and $\rho$ for given $Y$, $M$, $B$, and $K$. They can be solved for

---

[3] An alternate procedure is to specify three asset demand functions explicitly and then recognize that only two of them are independent due to the balance sheet constraint of the wealth. For example, we specify $M/P = \alpha W$, $qk = \beta W$, and $B/rP = \gamma W$, then use two ratios, such as $qk/(M/P) = \beta/\alpha$ and $(B/r)qk = \gamma/\beta$, as two independent equations.

## 3.4 Long-Run Equilibrium

$r$ and $\rho$ explicitly locally, i.e., in some neighborhood of $r$ and $\rho$ satisfying the equations by the implicit function theorem if the Jacobian does not vanish.

We write the solutions as

(7) $$r = h_1(Y; M, B, K)$$

and

(8) $$\rho = h_2(Y; M, B, K).$$

These equations are two-dimensional analogs of the standard $LM$ curve. Regarding (4) as a function of $Y$ in terms of $r$ and $\rho$ for given $M, B, K$, and $G$, we solve (4) for $Y$. This is possible at least locally by the implicit function theorem when the relevant Jacobian is nonzero:

(9) $$Y = h_3(r, \rho; M, B, K).$$

The momentary equilibrium of this model is then defined by the three equations (7), (8), and (9). These equations express feedbacks that exist between the asset sector and the real sector; (7) and (8) determine $r$ and $\rho$ for a given level of output $Y$, while $Y$ is determined by (9) for given values of $r$ and $\rho$. Jointly, $r, \rho$, and $Y$ are determined by solving (7), (8), and (9) simultaneously for historically given stocks of $M, B$, and $K$ and for a given level of the fiscal expenditure $G$. Let us write the reduced forms of $r, \rho$, and $Y$ as

(10) $\quad Y = F(M, B, K, G), \qquad \rho = H(M, B, K, G), \qquad r = J(M, B, K, G).$

These equations describe the momentary equilibrium state of this model.

### 3.3 Dynamics

The momentary equilibrium thus defined shifts with time since the stocks of money, bonds, and capital generally change with time. These changes are governed by two dynamic equations: the government budget constraint and investment. The government constraint is

(11) $$\dot{M} + \dot{B}/r = G + B - T(Y + B).$$

The capital stock grows according to

(12) $$\dot{K} = I(\rho, Y, K).$$

### 3.4 Long-Run Equilibrium

The long-run equilibrium of this model is defined by setting the right-hand sides of (11) and (12) to zero. Since the model does not specify the labor force, we assume for simplicity that the labor force is exogenously fixed and that there exists a stationary equilibrium. We concentrate on analyzing deviations of the economy about momentary equilibrium of time paths leading to long-run equilibrium.

## 3.5 Variational Relations: Shifting Momentary Equilibrium

We next describe how the momentary equilibrium shifts. Such shifts may occur for a number of reasons. We describe the shifts in two steps. First we let only $G$ vary. This gives rise to deviations in the momentary equilibrium due to changes in $G$. Then we investigate the effects of changing stocks of $M$, $B$, and $K$. Changes in stocks affect the time paths to long-run equilibrium.

Suppose $M$, $B$, and $K$ are held constant. Then the variational equations involve only the variations of $r$, $\rho$, and $Y$. The two variational equations of (5) and (6) determine the variations in $r$ and $\rho$ as functions of the variation of $Y$. They are the solutions of

(13) $\quad Z_r \, \delta r + Z_\rho \, \delta \rho = -Z_Y \, \delta Y, \quad L_r \, \delta r + L_\rho \, \delta \rho = -L_Y \, \delta Y.$

The solutions are expressible as follows. They are equal to the expressions obtained by a variation of (7) and (8):

(14) $\quad\quad\quad\quad \delta r = (\psi_1/\psi) \, \delta Y, \quad \delta \rho = (\phi_1/\psi) \, \delta Y,$

where

$$\psi_1 = Z_\rho L_Y - L_\rho Z_Y \quad \text{and} \quad \phi_1 = L_r Z_Y - Z_r L_Y$$

and where

$$\psi = Z_r L_\rho - Z_\rho L_r > 0.$$

The signs of the partial derivatives are

$$Z_r = \beta_1 W + \beta(-B/r^2)$$
$$= (\beta W/r)\{(\beta_1 r/\beta) - (1 - \alpha - \beta)\} < 0,$$
$$Z_\rho = \beta_2 W + \beta(-RK/\rho^2) + RK/\rho^2$$
$$= (\beta W/\rho)\{(\beta_2 \rho/\beta) + (1 - \beta)\} > 0,$$
$$L_r = \alpha_1 W + \alpha(-B/r^2)$$
$$= (\alpha W/r)\{(\alpha_1 r/\alpha) - (1 - \alpha - \beta)\} < 0,$$
$$L_\rho = \alpha_2 W + \alpha(-RK/\rho^2)$$
$$= (\alpha W/\rho)\{(\alpha_2 \rho/\alpha) - \beta\} < 0,$$
$$Z_Y = \beta_3 W - (1 - \beta) R_Y K/\rho,$$
$$L_Y = \alpha_3 W + \alpha R_Y K/\rho > 0.$$

## 3.5 Variational Relations: Shifting Momentary Equilibrium

If $Z_Y$ is negative, then $\phi_1$ is positive. (If $\beta_3 \leq 0$, then $Z_Y < 0$. Since $R_Y > 0$, $Z_Y$ may be negative for small positive $\beta_3$). When $Z_Y$ is negative, the sign of $\psi_1$ is indeterminate. If $Z_Y$ is positive, $\psi_1$ becomes positive.

From the goods market equilibrium condition for given $M$, $B$, and $K$ in Eq. (4), we derive another relation for the variations $\delta Y$, $\delta r$, and $\delta \rho$. This is a generalized IS relation for the variational variable. We next solve this together with Eq. (14) for $\delta Y$, $\delta r$, and $\delta \rho$ as functions of $\delta G$, for given $M$, $B$, and $K$. The result is the variational expression of the momentary equilibrium in response to $\delta G$. Later we shall examine how these relations are shifted when we allow $M$, $B$, and $K$ to vary.

In terms of the variational variables, a variation of (4) yields

$$\theta \, \delta Y = \delta G - \xi \, \delta \rho + (S_W B/r^2) \, \delta r, \tag{15}$$

where

$$\theta = S_Y(1 - T') + T' - I_Y + S_W K R_Y/\rho > 0, \qquad \xi = -I_\rho - S_W KR/\rho^2 > 0.$$

Where (14) and (15) are solved together, variations $\delta r$, $\delta \rho$, and $\delta Y$ are given in response to the variation in the fiscal variable $\delta G$ for given $M$, $B$, and $K$:

$$\delta r = \{(\psi_1/\psi)/\Delta\} \, \delta G, \qquad \delta \rho = \{(\phi_1/\psi)/\Delta\} \, \delta G, \qquad \delta Y = \delta G/\Delta,$$

where

$$\Delta = \theta + \xi(\phi_1/\psi) - (\psi_1/\psi)S_W B/r^2.$$

These expressions also determine the impact fiscal multipliers, since these are the variations in $r$, $\rho$, and $Y$ in response to a change in $G$ and are derived on the assumption that $M$, $B$, and $K$ remain constant. Over time, changes in $G$ from the equilibrium value will change the stock variables assumed constant. To evaluate how the momentary equilibrium conditions shift over time, we must incorporate variations in $M$, $B$, and $K$ in our analysis. Shifts of the LM relation are caused by nonzero $\delta M$, $\delta B$, and $\delta K$. When they are taken into account, Eq. (13) is modified into

$$\begin{aligned} L_r \, \delta r + L_\rho \, \delta \rho &= -L_Y \, \delta Y - L_M \, \delta M - L_B \, \delta B - L_K \, \delta K, \\ Z_r \, \delta r + Z_\rho \, \delta \rho &= -Z_Y \, \delta Y - Z_M \, \delta M - Z_B \, \delta B - Z_K \, \delta K, \end{aligned} \tag{13'}$$

where

$$L_M = -1 + \alpha < 0, \qquad\qquad Z_M = \beta > 0,$$

$$L_B = \alpha/r > 0, \qquad\qquad Z_B = \beta/r > 0,$$

$$\begin{aligned} L_K &= \alpha R/\rho + \alpha R_K K/\rho & Z_K &= (R/\rho + R_K K/\rho)(-1 + \beta) \\ &= (\alpha R/\rho)(1 + R_K K/R), & &= -(1 - \beta)(R/\rho)(1 + R_K K/R). \end{aligned}$$

The solutions are also changed:

$$\delta r = \{\psi_1 \, \delta Y + (\psi_2/r) \, \delta B - \psi_3 \, \delta M + \psi_4 \, \delta K\}/\psi,$$

$$\delta \rho = \{\phi_1 \, \delta Y + (\phi_2/r) \, \delta B - \phi_3 \, \phi M + \phi_4 \, \delta K\}/\psi,$$

where the coefficients are determined by

$$\begin{bmatrix} \phi_2 & -\phi_3 & \phi_4 \\ \psi_2 & -\psi_3 & \psi_4 \end{bmatrix} = \begin{bmatrix} Z_r & -L_r \\ -Z_\rho & L_\rho \end{bmatrix} \begin{bmatrix} -\alpha & 1-\alpha & -L_K \\ -\beta & \beta & -Z_K \end{bmatrix}$$

and where $\psi$ stands for $L_\rho Z_r - L_r Z_\rho > 0$.

The sign of $\phi_3$ is positive. Thus $\delta M > 0$ implies $\delta \rho < 0$. Note that $\delta B > 0$ implies $\delta \rho > 0$ if and only if $\phi_2 > 0$. From the above,

$$\phi_2 = L_r \beta - Z_r \alpha = (\alpha \beta W/r)(-\psi_L + \psi_E),$$

where

$$\psi_L = -\alpha_1 r/\alpha; \qquad \psi_E = -\beta_1 r/\beta.$$

Thus $\phi_2$ is positive if and only if the interest elasticity of demand for real balances is less than the interest elasticity of demand for equities.

Following Cohen and McMenamin, we say that bonds are closer substitutes for equities than for money if $\psi_E > \psi_L$ and that bonds are closer substitutes for money than for equities if $\psi_E < \psi_L$. Tobin (1969) refers to the former as the *traditional assumption*.

Similarly, when the shifts of the *IS* relation, due to changing stocks, are incorporated, Eq. (15) is changed into

(15') $\quad \theta \, \delta Y + \xi \, \delta \rho - S_W(B/r^2) \, \delta r = -S_W \, \delta M + \zeta_1 \, \delta B + \zeta_2 \, \delta K + \delta G,$

where

$$\zeta_1 = (1 - T')(1 - S_Y) - S_W/\rho > 0, \qquad \zeta_2 = I_K - S_W E_K,$$

where

$$E_K = (R + R_K K)/\rho = R(1 + R_K K/R)/\rho.$$

Solving (13') and (15') simultaneously, the variations $\delta Y$, $\delta \rho$, and $\delta r$ are given as the solution of

(16) $\quad \begin{bmatrix} \theta & \xi & -S_W B/r^2 \\ -\phi_1 & \psi & 0 \\ -\psi_1 & 0 & \psi \end{bmatrix} \begin{bmatrix} \delta Y \\ \delta \rho \\ \delta r \end{bmatrix} = \begin{bmatrix} -S_W & \zeta_1 & \zeta_2 & 1 \\ -\phi_3 & \phi_2/r & \phi_4 & 0 \\ -\psi_3 & \psi_2/r & \psi_4 & 0 \end{bmatrix} \begin{bmatrix} \delta M \\ \delta B \\ \delta K \\ \delta G \end{bmatrix}.$

The solutions are the same as those we obtain by taking a variation of (10). The solution of (16) yields reduced form expressions for $\delta r$, $\delta \rho$, and $\delta Y$ in terms of the state variables $\delta M$, $\delta B$, and $\delta K$ of the variational equations, which we next derive, and in terms of $\delta G$ the solutions coincide with variational expressions for $\delta r$, $\delta \rho$, and $\delta Y$ obtained by the variations of (10). See the Appendix of this chapter for the derivation of explicit relations.

Impact multipliers can be calculated from (16). For example, by solving (16) with $\delta G$ being the only nonzero variation on the right hand side, we derive the fiscal impact multipliers as

$$\begin{bmatrix} \partial Y/\partial G \\ \partial \rho/\partial G \\ \partial r/\partial G \end{bmatrix} = \Gamma \begin{bmatrix} \psi \\ \phi_1 \\ \psi_1 \end{bmatrix},$$

where $\Gamma^{-1} = \xi \phi_1 + \theta \psi - \psi_1 S_W B/r^2$.

Dependence of the fiscal impact multiplier on the parameters of the economy can be read off from the above as $\Gamma \psi$, for example. With zero $S_W$, the parameter $\theta$ and $\xi$ are determined by the characteristics of the real sector of the economy, while $\psi$ and $\phi_1$ depends on the characteristics of the financial sector. Larger $\xi$, $\phi$ or $\phi_1/\psi$ produce smaller fiscal impact multipliers. Smaller $\phi_1/\psi$ produces larger fiscal impact multipliers. Nonzero $S_W$ introduces a coupling between the two sectors so that $\theta$, $\xi$, and $\Gamma$ are influenced to some extent by the portfolio of the asset sector as well.

The monetary impact multipliers $\partial Y/\partial M$, $\partial \rho/\partial M$, $\partial r/\partial M$ can be similarly obtained by solving (16) after setting $\delta B$, $\delta K$, and $\delta G$ to zero on the right-hand side.

## 3.6 Variational Dynamics

### 3.6.1 Money Financing of Deficit

Consider 100% money financing of the variational government budget deficit. Then $\delta \dot{B} = 0$. The variation of Eq. (11) becomes, noting the dependence of $T$ on $Y$, assuming constant $B^0$,

$$\delta \dot{M} = \delta G - T' \delta Y.$$

The variation of Eq. (12) yields

(17) $$\delta \dot{K} = I_\rho \, \delta \rho + I_K \, \delta K + I_Y \, \delta Y.$$

Jointly they determine the dynamic equation for the state vector $z' = (\delta M, \delta K)$, which describes the dynamics for variational variables:

$$\frac{dz}{dt} = \begin{bmatrix} 0 \\ I_K \end{bmatrix} \delta K + \begin{bmatrix} -T' \\ I_Y \end{bmatrix} \delta Y + \begin{bmatrix} 0 \\ I_\rho \end{bmatrix} \delta \rho + \begin{bmatrix} 1 \\ 0 \end{bmatrix} \delta G,$$

where $\delta\rho$ and $\delta Y$ are related to $z$ and $\delta G$ by the solutions of (16). Since they are variations of (10), we can express them as

$$\delta Y = F_M \, \delta M + F_K \, \delta K + F_G \, \delta G, \qquad \delta\rho = H_M \, \delta M + H_K \, \delta K + H_G \, \delta G.$$

When $\delta\rho$ and $\delta Y$ are substituted out, the dynamics become

(18) $$\frac{dz}{dt} = D_M \, dz + U_M \, \delta G,$$

where

$$D_M = \begin{bmatrix} 0 & 0 \\ 0 & I_K \end{bmatrix} + \begin{bmatrix} -T' \\ I_Y \end{bmatrix} [F_M \quad F_K] + \begin{bmatrix} 0 \\ I_\rho \end{bmatrix} [H_M \quad H_K]$$

and

$$U_M = \begin{bmatrix} 1 \\ 0 \end{bmatrix} + \begin{bmatrix} -T' \\ I_Y \end{bmatrix} F_G + \begin{bmatrix} 0 \\ I_\rho \end{bmatrix} H_G.$$

The coefficients $F_M$ and $F_G$ are the impact multipliers of the monetary and fiscal instruments on real income, i.e., $\Delta Y/\Delta M$ is equal to $F_M$ and $\Delta Y/\Delta G$ to $F_G$. The Appendix calculates them as $F_G = \Omega^{-1}\theta^{-1}$ and

$$F_M = \Omega^{-1}(-\theta^{-1} S_W + n_1 \phi_3 - n_2 \psi_3).$$

By noting that $-\phi_3/\psi$ and $-\psi_3/\psi$ equal $\Delta r/\Delta M$ and $\Delta\rho/\Delta M$, respectively, the ratio $F_M/F_G$ is greater than one if and only if

$$(I_\rho + S_W KR/\rho^2)(\Delta\rho/\Delta M) + S_W(B/r^2)(\Delta r/\Delta M) - S_W > 1,$$

where the definition for $\xi$ given below (15) is substituted out, or

$$I_\rho \, \Delta\rho/\Delta M > 1 + S_W \, \Delta W/\Delta M$$

because $\Delta W/\Delta M$ equals $1 + (\partial/\partial r)(B/r)(\Delta r/\Delta M) + (\partial/\partial\rho)(KR/\rho) \, \Delta\rho/\Delta M$. We can, therefore, state that the monetary instrument has a greater impact on income than the fiscal instrument if and only if its effect on investment by causing changes in the rate of return on equity is greater than its effect on saving, $S_W \, \Delta W/\Delta M$ by more than one.

Cohen and McMenamin discuss stability of $D_M$. For stability of $D_M$ in absence of the Pigou effect, i.e., $S_W = 0$ in (5), Aoki (1980b) corrects their error (their Proposition 5b is erroneous).

The (variational) dynamic fiscal multiplier is computed from (18). The dynamic matrix $D_M$ determines the dynamic behavior of the model near the long-run equilibrium state.[4]

---

[4] Aoki (1980b) discusses the implications of the vanishing determinant $D_M$.

## 3.6.2 Bond Financing of Deficit

We next analyze the dynamic consequences of 100% bond financing of the government deficit. Assuming that $\delta \dot{M} = 0$, variation of (11) yields

$$\delta \dot{B}/r - (\dot{B}/r)(\delta r/r) = \delta G + \delta B - T'(\delta Y + \delta B).$$

This and Eq. (17) determine the variational dynamics. Instead of (18), the variational time path to the long-run equilibrium is governed by

$$\frac{d}{dt}\begin{bmatrix}\delta B \\ \delta K\end{bmatrix} = \begin{bmatrix}r(1-T') & 0 \\ 0 & I_K\end{bmatrix}\begin{bmatrix}\delta B \\ \delta K\end{bmatrix} + \begin{bmatrix}-rT' \\ I_Y\end{bmatrix}\delta Y$$

$$+ \begin{bmatrix}0 \\ I_\rho\end{bmatrix}\delta\rho + \begin{bmatrix}\dot{B}/r \\ 0\end{bmatrix}\delta r + \begin{bmatrix}r \\ 0\end{bmatrix}\delta G.$$

To put this into state-space form, we substitute $\delta r$, $\delta\rho$, and $\delta Y$ out by the solutions of (16); i.e., the variations of (10) (see the Appendix of this chapter for details):

$$\delta Y = F_B\,\delta B + F_K\,\delta K + F_G\,\delta G, \qquad \delta r = J_B\,\delta B + J_K\,\delta K + J_G\,\delta G,$$

and

$$\delta\rho = H_B\,\delta B + H_K\,\delta K + H_G\,\delta G.$$

The state-space representation of the dynamics under 100% bond financing of the government deficit is then

(19)
$$\frac{d}{dt}\begin{bmatrix}\delta B \\ \delta K\end{bmatrix} = D_B\begin{bmatrix}\delta B \\ \delta K\end{bmatrix} + U_B\,\delta G,$$

where

$$D_B = \begin{bmatrix}r(1-T') & 0 \\ 0 & I_K\end{bmatrix} + \begin{bmatrix}-rT' \\ I_Y\end{bmatrix}[F_B \ \ F_K] + \begin{bmatrix}0 \\ I_\rho\end{bmatrix}[H_B \ \ H_K]$$

and

$$U_B = \begin{bmatrix}r \\ 0\end{bmatrix} + \begin{bmatrix}-rT' \\ I_Y\end{bmatrix}F_G + \begin{bmatrix}0 \\ I_\rho\end{bmatrix}H_G.$$

The term $\dot{B}/r$ vanishes since $\dot{B} = 0$ at the long-run equilibrium.

We can calculate the dynamic fiscal multiplier from (19), which is the subject of the next chapter.

## Appendix

Decompose the matrix in Eq. (16) as $N - \mathbf{n}\mathbf{e}'$, where

$$N = \begin{bmatrix} \theta & \xi & -S_W B/r^2 \\ 0 & \psi & 0 \\ 0 & 0 & \psi \end{bmatrix}, \quad \mathbf{n} = \begin{bmatrix} 0 \\ \phi_1 \\ \psi_1 \end{bmatrix}, \quad \mathbf{e} = \begin{bmatrix} 1 \\ 0 \\ 0 \end{bmatrix}.$$

The inverse $(N - \mathbf{n}\mathbf{e}')^{-1}$ is $N^{-1} + N^{-1}\mathbf{n}\mathbf{e}'N^{-1}/(1 - \mathbf{e}'N^{-1}\mathbf{n})$, where

$$N^{-1} = \begin{bmatrix} \theta^{-1} & -n_1 & n_2 \\ 0 & \psi^{-1} & 0 \\ 0 & 0 & \psi^{-1} \end{bmatrix},$$

where

$$n_1 = \xi/(\theta\psi), \qquad n_2 = S_W(B/r^2)/(\theta\psi).$$

The solution of Eq. (16) is

$$\begin{bmatrix} \delta Y \\ \delta \rho \\ \delta r \end{bmatrix} = (N - \mathbf{n}\mathbf{e}')^{-1} \left\{ -\begin{bmatrix} S_W \\ \phi_3 \\ \psi_3 \end{bmatrix} \delta M + \begin{bmatrix} \zeta_1 \\ \phi_2/r \\ \psi_2 \end{bmatrix} \delta B + \begin{bmatrix} \zeta_2 \\ \phi_4 \\ \psi_4 \end{bmatrix} \delta K + \begin{bmatrix} 1 \\ 0 \\ 0 \end{bmatrix} \delta G \right\}.$$

For example, in the case where $\delta B = 0$, we can write $\delta Y$ as

$$\delta Y = \begin{bmatrix} F_M & F_K & F_G \end{bmatrix} \begin{bmatrix} \delta M \\ \delta K \\ \delta G \end{bmatrix},$$

where we use the expression for the inverse shown above to identify terms as

$$(F_M, F_K, F_G) = \Omega^{-1}(-\theta^{-1}S_W + n_1\phi_3 + n_2\psi_3, \theta^{-1}\zeta_2 - n_1\phi_4 + n_2\psi_4, \theta^{-1}),$$

where

$$\Omega = 1/(\Gamma\theta\psi).$$

Similarly,

$$\delta\rho = \begin{bmatrix} H_M & H_K & H_G \end{bmatrix} \begin{bmatrix} \delta M \\ \delta K \\ \delta G \end{bmatrix},$$

where

$$(H_M, H_K, H_G) = \Omega^{-1}\psi^{-1}(-\phi_3, \phi_4, \phi_1).$$

# 4 | Dynamic Policy Multipliers (Impulse Response Functions)[1]

This chapter derives the expressions for impact and dynamic multipliers of variational dynamic systems in state-space representation for continuous time models and discrete time models in Sections 4.1 and 4.2, respectively. Impact and dynamic multipliers of the fiscal and monetary instruments of a small open economy are calculated in Section 4.3 as illustration.

## 4.1 Dynamic Multipliers of Continuous Time Models

Policy multipliers of an economic model convey useful information on magnitudes and timings of policy instruments' influences on endogenous variables. Suppose that an economy is moving along a planned time path. How much does a change of an instrument from its planned path cause endogenous variables to deviate from their respective planned time paths? Calculating dynamic policy multipliers will provide the answers. Special types of dynamic multipliers are the well-known impact multipliers, which show immediate or impact effects, and the long-run multipliers, which indicate permanent effects on endogenous variables caused by changes in instruments.

There are as many multipliers as there are pairs of targets and instruments. In a multidimensional dynamic system with several instruments and targets, we have a multiplier matrix rather than a scalar multiplier. Each element of the matrix is the dynamic policy multiplier of a target and instrument pair. When there are preferred or assigned pairings of targets and instruments, diagonal elements of the multiplier matrix show the effects of instruments on the intended or assigned targets; off-diagonal elements show spill-over

---

[1] Appendix A further discusses policy multipliers of discrete-time models.

or unintended effects of instruments on nonassigned targets, if the pairs are numbered by the same subscripts.

Individual elements of a multiplier matrix may reach their maximum values some time after the change in the instrument has taken place or may exhibit monotone decay. The times at which the dynamic multipliers reach their maximum value, if they exist, may be different for different endogenous variables even for the same instruments. Both the maximum values of the multipliers and the times at which they are reached reveal important information about the power and timings of policy instruments. Here is a general procedure for calculating a dynamic multiplier matrix and the times at which the maxima are attained. Instead of policy multipliers of a nonlinear macroeconomic model, we calculate policy multipliers of the variational dynamic system derived from the nonlinear model, i.e., the variational policy multipliers. Our primary interest lies in the changes in some target variables from their reference time path values produced by changes in some policy instruments from their reference time paths.[2] Variational policy multipliers are very easy to compute once we put the models' dynamics in state-space representation. (Dynamic multipliers are easier to derive from state-space representation. Appendix A gives a procedure for converting autoregressive moving average models into state-space form.) Our model is already in state-space form.

To compute variational dynamic multipliers, we must use the variational dynamics about some chosen time path or about an equilibrium state. Then we can represent a model by the next two equations without losing generality: The dynamic equation is

$$\dot{z} = Az + Bx, \tag{1}$$

and the target equation is

$$q = Cz + Dx, \tag{2}$$

where $z$ denotes the state vector, $x$ the instrument vector, and $q$ the target vector. The multiplier matrix is dim $q$ by dim $x$. A simpler case conveying the same information about calculating the dynamic policy multiplier results in specializing our discussion to the dynamic system with a scalar instrument. The matrix $B$ then becomes a vector $b$, and the multiplier matrix a vector of dimension $q$.

---

[2] What we calculate may therefore be thought of as incremental dynamic multipliers which relate incremental changes in instruments to incremental induced changes in endogenous variables, all measured from respective reference paths.

## 4.1 Dynamic Multipliers of Continuous Time Models

To isolate effects of instrument changes, we solve (1) with the zero initial condition. The solution is given by

$$z(t) = e^{At} \int_0^t e^{-A\tau} bx(\tau)\, d\tau.$$

Consequently the target vector is related to the instrument by

$$q(t) = Ce^{At} \int_0^t e^{-A\tau} bx(\tau)\, d\tau + Dx(t).$$

The nonzero vector $D$ represents impact effects. With zero $D$, the instruments affect target vectors only through integral effects of past values of the instruments. The function $Ce^{A(t-s)}b$ is known as the impulse response function in the system literature.

We consider two types of change: temporary change of the instrument,

$$x(t) = \begin{cases} \bar{x}, & \text{for } 0 \le t \le \bar{t}, \\ 0, & \text{otherwise,} \end{cases}$$

and permanent (one-and-for-all) change, $x(t) = \bar{x}$ for all $t \ge 0$. With the temporary change, the impact multiplier is

$$\mu(0) = D.$$

Assuming that $A$ is a stable matrix, the long-run multiplier is

$$\mu(\infty) = 0,$$

where we use $\mu(t)$ to denote a dynamic multiplier. With permanent change, the impact and the long-run multiplier are given, respectively, by

$$\mu(0) = D \quad \text{and} \quad \mu(\infty) = -CA^{-1}b + D.$$

With temporary change, the finite time-dynamic multiplier is[3]

(3) $$\mu(t) = CA^{-1}(e^{At} - I)b + D, \quad \text{for } t \le \bar{t},$$

and

(4) $$\mu(t) = CA^{-1}e^{At}(I - e^{-A\bar{t}})b, \quad \text{for } t > \bar{t}.$$

For the permanent change, the multiplier vector is given by

(5) $$\mu(t) = CA^{-1}(e^{At} - I)b + D.$$

Note that (5) is the same as (4) if $D$ is zero. When we measure the multiplier vector from its steady-state or long-run level as $\mu(t) - \mu(\infty)$, we note that the

---

[3] We assume that the inverse of $A$ exists. Otherwise, the multipliers cannot be written conveniently as shown.

expressions of the multipliers for temporary and permanent changes both have the same structure. The only difference is that the vector $b$ is replaced with the vector $(I - e^{-At})b$ in the former.

The multiplier for a specific target can be extracted quite easily from the expression for the multiplier vector. For example, the multiplier for the first component of the target vector $q$ is obtained by forming the inner product of the multiplier with a vector $u$ which is zero except for the unit element in the first component. The multiplier attains a relative maximum value, if such exists, when its time derivative vanishes for the first time after $t = 0$. Since $\mu(t) - \mu(\infty)$ is of the form $CA^{-1}e^{At}\beta$, the equation

$$(6) \qquad 0 = u'\, d\mu/dt = u'Ce^{At}\beta$$

determines the time at which an instrument change exerts its maximum effects on the first component of $q$, where the vector $\beta$ is $b$ in the case of permanent shift in the instrument and $(I - e^{-A\bar{t}})b$ in the case of temporary change in $x$.

We emphasize that multipliers of a first-order dynamics and multidimensional dynamics can exhibit fundamentally different behavior. The multiplier decreases monotonically for any stable one-dimensional dynamic system and does not exhibit any peak. Finite time multipliers are always less than the corresponding impact multipliers. With a multidimensional system, the multiplier can have one or more relative maxima some of which may be larger than the impact multiplier.

### An Example

Let us suppose that the matrix $A$ is given by

$$\begin{bmatrix} -1 & 0 \\ 1 & -2 \end{bmatrix},$$

$b$ by

$$\begin{bmatrix} 1 \\ 0 \end{bmatrix},$$

and $C$ by $[1 \ -2]$. Then, from (5), noting that $A$ is a stable matrix

$$\mu(t) - \mu(\infty) = CA^{-1}e^{At}b = e^{-t} - e^{-2t}.$$

This function is plotted in Fig. 1. It shows that the dynamic multiplier reaches its maximum value at $t = \ln 2$.

### 4.3 Multiplier in a Small Open Economy: An Example

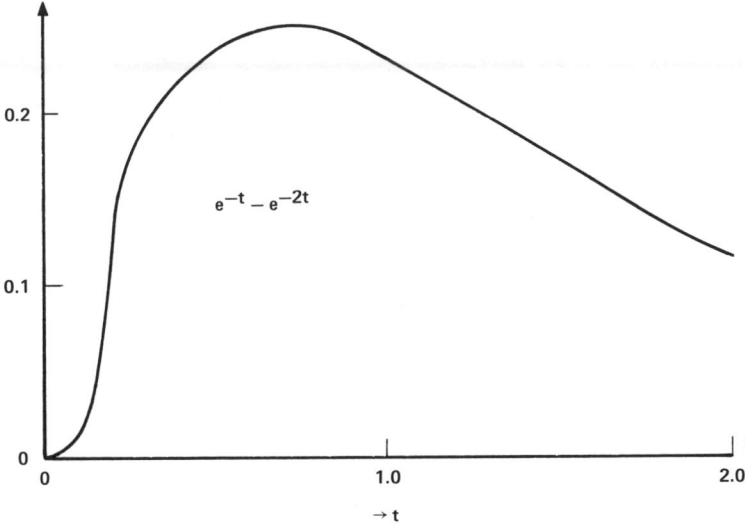

*Figure 1* Time profile of a dynamic multiplier.

### 4.2 Discrete-Time Policy Multiplier

Effects of the instruments in (1) can alternatively be evaluated by converting (1) into a difference equation by integrating (1) over a time interval of duration $h$. Denote $z(kh)$ by $z(k)$ and $x(kh)$ by $x(k)$. Then (1) becomes

$$z(k + 1) = (I + A \Delta)z(k) + B \Delta x(k).$$

Let $z(0) = 0$. Then the initial effect of $x(0)$ held over one period propagates with time as

$$z(1) = B \Delta x(0),$$
$$z(2) = (I + A \Delta)B \Delta x(0),$$
$$z(k + 1) = (I + A \Delta)^k B \Delta x(0).$$

Thus $(I + A \Delta)^k B$ is the policy multiplier.

### 4.3 Multiplier in a Small Open Economy: An Example

Impact and dynamic multipliers are calculated using an abbreviated model of a small open economy. More fully specified models are discussed in Chapter 8 and in Part Two.

### 4.3.1 Model

The private sector of this economy holds stock of domestic money which is a nontraded financial asset, and stock of internationally traded bonds $F$, expressed in foreign exchange with an exogenously given interest rate $i^*$. The asset sector is specified by the two demand equations:[4]

(7) $$M/P = a(i^*, Y)A/P, \qquad \alpha_Y > 0,$$

and

$$EF/P = \beta(i^*, Y)A/P, \qquad \beta_Y = -\alpha_Y,$$

where $\alpha$ and $\beta$ sum up to one, and where $A$ is nominal wealth.

The government does not intervene in the foreign market. The money stock remains constant by assuming a balanced budget. The capital stock is also assumed constant. In this abbreviated model then, the dynamics come only from changing stock of the international bonds held by the private sector of the economy. The stock of the international bonds changes according to

(8) $$\dot{F} = B_T + i^*F,$$

where $B_T$ is the trade balance specified as

(9) $$B_T = U(Y, E/P), \qquad U_1 < 0, \quad U_2 > 0,$$

where $P^*$ is normalized to one.

The economy produces a single (composite bundle of) good which is an imperfect substitute for the world good. The aggregate demand is supposed to equal

(10) $$Y = H(Y - T) + G + X(Y, E/P), \qquad H' > 0, \quad X_1 < 0, \quad X_2 > 0,$$

and the aggregate supply depends on $P$,

(11) $$Y = Y(P), \qquad Y' > 0,$$

where real tax receipt $T$ equals $G$ by the balanced budget condition. The interest receipt $i^*F$ and capital gains are ignored in the expression for the disposable income which is approximated by $Y - T$. Static expectations on the inflation and the exchange rate are assumed also for simplicity.

---

[4] Demand for real balances may be thought to depend on real wealth through opportunity cost for time, for example.

## 4.3 Multiplier in a Small Open Economy: An Example

### 4.3.2 Variational Equations

Initially, the economy is supposed to be in its long-run equilibrium state in which $P, Y, G, M$, and $F$ are all constant. We next derive variational equations. In (7) only one equation is independent because of the balance sheet constraint. We take it to be the ratio $M/EF$. Taking its variation, we derive

(12) $$m - e - f = \mu y,$$

where

$$\mu = \alpha_Y Y/(\alpha\beta) > 0.$$

From (8), recalling that $\dot{F}/F$ is zero at the long-run equilibrium

(13) $$\dot{f} = i^*f + \delta B_T/F = i^*f - \Omega_1 y + \Omega_2(e - p)$$

follows noting that the variational expression for the trade balance follows from (9):

$$\delta B_T = U_1 Yy + U_2(E/P)(e - p).$$

Hence

$$\delta B_T/F = -\Omega_1 y + \Omega_2(e - p),$$

where

$$\Omega_1 = -U_1 Y/F > 0, \qquad \Omega_2 = U_2(E/P)/F > 0.$$

From variations of (10) and (11) we obtain the variational expressions for $Y$ and $P$. First, from (10),

$$\delta Y = (1 - H' - X_1)^{-1}\{(1 - H')\delta G + (X_2 E/P)(e - p)\}$$

or

(14) $$y = d_0 g + d_1(e - p),$$

where

$$d_0 = (1 - H' - X_1)^{-1} Y^{-1}(1 - H')G > 0,$$
$$d_1 = (1 - H' - X_1)^{-1}(X_2 E/P) > 0.$$

Then from (11), $y = \sigma p$ where $\sigma$ is defined to be $(Y'P/Y) > 0$. Substituting $\sigma p$ for $y$ in (14), we solve it for $p$ as

$$p = (\sigma + d_1)^{-1}(d_0 g + d_1 e).$$

This, together with (12), determines $e$, $p$, and $y$:

(15) $\quad e = (\sigma + d_1 + \mu\sigma d_1)^{-1}\{(\sigma + d_1)(m - f) - \mu\sigma d_0 g\},$

(16) $\quad p = (\sigma + d_1 + \mu\sigma d_1)^{-1}\{d_0 g + d_1(m - f)\},$

and

(17) $\quad y = \sigma(\sigma + d_1 + \mu\sigma d_1)^{-1}\{d_0 g + d_1(m - f)\}.$

### 4.3.3 Impact Multipliers

Effects of instantaneous changes in $G$, $M$, or $F$ can be read off from Eqs. (15)–(17). For example from (17), keeping $M$ and $F$ fixed,

$$y/g = \sigma(\sigma + d_1 + \mu\sigma d_1)^{-1} d_0$$

or

(18) $\quad \dfrac{\Delta Y}{\Delta G} = \dfrac{Y}{G}\sigma(\sigma + d_1 + \mu\sigma d_1)^{-1} d_0.$

If the central bank (the government) sells international bonds to the private sector so that $\Delta M = -E\,\Delta F > 0$, then $\Delta F/F$ equals $-(\Delta M/M)(M/EF)$; hence $m - f$ in (15)–(17) equals $(\Delta M/M)(1 + M/EF)$. Then from (15), the exchange rate instantly depreciates by the amount given by

$$\Delta E/E = (\sigma + d_1)(\sigma + d_1 + \mu\sigma d_1)^{-1}(1 + M/EF)(\Delta M/M).$$

### 4.3.4 Dynamic Multipliers

To obtain the expression for dynamic multipliers, we write a state-space representation of the differential equation for $f$ from (13), (15), (16), and (17). From the definition of $d_0$ we note that the closer $H'$ is to one, the closer the fiscal impact multiplier is to zero. The differential equation becomes

(19) $\quad \dot{f} = -\lambda f - \lambda_g g + \lambda_m m,$

where

$$\lambda = -i^* + \lambda_m, \qquad \lambda_g = \{\Omega_1 \sigma + \Omega_2(1 + \mu\sigma)\} d_0 > 0,$$

and

$$\lambda_m = (\sigma + d_1 + \mu\sigma d_1)^{-1}\sigma(-\Omega_1 d_1 + \Omega_2).$$

## 4.3 Multiplier in a Small Open Economy: An Example

Stability of (19) requires that $\lambda$ be positive, i.e., $\lambda_m$ is greater than $i^*$. To obtain the fiscal dynamic multiplier, we set $m$ to zero and integrate (19) as

$$f = e^{-\lambda t}f(0) - \lambda_g \int_0^t e^{-\lambda(t-s)}g(s)\,ds.$$

To illustrate, let $f(0)$ be zero and consider a once-and-for-all change in $g$, i.e.,

$$g(s) = \bar{g}, \quad s \geq 0.$$

Then

(20) $$f(t) = -(\lambda_g \bar{g}/\lambda)(1 - e^{-\lambda t}).$$

This, together with (15), shows that

$$e(t)/\bar{g} = (\sigma + d_1 + \mu\sigma d_1)^{-1}\{-\mu\sigma d_0 - (\sigma + d_0)(\lambda_g/\lambda)(1 - e^{-\lambda t})\}.$$

The first term in bracket shows the impact effect; an instantaneous appreciation of the exchange rate. The second term is due to the dynamics, i.e., gradual decumulation of the international bonds as expressed by (20).

In the case of an open market operation $\Delta F = -\Delta M$, where we set $\bar{E}$ to one, the initial condition of (19) is given by $f(0) = \Delta F/F = -(\Delta M/M)(M/F)$. Keeping $G$ at the equilibrium value in (19), $f$ changes with time according to

$$f(t) = f(0)e^{-\lambda t} + \lambda_m \int_0^t e^{-\lambda(t-s)}m\,ds = f(0)e^{-\lambda t} + \lambda_m(\bar{m}/\lambda)(1 - e^{-\lambda t}),$$

where $\bar{m} = (\Delta M/M)$.

Substituting $f(0)$ out from the above,

$$f(t)/\bar{M} = -(M/F)e^{-\lambda t} + (\lambda_m/\lambda)(1 - e^{-\lambda t}).$$

After an instantaneous decrease, $F$ is gradually accumulated to the final stock given by $(F(\infty) - \bar{F})/(\bar{F}\bar{m}) = f(\infty)/\bar{m} = \lambda_m/\lambda$.

The exchange rate behavior is calculated from the above and (15).

### 4.3.5 Elaborations

When the menu of the financial assets is expanded to include stocks of domestic bonds $B$ and foreign bonds $F$, which are imperfect substitutes, then both the domestic interest rate $i$ and the international rate $i^*$ appear in the asset demand functions:

$$M/P = \alpha(i, Y),$$

$$B/P = \beta(i, i^*, Y)(A - M)/P,$$

$$EF/P = \gamma(i, i^*, Y)(A - M)/P,$$

where $\beta$ and $\gamma$ sum up to one. We assume for simplicity that $i^*$ does not appear in the demand equation for real balances. We use the equation for real balances and the ratio $EF/B = \gamma/\beta$ as the two independent equations. The variational equations for the asset sector variables $\delta i$ and $e$ are

$$\mu_1 \delta i = -m + p + \mu_2 y,$$

where

$$\mu_1 = -\alpha_1/\alpha > 0, \qquad \mu_2 = \alpha_2 Y/\alpha > 0,$$

and

$$v_1 \delta i + e = b - f - v_2 y,$$

where

$$v_1 = -\gamma_1/\gamma + \beta_1/\beta > 0, \qquad v_2 = (-\gamma_2/\gamma + \beta_2/\beta)Y.$$

These two equations can be solved for $\delta i$ and $e$ holding $p$ and $y$ exogenous:

(21) $\begin{bmatrix} \delta i \\ e \end{bmatrix} = \mu_1^{-1} \left\{ \begin{bmatrix} 1 \\ v_1 \end{bmatrix} m + \mu_1 \begin{bmatrix} 0 \\ 1 \end{bmatrix} (b - f) - \begin{bmatrix} 1 \\ v_1 \end{bmatrix} p - \begin{bmatrix} \mu_2 \\ \mu_1 v_2 + v_1 \mu_2 \end{bmatrix} y \right\}.$

To obtain variations in $Y$ and $P$, we replace $H(Y - T)$ by $H(Y - T, i)$, with $H_2 < 0$. Consequently, (14) is replaced by $y = d_0 g + d_1(e - p) - d_2 \delta i$, where $d_2 = -(1 - H_1 - X_1)^{-1} Y^{-1} H_2 > 0$. The variational supply expression remains as before; $y = \sigma p$. The equilibrium in the real sector implies then that $p$ and $y$ are the solutions of

$$\begin{bmatrix} \sigma & -1 \\ d_1 & 1 \end{bmatrix} \begin{bmatrix} p \\ y \end{bmatrix} = (d_0 g + d_1 e - d_2 \delta i) \begin{bmatrix} 0 \\ 1 \end{bmatrix},$$

or

(22) $\quad p = (\sigma + d_1)^{-1}(d_0 g + d_1 e - d_2 \delta i) \qquad$ and $\qquad y = \sigma p.$

Solving (20) and (21) simultaneously,

(23) $\quad p = \{\sigma + d_1 - (\rho_1 + \rho_2 \sigma)/\mu_1\}^{-1} \{((d_1 v_1 - d_2)/\mu_1)m + d_0 g\}$

and

$$y = \sigma p,$$

where

$$\rho_1 = d_2 - d_1 v_1 \qquad \text{and} \qquad \rho_2 = d_2 \mu_2 - d_1(\mu_1 v_2 + \mu_2 v_1).$$

The fiscal impact multiplier now becomes

$$\Delta Y/\Delta G = (Y/G)\sigma\{\sigma + d_1 - (\rho_1 + \rho_2 \sigma)/\mu_1\}^{-1} d_0.$$

## 4.3 Multiplier in a Small Open Economy: An Example

Comparing this with its counterpart (18), we note that the fiscal impact multiplier of our simpler two-asset model is greater if and only if

$$\mu\sigma d_1 < d_1(v_1/\mu_1 + \sigma v_2 + \sigma\mu_2 v_1/\mu_1) - d_2(1 + \mu_2\sigma)/\mu_1,$$

where $\mu$ of (18) corresponds to $v_2$. This inequality can be satisfied if $v_1$ is sufficiently large, i.e., as the home and foreign bonds become closer substitutes, then $\beta_1$ becomes larger and hence $v_1$ becomes larger. In the limiting case of $v_1$ approaching infinity, i.e., $i = i^*$, then $\Delta Y/\Delta G$ becomes zero, i.e., under floating exchange rate regimes with home and foreign bonds as perfect substitutes, the fiscal impact multiplier is zero. [Because $v_1$ appears in the coefficient of $m$ in (22), $\Delta Y/\Delta M$ is not zero in this limiting case.] As pointed out by Branson (1980), however, this Mundellian result (Mundell, 1968) is not robust. It is destroyed if real balances depend on the exchange rate, for example, by redefining real balances by $M/P_I$, where $P_I$ is the consumer price index which is a function of $P$ and $E$. Alternatively, a respecification of $M/P$ as $\alpha(i, Y)W$ would also destroy this well-known result.

Other simple illustrations of dynamic multiplier calculations are found in Section 12.2, for example.

# 5 How to Evaluate Structural Differences: Application of Perturbation Theory

Why do countries respond differently when their economies are subjected to common exogenous shock? How much of response differences is due to structural differences of these economies, how much is due to differential policy responses, and how much is due to their mutual interdependence? How different are the policy reaction functions which are called for to counter the same exogenous shocks when economies differ in some structural characteristics? To answer these questions, we need a systematic procedure for evaluating and comparing dynamic responses of two (or more) different economies. This chapter describes our second method of conducting comparative dynamic analysis which amplifies our observation made in Section 2.4 and complements the root-locus method presented there. In Chapter 2, which described our first procedure, we showed that neighboring time paths of a model moving along some reference time path can be evaluated by variational analysis of the model dynamics. Here we compare dynamic behavior of two models with similar structures and show that differences in their behavior can be analyzed by treating structural changes or different parameter values as perturbations. Models differing in some small detail from a given one due to refinements or elaborations on basic structures can often be treated this way.

The basic notion is given in Section 5.1 and is elaborated on in Sections 5.2 and 5.3. Section 5.4 presents one example.

## 5.1 Basic Procedure

Let a model's variational dynamics be given by

(1) $$\dot{z} = Az + Bx,$$

where $z$ is a state vector and $x$ is a vector of instruments.

## 5.1 Basic Procedure

We view (1) as the variational dynamic equation of a basic model so that (1) is a detrended log-linear model of the basic model about a "control" solution. Suppose we wish to investigate the dynamic behavior of another model similar to the basic one with variational dynamics

(2) $$\dot{z} = (A + \zeta C)z + (B + \zeta D)x,$$

where the matrices $C$ and $D$ are compatible with $A$ and $B$, respectively, and the parameter $\zeta$ symbolically indicates that the model (2) differs from (1) only by "small" perturbation of the matrices in (1). In other words, we regard (1) and (2) as similar except for "small" detail. One may interpret (1) and (2) as variational dynamics of a same small open economy, where $\zeta C$ stands for some additional transmission paths or dynamics ignored in the basic model, or $\zeta C$ could stand for changes in some model parameters.

We want to approximate the solution of (2) without solving it explicitly by operating on the solution of (1), when (1) is easier to solve, because calculating state transition matrices of (1) or (2) can be complicated. This, in essence, is the aim of our perturbation analysis procedure. If one country in a two-country model of the world is treated as a small open economy, then the dynamic behavior of the model can be recursively determined. The ignored feedback effects from the country so treated may then be included in the total analysis as perturbation terms. Three-country model of the world may be similarly analyzed, i.e., first, choose a benchmark model by ignoring some interaction terms to introduce some recursive structure into the model. Ignored interaction terms are then included in the final analysis as perturbation terms. The matrix $A$ would be block triangular, and the matrix $C$ has one or more nonzero off-diagonal submatrices in these cases.

The dynamic response of (1) is

$$z(t) = \Phi(t, 0)z(0) + (\Phi, Bx),$$

where the first term describes dynamic effects of the initial disturbance to the state vector and the second term shows how the instrument variation affects the state vector. In our notation we write this second term simply as $(\Phi, Bx)$, where $\Phi$ stands for the state transition matrix, i.e., the fundamental solution matrix. See the explanation in the Notation section at the beginning of the book.

Practically speaking, evaluation of the effects of the initial disturbance or change in exogenous variables or the instrument vector can be complicated because the expression for $\Phi$ is involved. Instead of solving (2) directly, we relate its solution to that of (1) plus a correction term.[1] Denote the solution

---

[1] Perturbation analysis can be used to relate these two matrix exponential functions. See Appendix F for further detail.

of (1) by $z^0$, that of (2) by $z$, and define $\delta z$ by their difference

$$\delta z = z - z^0.$$

This variable expresses changes in the state vector due to nonzero $\zeta$ in (2). It obeys the differential equation

(3) $$\delta \dot{z} = A\, \delta z + \zeta C z^0 + \zeta D x, \qquad \delta z(0) = 0.$$

Here the cross-product term $\zeta C\, \delta z$ is ignored as of second order of smallness. The initial condition is zero because (1) and (2) are solved with the same initial condition to evaluate the effects of nonzero $\zeta$.[2]

Solving (3), we can express the correction term as

$$\delta z = (\Phi, \zeta C z^0 + \zeta D x) = \zeta(\Phi, C z^0) + \zeta(\Phi, D x).$$

Substitute the solution of (1) into the first term. Then it becomes

$$(\Phi, C z^0) = (\Phi, C(\Phi, B x)) + \text{a term depending on } z^0(0).$$

We can thus express the dependence of $\delta z$ on $x$ simply as

$$\delta z = \zeta(Z, x) + \text{a term depending on } z^0(0),$$

where

$$Z = \Phi D + (C\Phi)*\Phi B$$

in our notation, which stands for

$$Z(t, s) = \Phi(t, s)D + \int_s^t \Phi(t, \tau) C \Phi(\tau, s) B\, d\tau.$$

We use this expression in Parts Two and Three of this book.

---

[2] The only reason for ignoring the cross-product term $\zeta C\, \delta z$ is to avoid computing the state transition matrix for $A + \zeta C$ and use that for $A$ which is used to calculate $z^0$. As an alternative to dropping the cross term altogether, a successive approximation procedure may be employed by generating a sequence of approximations $\delta z^{(n)}$ by

$$\delta \dot{z}^{(n)} = A\, \delta z^{(n)} + \zeta C z^0 + \zeta C\, \delta z^{(n-1)} + \zeta D x.$$

The successive improvement is governed by

$$\delta \dot{z}^{(n)} - \delta \dot{z}^{(n-1)} = A(\delta z^{(n)} - \delta z^{(n-1)}) + \zeta C(\delta z^{(n-1)} - \delta z^{(n-2)}),$$

where $\delta z^{(0)} = 0$. Therefore if

$$\int_0^t \|\Phi_0(t, \tau) \zeta C(\tau)\|\, d\tau < 1,$$

then this approximation scheme converges.

## 5.2 Structural Perturbation Method[3]

In Part Three we have several occasions for comparing behavior of a model described by the differential equation

(4)
$$\frac{d}{dt}\begin{bmatrix} z_1^0 \\ z_2^0 \end{bmatrix} = \begin{bmatrix} A_1 & 0 \\ 0 & A_2 \end{bmatrix}\begin{bmatrix} z_1^0 \\ z_2^0 \end{bmatrix} + \begin{bmatrix} B_1 \\ 0 \end{bmatrix} x_1 + \begin{bmatrix} 0 \\ B_2 \end{bmatrix} x_2$$

with that of

(5)
$$\frac{d}{dt}\begin{bmatrix} z_1 \\ z_2 \end{bmatrix} = \begin{bmatrix} A_1 & \zeta A_{12} \\ \zeta A_{21} & A_2 + \zeta A_{22} \end{bmatrix}\begin{bmatrix} z_1 \\ z_2 \end{bmatrix} + \begin{bmatrix} B_1 \\ \zeta B_{21} \end{bmatrix} x_1 + \begin{bmatrix} \zeta B_{12} \\ B_2 \end{bmatrix} x_2.$$

Equation (4) states that the vectors $z_1$ and $z_2$ are governed by two entirely independent equations.[4] These vectors are not therefore coupled together by mutual interactions. Nonzero $\zeta$ introduces interdependence between these two vectors, both through dynamic coupling terms, i.e., through nonzero off-diagonal submatrices in the dynamic matrix and by impact effects represented by the nonzero submatrices $B_{12}$ and $B_{21}$. For example, a nonzero $B_{21}$ means that changes in $x_1$ will have a direct effect on the derivatives of $z_2$. Equation (5) also allows for the possibility that $A_2$ itself could change for nonzero $\zeta$.

Rather than solving (5) directly, it is much easier to approximate the solution of (5) as the sums of $z_i^0$ with $\delta z_i$, where

$$\delta z_i = z_i - z_i^0, \quad i = 1, 2.$$

They are governed by the differential equation

(6)
$$\frac{d}{dt}\begin{bmatrix} \delta z_1 \\ \delta z_2 \end{bmatrix} = \begin{bmatrix} A_1 & 0 \\ 0 & A_2 \end{bmatrix}\begin{bmatrix} \delta z_1 \\ \delta z_2 \end{bmatrix} + \zeta \begin{bmatrix} 0 & A_{12} \\ A_{21} & A_{22} \end{bmatrix}\begin{bmatrix} z_1^0 \\ z_2^0 \end{bmatrix} + \begin{bmatrix} \zeta B_{12} \\ 0 \end{bmatrix} x_2 + \begin{bmatrix} 0 \\ \zeta B_{21} \end{bmatrix} x_1.$$

The initial conditions for $\delta z_i$, $i = 1, 2$, are again zero. $\delta z_1$ and $\delta z_2$ can now be solved separately:

$$\delta z_1 = \zeta(\Phi_1, A_{12} z_2^0) + \zeta(\Phi_1, B_{12} x_2)$$

and

$$\delta z_2 = \zeta(\Phi_2, A_{21} z_1^0) + \zeta(\Phi_2, B_{21} x_1) + \zeta(\Phi_2, A_{22} z_2^0),$$

where $\Phi_i$ stands for the matrix exponential function for $A_i$, $i = 1, 2$. Since $z_2^0$ depends on $x_2$ alone, $\delta z_1$ will depend only on $x_2$, while $\delta z_2$ depends both

---

[3] For a related discussion, see Aoki (1980d).

[4] If the submatrix $\zeta A_{12}$ is included in (4), then (4) describes a world composed of a small open economy, the state of which evolves with time according to $z_1^0$, plus a large economy whose state provides the exogenous environment for the small open economy.

on $x_1$ and $x_2$. Further discussion of this method and its application to evaluate distributional effects of national policies in a multiple-country model of the world are found in Chapters 13 and 15.

More generally, consider a two-country model of the world described by

(7) $$\frac{d}{dt}\begin{bmatrix} z \\ z^* \end{bmatrix} = \begin{bmatrix} A_1 & A_2 \\ A_3 & A_4 \end{bmatrix}\begin{bmatrix} z \\ z^* \end{bmatrix} + \begin{bmatrix} B_1 \\ B_2 \end{bmatrix}x + \begin{bmatrix} B_3 \\ B_4 \end{bmatrix}x^*,$$

where $z$ and $z^*$ are the state vectors for the two countries and $x$ and $x^*$ are the exogenous (instrument) vectors.[5] In the world of (7) two countries have different characteristics. For example, $A_1$ need not equal $A_4$ and $A_2$ and $A_3$ can be different. Instead of solving this equation directly, we compare its dynamic behavior with that of

(8) $$\frac{d}{dt}\begin{bmatrix} z^0 \\ z^{*0} \end{bmatrix} = \begin{bmatrix} \bar{A}_1 & \bar{A}_2 \\ \bar{A}_2 & \bar{A}_1 \end{bmatrix}\begin{bmatrix} z^0 \\ z^{*0} \end{bmatrix} + \begin{bmatrix} \bar{B}_1 \\ \bar{B}_2 \end{bmatrix}x + \begin{bmatrix} \bar{B}_2 \\ \bar{B}_1 \end{bmatrix}x^*,$$

where

$$\bar{A}_1 = (A_1 + A_4)/2, \qquad \bar{A}_2 = (A_2 + A_3)/2,$$
$$\bar{B}_1 = (B_1 + B_4)/2, \qquad \bar{B}_2 = (B_2 + B_3)/2.$$

The world represented by (8) consists of two countries with the same average characteristics of the two countries in (7). The differences between these two models are described by the differences of the state vectors

$$\delta z = z - z^0 \qquad \text{and} \qquad \delta z^* = z^* - z^{*0}.$$

They obey the differential equation

(9) $$\frac{d}{dt}\begin{bmatrix} \delta z \\ \delta z^* \end{bmatrix} = \begin{bmatrix} \bar{A}_1 & \bar{A}_2 \\ \bar{A}_2 & \bar{A}_1 \end{bmatrix}\begin{bmatrix} \delta z \\ \delta z^* \end{bmatrix} + \begin{bmatrix} A_1 - \bar{A}_1 & A_2 - \bar{A}_2 \\ A_3 - \bar{A}_2 & A_4 - \bar{A}_1 \end{bmatrix}\begin{bmatrix} z^0 \\ z^{*0} \end{bmatrix}$$
$$+ \begin{bmatrix} B_1 - \bar{B}_2 \\ B_2 - \bar{B}_1 \end{bmatrix}x + \begin{bmatrix} B_3 - \bar{B}_2 \\ B_4 - \bar{B}_1 \end{bmatrix}x^*,$$

---

[5] If submatrices $A_2$ and $B_3$ are set to zero in (7), the model becomes one where the foreign country is treated as small since home country affects the state of the foreign country but not conversely. If this model is taken to be the standard case, then the model represented by (7) may be approximately analyzed by the differential equation that describes dynamic behavior of the difference of the state vector from the reference case

$$\frac{d}{dt}\begin{bmatrix} \delta z \\ \delta z^* \end{bmatrix} = \begin{bmatrix} A_1 & A_2 \\ A_3 & A_4 \end{bmatrix}\begin{bmatrix} \delta z \\ \delta z^* \end{bmatrix} + \begin{bmatrix} A_2 \\ 0 \end{bmatrix}z^{*0} + \begin{bmatrix} B_3 \\ 0 \end{bmatrix}x^*.$$

If the product $A_2 \, \delta z^*$ is regarded small, then the dynamics simplify to

$$\delta \dot{z} = A_1 \, \delta z + A_2 z^{*0} + B_3 x^* \qquad \text{and} \qquad \delta \dot{z} = A_3 \, \delta z + A_4 \, \delta z^*.$$

Similar simplified approximate analysis can be carried out for three-country models of the world such as the one in Chapter 15.

## 5.2 Structural Perturbation Method

where cross-product terms such as $(A_1 - \bar{A}_1)\delta z^0$ are neglected as second order of smallness.

To facilitate solving (9), we diagonalize the dynamic matrix of (9) by changing the variables to

$$\delta z_a = (\delta z + \delta z^*)/2 \quad \text{and} \quad \delta z_\delta = (\delta z - \delta z^*)/2.$$

These new vectors are governed by

(10) $\quad \dfrac{d}{dt}\begin{bmatrix}\delta z_a \\ \delta z_\delta\end{bmatrix} = \begin{bmatrix}A_a & 0 \\ 0 & A_\delta\end{bmatrix}\begin{bmatrix}\delta z_a \\ \delta z_\delta\end{bmatrix} + \begin{bmatrix}0 & A_{a\delta} \\ A_{\delta a} & 0\end{bmatrix}\begin{bmatrix}z_a^0 \\ z_\delta^0\end{bmatrix} + \begin{bmatrix}0 \\ B_{\delta a}\end{bmatrix}x_a + \begin{bmatrix}B_{a\delta} \\ 0\end{bmatrix}x_\delta,$

where $z_a^0$, $z_\delta^0$, $x_a$, and $x_\delta$ are defined analogously to $\delta z_a$ and $\delta z_\delta$, and $A_a = \bar{A}_1 + \bar{A}_2$, $A_\delta = \bar{A}_1 - \bar{A}_2$, $A_{a\delta} = A_1 - \bar{A}_1 + A_3 - \bar{A}_2$, $A_{\delta a} = A_1 - \bar{A}_1 - (A_3 - \bar{A}_2)$, $B_{a\delta} = B_1 - \bar{B}_1 + B_3 - \bar{B}_2$, and $B_{\delta a} = B_1 - \bar{B}_1 - (B_3 - \bar{B}_2)$.

The solution of (10) is

(11) $\quad \delta z_a = (\Phi_a, A_{a\delta}z_\delta^0 + B_{a\delta}x_\delta) \quad \text{and} \quad \delta z_\delta = (\Phi_\delta, A_{\delta a}z_a^0 + B_{\delta a}x_a)$

because $\delta z_a(0)$ and $\delta z_\delta(0)$ are both zero.

From (8) we note that $z_a^0$ and $z_\delta^0$ are governed by

$$\dfrac{d}{dt}\begin{bmatrix}z_a^0 \\ z_\delta^0\end{bmatrix} = \begin{bmatrix}A_a & 0 \\ 0 & A_\delta\end{bmatrix}\begin{bmatrix}z_a^0 \\ z_\delta^0\end{bmatrix} + \begin{bmatrix}B_a \\ 0\end{bmatrix}x_a + \begin{bmatrix}0 \\ B_\delta\end{bmatrix}x_\delta,$$

where

$$\bar{B}_a = \bar{B}_1 + \bar{B}_2 \quad \text{and} \quad \bar{B}_\delta = \bar{B}_1 - \bar{B}_2.$$

The solutions are

$$z_a^0 = \Phi_a(t, 0)z_a^0(0) + (\Phi_a, B_a x_a)$$

and

$$z_\delta^0 = \Phi_\delta(t, 0)z_\delta^0(0) + (\Phi_\delta, B_\delta x_\delta).$$

Alternatively,

(11') $\quad \begin{pmatrix}z^0 \\ z^{*0}\end{pmatrix} = \dfrac{1}{2}\begin{bmatrix}\Phi_a + \Phi_\delta & \Phi_a - \Phi_\delta \\ \Phi_a - \Phi_\delta & \Phi_a + \Phi_\delta\end{bmatrix}\begin{bmatrix}z^0(0) \\ z^{*0}(0)\end{bmatrix}$

$\qquad + \dfrac{1}{2}\begin{bmatrix}\Phi_a B_a + \Phi_\delta B_\delta & \Phi_a B_a - \Phi_\delta B_\delta \\ \Phi_a B_a - \Phi_\delta B_\delta & \Phi_a B_a + \Phi_\delta B_\delta\end{bmatrix}\begin{bmatrix}x \\ x^*\end{bmatrix}.$

Note that effects of nonzero initial conditions and $x$ and $x^*$ are symmetrical in this symmetric world.

Substituting these into (11), we can express the differences of the state vector for (7) and (8) as

$$\delta z = \delta z_a + \delta z_\delta \quad \text{and} \quad \delta z^* = \delta z_a - \delta z_\delta,$$

where
$$\delta z_a = (S_{a\delta}, x_\delta) + \text{a term depending on } z_\delta^0(0)$$
and
$$\delta z_\delta = (S_{\delta a}, x_a) + \text{a term depending on } z_a^0(0),$$
where
$$S_{a\delta} = \Phi_a B_{a\delta} + (A_{a\delta}\Phi_\delta)^*\Phi_a B_\delta \quad \text{and} \quad S_{\delta a} = \Phi_\delta B_{\delta a} + (A_{\delta a}\Phi_a)^*\Phi_\delta B_a.$$

We can usefully summarize the differences of models given by (7) and (8) in matrix form:

(12)
$$\begin{pmatrix} \delta z \\ \delta z^* \end{pmatrix} = \frac{1}{2}\begin{bmatrix} S_{a\delta} + S_{\delta a} & -S_{a\delta} + S_{\delta a} \\ S_{a\delta} - S_{\delta a} & -(S_{a\delta} + S_{\delta a}) \end{bmatrix}\begin{bmatrix} x \\ x^* \end{bmatrix}.$$

Note that this matrix is antisymmetric. We utilize this representation later in Part Three when distributional effects of common and different changes of $x$ and $x^*$ on individual countries are discussed.

## 5.3 Choice of State Vectors in Models of Interdependent Economies

Later in Part Three of this book, we construct two- and three-country models of the world and ask, among several questions we address with these models, how a particular exogenous shock or a change of policy instrument impinges differentially on individual countries in the model. I distinguish between effects of changes common to all countries and those which differ in individual countries. This distinction helps our study of coordination of national policies and our analysis of distributional effects of exogenous disturbances and policy changes.

Given that such a distinction is useful, our procedure introduced in Sections 5.1 and 5.2 offers a handy choice of state variables in a multiple-country world model. Theoretically, any choice of the state vector describes the dynamics. Practically, some choices lead to a simpler description of dynamics than other choices. We have shown that it is much simpler to write dynamic equations for the national averages and for the vector of national differences rather than to write dynamics for the state variables of the model and later calculate the averages and the differences. This is particularly so if the individual countries are "similar" in structure and enter symmetrically into the model because the equations determining averages and differences completely separate; i.e., dynamic matrices become diagonal if sectors of the economies are identically specified for all the countries as (10) shows. The equations become approximately decoupled if the economies are similar but not identical. Theory of perturbation can be applied to analyze these models as shown in Section 5.2. This mode of dynamic representation has significant implications for the study of coordination of national policies. We take up this important point in Part Three.

Because our procedure is better conveyed by examples than abstract description, we mention one example in this section. It is a static model and is used to examine the impact effect on national incomes of changes in exogenous shift parameters such as government expenditures. Dynamic examples are found in Chapters 13 and 15.

## 5.4 Example: Effects of Trade on National Incomes

This model is directly related to the one Metzler (1951) discusses. Cooper (1973) uses it to analyze interdependence of countries trading among themselves. No asset sectors are modeled. Cooper's model serves as a vehicle for illustrating our procedure for examining distributional effects of exogenous shocks. A country in this model is described by the following set of equations:

$$Y = C + X - I_m + Z, \quad C = C(Y), \quad I_m = I_m(Y), \quad X = X(Y^*) = I_m^*(Y^*),$$

where $Y$ is national income, $C$ consumption, and $X$ the export of goods and services, all in constant prices. The exchange rate is fixed in this model as well. The variable $Z$ represents all other autonomous expenditures.

Let $s = 1 - C'$ and $m = I_m'$. Equation (13) determines the impact effects of the sudden changes in $Z$ or $Z^*$ on the national incomes:

(13) $$M_2 \, d\mathbf{Y} = d\mathbf{Z},$$

where

$$M_2 = \begin{bmatrix} s + m & -m^* \\ -m & s^* + m^* \end{bmatrix}, \quad d\mathbf{Y} = \begin{bmatrix} dY \\ dY^* \end{bmatrix}, \quad d\mathbf{Z} = \begin{bmatrix} dZ \\ dZ^* \end{bmatrix}.$$

The parameters $m$ and $m^*$ measure the degree of interdependence through trade.

In a three-country model, the basic equation determining the impact effects on the national incomes becomes

(14) $$M_3 \, d\mathbf{Y} = d\mathbf{Z},$$

where

$$M_3 = \begin{bmatrix} s_1 + m_1 & -m_{12} & -m_{13} \\ -m_{21} & s_2 + m_2 & -m_{23} \\ -m_{31} & -m_{32} & s_3 + m_3 \end{bmatrix}, \quad d\mathbf{Y} = \begin{bmatrix} dY_1 \\ dY_2 \\ dY_3 \end{bmatrix}, \quad d\mathbf{Z} = \begin{bmatrix} dZ_1 \\ dZ_2 \\ dZ_3 \end{bmatrix},$$

and where $m_{ij}$ is the marginal propensity of country $j$ to import from country $i$.

In (13) and (14) if $Z$s are interpreted as fiscal expenditures, then the solutions of the algebraic equations yield the impact effects of the fiscal policies on national outputs.

What are the implications of (13) for interdependence of national income disturbances due to shifts of autonomous expenditures in the individual countries? We can invert (13) to obtain $\delta Y$ and $\delta Y^*$, then use the result to calculate the average $(dY + dY^*)/2$ and the difference $(dY - dY^*)/2$ to examine how the shift parameters $dZ$ and $dZ^*$ affect the world average output and to see if individual countries are differentially affected. This straightforward solution method works for the two-country model but is algebraically tedious for the three-country model. Even in the two-country model, our alternate procedure for first calculating the world average and the national differences of the outputs and then calculating $dY$ and $dY^*$ for them is algebraically simpler. We now illustrate:

Define the averages and the difference vectors of the national incomes and the shift parameters as

$$dY_a = (dY + dY^*)/2, \qquad dY_\delta = (dY - dY^*)/2,$$
$$dZ_a = (dZ + dZ^*)/2, \qquad dZ_\delta = (dZ - dZ^*)/2.$$

Then we can write impact changes in the national incomes $dY$ and $dY^*$ as a vector

$$d\mathbf{Y} = dY_a \begin{bmatrix} 1 \\ 1 \end{bmatrix} + dY_\delta \begin{bmatrix} 1 \\ -1 \end{bmatrix}.$$

Similarly for $dZ$ and $dZ^*$,

$$d\mathbf{Z} = dZ_a \begin{bmatrix} 1 \\ 1 \end{bmatrix} + dZ_\delta \begin{bmatrix} 1 \\ -1 \end{bmatrix}.$$

Assuming that $s$ is the same as $s^*$, we derive the relation for the average variables by multiplying (13) from the left by $\frac{1}{2}[1 \; 1]$, which results in

(15) $$s \, dY_a = dZ_a,$$

where $[1 \; 1] \, d\mathbf{Y}_\delta$ and $[1 \; 1] \, d\mathbf{Z}_\delta$ both vanish by definition.

Equation (15) states that the average national income change is determined only by the world average of the exogenous shift variables $dZ_a$. Now multiply (13) from the left by $\frac{1}{2}[1 \; -1]$ to obtain

(16) $$(s + m + m^*) \, dY_\delta + (m - m^*) \, dY_a = dZ_\delta.$$

Substitute (15) for $dY_a$ in (16). Then we can solve (16) for $dY_\delta$ as

(17) $$dY_\delta = (s + m + m^*)^{-1} \{dZ_\delta - (m - m^*) \, dZ_a/s\}.$$

## 5.4 Example: Effects of Trade on National Incomes

Note that the difference of the national incomes depends not only on the difference of the shift variables but also on their average unless $m$ is equal to $m^*$. For example, an increase in $dZ_a$, while keeping the difference $dZ_\delta$ the same, causes a greater divergence between the two countries' national incomes. The average and the difference can be determined separately, i.e., the equations for determining the average and the difference are decoupled if and only if $m$ is equal to $m^*$.

The expressions for the national income are

$$dY = dY_a + dY_\delta = \{(s + m + m^*)\}^{-1}\{(s + m^*)\, dZ/s + m^*\, dZ^*/s\}$$

and

$$dY^* = dY_a - dY_\delta = \{(s + m + m^*)\}^{-1}\{m\, dZ/s + (s + m^*)\, dZ^*/s)\}.$$

The advantages of our procedure over the more direct calculations are implied by the above derivations but become even clearer when we analyze (14) for the distributional effects. The direct inversion of (14) and the subsequent averaging and differencing is much messier than the alternate procedure we now demonstrate. To analyze the three-country case, Cooper makes an assumption on the trading pattern among the three nations. First, he assumes that $s_i$ is the same for all three countries. Second, he introduces the notion of "economic" distance and assumes that country 2 is equally likely to trade with countries 1 and 3, but country 1 trades more with 2 than with 3 because countries 1 and 3 are further apart economically. Similarly, country 3 trades more with country 2 than with country 1. This trading pattern is reflected on his assumption that $m_{31} \leq m_{21}, m_{12} = m_{32}$, and $m_{13} \leq m_{23}$. We somewhat relax Cooper's assumption. Instead of assuming that country 1 and country 3 are far apart in economic distance we first examine (14) under the assumption that the economic distance between country 1 and country 3 is merely different from the economic distance between countries 1 and 2 and 2 and 3, i.e., we assume $m_{12} = m_{21} = m_{32} = m_{23}$, $m_{13} = m_{31}$. This assumption renders the matrix $M_3$ symmetric. Let $a = m_{12}$, and $b = m_{13}$. When $b$ is taken to be zero, countries 1 and 3 do not trade mutually, as in Cooper's extreme case.

When $b$ is taken to be the same as $a$, all three countries are at equal economic distance—a case Cooper did not consider. Here is a simple case where $a$ is assumed to be the same as $b$ and all $s_i + m_i$ are the same for all $i = 1, 2, 3$.

Under the assumed trading pattern, the matrix $M_3$ is written as

$$M_3 = (s + m + a)I - a \begin{bmatrix} 1 \\ 1 \\ 1 \end{bmatrix} [1 \quad 1 \quad 1].$$

Multiply (14) from the left by $\frac{1}{3}[1\ 1\ 1]$ to obtain

(18) $$(s + m - 2a)\,dY_a = dZ_a.$$

Note that $[1\ 1\ 1]\,d\mathbf{Y}_\delta$ and $[1\ 1\ 1]\,d\mathbf{Z}_\delta$ both vanish by definition, where we define the difference vectors by

$$d\mathbf{Y}_\delta = d\mathbf{Y} - dY_a \begin{bmatrix} 1 \\ 1 \\ 1 \end{bmatrix} \quad \text{and} \quad d\mathbf{Z}_\delta = d\mathbf{Z} - dZ_a \begin{bmatrix} 1 \\ 1 \\ 1 \end{bmatrix},$$

respectively.

From (14) and (18), we deduce that $d\mathbf{Y}_\delta$ satisfies

(19) $$M_3\,d\mathbf{Y}_\delta = d\mathbf{Z}_\delta.$$

Equation (19) shows that the national income differences themselves obey (14), i.e., the average and the differences decouple under the assumed trading pattern. The inverse of $M_3$ can be written as (see Aoki (1976, p. 390), for example)

$$M_3^{-1} = (s + m + a)^{-1}I + (s + m - 2a)^{-1}(s + m + a)^{-1}a \begin{bmatrix} 1 \\ 1 \\ 1 \end{bmatrix}[1\ 1\ 1].$$

Now, because $[1\ 1\ 1]\,d\mathbf{Z}_\delta = 0$, (19) can be solved as

$$d\mathbf{Y}_\delta = (s + m + a)^{-1}\,d\mathbf{Z}_\delta.$$

In words, when the economic distance of the three countries are the same, there is no interaction term in the national incomes, i.e., disturbances originating in a country do not spread internationally through trade.

Even when $a$ is not equal to $b$, if we assume that $m_1 - a - b = m_2 - 2a = m_3 - a - b$, then the averages and the differences still separate. Equation (18) is replaced by

(18′) $$(s + m_1 - a - b)\,dY_a = dZ_a.$$

Equation (19) remains valid for this case as well. Suppose only one country autonomously expands, say $dZ_1$ is positive, $dZ_2$ and $dZ_3$ remain zero. Then $dZ_a$ equals $dZ_1/3$, and $dZ_\delta = (dZ_1/3)[2\ -1\ -1]$. Thus $dY_1$ is given by the expression $(s + m - a)(s + m + a)^{-1}(s + m - 2a)^{-1}\,dZ_1$, and $dY_2$ and $dY_3$ are equal to $a(s + m + a)^{-1}(s + m - 2a)^{-1}\,dZ_1$. If two out of the three countries expand, say $dZ_1 = dZ_2 > 0$, $dZ_3 = 0$, then $dZ_a = 2dZ_1/3$ and $dZ_\delta = (dZ_1/3)[1\ 1\ -2]$. Consequently, individual countrys' outputs change according to $dY_1 = D(s + m)$, $dY_2 = D(s + m)$, and $dY_3 = 2aD$, where $D$

## 5.4 Example: Effects of Trade on National Incomes

stands for $(s + m - 2a)^{-1}(s + m + a)^{-1} dZ_1$. Consequences of other patterns of expansions can be similarly analyzed.

When $m_1 - a - b$, $m_2 - 2a$, and $m_3 - a - b$ are not the same, then the averages and the differences no longer decouple.

We now investigate (14) by abandoning any specific assumption on the economic distances among the trading countries. The assumption that $s_i$ is the same for all three countries is retained. The matrix $M_3$ can be written as

$$M_3 = \text{diag}[d_1 \ d_2 \ d_3] - \begin{bmatrix} b & a & b \\ a & a & a \\ b & a & b \end{bmatrix},$$

where $d_1 = s + m_1 + b$, $d_2 = s + m_2 + a$, $d_3 = s + m_3 + b$. We note that

$$\begin{bmatrix} b & a & b \\ a & a & a \\ b & a & b \end{bmatrix} = \begin{bmatrix} 1 & 1 \\ 1 & 0 \\ 1 & 1 \end{bmatrix} \begin{bmatrix} a & 0 \\ 0 & b-a \end{bmatrix} \begin{bmatrix} 1 & 1 & 1 \\ 1 & 0 & 1 \end{bmatrix}.$$

In other words, we can write $M_3$ as

$$M_3 = D - VSV',$$

where

$$D = \text{diag}[d_1 \ d_2 \ d_3], \quad S = \text{diag}[a \ \ b-a], \quad V' = \begin{bmatrix} 1 & 1 & 1 \\ 1 & 0 & 1 \end{bmatrix}.$$

In this form the inverse of $M_3$ is given by [see Householder (1964, p. 124)]

$$M_3^{-1} = D^{-1} - D^{-1} V T V' D^{-1}, \quad T^{-1} + S^{-1} = V' D^{-1} V,$$

if all the indicated inverses exist.

Equation (18) is replaced by

(20) $\quad (s + \sigma) d Y_a + \frac{1}{3}(\tau_1, \tau_2, \tau_3) d \mathbf{Y}_\delta = dZ_a,$

where

$$\sigma = \sum_i \sigma_i, \quad \sigma_i = m_i - \sum_{j \neq i} m_{ij},$$

$$\tau_i = s + m_i - \sum_{j \neq i} m_{ji}.$$

The national differences of the impact effects induced by $d\mathbf{Z}_\delta$ are given by

$$dY_a \{M_3 - (s + \sigma)I\} \mathbf{e} + (M_3 - \tfrac{1}{3}\mathbf{e}\tau') d\mathbf{Y}_\delta = d\mathbf{Z}_\delta,$$

where

$$\mathbf{e}' = [1 \ 1 \ 1] \quad \text{and} \quad \tau' = [\tau_1 \ \tau_2 \ \tau_3] = \mathbf{e}' M_3.$$

After substituting $dY_a$ out by (20), $d\mathbf{Y}_\delta$ is determined as the solution of

$$M_3\left\{I - \frac{1}{3(s+\sigma)} \mathbf{e}\tau'\right\} d\mathbf{Y}_\delta = d\mathbf{Z}_\delta + \left(\mathbf{e} - \frac{1}{s+\sigma}\tau\right) dZ_a.$$

After some algebra, noting that $\tau = M_3\mathbf{e}$ by definition, $d\mathbf{Y}_\delta$ can be expressed as

(21) $$d\mathbf{Y}_\delta = M_3^{-1} d\mathbf{Z}_\delta + (M_3^{-1}\mathbf{e}) dZ_a.$$

In the expression for the inverse of $M_3$ of the first term, the term $D^{-1}VTV'$ represents interactions due to trade among the three countries. The second term represents the distributional effects of $dZ_a$ due to the different national characteristics, i.e., the different $m_{ij}$s.

# 6 | Controllability and Theory of Economic Policy

This chapter summarized some system theoretic results which bear on design and effectiveness of policy instruments. They are all related to the notion of controllability introduced in Section 6.1. This section and Section 6.2 deal with the question of existence of a set of instruments to modify time paths of some selected endogenous variables. Section 6.3 generalizes the assignment problem [see Aoki (1976, p. 176, 236) for example] and discusses the existence of instruments which can affect only those target variables at which they are aimed with no spill-over effects on other endogenous variables. Section 6.4 considers instruments' ability to stabilize (otherwise) unstable dynamic systems. A small example illustrates this last topic in Section 6.5.

## 6.1 Controllability

Design of good policy regimes requires sound understanding of how each instrument affects endogenous variables in economy. Because the economy is complex, many obstacles surround this objective. Setting aside various practical difficulties, such as parameter uncertainty, random shocks, and exogenous shifts, consider how policy makers may formalize the notion of effectiveness of a given instrument. One way would be to calculate (dynamic) policy multipliers. We discuss this approach in Chapter 4. This formalization of the effectiveness of the policy instrument is too quantitative and too specific, however, because the multiplier is tied to a specific time path profile of the instrument. To calculate the multiplier, policy makers must first decide on a time path of a given instrument, then evaluate changes in endogenous variables produced by changes in the instrument.[1] To policy makers, it

[1] In nonlinear models, doubling dosage of some instruments generally does not produce twice the effects. Only in variational dynamic multipliers discussed in Chapter 4, this linear relation between the dosage and effects approximately holds.

would be more useful to have a more qualitative measure of instrument effectiveness which does not require prior choice of instrument time path but which broadly describes capability of any instrument to affect economy in a given class of instruments.

Controllability is such a notion. A dynamic model or a set of target variables of a dynamic economic model is controllable if the state vector or the target vector can be moved in any arbitrary direction with a given set of instruments. Controllability ensures that an instrument time path can be found to achieve given target value, without actually choosing the instrument time path beforehand. Thus, controllability can be thought of as an existence condition of a dynamic policy. We say that a deterministic system $\dot{z} = f(t, z, x)$ is (completely) controllable at time $t_0$ if for each pair of states $z_0$ and $z_1$, there exists a feasible instrument vector $x(\cdot)$ on some finite interval $t_0 \leq t \leq t_1$ such that the system moves from the state $z_0$ at time $t_0$ to $z_1$ at time $t_1$. Problems associated with the existence and the design of policy instruments to achieve a set of targets were considered, for example, by Tinbergen for a static economic system (Tinbergen, 1955). Controllability generalizes his approach to dynamic models. When a static economic model is replaced by a dynamic one, then feasible or attainable targets mean that these targets can be achieved at any specific future time by instruments satisfying all the constraints imposed for economic, political, and other reasons.

In other words, the concept of controllability naturally arises when we examine the geometry of the set of time paths attainable by a dynamic system using feasible controls (i.e., controls satisfying all the constraints imposed on them).

For variational dynamic systems with which we are mostly concerned, the set of attainable state vectors starting from zero initial conditions is simply given by

$$R(t_0, t_1) = \left\{ z : z = \int_{t_0}^{t_1} \phi(t_1, \tau) B(\tau) x(\tau) \, d\tau, \, x(\cdot) \text{ feasible} \right\},$$

where $\phi(t_1, \tau)$ is the state transition matrix (fundamental matrix of solutions) of the variational dynamics. This set is a subspace because we allow any continuous instrument time path over an interval $[t_0, t_1]$ as a feasible time path. This set is the entire $n$-dimensional Euclidean space if and only if the state vector is controllable by $x$ where $n$ is the dimension of the state vector. We can characterize this set in several ways. For example, it is known that this subspace is the same as the range (also known as image) space of the matrix

$$W^2 = \int_{t_0}^{t_1} \phi(t_1, \tau) B(\tau) B(\tau)' \phi(t_1, \tau)' \, d\tau.$$

## 6.2 Path Controllability

This fact can be stated as

**Lemma.** The image space of $R(t_0, t_1)$ satisfies

$$\text{Im}(R(t_0, t_1)) = \text{Im}(W^2) = \text{Im}(W),$$

where $W$ is the positive definite square root matrix of $W^2$.

See, for example, Brockett (1970) for proof. When controllability of $q = Cz(t)$ is the issue, $C\phi(t_1, \tau)$ replaces $\phi(t_1, \tau)$ in the definitions of $R$ and $W^2$. When the variational differential equations are of constant coefficient variety (they often are time invariant if the reference time paths are balanced growth paths or long-run equilibrium state paths), then the state transition matrix is $\phi(t, \tau) = e^{A(t-\tau)}$ and $W^2$ can be written for any $t > 0$ as

$$W^2 = \int_0^t S(t - \tau)S'(t - \tau) \, d\tau,$$

where $S(t) = Ce^{At}B$.

It can be shown that the geometry of $W^2$, i.e., its range and the null space coincide with the range and the null space of $QQ'$ where the matrix $Q$ is

$$Q = [B \quad AB \quad \cdots \quad A^{n-1}B],$$

where $n$ is the dimension of the state vector.

Therefore, the range space of $W$ is the entire $n$-dimensional Euclidean space if and only if the rank of $Q$ is equal to $n$. Thus we have another equivalent characterization of controllability in terms of the rank of $Q$ or of the range space of $W^2$. [See Aoki (1976, pp. 78–97) or Brockett (1970, p. 79).]

Some economists dismiss the concept of (point) controllability as being of limited interest for the theory of economic policy (Nyberg and Viotti, 1976), while others regard it as crucial (Buiter and Gersovitz, 1979). We view controllability and its several extensions as very important in any dynamic policy analysis, inasmuch as it implies the existence of policies with some desirable characteristics, such as policies that can cause target vectors to follow desired time paths, policies that stabilize otherwise unstable models, policies that have no spill-over effects, and so on. We shall take up these policies in turn and comment briefly on them. To distinguish the basic notion of controllability just discussed from related notions derived from it, we call it the basic notion point controllability.

### 6.2 Path Controllability

Although point controllability is important, it does not contain the notion associated with guiding the economy back to an equilibrium or to a trend or growth path. Point controllability focuses on moving the economy to a prespecified state at a prespecified time but expresses nothing about the economy once it reaches its target. Are the instruments numerous or powerful enough to keep the economy in the desired state forever once it gets there? Can a policy maker specify the time path along which he wishes to decrease inflation rates?

A concept stronger than point controllability is needed to ensure that a given target variable can be guided along a chosen time path. This is the concept of path controllability. When $A$ and $B$ are constant matrices in (1) of Chapter 4, it is known that the state vector $z$ of (1) is path controllable if and only if the matrix defined below has rank $n^2$ where $n$ is the dimension of the vector $z$:

$$\begin{bmatrix} B & AB & \cdots & A^{2n-2}B \\ 0 & B & & \\ \vdots & \vdots & \ddots & \\ 0 & 0 & \cdots & B & \cdots & A^{n-1}B \end{bmatrix}.$$

[See Aoki (1976, p. 89).]

When a target vector $q$ is defined by (2) of Chapter 4 the target vector $q$ is path controllable if and only if

$$\begin{bmatrix} D & CB & CAB & \cdots & CA^{n-1}B & \cdots & 0 \\ 0 & D & CB & & & & \\ \vdots & & \ddots & \ddots & & & CA^{n-2}B \\ 0 & & & & D & CB & \cdots & CA^{n-1}B \end{bmatrix}$$

has rank $m(m + 1)$ where $m$ is the dimension of $q$.

Since these rank conditions are cumbersome to verify, we also give a set of sufficient conditions which seem to cover most macroeconomic applications. They are [see Aoki and Canzoneri (1980) for proof]:

### 6.2.1 Sufficient Conditions for Path Controllability

The target vector $q = Cz + Dz$ subject to the dynamics $\dot{z} = Az + Bx$ is path controllable by $x$ if any one of the following four conditions is met

(i) $|D| \neq 0$,
(ii) $D = 0, |CB| \neq 0$,
(iii) $|D - CA^{-1}B| \neq 0$,
(iv) rank $DC$ is $l$, which is less than $m = \dim q$, and there exists a nonsingular matrix $P$ such that

$$[PC \quad PD] = \begin{bmatrix} C_1 & D_1 \\ C_2 & 0 \end{bmatrix},$$

## 6.4 Stabilizability

where $D_1$ is $l \times m$ and

$$\begin{bmatrix} D \\ C_2 B \end{bmatrix}$$

has rank $n$. (The matrix $P$ represents a series of elementary row operations to reduce $D$ to the form $\begin{bmatrix} D_1 \\ 0 \end{bmatrix}$.)

We shall use several of these sufficient conditions when discussing interactions of national macroeconomic policies, because path controllability is more pertinent than (point) controllability in our examination both of dynamic interdependence of economies and of interactions (or spill-over effects) of monetary and fiscal policy instruments of different policy makers. Illustrations of the concept of path controllability will be postponed until Part Three because this point can be made more easily and shall become almost self-evident only after we develop the dynamic equations for national averages and the vectors made up of national differences in a multiple-country model of the world.

### 6.3 Policies with No Spill-Over Effects

Another important policy question is whether some targets can be changed without changing other target values. [This question is known as the decoupling problem in control literature (Falb and Wolovich, 1967).] This turns out to be a generalized version of the so-called assignment problem (Mundell, 1968); subsets of instruments are assigned, one to one, to subsets of targets so that instruments in one subset influence only a limited number of targets to achieve noninteraction of some groupings of targets. For linear dynamic systems at least, all these questions are closely connected with the controllability property. See, for example, Aoki (1976), Chapter 8). Sufficient conditions for path controllability also serve as sufficient conditions for decoupling. See Aoki and Canzoneri (1978b) for proof.

### 6.4 Stabilizability

Controllability is also important since it appears as a technical condition in many optimization questions. For example, we know that a certain canonical or standard state-space representation is guaranteed to exist for controllable systems. Controllability suffices also for the existence of optimal solutions to certain quadratic programming problems arising in the regulation of linear dynamic systems.

The remainder of this section shall define the implication of controllability on the existence and design of stabilizing policy reaction functions (stabilization policies for short).

As we showed in Section 2.3, the relative deviational variables are governed by linear dynamic equations. Although we can give conditions for controllability and stabilizability for general linear dynamic systems, the conditions simplify considerably if $A$ and $B$ are time invariant, i.e., constant matrices in (1) of Chapter 4. Therefore, we give conditions for this simpler case here. [See Aoki (1976, Theorems 3 and 4, pp. 82–83) for the statements of the general conditions.] This would be the case if (i) the reference path is actually an equilibrium point or (ii) the reference path is a balanced growth path on which $Z^0$ and $X^0$ assume constant values (for example, if $Z$ and $X$ refer to intensive form variables such as per capita income or per capita money stock).

Consider a feedback rule $x = -\Gamma z$ which ties (deviation of) instruments $x$ to (deviation of) state variables $z$ by a set of constant coefficients. The resulting dynamic equation is

$$\dot{z} = (A - B\Gamma)z.$$

This policy behavior is, therefore, characterized by partial adjustment of deviations. Buiter and Gersovitz (1979) state "... the simplest and most intuitive form of response to disequilibrium. To know that any system that is dynamically point controllable can be stabilized in so simple a manner is clearly of great interest."

Note that the dynamic matrix $A$ of (1) of Chapter 4 is modified to $(A - B\Gamma)$ by adopting this reaction function. If $\Gamma$ can be chosen to make the modified dynamic matrix stable, i.e., if all the eigenvalues of $A - B\Gamma$ have negative real parts, then we say that the policy reaction function $x = -\Gamma z$ stabilizes the dynamic system. We have

***Proposition 1.*** If the dynamic system (1) of chapter 4 is point controllable by $x$, then $(A, B)$ is a stabilizable pair, i.e., there exists a constant matrix $\Gamma$ such that $A - B\Gamma$ is a stable matrix.

We call $(A, B)$ a controllable pair when the dynamic system is point controllable. The constant policy reaction matrix $\Gamma$ can be thought of as arising from the following intertemporal optimization problem for the decision maker. If a policy maker uses a quadratic cost

$$\int_0^\infty (z'Qz + x'Rx)\, dt, \qquad R > 0, \quad Q \geq 0$$

subject to the dynamics (1) of Chapter 4 to penalize deviations of the economy from the reference time paths [i.e., the path along which $z = 0$ and $x = 0$

since $z$ and $x$ are measured from trend time paths $Z^0(t)$ and $X^0(t)$], we can show [see, for example, Aoki (1976, Section 5.42)] that the optimal policy reaction function is linear in $z$, $x = -\Gamma z$ where $\Gamma$ is given by $\Gamma = -R^{-1}B'S$, where $S$ is a positive definite symmetric matrix solution of

$$A'S + SA' - SBR^{-1}B'S + Q = 0.$$

This equation is known as the algebraic Riccati equation. It is known that a positive definite solution $S$ exists if $(A, B)$ is a controllable pain and if $(A', C')$ is a controllable pair, where $C$ comes from decomposing $Q$ as $C'C$. (Such a decomposition of any positive semidefinite matrix always exists.) If one replaces the infinite planning horizon with a finite one with a cost to terminal deviation

$$z'(T)S_0 z(T) + \int_0^T \{z'(t)Qz(t) + x'(t)R(t)x(t)\}\, dt,$$

where $T$ is the length of a planning horizon, then the optimal policy is still of the form $x(t) = -\Gamma(t)z(t)$. The policy reaction matrix $\Gamma(t)$ is now a time-varying matrix. It is given by $R^{-1}(t)B'(t)S(t)$, where $S(t)$ is now a solution of

$$-\dot{S}(t) = A'(t)S(t) + S(t)A(t) - S(t)B(t)R(t)^{-1}B'(t)S(t) + Q(t),$$

$$S(T) = S_0.$$

Note that $A$ and $B$ need not be constant. It is known that $A(t) - B(t)\Gamma(t)$ is also a stable matrix [see, for example, Aoki (1976, Section 5.4.1)].

## 6.5 Example

The model, expressed in variational, i.e., log-linear form, is specified as follows:

(1) $\qquad \dot{w} = -v(w - p), \qquad v > 0,$

(2) $\qquad \dot{m} = -\mu_1 y + \mu_2 p + x, \qquad \mu_1, \mu_2 > 0,$

where

(3) $\qquad y = -a\{(1 - \rho_1)w - \rho_2 m\},$

(4) $\qquad p = \rho_1 w + \rho_2 m, \qquad \rho_1 < 1, \quad \rho_2 > 0.$

Equation (1) states that the wage rate adjusts to close a "gap" between a constant, exogenously set desired and the actual real wage wage rate.[2] Equation

---

[2] Variation of the desired real wage rate therefore does not appear in (1).

(2) is the variational government budget constraint equation in which the unplanned budget deficit or surplus is monetized 100%. The fiscal variable is constant in this example. Changes in the output from the planned rate cause the tax receipt changes, which are assumed to be proportional to $y$.

The variable $x$ is the instrument in this model. Equations (3) and (4) are reduced forms stating how $y$ and $p$ are related to the state variable $w$ and $m$. Equation (4) shows that price changes are caused by wage rate increases (mark-up pricing) and increases caused by money stock increase. Equation (3) follows from the output supplies responding to real wage rates changes by $y = -a(w - p)$. The dynamic equation, then, is

$$\frac{d}{dt}\begin{bmatrix} w \\ m \end{bmatrix} = \begin{bmatrix} -v & 0 \\ 0 & 0 \end{bmatrix}\begin{bmatrix} w \\ m \end{bmatrix} + \begin{bmatrix} 0 \\ -\mu_1 \end{bmatrix} y + \begin{bmatrix} v \\ \mu_2 \end{bmatrix} p + \begin{bmatrix} 0 \\ 1 \end{bmatrix} x.$$

After substituting $y$ and $p$ out by (3) and (4) the state equation becomes

(5) $$\frac{d}{dt}\begin{bmatrix} w \\ m \end{bmatrix} = \phi \begin{bmatrix} w \\ m \end{bmatrix} + \begin{bmatrix} 0 \\ 1 \end{bmatrix} x,$$

where

$$\phi = \begin{bmatrix} -v(1 - \rho_1) & v\rho_2 \\ a\mu_1(1 - \rho_1) + \mu_2\rho_1 & -a\mu_1\rho_2 + \mu_2\rho_2 \end{bmatrix}.$$

The trace of the matrix $\phi$ is assumed negative by postulating that

$$\mu_2\rho_2 < a\mu_1\rho_2 + v(1 - \rho_1).$$

The dynamics (5) are unstable since the determinant of $\phi$ is negative, being equal to $-\mu_2\rho_2 v$.

Consider policy reaction functions of the form

(i) $x = -\chi p$ and (ii) $x = -\gamma(\chi w + m)$

to stabilize (5). The policy reaction function (i) stabilizes the dynamics if $\chi > \mu_2$, since $\mu_2$ in (2) is replaced with $(\mu_2 - \chi)$, and the determinant of the modified dynamics equals $-v(\mu_2 - \chi)\rho_2$. With (ii), the dynamic matrix $\phi$ changes into

$$\phi' = \phi - \gamma \begin{bmatrix} 0 \\ 1 \end{bmatrix} [\chi \quad 1].$$

Its characteristic equation is

$$\lambda^2 + \lambda\{v(1 - \rho_1) + (a\mu_1 - \mu_2)\rho_2\} - \mu_2\rho_2 v = -\gamma\{\lambda + v(1 - \rho_1 + \rho_2\chi)\}.$$

With $\gamma$ zero, this has one unstable root. With a positive $\chi$ the two roots eventually become negative for large $\gamma$ and $\chi$.

# 7 Linkages of National Economies

## 7.1 Introduction

Howe *et al.* (1979) have made preliminary quantitative estimates of the importance of interdependency by evaluating the effects of the monetary and fiscal policies of Japan, West Germany, and the United States on the Federal Reserve Board (FRB) multicountry econometric model.[1]

Linkages among economies may be classified either as:

(i) the direct effects of policies in one country on other economies or

(ii) indirect or feedbacks of a policy change on the initiating country via foreign repercussions.

In various variational models we examine in Part Three, the first type of effects are apparent from the model by having nonzero (submatrix) entries in the instrument matrix: For example, $\psi_{21}$ and $\psi_{12}$ are possibly nonzero in a two-country model of the world:

$$\frac{d}{dt}\begin{bmatrix} z \\ z^* \end{bmatrix} = \phi \begin{bmatrix} z \\ z^* \end{bmatrix} + \begin{bmatrix} \psi_{11} \\ \psi_{21} \end{bmatrix} x + \begin{bmatrix} \psi_{12} \\ \psi_{22} \end{bmatrix} x^*.$$

Several indirect or feedback paths are present in (ii).[2]

---

[1] There are several other econometric studies on interdependence. They are mostly done under fixed exchange rate regimes. See Hickman and Schleifer (1978), Deardorff and Stern (1978), and the models referred to in these two studies. Black (1978) assesses the nature of disturbances in the 1970s and discusses policy responses of several major countries.

[2] Additionally, economies can be affected by common exogenous disturbances which may set off (synchronized) deviations in some macroeconomic variables and various policy responses from policy makers of individual countries. Interactions among economies tied together with trade in goods and financial assets may accentuate or dampen such disturbances, depending on the policy responses of the countries involved. Because these are best studied in stochastic context, we leave their comprehensive analysis to a separate study.

Foreign economies affect home economy through many transmission paths.[3] Here we briefly describe the four more important interactions, some direct and some feedback or induced, among different nations. They are interest rate linkage, exchange rates and price linkage, terms-of-trade linkage, and linkage due to expectations. These mechanisms are incorporated in some of the models, and their effects are analyzed in Parts Two and Three.

## 7.2 Interest Rate Linkage

Foreign or "world" interest rates affect domestic economy most directly when the interest rate parity (covered or uncovered arbitrage) assumption is adopted. See Aliber's comments (1976) on the interest rate parity condition, for example. Frequently, only one type of bond is assumed to be traded internationally, or domestic and foreign bonds are assumed to be perfect substitutes.[4] Under this assumption, the home interest rate is tied to the foreign or "world" rate by

$$(1) \qquad i = i^* + \varepsilon,$$

where $i^*$ is the foreign interest rate and $\varepsilon$ is the expected rate of depreciation of the exchange rate.

The assumption (1) is, however, highly idealized. Because of political risk and other reasons, the home bonds and foreign bonds are really imperfect substitutes even when their yields are the same. In some models, then, we drop this perfect substitutability of domestic bonds with foreign bonds. There is no tight linkage of the economy to the world economic situation as there would be under the assumption of the interest rate parity condition. Interest, income, and wealth elasticities of demands for domestic and foreign financial assets are then different and will jointly determine responses of domestic interest rates and exchange rates to instruments of domestic government or exogenous shocks.

## 7.3 Price Linkages[5]

There are many studies on empirical validity of the purchasing power parity condition. The consensus of econometric evidence supports the

---

[3] Salant (1977) discusses several specific mechanisms of international transmission of inflation both under fixed and flexible exchange rates as well as the question of convergence of national inflation rates.

[4] Frankel (1980) discusses the differences of assuming perfect capital mobility and perfect substitutability.

[5] Traded and nontraded goods are distinguished in some models, as in Calvo and Rodriguez (1977) and Flood (1977). Oppenheimer (1974) summarizes the significance of models containing

## 7.3 Price Linkages

conclusion that, in the short run at least, both the absolute and the relative versions of the purchasing power parity condition do not hold. See the May 1978 issue of the *J.I.E.*, for example.

Many papers have identified transmission paths whereby foreign prices influence domestic price formation. See Turnovsky and Kaspura (1974) or Modigliani and Padova–Schioppa (1978), for example. The direct as well as indirect channels through which foreign price levels affect domestic prices are

(i) a domestic price index when foreign goods are included in the bundles of goods consumed domestically,

(ii) imported intermediate goods prices affecting the price level of the national output (either by marginal cost pricing or mark-up pricing schemes),

(iii) foreign demands affecting demands of foreign substitute goods hence domestic price levels, and

(iv) domestic wage rate formation where expectations of inflation of the domestic price level are influenced by foreign price level inflation.

Channel (i) is often modeled as

$$P_I = P^{1-b}(EP^*)^b, \tag{2}$$

where $P$ is the national output price, $P^*$ is the "foreign" goods price in foreign currency, and the parameter $b$ indicates the proportion of domestic goods in the basket of goods used to compute the consumer price index. The parameter $b$ is a measure of "openness" of domestic economy. Discussions of the other channels will reveal two additional measures.

Channel (ii) suggests another measure of openness. The unit cost of the national output will contain the cost of imported raw materials or intermediate goods, in addition to costs of domestic factors of production of which

---

nontraded goods sector as follows:

> Non-traded goods cannot play a pivotal role in balance-of-payments equilibrium if they are highly substitutable for traded goods in either production or consumption, or if the non-traded goods sector is very small. On the other hand, a country which is a perfect competitor in world markets cannot change its terms of trade. If such a country produces only or predominantly traded goods, devaluation will not change any relative prices, and so will not help to maintain internal balance.

> In other words, in models in which policy instruments can cause relative prices to change, nontraded goods sectors do not add any essential new dynamic adjustment mechanisms. However, nontraded goods are essential in models which otherwise have no mechanisms for changing relative prices in response to policy instruments. Henderson (1977) and Mussa (1979) also expressed similar opinions.

the labor cost is dominant. Letting $v$ be the mark up, the price $P$ in (2) may be related to the costs of the imported material by[6]

(3) $$P = (1 + v)\{W^{\gamma}(EP_0^*)^{1-\gamma}\},$$

where $P_0^*$ is the price of the imported material in foreign currency and where the wage rate $W$ is chosen as a representative of domestic factor costs. Aoki and Canzoneri (1979) have analyzed a small open economy which imports oil. Using an equation somewhat different from (3), they demonstrated that the parameters $b$ in (2) and $\gamma$ in (3) affect dynamics of home economy differently.

We may capture a major portion of direct influence of foreign prices through competition in both international and domestic markets, i.e., channel (iii) by suitably combining (2) and (3).

Channel (iv) has recently received much attention, especially in performance analysis of macroeconomic models with wage indexation, such as Modigliani and Padova–Schioppa (1978), Sachs (1980), and Eichengreen (1979).

One way of modeling this channel is to posit (in log-linear form)

(4) $$\dot{w} = \theta\{\omega - (w - p_i)\} + \rho_i,$$

where $\omega$ is the "desired" real wage rate, $\rho_i$ is the expected rate of inflation of the consumer price index, and $\theta$ is the adjustment speed coefficient.

Aoki and Canzoneri (1979) use this equation. Alternatively, Modigliani and Padova–Schioppa (1978) use (in our notation) $W = \theta(a_1 P_I + a_2 EP^*)$ or its lagged version. Here $a_2$ provides yet another measure of openness of the economy.

In addition to affecting domestic economy through channels similar to the price channels, as indicated in (2) and (3), exchange rate changes affect home economy through valuation effects; domestic currency value of foreign assets in the domestic private sector varies in direct proportion with exchange rate changes. Changes in domestic private sector real wealth then affect demands for assets and real goods.

## 7.4 Terms-of-Trade Linkage

In aggregate demand functions for domestic goods, exports, and imports, the (final good) terms of trade appears as one of the important arguments. We model the volumes of exports $X$ and imports $I_m$ as functions of the terms

---

[6] Modigliani and Padova–Schioppa (1978) uses an additive formula. Here we use the geometric average form to express $P$ in a form analogous to (2).

## 7.5 Expectations

of trade among other variables. We use $Y$ or disposable income $Y'$ as the scale variable in the import function.

### 7.5 Expectations

Expectations on the inflation rates or the exchange rate changes affect home economy through many channels. We have already encountered the expected exchange rate depreciation $\varepsilon$ in (1) and the expected inflation rate of consumer price index $\rho_i$ in (4).

Since their effects must be evaluated in general equilibrium models, we leave detailed examination to Parts Two and Three where individual models incorporating some of the linkages are analyzed in detail. See also Example in Appendix C which describes a two-country model of the world under perfect foresight assumption on the exchange rate changes, i.e., $\varepsilon = \dot{e}$.

# 8 | Sources of Dynamics and Their Interactions

It is well known that changing stocks of assets due to nonzero flows contribute to dynamics. Stocks of capital or bonds may change due to investment or government budget deficits. In open economies, stocks of foreign assets held by the domestic residents or stocks of domestic assets held by foreigners may change because of nonzero current account. Changes in stocks of assets held in the private sector of the economy generally cause shifts among some variables in the asset demand functions, such as the domestic interest rate and the exchange rate. Consequently, some variables in the real sectors or labor sectors vary. There are also dynamics not due to changing stocks such as wage rate changes and changes in expectations.

We list and briefly discuss these and other factors that contribute to dynamics of open economies and derive variational differential equations governing such changes. Our example of variational dynamics of a closed economy in Chapter 3 has already demonstrated how changing stocks of domestic government debts and changing stocks of capital determine the total dynamics in a closed economy.

This chapter introduces our procedure for deriving dynamics due to changing stocks in open economies. The basic procedure is the same as in Chapter 3, although details are considerably different. We focus on two sources of dynamics due to changing stocks that are frequently mentioned in the literature: the government budget constraint and the current account. Since all the sources of dynamics are intercoupled, we cannot really set aside other sources of dynamics, such as capital growth, expectation dynamics, or wage rate dynamics due to some indexation schemes and the like, and derive dynamics solely due to these sources by themselves without some simplifying assumptions. However, to attempt an all inclusive dynamic analysis now would lead to very complex models which can best be analyzed after various components of dynamics have been examined. Besides, the exact nature of interactions or feedbacks among sources of dynamics depends on model

## 8.1 Variational Dynamic Equations

specification and cannot conveniently be discussed in general terms even when such undertakings are feasible. Here, we resort to partial analysis for expositional purposes and concentrate on the interactions of the government budget equation and the current account equation, since even this limited scope of analysis of interactions among different sources of dynamics seems to be lacking in the existing literature. For example, a number of writers have focused on dynamics due to the government budget constraint in the recent literature on closed and open economies.[1] Several recent writers have included the current account as an important factor in their explanation of exchange rate dynamics.[2] Although dynamics due to one or the other of these two sources has been examined, the combined dynamics and the process of interaction of these two dynamics have not been examined even in a relatively simple macroeconomic model of open economy with bonds under flexible exchange rate regimes, in which both domestic output and its price are allowed to vary.[3] These two sources of dynamics generally interact and can have important effects on the ways monetary and fiscal policies affect the economy. Only under special circumstances can the two dynamics be treated separately.

By imposing some simplifying assumptions which do not destroy the essential features of the combined dynamics, we exhibit and analyze the interactions between these two sources of dynamics in a simple and straightforward way.

Effects of these interacting dynamics on short-run stability and policy effectiveness are further elaborated on in the examples of Sections 8.2 and 8.4 following the general exposition in Section 8.1 as well as in individual models later in Parts Two and Three of the book. Since debt service terms are important as a determinant of long-run policy effectiveness, as pointed out for example by Rodriguez (1979), the service terms are included in the budget equation and the current account equation jointly describe the rates with which some components of the domestic private sector wealth are changing. We treat stock of the government bonds as part of the private sector nonhuman wealth in this book. (To be definite in our analysis, we assume that

---

[1] See, for example, Turnovsky (1977).
[2] See, for example, Branson (1976b) and Rodriguez (1979).
[3] For example, Turnovsky (1977) considers the problem under a fixed exchange rate regime. Branson (1976a) considers flexible exchange rates. However, his model does not contain foreign bonds. Kouri (1976) considers domestic and foreign currencies as financial assets but not interest bearing assets. Calvo and Rodriguez (1977) similarly treat a model with domestic and foreign currencies as the only financial assets. Rodriguez (1979) focuses on the stock of domestically held international bonds and the service term as an important determinant of the effectiveness of monetary and fiscal policies in the long run while he keeps the stock of the government debt constant by assuming a balanced budget.

deviation of the equity is zero, i.e., investment is autonomous and is proceeding according to the plan, i.e., deviation of capital stock and equity from the reference time paths are zero.)

## 8.1 Variational Dynamic Equations

### 8.1.1 Government Budget Constraint

Under the 100% bond financing of the unplanned government budget deficit,[4] variation in the budget deficit from a reference or "control" solution value is financed by issues of new government bonds. This causes the stock of the government bonds to deviate from the "planned" rate, namely, the rate of the reference or "control" case, corresponding to the original plan of the government instrument paths. We denote the planned rate of bond growth by $l_B$, i.e., the value of $\dot{B}/B$ along the reference (planned) time path is $l_B$, where a dot denotes differentiation with respect to time. $l_B$ can be varying with time.[5] We treat the government bonds and foreign bonds as fixed in nominal value with variable rates of return. The variational expression of the government budget constraint is given by the following:

$$(1) \qquad \delta \dot{B} = \delta D_f,$$

where the budget deficit is denoted by $D_f$. Its exact expression depends on the specification of the asset sector but is of the general form[6]

$$(2) \qquad D_f = P(G - T) + \text{debt service terms}.$$

The differential equation for the relative deviation of the bond stock is obtained from (1) as

$$(3) \qquad \dot{b} = -l_B b + \delta \dot{B}/B = -l_B b + \delta D_f / B.$$

The exact expression for $\delta D_f$, left unspecified for now, depends on specific models and will generally contain variations of variables such as interest rates and price levels.

---

[4] Dynamics when the budget imbalance is partially financed by new money and partially by new bond issue can be similarly discussed.

[5] The rates of growth of the stocks of the domestic and foreign bonds need not be zero at a point of a reference path. They must be consistent with the asset sector equilibrium condition as pointed out in Section 1.3. More explicit characterization of the reference paths is found in the next section as well as in Parts Two and Three.

[6] We assume that the central bank uses the interest received on the stock of reserves to offset the government budget deficit.

## 8.1 Variational Dynamic Equations

### 8.1.2 Current Account

The current account equation describes the rate of change in the home country's holdings of the foreign (international) asset. The variation in the rate of acquisition of the foreign financial assets by the domestic country is given by

(4) $\qquad \delta\dot{R} + \delta\dot{F} =$ variation in the current account,

where $R$ is the central bank's holding of the foreign asset and $F$ is the domestic private sector holdings of the foreign bonds in foreign currency.[7] For simplicity, we assume that the foreigners do not hold domestic bonds. Models in which foreigners hold domestic bonds are discussed in Parts Two and Three.

The current account $U$ is expressible as

$$U = B_T + i^*(F + R) \qquad \text{in foreign currency,}$$

where $B_T$ is the trade balance and $i^*$ is the interest rate on foreign bonds.

Denote the reference rate of change in $F$ by $l_F$, i.e., $l_F = \dot{F}/F$. The central bank may decide that $\sigma\%$ of $\delta U$ is allocated to $\delta\dot{R}$, i.e.,

$$\delta\dot{R} = \sigma\,\delta U$$

and the remainder is absorbed by the private sector[8]

$$\delta\dot{F} = (1 - \sigma)\,\delta U.$$

The variable $\sigma$ is a policy instrument of the central bank.

The variational equation (4) can be expressible as

(4') $\qquad \dot{r} = -l_R r + \sigma\,\delta U/R, \qquad \dot{f} = -l_F f + (1 - \sigma)\,\delta U/F,$

where $l_R = \dot{R}/R$ is the planned rate of growth of the central bank holdings of the stock of international reserve. When the central bank does not intervene

---

[7] The original equation, $\dot{R} + \dot{F} =$ current account, states that the holdings of the foreign (international) currency of the domestic economy can increase in the aggregate only by the balance-of-payments surplus. This assumes that the home currency can be freely converted to the foreign currency. We do not discuss a possibility where the rest of the world is reluctant to convert the home currency to the "foreign" currency.

[8] The central bank intervenes in the foreign exchange market. These foreign exchange and open market operations produce discontinuous changes in some stocks of financial assets. Rather than directly analyzing consequences of a sequence of these discontinuous operations, we approximate them by flows as smoothed average over some time interval. Alternatively, we may regard this equation as a policy reaction function.

in the foreign exchange market in reacting to deviation from the trend path, then $\sigma = 0$ and $\delta R \equiv 0$ because $R$ is growing according to the planned rate by setting $\sigma$ to zero. The differential equation for the relative deviation $f = \delta F/F$ then is obtained from (4')

(5) $$\dot{f} = -l_F f + \delta U/F.$$

For simplicity, we exhibit the dynamics with $\sigma = 0$. Then from (3) and (5)

(6) $$\frac{d}{dt}\begin{bmatrix} b \\ f \end{bmatrix} = \begin{bmatrix} -l_B & 0 \\ 0 & -l_F \end{bmatrix}\begin{bmatrix} b \\ f \end{bmatrix} + \begin{bmatrix} 0 \\ 1 \end{bmatrix}\frac{\delta U}{F} + \begin{bmatrix} 1 \\ 0 \end{bmatrix}\frac{\delta D_f}{B}.$$

The diagonal elements $-l_B$ and $-l_F$ are there due to our choice of relative rather than actual deviations as the state variables. This equation is not yet in state-space form because $\delta U$ and $\delta D_f$ are not expressed in terms of $b$ and $f$. One may mistakenly conclude from (6) that no interactions exist between the dynamics for $b$ and $f$ since deviation in the current account affects only $\dot{f}$, and $\dot{b}$ is affected only by the unbalanced budget. To perceive that the dynamics for $b$ and $f$ interact, we must express $\delta U$ and $\delta D_f$ in terms of the basic (state) variables, which include $b$ and $f$. The state variables are variables which completely and uniquely determine future time evolution of the model for given time paths of instruments and will generally contain other variables in addition to $b$ and $f$.

This step must be carried out in the context of specific models, since exact dependence of $\delta U$ and $\delta D_f$ on state variables cannot be known without more fully specifying the structure of the macroeconomic model. An example at the end of this chapter illustrates this step. Parts Two and Three of the book contain more complex examples. Suffice it to note that $\delta U$ will depend on the deviation of the interest rate from the trend rate which in turn depends on $b$, while $\delta D_f$ will depend on deviations of the domestic price level, output, and the exchange rate from the trend values, all of which are influenced by $f$ among others. Therefore, in the state-space representation of the dynamics, a state vector $z$ will be of the form

$$z = \begin{bmatrix} b \\ f \\ \zeta \end{bmatrix},$$

where $\zeta$ represents some other variables without which the future time path of the economy cannot be specified uniquely. (What constitutes $\zeta$ depends on the specific models and the matrix $\Phi$ in the dynamic equation $\dot{z} = \Phi z$ will not be diagonal, i.e., there are cross effects in general.) To put this analysis concretely, we shall consider a simple model after mentioning other sources of dynamics which are not due to changing stocks.

### 8.1.3 Expectations

We find that the perfect foresight assumption and some regressive mechanisms of expectation generation are the most common specifications adopted in the literature on expectational variables. The perfect foresight assumption posits that expected rates of changes of some variables are equal to their actual rates of changes. For example, deviation of the expected rate of depreciation of the exchange rate from a specified trend rate or reference rate equals the actual rate of change of the relative deviation of the exchange rate, $\delta\varepsilon = \dot{e}$. Or, again, the variation of the expected rate of inflation of the domestic output price equals the actual rate of change of the relative deviation of the price level $\delta\pi = \dot{p}$ where $\varepsilon$ and $\pi$ are the expected rate of changes of the exchange rate and the inflation rate of the home output price, respectively, i.e., expected values of $\dot{E}/E$ and $\dot{P}/P$, respectively.

Autoregressive mechanisms for expectations posit that variation in the expected rates of changes such as $\delta\varepsilon$ or $\delta\pi$ are proportional to the deviations of the variables from their reference paths. For example, hypotheses such as

$$(7) \qquad \delta\varepsilon = -ve \quad \text{or} \quad \delta\pi = -\theta p$$

have been used in the literature. More generally, $\delta\varepsilon$ should be proportional to the deviations of the state vector components and instruments, not merely to $e$,[9] and $\delta\pi$ should not be proportional solely to $p$ but similarly should depend on state variables and instruments of the model. This is because spill-over effects exist in the economy. For example, the specification

$$(8) \qquad \delta\varepsilon = v_0 g - v_1 e - v_2 b - v_3 f$$

is more general than the popular autoregressive expectations equation.

These more general regressive mechanisms can be justified in two ways. First, one could apply the general weighted mean-square estimation schemes for the dynamic system (Kalman filter). In this approach, the dynamics in the stochastic continuous time model are usually given by the stochastic differential equation of the form

$$d\hat{z} = A\hat{z}\, dt + k\, dv,$$

where $dv$ is the innovation process, i.e., the process representing the new information carried by the new observation on the state vector. In the state-space model of the economy, the state vector would contain the expectational variables as parts of the vector. Consequently the differential equation

---

[9] For example, deviations of the interest rate, output, and its prices all are expected to affect the current account. These variables, then, would affect $\varepsilon$. Because these variables are expressible as linear combinations of the state variables, $\varepsilon$ would depend on some components of state variables. See Appendix C for further discussions on these and related points.

for the expectational variables is embedded in the Kalman filter and would be of the general form given above as (8). Alternatively, we could prove that our more general regressive mechanisms can be made to coincide with perfect foresight models with suitable choices of coefficients such as $v_1 \sim v_3$ in (8). Appendix C demonstrates this possibility and discusses regressive expectations mechanisms and their consistency or uniqueness questions in detail.

### 8.1.4 Wage Rate Dynamics and Output Pricing Equation

Specification of wage rate changes in a model has important implications on the model dynamics. For example, if wages are postulated to change according to some wage indexation scheme, it matters whether the wage rate to be held constant by indexation is the nominal wage rate or a suitably defined wage rate. [See Bruno and Sachs (1979), Sachs (1979), Fischer (1977), Gray (1975), Modigliani–Padova–Schioppa (1978) for some preliminary analyses of these issues.]

Different schemes for setting wage rates can be subsumed in a general wage rate equation (in relative variational variables)

$$(9) \qquad \dot{w} = f(w, y, p_i, \rho_i),$$

where $p_i$ is the consumer price index and $\rho_i$ its expected rate of changes.

When mark-up pricing schemes are incorporated into models, they usually take the form [see Gordon (1972, 1976), Nordhaus (1971), for example]

$$\dot{P}/P = \dot{W}/W + \alpha(\hat{P}_I/P_I),$$

where $W$ is the nominal wage rate and $P_I$ is a consumer price index or in variational form

$$(10) \qquad \dot{p} = \dot{w} + \alpha\rho_i,$$

since $\dot{p} = \delta(\dot{P}/P)$ and $\dot{w} = \delta(\dot{W}/W)$. Equation (9) or (10) further adds to the dynamics of open economy models as we later show in Parts Two and Three.

## 8.2 Example 1: A Small Open Economy with Full Employment and Purchasing Power Parity

We have outlined a general procedure for deducing the dynamics arising from an unbalanced government budget and a nonzero current account. Our analysis has been purposely left incomplete since we outlined a general procedure common to all models while omitting details specific to a par-

## 8.2 A Small Open Economy with Full Employment and Purchasing Power Parity

ticular model. We now apply the procedure to a simple model and supply the omitted details to illustrate the derivation of the dynamics and examinations of the dynamic behavior of the model. A small open economy producing a (composite) tradeable good, which is a perfect substitute for the world good, shall illustrate. We therefore impose the purchasing power parity condition here. The "foreign" price level $P^*$ is assumed constant, and is set to one without loss of generality. A more general economy, producing a (composite) tradeable good distinct from the world good, shall be discussed later in Part Two.

Our main results are the derivation of differential equation for short-run dynamics and the elucidation of the role of the money stock growth rate in stability of short-run dynamics. These results illustrate the more general fact that short-run stability depends on the long-run policy objectives which determine the reference path that the economy is designed to follow. We return to this point later in Part Two of the book. Appendix D provides further analysis of this interdependence.

### 8.2.1  Asset Sector

There are two financial assets: domestic money, which is nontraded internationally, and bonds which are traded internationally. Let $M$ denote the stock of money in domestic currency and $F$ the stock of international bonds in foreign currency held by the private sector of the small economy. To simplify, we assume that the government neither issues bonds nor holds international bonds. The domestic currency value of the stock of international bonds is $EF$ where $E$ is the exchange rate. The domestic interest rate $i$ is assumed to be equal to $i^* + \varepsilon$, where $\varepsilon$ is the expected rate of depreciation of the exchange rate and $i^*$ the exogenously fixed world interest rate.[10] Since the nominal rates of return to holding stocks of money and bonds are 0 and $i^* + \varepsilon$, respectively, proportions of the domestic private sector wealth, held as money and bonds, depend on $\varepsilon$. For the moment, we ignore the possibility that stock holdings may depend on some variable representing a level of economic activity.[11] Thus, we assume that the asset demand functions are given by

$$(11) \qquad M = \alpha(\varepsilon)A, \qquad \alpha' < 0,$$

$$(12) \qquad EF = \beta(\varepsilon)A, \qquad \beta' > 0,$$

---

[10] We later discuss models in which domestic and foreign bonds are treated as imperfect substitutes.

[11] This aspect is taken up later in Part Two.

where

$$A = M + EF; \quad \text{hence} \quad \alpha + \beta = 1,$$

in domestic currency and where changes in $\varepsilon$ are governed by a regressive mechanism to be discussed later, which is a generalization of adaptive expectations mechanisms often found in the literature. [See, for example, Dornbusch (1976b).]

Because of the balance sheet constraint, i.e., $\alpha + \beta = 1$, there is only one independent equation in the asset sector. We choose the ratio of (11) over (12) $M/EF = \alpha(\varepsilon)/\beta(\varepsilon)$ and later use it to derive a variational relation between $e$ and $\delta e$.

Even though the capital stock is constant by assumption, it still is a component of the private sector's portfolio as we have shown in Chapter 3.

The asset sector should really be specified by the three asset demand functions:

$$M = \alpha(\varepsilon, \rho)A, \quad EF = \beta(\varepsilon, \rho)A, \quad \text{and} \quad qK = \gamma(\varepsilon, \rho)A,$$

where $q = R(Y, K)/\rho$ as in Chapter 3, and $\rho$ is the rate of return on equity capital.

Variations of two independent equations out of these three equations are solved for $\delta\rho$ and $e$. The expression for $e$ becomes

$$e = \omega_1 m - \omega_2 f - \omega_3 y$$

rather than Eq. (25) to follow. However, if we assume that $\alpha_2/\alpha = \beta_2/\beta$, i.e., the private sector is equally likely to shift out (into) from money and bonds into (out of) equity in response to changes in $\rho$, then $\omega_1$ equals $\omega_2$ and $\omega_3$ vanishes leaving $e$ as given in Eq. (25). We assume this condition to avoid the complication of including the equity capital in our analysis. Long-run equilibrium must also be modified. Either we assume stationary states in which all variables are constant or assume $(R_1/R)(\dot{Y}/Y) = \dot{M}/M = \dot{E}/E$ and all others are constant. Here nonzero $\dot{Y}/Y$ may be interpreted as due to technical progress.

See Chapter 9 for analysis which includes $qK$ explicitly.

### 8.2.2 Government Budget Deficit Variation

Because of the absence of domestic government bonds, the expression for the budget deficit is simply

(13) $$D_f = P(G - T).$$

Its variational expression is

(14) $$\delta D_f/M = m_1 e + m_0 g,$$

## 8.2 A Small Open Economy with Full Employment and Purchasing Power Parity

where
$$m_0 = PG/M, \quad m_1 = P(G - T)/M,$$
because of the equality of $p$ with $e$ by the purchasing power parity condition. We treat the real output $Y$ as fixed at full employment level $\bar{Y}$ because of flexible prices and wages which are implicit in this model. Hence we assume that $\delta T = 0$ because $T$ is assumed to be a function of $\bar{Y}$ only.[12] Note that $\dot{M}/M = m_1$.

The current account is
$$U = B_T + i^*F,$$
where the trade balance is (assuming investment to be autonomous, i.e., $I = \bar{I}$)

(15)
$$B_T = \bar{Y} - C - \bar{I} - G,$$

where we specify consumption $C$ as
$$C = C(Y', A/P), \quad 0 < C_1 < 1, \quad 0 < C_2,$$
and where the disposable income is

(16)
$$Y' = \bar{Y} - T + i^*F - \varepsilon A/P.$$

The last term in Eq. (16) represents loss of real wealth due to inflation. Here, as a consistency condition for expectations, we posit the equality of the expected rate of inflation with the expected rate of depreciation of the exchange rate by the purchasing power parity condition.

### 8.2.3 Long-Run Properties

Let $N = M/E$. Then $\dot{N}/N = \dot{M}/M - \dot{E}/E$. The equality $\bar{N}/\bar{F} = \alpha(\varepsilon)/\beta(\varepsilon)$ holds on the reference path, where an overbar denotes the long-run value. Because the expected rate of depreciation should be equal to the actual rate in the long run, $\dot{E}/E = \varepsilon$ holds on the reference path. Because the asset sector is assumed to be in equilibrium at all times, the relation $\dot{M}/M - \dot{E}/E - \dot{F}/F = (\alpha'/\alpha - \beta'/\beta)\dot{\varepsilon}$ must hold. We consider a reference path along which $\varepsilon$ equals a constant $\bar{\varepsilon}$. This implies that $\dot{M}/M$ must equal $\dot{E}/E + \dot{F}/F$. To consider a simple case, we choose the reference path along which $\dot{F}/F$ is zero, i.e., $l_F$ is zero.

Thus the reference path is characterized by
$$\mu = \overline{(\dot{M}/M)} = \overline{(\dot{E}/E)} = \bar{\varepsilon}.$$

---

[12] With $T = T(\bar{Y}, P)$, $\delta T$ equals $(T_2 P)p$ or $(T_2 E)e$. This alternate specification of $T$ thus modifies $m_1$.

Here we treat $\mu$ as the monetary instrument. Therefore, the coefficient in Eq. (14) becomes $\bar{m}_1 = \mu$. We later examine the consequences of choosing different $\mu$ values for which the variational dynamics remain stable.

The effects of $\mu$ on the long-run equilibrium value of disposable income or consumption can be easily deduced. From the government budget equations, $\mu$ and $\bar{N}$ are selected by $\mu = (\bar{G} - \bar{T})/\bar{N}$, given $\bar{G} - \bar{T}$. The asset sector equilibrium condition $\bar{N}/\bar{F} = \alpha(\mu)/\beta(\mu) = \gamma(\mu)$ can be solved for $\bar{N}$ as $\bar{N} = (\bar{G} - \bar{T})/\mu$. Hence $\mu \bar{F} = (\bar{G} - \bar{T})/\gamma(\mu)$. The disposable income is determined by the implicit equation

$$\bar{Y} = C(\bar{Y} - \bar{T} + i^*\bar{F} - \mu(\bar{N} + \bar{F}), \bar{N} + \bar{F}) - i^*\bar{F} + \bar{G},$$

where $\bar{T} = \bar{G} - \mu\bar{N}$ and $\bar{B}_T = -i^*\bar{F}$ has been used, which is derived from the long-run equilibrium condition in the current account, i.e., $\dot{F} = 0$ on the reference path. The disposable income declines monotonically with increasing $\mu$. Because of this, it is of some interest to obtain a range of $\mu$ for which the long-run equilibrium state is stable. Later in our discussion on stability of the variational dynamics about the long-run equilibrium, we derive a set of conditions on $i^*$, $C_1$, and $C_2$ to ensure stability of the variational equation where $C_i$ is the partial derivative of $C$ with respect to the $i$th argument of $C$.

### 8.2.4 Variational Equations

The variation of the current account equation is (recalling that $l_F$ is zero)

(17) $$\dot{f} = i^*f + \delta B_T/F,$$

where, from (15),

(18) $$\delta B_T = -\delta C - \delta G = -C_1 \delta Y' - C_2\{\delta A/E - (A/E)e\} - \delta G.$$

Taking the variation of the disposable income expression given by Eq. (16)

$$\delta Y' = i^* \delta F - (A/E) \delta \varepsilon + \varepsilon(A/E)e - \varepsilon \delta A/E,$$

where

$$\delta A = Mm + EF(e + f).$$

In relative deviation terms, we write the above expression as

(19) $$y' = l_1 f + l_2(e - m) - l_3 \delta\varepsilon,$$

where

$$l_1 = (i^* - \varepsilon)F/Y', \qquad l_2 = \varepsilon M/EY', \qquad l_3 = A/EY'.$$

## 8.2 A Small Open Economy with Full Employment and Purchasing Power Parity

We rewrite (18) more explicitly as

$$\delta B_T/F = -\Omega_1 y' - \Omega_2(m-e) - C_2 f - \Omega_0 g,$$

where

$$\Omega_1 = C_1 Y'/F, \qquad \Omega_2 = C_2 M/EF, \qquad \Omega_0 = G/F.$$

When this expression is substituted into (17), we obtain the variational differential equation of the current account which shows the dependence of $\dot{f}$ on $m, f, e,$ and $y'$,

(20) $$\dot{f} = (i^* - C_2)f - \Omega_1 y' - \Omega_2(m-e) - \Omega_0 g.$$

From (14), the variational differential equation for the money stock is given by

(21) $$\dot{m} = -\mu m + m_1 e + m_0 g.$$

Equations (20) and (21) jointly determine the dynamics for $m$ and $f$

(22) $$\frac{d}{dt}\begin{bmatrix} m \\ f \end{bmatrix} = \begin{bmatrix} -\mu & 0 \\ -\Omega_2 & i^* - C_2 \end{bmatrix}\begin{bmatrix} m \\ f \end{bmatrix} + \begin{bmatrix} m_1 \\ \Omega_2 \end{bmatrix}e - \Omega_1\begin{bmatrix} 0 \\ 1 \end{bmatrix}y' + \begin{bmatrix} m_0 \\ -\Omega_0 \end{bmatrix}g.$$

We need to express $e$ and $y'$ in terms of $m$ and $f$ to render this dynamic equation in state-space form.[13] For this purpose, we take the variation of the asset sector equilibrium condition to relate $e$ and $\delta\varepsilon$ by the equation

(23) $$-m + e + f = \theta\,\delta\varepsilon,$$

where

$$\theta = (\beta'/\beta - \alpha'/\alpha) > 0.$$

We adopt a simple autoregressive expectation mechanism to relate $\delta\varepsilon$ to $e$ by[14]

(24) $$\delta\varepsilon = -ve, \qquad v \geq 0.$$

We then solve (23) and (24) simultaneously for $e$ and $\delta\varepsilon$ to obtain their reduced form expressions as

(25) $$e = \omega(m - f),$$

---

[13] Instead of $m$ and $f$, other choices of state vectors are possible. To exhibit directly the effects of current account on dynamics, for example, we may choose $m$ and $\delta Z$ as the components of the state vector, where $Z$ is defined to be $U/F$. (Because $\bar{U}$ is zero, we use $\delta Z$ rather than $\delta Z/\bar{Z}$.) Noting that $\delta Z = \delta U/F - \bar{Z}f = \delta U/F$ and that $\delta U = \delta B_T/F + i^* f$, we can replace $f$ by $\delta Z$ in (22) and (22') below.

[14] More generally, one should relate $\delta\varepsilon$ to other variables such as $m, f$ and $g$. (See Appendix C on the relationship between such regressive expectation generation schemes and consistency of expectations.)

where

$$\omega = (1 + \theta v)^{-1}$$

and

(26) $$\delta\varepsilon = -v\omega(m - f).$$

Substituting (25) and (26) into (19), we derive the reduced form expression for $y'$

(27) $$y' = -\eta_1 m + \eta_2 f,$$

where

$$\eta_1 = l_2(1 - \omega) - l_3 v\omega \quad \text{and} \quad \eta_2 = l_1 - (l_2 + vl_3)\omega.$$

When (25) and (27) are substituted into (22), the state-space dynamic equation for $m$ and $f$ results:

(22') $$\frac{d}{dt}\begin{bmatrix} m \\ f \end{bmatrix} = \Phi \begin{bmatrix} m \\ f \end{bmatrix} + \begin{bmatrix} m_0 \\ -\Omega_0 \end{bmatrix} g,$$

where

$$\Phi = \begin{bmatrix} -\mu & 0 \\ -\Omega_2 & i^* - C_2 \end{bmatrix} + \omega \begin{bmatrix} m_1 \\ \Omega_2 \end{bmatrix} [1 \quad -1] - \Omega_1 \begin{bmatrix} 0 \\ 1 \end{bmatrix} [-\eta_1 \quad \eta_2]$$

$$= \begin{bmatrix} -\mu & 0 \\ -\Omega_2 + \Omega_1\eta_1 & i^* - C_2 - \Omega_1\eta_2 \end{bmatrix} + \omega \begin{bmatrix} m_1 \\ \Omega_2 \end{bmatrix} [1 \quad -1].$$

Along the reference path, $\bar{m}_1 = \mu$, hence the dynamic matrix evaluated along the reference path is

$$\bar{\Phi} = \begin{bmatrix} -\mu(1 - \omega) & -\mu\omega \\ -\Omega_2(1 - \omega) + \Omega_1\eta_1 & i^* - C_2 - \Omega_1\eta_2 - \omega\Omega_2 \end{bmatrix}.$$

### 8.2.5 Interactions

Nonzero off-diagonal elements of $\bar{\Phi}$ indicate mutual interactions between dynamics for $m$ and $f$, i.e., mutual interactions between the dynamics of $m$ and $f$ exists if and only if $\mu \neq 0$ and $\bar{\Phi}_{21} = -\Omega_2(1 - \omega) + \Omega_1\eta_1 \neq 0$. If $\mu = 0$ but the $\bar{\Phi}_{21} \neq 0$, then the dynamics become recursive: $m$ affects the dynamics of $f$ but not conversely. Generally, we see that $\bar{\Phi}_{21} \neq 0$. Another way for interactions to vanish is to assume static expectations; i.e., $v = 0$. Then $\omega$ becomes one and $\eta_1$ reduces to zero; i.e., the money stock variation is affected by variation in $F$ but not conversely.

## 8.2 A Small Open Economy with Full Employment and Purchasing Power Parity

### 8.2.6 Policy Effects

We exhibit that nonzero off-diagonal elements of $\Phi$, i.e., dynamic coupling, implies a possibility of a fiscal change reaching its maximum effects sometime after the change has taken place. Without dynamic interaction between deviations in stocks of money and bonds, the dynamic fiscal multiplier monotonically declines with time.

This possibility is illustrated with deviations in the money stock itself. Now, with $m(0)$ and $f(0)$ zero, integrate (22') to obtain

$$m(t) = [1 \ 0]\begin{bmatrix}m\\f\end{bmatrix}(t) = [1 \ 0]\int_0^t e^{\Phi(t-\tau)}\begin{bmatrix}m_0\\-\Omega_0\end{bmatrix}g(\tau)\,d\tau.$$

Denote the dynamic multiplier by $h(t)$, i.e.,

$$h(t) = [1 \ 0]e^{\Phi t}\begin{bmatrix}m_0\\-\Omega_0\end{bmatrix} = \zeta_1 e^{-\lambda_1 t} - \zeta_2 e^{-\lambda_2 t},$$

where

$$\zeta_i = -(\lambda_2 - \lambda_1)^{-1}\{m_0(\lambda_i + \phi_{22}) + \Omega_0\phi_{12}\}, \quad i = 1, 2,$$

where $-\lambda_1$ and $-\lambda_2$ are the eigenvalues of $\Phi$.[15]

We assume that $\lambda_2 - \lambda_1$ is positive without loss of generality. Now, even when $\lambda_1$ and $\lambda_2$ are real, $h(t)$ reaches its maximum value for some $t > 0$ if and only if $\lambda_2\zeta_2/\lambda_1\zeta_1$ is greater than one. The condition can equivalently be stated as

$$\Omega_0\phi_{12} \gtreqless m_0\phi_{11} \quad \text{if} \quad m_0(\lambda_1 + \phi_{22}) + \Omega_0\phi_{12} \gtreqless 0.$$

Substituting the expression for $\phi_{ij}$ in the above and noting that $\Omega_0/m_0$ equals $M/EF$, i.e., $\alpha/\beta$, we arrive at the conditions

If $\alpha/\beta < (\lambda_1 + \phi_{22})/\mu\omega,$ then $\alpha/\beta < \theta v.$

If $\alpha/\beta > (\lambda_1 + \phi_{22})\mu\omega,$ then $\alpha/\beta > \theta v.$

---

[15] More generally, suppose an endogenous variable $q$ is related to $m$ and $f$ by

$$q = (a, b)\begin{bmatrix}m\\f\end{bmatrix}.$$

Then

$$(a, b)e^{\Phi t}\begin{bmatrix}m_0\\-\Omega_0\end{bmatrix}$$

is the relevant fiscal multiplier, which equals $\zeta_1 e^{-\lambda_1 t} - \zeta_2 e^{-\lambda_2 t}$ when we redefine

$$\zeta_i = (\lambda_2 - \lambda_1)^{-1}\{-a[m_0(\lambda_i + \phi_{22}) + \Omega_0\phi_{12}] + b[m_0\phi_{21} + \Omega_0(\lambda_i + \phi_{11})]\}, \quad i = 1, 2.$$

Thus, if $\lambda_1 + \phi_{22}$ is negative, $\alpha/\beta > \theta v$ is the only binding condition, i.e., The coefficient $v$ in the regressive expectation equation (24) cannot be too large for this dynamic phenomenon to exist. If $\lambda_1 + \phi_{22}$ is positive, either of these two possibilities could obtain. The expression $\lambda_1 + \phi_{22}$ is positive if and only if $\phi_{22} > \phi_{11}$ (i.e., the dynamics associated with money stock adjustment is faster than that of foreign bond deviations) and $\phi_{12}\phi_{21}$ is negative, i.e., cross effects of $m$ on $f$ and $f$ on $m$ are of opposite signs.

### 8.2.7 Stability Analysis

*Constant Money Stock*

When $\mu$ is zero, $m$ is identically zero and the dynamics reduce to a single differential equation for $f$. The dynamics for $f$ are stable if and only if $\overline{\Phi}_{22}$ is negative. The inequality $\overline{\Phi}_{22} < 0$ can be rewritten as

$$i^* - C_2 - \Omega_1\eta_2 - \omega\Omega_2 < 0$$

or because $\bar{\varepsilon}$ is also zero when $\mu$ is zero,[16]

(28) $\qquad (v\omega/\beta)C_1 + (1 - C_1)i^* < C_2(1 + \omega\alpha/\beta).$

The inequality (28) can be rewritten as

(28') $\qquad v\{\theta(1 - C_1)i^* + C_1/\beta - C_2\theta\} < C_2/\beta - (1 - C_1)i^*.$

Assuming that the right hand side is positive, this inequality bounds $v$ from above if the expression in bracket is positive on the left hand side. With a negative bracketed expression, any positive $v$ will satisfy this inequality. If $C_2 > i^*(1 - C_1)$, then a sufficiently large $\theta$ will cause the bracketed expression to become negative (large $\theta$ is implied by very sensitive portfolio behavior to changes in $\varepsilon$).

We later show that as $v$ becomes very large (assuming that dynamics remain stable, i.e., the bracketed expression remains negative) the model behavior becomes similar to that under perfect foresight expectations discussed in the next section.

*Static Expectations*

When $v$ is set to zero in (24), the expectations become stationary and the coefficient $\omega$ in (25) becomes one. The dynamics (22') specializes to $\dot{m} = -\mu f$

---

[16] From the definitions below (19) and (27), $\Omega_1\eta_2$ simplifies to $C_1(i^* - v\omega/\beta)$.

## 8.3 Regressive Expectations and Consistency cum Stability

and $\hat{f} = \bar{\Phi}_{22} f$ because $\eta_1$ vanishes in this case causing $\bar{\Phi}_{21}$ to vanish as well. The element $\bar{\Phi}_{22}$ if negative if and only if

$$(1 - C_1)i^* < C_2(1 + \alpha/\beta).$$

This condition states that the wealth effect on consumption must be sufficiently large for the dynamics to be stable under stationary expectations.

### General Case

The stability conditions with nonzero $\mu$ and $v$ are

$$\text{tr } \bar{\Phi} < 0 \quad \text{and} \quad \det \bar{\Phi} > 0.$$

In the original model parameters, the trace condition can be stated as

$$i^* - C_2 - \Omega_1 \eta_2 - \omega \Omega_2 < \mu(1 - \omega).$$

This can be put into a form analogous to (28') as

(29) $\quad v\{\theta(1-C_1)i^* + C_1(\mu\theta + 1/\beta) - (C_2+\mu)\theta\} < C_2/\beta - (1-C_1)i^* - \mu C_1/\beta,$

to which comments similar to those below (28') apply as well.

The determinant condition becomes

$$i^* - C_2 - \Omega_1 \eta_2 - \omega \Omega_2 < \omega(1-\omega)^{-1}\{\Omega_1 \eta_1 - \Omega_2(1-\omega)\},$$

or

(30) $\quad (1 - C_1)i^* + \{\mu + 1/(\beta\theta)\}C_1 < C_2, \quad \text{for} \quad \mu > 0.$

Equation (30) bounds $\mu$ from above.

## 8.3 Regressive Expectations and Consistency cum Stability

The analysis of Example 1 has been carried out on the assumption that the expectation is generated autoregressively by (24). Here we discuss consequences of respecifying (24) by a more general regressive expectation $\delta\varepsilon = -v_1 m + v_2 f$. We refer the reader to Appendix C for further discussion on the reason for such a respecification. We then show that appropriate choices of $v_1$ and $v_2$ determined as suitable roots of algebraic equations can lead to the perfect foresight model. This provides another example of how consistency plus stability requirements can generate self-fulfilling stable expectation.[17]

With (24) replaced by

(24')
$$\delta\varepsilon = -v_1 m + v_2 f,$$

(25) changes into

(25')
$$e = \omega_m m - \omega_f f,$$

where

$$\omega_m = 1 - \theta v_1, \qquad \omega_f = 1 - \theta v_2.$$

From (19), (24'), and (25') the expression for $y'$ now becomes

(27')
$$y' = -\eta_1 m + \eta_2 f,$$

where

$$\eta_1 = l_2(1 - \omega_m) - l_3 v_1 = (l_2 \theta - l_3)v_1,$$
$$\eta_2 = l_1 - l_2 \omega_f - l_3 v_2 = l_1 - l_2 + (l_2 \theta - l_3)v_2.$$

From (22), (25'), and (27'), the dynamic matrix $\Phi$ is consequently changed to

$$\Phi = \begin{bmatrix} -\mu & 0 \\ -\Omega_2 + \Omega_1 \eta_1 & i^* - C_2 - \Omega_1 \eta_2 \end{bmatrix} + \begin{bmatrix} m_1 \\ \Omega_2 \end{bmatrix} [\omega_m \quad -\omega_f].$$

For later purpose, we rewrite it as

$$\Phi = \Phi^0 + \Phi^1,$$

where

$$\Phi^0 = \begin{bmatrix} -\mu + m_1 & -m_1 \\ 0 & \phi \end{bmatrix},$$

where

$$\phi = i^* - C_2 - \Omega_1(l_1 - l_2) - \Omega_2 \quad \text{and} \quad \Phi^1 = \begin{bmatrix} m_1 \theta \\ \sigma \end{bmatrix} [-v_1 \quad v_2],$$

where $\sigma = \theta \Omega_2 - (l_2 \theta - l_3)\Omega_1$.

The consistency requirement demands that the expectation be self-fulfilling,[17] i.e., the relation given by

$$\delta\varepsilon = \dot{e}$$

---

[17] Dornbusch (1976b) provides a single dimensional dynamic example of this fact.

## 8.3 Regressive Expectations and Consistency cum Stability

is satisfied on any $m$ and $f$.[18] From (24'), (25') and the dynamics, this relation can equivalently be put as

(31) $$[-v_1 \quad v_2] = [\omega_m \quad -\omega_f]\Phi.$$

(See Appendix C.)

Equation (31) can be simplified as

$$[-v_1 \quad v_2] = \{[1 \quad -1] + \theta[-v_1 \quad v_2]\}\Phi^0$$
$$+ \{m_1\theta - \sigma - \theta(m_1\theta v_1 - \sigma v_2)\}[-v_1 \quad v_2].$$

This equation is generally a nonlinear algebraic relation for $v_1$ and $v_2$ because $\Phi$, $\omega_m$, and $\omega_f$ are linear in $v_1$ and $v_2$. Along the reference path $m_1$ equals $\mu$; hence $\Phi^0$ becomes

$$\begin{bmatrix} -\mu \\ \phi \end{bmatrix}[0 \quad 1].$$

Hence

$$\{[1 \quad -1] + \theta[-v_1 \quad 0_2]\}\Phi^0 = \{-(\mu + \phi) + \theta(\mu v_1 + \phi v_2)\}[0 \quad 1].$$

Therefore, the coefficients $v_1$ and $v_2$ are the roots of

$$v_1 = v_1\{\mu\theta - \sigma - \theta(\mu\theta v_1 - \sigma v_2)\}$$

and

$$v_2 = v_2\{\mu\theta - \sigma - \theta(\mu\theta v_1 - \sigma v_2)\} - \mu - \phi + \theta(\mu v_1 + \phi v_2).$$

---

[18] Under the perfect foresight assumption, the dynamics are three dimensional: (23), (19) with (20), and (21) are the three coupled differential equations when $\dot{e}$ is substituted for $\delta \varepsilon$

$$\begin{bmatrix} 1 & 0 & 0 \\ 0 & 1 & 0 \\ -l_3\Omega_1 & 0 & 1 \end{bmatrix}\begin{bmatrix} \dot{e} \\ \dot{m} \\ \dot{f} \end{bmatrix} = \begin{bmatrix} 1/\theta & 1/\theta & 1/\theta \\ m_1 & -\mu & 0 \\ \tilde{\phi}_{31} & -\tilde{\phi}_{31} & \tilde{\phi}_{33} \end{bmatrix}\begin{bmatrix} e \\ m \\ f \end{bmatrix} + \begin{bmatrix} 0 \\ m_0 \\ -\Omega_0 \end{bmatrix}g,$$

where

$$\tilde{\phi}_{31} = -\Omega_1 l_2 + \Omega_2 \quad \text{and} \quad \tilde{\phi}_{33} = i^* - C_2 - \Omega_1 l_1.$$

Multiplying the above from the left by the inverse of the left-hand side matrix, the dynamics under the perfect foresight are governed by

$$\frac{d}{dt}\begin{bmatrix} e \\ m \\ f \end{bmatrix} = \begin{bmatrix} 1/\theta & -1/\theta & 1/\theta \\ m_1 & -\mu & 0 \\ \sigma/\theta & -\sigma/\theta & \zeta \end{bmatrix}\begin{bmatrix} e \\ m \\ f \end{bmatrix} + \begin{bmatrix} 0 \\ m_0 \\ -\Omega_1 \end{bmatrix}g,$$

where $\zeta = i^* - C_2 - \Omega_1\eta_2$ and $v_2$ is taken to be $1/\theta$. The characteristic equation associated with these dynamics is $\lambda\{\lambda^2 + (\mu - \zeta - 1/\theta)\lambda - \mu\zeta + \zeta/\theta - \sigma/\theta^2\}$. It has one zero eigenvalue and can be shown to have one unstable eigenvalue. (For example, the quadratic polynomial in bracket is unstable regardless of the sign of $\sigma$ for $\mu$ less than $1/\theta$.)

The roots are[19]

(i) $v_1 = 0$ and $v_2$ are the roots of $\theta\sigma v_2^2 + (\mu\theta - \sigma + \theta\phi - 1)v_2 - \mu - \phi = 0$, or

(ii) $v_1 \neq 0$ and $v_1$ and $v_2$ are determined by

$$\mu\theta v_1 - \sigma v_2 = \mu - \sigma/\theta \quad \text{and} \quad \mu v_1 + \phi v_2 = (\mu + \phi)/\theta,$$

i.e.,

$$v_1 = v_2 = \frac{\mu\phi + \sigma\mu/\theta}{\mu\theta\phi + \mu\sigma} = \frac{\phi + \sigma/\theta}{\theta\phi + \sigma} = \frac{1}{\theta} > 0.$$

With the perfect foresight, variation in $E$ turns out to be zero because $\omega_m$ and $\omega_f$ are both zero in (25'). The matrix $\Phi$ simplifies to

$$\Phi = \begin{bmatrix} -\mu & 0 \\ -\Omega_2 + \Omega_1\eta_1 & i^* - C_2 - \Omega_1\eta_2 \end{bmatrix}.$$

Thus the dynamics are recursive; the dynamics for $m$ are separate from $f$. The short-run variations are stable, then, if and only if $\mu > 0$, and $i^* - C_2 - \Omega_1\eta_2$ is negative. The latter equals $\sigma/\theta + \phi$, i.e.,

$$i^* - C_2 - \Omega_1(l_1 - l_3/\theta) < 0 \quad \text{if and only if} \quad \sigma/\theta + \phi < 0,$$

where the expression for $\eta_2$ has been substituted out. The latter inequality can be equivalently written as

$$i^*(1 - C_1) + C_1\mu + C_1/\{\beta(\mu)\theta\} < C_2,$$

because $A/EF$ equals $1/\beta(\mu)$ on the reference path.

---

[19] With zero $v_1$, the dynamics reduce to $\dot{f} = (\sigma v_2 + \phi)f$ and $\dot{m} = -\mu(1 - \theta v_2)f$, hence the $f$-dynamics are stable if $\sigma v_2 + \phi$ is negative. In case (ii), the dynamics are: $\dot{f} = (\sigma/\theta + \phi)f - (\sigma/\theta)m$ and $\dot{m} = -\mu f$ or $\ddot{f} - (\sigma/\theta + \phi)\dot{f} - \mu(\sigma/\theta)f = 0$, which is stable if and only if $\sigma/\theta + \phi$ and $\sigma$ are both negative (because $\mu/\theta$ is positive).

The negativity of $\sigma$ holds if and only if

$$C_1/\theta + C_2\alpha < \alpha\mu C_1.$$

The expression $\sigma/\theta + \phi$ is negative if and only if

$$i^* - C_2 - \Omega_1(l_1 - l_3/\theta)$$

is negative, or

(*) $\qquad (1 - C_1)i^* + C_1(\mu + 1/(\beta\theta)) < C_2.$

Note that this is identical to (30) in the previous section. In case (i), one of the roots of $v_2$ can be chosen to make $\sigma v_2 + \phi$ negative if $(\mu + \phi)\sigma$ is positive or under the assumption that $\sigma$ is negative if $\mu + \phi$ is negative if

$$i^*(1 - C_1) + C_1 + C_1(\mu + 1/\beta\theta) + \mu(1 + C_1) < C_2.$$

This latter inequality implies (*). Note that case (ii) is the limiting case of the regressive expectation model where $v \to \infty$.

This is an implicit inequality for $\mu$. Noting that $\beta'$ is positive, we see that the rate of money stock growth cannot be too large nor too small along the reference path for the short-run dynamics to be stable.

## 8.4 Example 2: Effects of Bond-Financed Budget Deficit on Short-Run Stability

### 8.4.1 The Model

In this example we allow the domestic government to issue its own bonds which are perfect substitutes for international bonds. The government can now finance part of the budget deficit by issuing its own bonds. This modifies the government budget equation, and stability conditions become more complex. The dynamics for the variational variable become three dimensional, involving stocks of money, domestic bonds, and international bonds. In another modification of the basic model, we can respecify the asset equation by including a scale variable to represent a level of economic activity. We take up this point later in Part Two of the book.

This model is used to evaluate influences of the extent of bond-financed unplanned government budget imbalances on short-run behavior of the model about the reference path. We can show that as the percentage of bond-financed imbalances increases the dynamics become sluggish under certain conditions, i.e., it takes longer to return to the reference path after exogenous disturbance even though the dynamics are stable.

When we allow the domestic government to issue its own bonds, which are perfect substitutes for international bonds, the variational dynamics governing the model becomes more complex. By assumption there are now three financial assets in the model: domestic money, which is a nontraded financial asset, and international and domestic bonds. Let $M$ be the stock of money, where $B$ denotes the stock of domestic government bonds and $F$, the domestically held stock of international bonds denominated in foreign currency. Domestic and foreign bonds are assumed to be perfect substitutes and both are fixed in nominal values with variable interest rates. As before, $E$ denotes the exchange rate, which is the domestic currency price of a unit of foreign currency. The total value of bonds held by the domestic private sector is therefore $B + EF$ in domestic currency.

The asset demand functions are specified by

(32) $$M = \alpha(\varepsilon)A, \qquad \alpha' < 0,$$

(33) $$B + EF = \beta(\varepsilon)A, \qquad \beta' > 0,$$

where

$$A = M + B + EF.$$

The long-run equilibrium that we consider in this section is characterized by

(34) $$\dot M/M = \dot B/B = \dot E/E = \bar\varepsilon = \mu.$$

and

(35) $$\dot F/F = 0.$$

The domestic interest rate $i$ equals $i^* + \varepsilon$ by the assumption of the perfect substitutability of domestic and foreign bonds. On the reference path $i$ equals $i^* + \bar\varepsilon$, i.e., $i^* + \mu$.

The central bank holds stock $V$ of the foreign bonds. The small economy thus holds a total of $(F + V)$ of the foreign securities. The current account $U$ is then the sum of the trade balance and the interest receipt

(36) $$U = B_T + i^*(F + V)$$

in foreign currency, where $B_T$ is the trade balance and is still given by

(37) $$B_T = \bar Y - C - \bar I - G.$$

In (37), we retain the same specification of consumption $C = C(Y', A/E)$, where the disposable income is given by $Y' = \bar Y - \bar T + i^*(B/E + F) - \varepsilon(M/E + F)$. Here we use the relation $i = i^* + \varepsilon$. We recall that $\pi = \varepsilon$ because of the purchasing power parity condition and $P^* = 1$. In our later analysis, the instrument $\mu$ is constrained to ensure short-run stability.

### 8.4.2 Variational Equations

The differential equation for the relative deviation $f = \delta F/F$ is still given by

(38) $$\dot f = \delta U/F = i^* f + \delta B_T/F,$$

where, for simpler analysis, we assume that $\delta V = 0$, that is, that the central bank does not intervene by selling or acquiring international bonds.

Variation of the trade balance is given by (18) of Example 1. We set $\delta G$ to zero since we merely investigate the dependence of short-run dynamics on the percentage of the budget imbalance financed by bonds.

The variational expression of $A$ now is given by

$$\delta A = \delta M + \delta B + EF(e + f).$$

From its definition,

$$\delta Y' = i^*(B/E)(b - e) + i^* \delta F - \delta\varepsilon(M/E + F) - \varepsilon(M/E)(m - e) - \varepsilon F f.$$

Hence

(39) $$y' = l_1 f + l_2(e - m) - l_3(e - b) - l_4 \delta\varepsilon,$$

## 8.4 Effects of Bond-Financed Budget Deficit on Short-Run Stability

where

$$l_1 = (i^* - \varepsilon)F/Y', \qquad l_2 = \varepsilon M/EY', \qquad l_3 = i^*B/EY', \qquad l_4 = (M/E+F)/Y',$$

and

(40) $\qquad \delta B_T/F = -\Omega_1 y' - \Omega_2(m-e) - \Omega_3(b-e) - C_2 f,$

where

$$\Omega_1 = C_1 Y'/F, \qquad \Omega_2 = C_2 M/EF, \qquad \Omega_3 = C_2 B/EF.$$

Using (40), (38) can be rewritten as

(41) $\qquad \dot f = (i^* - C_2)f - \Omega_1 y' - \Omega_2(m-e) - \Omega_3(b-e).$

The variational expression for the budget deficit is also more involved than that in Example 1. From $D_f = P(G-T) + iB$, we note that

$$\delta D_f = i\,\delta B + \delta\varepsilon B + P(G-T)e,$$

where $\delta T$ equals zero by the full employment assumption as in Example 1, and $\delta G$ is zero by assumption.

Now let $\zeta\%$ of $\delta D_f$ be financed by issuing bonds and the remainder by issuing government money. Then, the variational variables $m$ and $b$ are governed by[20]

(42) $\qquad\qquad\qquad \dot m + \mu m = (1-\zeta)\,\delta D_f/M$

and

(43) $\qquad\qquad\qquad \dot b + \mu b = \zeta\,\delta D_f/B.$

Equations (41)–(43) jointly determine the short-run dynamics of this model:

$$(44)\quad \frac{d}{dt}\begin{bmatrix} m \\ b \\ f \end{bmatrix} = \begin{bmatrix} -\mu & 0 & 0 \\ 0 & -\mu & 0 \\ 0 & 0 & i^* \end{bmatrix}\begin{bmatrix} m \\ b \\ f \end{bmatrix} + \begin{bmatrix} (1-\zeta)/M \\ \zeta/B \\ 0 \end{bmatrix}\delta D_f + \begin{bmatrix} 0 \\ 0 \\ 1 \end{bmatrix}\delta B_T/F$$

$$= \begin{bmatrix} -\mu & i\gamma(1-\zeta) & 0 \\ 0 & -\mu+\gamma\zeta i & 0 \\ -\Omega_2 & -\Omega_3 & i^* - C_2 \end{bmatrix}\begin{bmatrix} m \\ b \\ f \end{bmatrix} + \begin{bmatrix} (1-\zeta)m_1 \\ \gamma\zeta m_1 \\ \Omega_2 + \Omega_3 \end{bmatrix}e$$

$$-\Omega_1\begin{bmatrix} 0 \\ 0 \\ 1 \end{bmatrix}y' + \begin{bmatrix} (1-\zeta) \\ \zeta\gamma \\ 0 \end{bmatrix}\delta\varepsilon,$$

---

[20] When $\zeta$ is set to 0, the dynamics for $b$ separate from the rest as $\dot b = -\mu b$. The remainder becomes two dimensional, which behaves essentially as in Example 1. With $\zeta$ set to one, the dynamics for $m$ become $\dot m = -\mu m$ and separate from the rest.

These dynamics are more complicated due to the presence of the service term in the government budget constraint. The ratio $M/B$ on the reference path enter into the stability condition.

where
$$\gamma = M/B \quad \text{and} \quad m_1 = P(G - T)/M.$$

To express $e$, $y'$, and $\delta\varepsilon$ in reduced forms, we assume an autoregressive expectation mechanism,

(45) $$\delta\varepsilon = -ve.$$

From variation of the asset sector equilibrium, we derive

(46) $$e = -\theta_1 b - f + \theta_2 m + \theta_3 \delta\varepsilon,$$

where

$$\theta_1 = B/EF > 0, \quad \theta_2 = (1 + \theta_1) > 0, \quad \theta_3 = \theta_2(\beta'/\beta - \alpha'/\alpha) > 0.$$

Solving (45) and (46) jointly, we arrive at the reduced forms of $e$ and $\delta\varepsilon$:

(47) $$e = -\omega_1(\theta_1 b + f - \theta_2 m),$$

where $\omega_1 = (1 + v\theta_3)^{-1}$, and

(48) $$\delta\varepsilon = v\omega_1(\theta_1 b + f - \theta_2 m).$$

Finally, from (39), (47), and (48), we can put $y'$ in the form

(49) $$y' = -\eta_1 m + \eta_2 b + \eta_3 f,$$

where

$$\eta_1 = l_2 - (l_2 - l_3 + vl_4)\omega_1\theta_2,$$
$$\eta_2 = l_3 - (l_2 - l_3 + vl_4)\omega_1\theta_1,$$
$$\eta_3 = l_1 - (l_2 - l_3 + vl_4)\omega_1.$$

The dynamics (44) are set in state-space form by substituting $y'$, $e$, and $\delta\varepsilon$ out by their reduced forms given in (47)–(49). When this is done, the dynamic matrix along the reference path $\bar{\Phi}$ can be written as

(50) $$\bar{\Phi} = \Phi^0 + \mathbf{hn}',$$

where

$$\Phi^0 = \begin{bmatrix} -\mu & 0 & 0 \\ 0 & -\mu & 0 \\ \phi_{31} & \phi_{32} & \phi_{33} \end{bmatrix}, \quad \mathbf{h} = \begin{bmatrix} 1 - \zeta \\ \gamma\zeta \\ 0 \end{bmatrix}, \quad \mathbf{n}' = [\phi_1 \quad \phi_2 \quad -\phi],$$

and

$$\phi_{31} = -\Omega_2 + \Omega_1\eta_1 + \omega_1\theta_2(\Omega_2 + \Omega_3),$$
$$\phi_{32} = -\Omega_3 - \Omega_1\eta_2 - \omega_1\theta_1(\Omega_2 + \Omega_3),$$
$$\phi_{33} = i^* - C_2 - \Omega_1\eta_3 - \omega_1(\Omega_2 + \Omega_3),$$
$$\phi = \omega_1(\mu - v), \quad \phi_1 = \phi\theta_2, \quad \phi_2 = \bar{i} - \phi\theta_1, \quad \bar{i} = i^* + \mu.$$

## 8.4.3 Stability Analysis

This form is convenient to examine the dependence of the eigenvalues on $\zeta$, the percentage of bond-financed deficit.

The eigenvalues of $\bar{\Phi}$ are the roots of

$$0 = |\lambda I - \bar{\Phi}| = |\lambda I - \Phi^0|\{1 - \mathbf{n}'(\lambda I - \Phi^0)^{-1}\mathbf{h}\}$$

[see, for example, Aoki (1976, Appendix D)], where

$$|\lambda I - \Phi^0| = (\lambda + \mu)^2(\lambda - \phi_{33})$$

and

$$(\lambda I - \Phi^0)^{-1} = \begin{bmatrix} (\lambda + \mu)^{-1} & 0 & 0 \\ 0 & (\lambda + \mu)^{-1} & 0 \\ \phi_{31}\{(\lambda + \mu)(\lambda - \phi_{33})\}^{-1} & \phi_{32}\{(\lambda + \mu)(\lambda - \phi_{33})\}^{-1} & (\lambda - \phi_{33})^{-1} \end{bmatrix}.$$

The characteristic polynomial of $\bar{\Phi}$ becomes $(\lambda + \mu)q(\lambda)$, where

$$q(\lambda) = s(\lambda) + \zeta u(\lambda),$$

where

$$s(\lambda) = \lambda^2 + (\mu - \phi_{33} - \phi_1)\lambda + \phi_{33}(\phi_1 - \mu) + \phi\phi_{31},$$
$$u(\lambda) = (\phi_1 - \phi_2\gamma)\{\lambda + \lambda_0\},$$

where $\lambda_0 = -\phi_{33} - \phi(\phi_{31} - \gamma\phi_{32})(\phi_1 - \phi_2\gamma)^{-1}$.

One eigenvalue of $\bar{\Phi}$ thus equals $-\mu$, which is independent of $\zeta$. The other two are the roots of $q(\lambda)$: We use the root-locus method to examine their dependence on $\zeta$ by rewriting $q(\lambda) = 0$ as

$$(\lambda + \lambda_0)/s(\lambda) = -1/\kappa\zeta,$$

where $\kappa = (\phi_1 - \phi_2\gamma) = -\bar{i}\gamma + \phi(\theta_1\gamma + \theta_2)$.

We have already shown that $\zeta = 0$ reduces the dynamics to the case of Example 1, i.e., the two roots of $s(\lambda)$ are the ones of Example 1, and the third eigenvalue $\mu$ belongs to the dynamics $\dot{b} = -\mu b$. In Example 1 we have discussed the conditions under which the roots of $s(\lambda)$ are stable. Suppose that these conditions are met so that $s(\lambda)$ has stable roots for $\zeta$ zero. So we assume that $\mu$ and $\nu$ are such that, the inequalities

$$\mu - \phi_{33} - \phi_1 > 0 \quad \text{and} \quad \phi_{33}(\phi_1 - \mu) + \phi\phi_{31} > 0$$

are satisfied.

As $\zeta$ increases from zero, the percentage of bond-financed budget imbalance increases. The short-run stability thus crucially depends on the sign of $\lambda_0$ as follows.

We ask when the bond-financing is likely to be destabilizing. From the root-locus consideration, a negative $\lambda_0$ is sufficient for an increase in $\zeta$ to be destabilizing the dynamics, when $\kappa$ is positive. When $\kappa$ is negative a positive $\lambda_0$ is destabilizing, i.e., $\kappa\lambda_0 < 0$ is a sufficient condition.

Substituting the definitions, this inequality can be reduced to the one for $\mu$ and $v$.[21] The inequality $\kappa\lambda_0 < 0$ is equivalent to $\phi_{33}(\phi_1 - \phi_2\gamma) + \phi(\phi_{31} - \gamma\phi_{32}) > 0$. It is rather involved and does not seem to have an easy interpretation. With large $v$, however, $\omega_1$ becomes small hence $\phi$ becomes small. The inequality approximately becomes $(i^* - C_2 - \Omega_1\eta_3)\gamma\bar{i} > 0$ or $i^* - C_2 - \Omega_1\eta_3 > 0$. Substituting $\eta_3$ out, this can be equivalently put as $i^*(1 - C_1) + C_1\mu < C_2$, a condition similar to those derived in Section 8.2.7. With nonzero $\omega_1$ now, the inequality can be put as

$$\phi_{33}\phi_1 + \phi\{\Omega_1\eta_1 + \theta_2(\Omega_2 + \Omega_3)\omega_1\}$$
$$+ \gamma[-\phi_{33}\phi_2 + \phi\{\Omega_1\eta_2 + \theta_1(\Omega_2 + \Omega_3)\omega_1\}] > 0.$$

Therefore, if the expression in the square bracket is positive, smaller $\gamma$ (i.e., $B$ larger than $M$) implies that the stability condition is harder to satisfy. (The square bracketed expression is negative if $\phi$ is negative or if $v > \mu$. It is necessary that $\mu > v$ for the square bracketed expression to be positive.)

---

[21] The inequality does not seem to have an easy interpretation.
$$\phi_{33}(\phi_1 - \phi_2\gamma) + \phi(\phi_{31} - \gamma\phi_{32}) > 0,$$
where $\phi_1 - \phi_2\gamma = (\theta_2 + \gamma\theta_1)\phi - \bar{i}\gamma$, $\phi_{31} - \gamma\phi_{32} = \Omega_1(\eta_1 + \gamma\eta_2) + (\theta_2 + \gamma\theta_1)(\Omega_2 + \Omega_3)\omega_1$, and $\Omega_1(\eta_1 + \gamma\eta_2) = (C_1/EF)\{\bar{i}M - \xi(\theta_2 + \gamma\theta_1)\omega_1\}$, where $\xi = \mu M - i^*B - v(M/E - F)$, $\Omega_1\eta_3 = (C_1/EF)(i^* - \mu - \omega_1\xi)$, and $\Omega_2 + \Omega_3 = (C_2 B/EF)(1 + \gamma)$.

The stability dependence on $\gamma$ can be similarly analyzed by the root-locus method.

# Part Two | Small Open Economies

Parts Two and Three share two common objectives. One is to illustrate our techniques for analyzing dynamic behavior of open economies in response to exogenous shocks or instrument changes on models commonly found in the literature. Some of the more important techniques we use have been mentioned in Part One. The other objective is to add to results on policy effectiveness studies of open economies in dynamic settings.

Models of open economies seem to have undergone substantial changes during the period from the late 1960s to middle 1970s. As Henderson (1977) pointed out, general equilibrium models using a portfolio balance approach seem to have come to be used more frequently. For this reason, we also used models of this class. Other views and other forms of models, of course, exist. Some questions may very well call for other types of models or other modes of analysis. In this book we address questions which are essentially dynamic in nature. Changing stocks of financial assets, capital or public debts due to current account, investment, and government budget imbalances all contribute to dynamics, not to mention expectational dynamics and wage rate dynamics. There are feedbacks among various sectors of an economy as well as among countries. There are interactions between the long-run and short-run policy variables or objectives. Traditionally, questions related to policy effectiveness have been examined only at impact and at steady-state (long-run) equilibriums. In this study we evaluate behavior of open economies not only at the instant of exogenous shocks or changes in instruments but also after some time has elapsed since the last impacts. Put differently, we examine how much dynamics matter in analyzing policy effects on several models of open economies.

Part Two is devoted to models of small open economies. Questions related to interdependence of economies in which feedback effects among different countries cannot be ignored are examined in Part Three.

Analysis of a small open economy treats the rest of the world as exogenous and is characterized by a set of assumptions, or constraints, about the economy. For example, no changes in the states of the small open economy or its instruments shall affect the rest of the world by assumption, and there will be no repercussions from the rest of the world to policy changes or other disturbances originating in the small open economy. Feedback effects are thus entirely ignored in analysis of a small open economy.

This assumption takes on several forms: In analyzing asset sector behavior, it may be assumed that only one type of bonds is internationally traded (i.e., by assumption home and foreign securities are perfect substitutes with identical rates of return and risk characteristics) and that because of the uncovered arbitrage, the domestic rate of yield is constrained to equal the exogenous "world" rate of interest rate plus the expected rate of depreciation of the exchange rate. Another common assumption is that the output price of an economy is tied to the exogenously fixed "world" price by some variant of the purchasing power parity assumption.

To reiterate, then, the notion of a small open economy is not an intrinsic property of a country but rather denotes a theoretical construct embodying several common assumptions used in analyzing economic behavior of a country. We can treat a country as a small open economy or as one country in a multiple-country model of the world, depending on the assumptions we used to eliminate or simplify transmission paths between it and the rest of the world. In analyzing a small open economy, the rest of the world is exogenous and is usually specified only to the extent that some variables facing the small open economy are compatibly determined in the rest of the world. Typically, the world price level, income, inflation rate, or interest rates are treated as exogenously fixed outside the country. With most or all variables in the rest of the world thus exogenously specified, we then have a small open economy. We also disregard foreign repercussions to domestic policy changes in the small open economy because the foreign variables are treated as exogenous variables.

How valid are the assumptions surrounding the treatment of an economy as a small open economy? The justification often advanced in the literature for this mode of analysis is that the economy is too small in the world markets to influence significantly the intrinsic economic variables in the rest of the world. This does not mean that the economy is necessarily a price taker in the market for goods or assets that originate domestically. (This is a separate issue.) To characterize smallness and determine its effects in the analysis, a two- or multiple-country model of the world must be specified and the results compared. We return to this point later in Part Three.[1] Collective assump-

---

[1] Krugman (1980) uses a dynamic three-country partial equilibrium model of the world to show that some small country treatments in the literature in analyzing the effects of oil price increases are not justified.

# Small Open Economies

tions used to analyze a small open economy may reasonably approximate conditions in a given real country. Even when the assumptions do not reasonably approximate reality, this mode of analysis may be justified as a first iteration of the analysis. Foreign repercussions can be taken into account in the second round of iterations of the analysis.

Chapter 9 illustrates influences of capital growth on policy effects by calculating the dynamic fiscal policy multiplier of a growing small open economy. We show that the dynamic multiplier could exhibit oscillatory behavior and reach a peak some time after a change in the fiscal instrument, while the fiscal multiplier monotonically decays if there is no capital growth, i.e., the dynamic multiplier is always smaller than the impact multiplier with no capital growth.

Chapter 10 discusses stabilization policies, i.e., policy reaction functions which stabilize an otherwise unstable economy or which increase the "degree" of stability. This chapter analyzes influences of long-run policy choices on the government budget imbalance and current account on short-run stability in an economy in which the purchasing power parity and the interest rate parity conditions hold. In addition to providing illustrations of the root-locus method of Chapter 2 for describing the influences of stabilizing feedback, the main result of this chapter is the demonstration that the short-run stability requirements impose joint constraints on long-run policy objectives and that these constraints cannot generally be separately stated for the size of the current account and the size of the budget imbalance.

In Chapter 11, the assumption of the purchasing power parity and the interest rate parity conditions are dropped. The model of this chapter is used to answer, among other questions, whether variable wage rates are more inflationary than rigid wage rates. Analysis of this question provides the first illustration of our structural sensitivity or perturbation analysis method of Chapter 5. (We shall see more applications of this method in Part Three.) We compare the inflation rate of the model having variable wage rates with that of the model having rigid wage rates by treating the former as a structural perturbation of the latter.

# 9 A Growing Economy: Influences of Capital Growth on the Dynamic Multiplier

The model of this chapter illustrates that growth in capital can have important effects on the policy effectiveness. In the model of a growing economy we discuss here, the dynamic fiscal multiplier reaches a peak some time after a change in the fiscal policy, while the fiscal multiplier monotonically decreases if there is no growth in capital.

To simplify the analysis, we treat a model in which domestic money and international bonds are the only two types of financial assets available to the residents of the small open economy, and impose the interest rate parity condition $i = i^*$, assuming that the expectation on the exchange rate depreciation is zero. This is consistent with our choice of the reference path discussed later in this chapter.

## 9.1 The Model

### 9.1.1 The Asset Sector

We assume that domestic residents hold stocks of capital and domestic money, both of which are nontraded assets, and a stock of internationally traded bonds. The domestic government does not issue bonds of its own. The world interest rate $i^*$ is exogenously fixed. Since $E$ is constant, on the long-run path we later choose, we assume $i = i^*$ setting $\varepsilon$ to zero. The asset demand functions are assumed to be given by

$$M = \alpha(r, PY/A)A, \qquad \alpha_1 < 0, \quad \alpha_2 > 0,$$

and

$$EF = \beta(r, PY/A)A, \qquad \beta_1 < 0, \quad \beta_2 < 0,$$

and

$$qK = \gamma(r, PY/A)A, \qquad \gamma_1 > 0, \quad \gamma_2 < 0,$$

where

$$q = R(K, \overset{+}{Y})/r$$

and

(1) $$A = M + EF + qK,$$

where $M$ is domestic money stock, $F$ is foreign bond stock in foreign currency, and $r$ is the rate of return on equity capital. The expression for $q$ is the same as the one in Chapter 3. Because of the balance sheet constraint there are only two independent equations in the asset sector. We take it to be the ratios:

(2) $$EF/M = \phi(r, PY/A),$$

where $\phi = \beta/\alpha$, and

(3) $$qK/EF = \psi(r, PY/A),$$

where $\psi = \gamma/\beta$.

To simplify algebra, we assume that $\alpha_1/\alpha$ equals $\beta_1/\beta$ and $\beta_2/\beta$ equals $\gamma_2/\gamma$; i.e., the private sector shifts out (into) equally from money and bond into (out of) equity as $r$ changes. As the scale variable $PY/A$ changes, the private sector moves out of (into) money equally into (from) bonds and equity. These two assumptions simplify the ensuing analysis without essential changes of transmission paths in the model.

### 9.1.2 Real Sector

The economy produces a traded (composite) good which is an imperfect substitute for the world good. The supply equation is taken to be a function of $w/P$ and capital stock $K$

(4) $$Y^s = Y(w/P, K),$$

where $w$ is the nominal wage rate which is assumed constant.[1]

The demand equation is given by

(5) $$Y = C(Y') + I(q, Y, K) + G + X(Y^*),$$

where $I$ is real investment and export $X$ is a function of a foreign scale variable which is taken to be $Y^*$. $C$ is the real purchase of goods by the home residents which is assumed to be unit elastic with respect to $Y'$. It is specified as a function of $Y'$ where $Y'$ is the disposable income given by

(6) $$Y' = (1 - \tau)(Y + i^*EF) - \lambda K,$$

---

[1] The wage rate dynamics are discussed in Chapter 11.

## 9.1 The Model

where $\tau$ is the tax rate and $\lambda$ is the rate of depreciation of capital per unit capital. The investment is assumed to be a function of $q$, $Y$, and $K$ only, since $i^*$ is exogenously fixed. More realistically, both $C$ and $X$ will depend on the (final good) terms of trade $P/EP^*$. To simplify the ensuing analysis we first assume that dependence of $C$ and $X$ on the terms of trade is negligible in the short run. Later we elaborate on consequences of not making this simplifying assumption. (We also investigate the effects of the terms of trade in Chapter 11.)

### 9.1.3 Dynamics

The dynamics come from the government budget constraint, from the current account relation, and from the growth of capital stock. Assume that the domestic government does not intervene in the foreign exchange market and that the government budget constraint equation is simply given by[2]

(7) $$\dot{M} = P(G - T).$$

The private holding of the international bonds change according to

(8) $$\dot{F} = B_T + i^*F \quad \text{in foreign currency,}$$

where the trade balance is given by

$$B_T = PX/E - P^*I_m,$$

where $I_m$ is the imports. Imports are specified to depend on only $Y'$ for simplicity of analysis. Equations (7) and (8) are both simplifications of more complicated functional dependence.

The specification of dynamics is completed by positing

(9) $$\dot{K} = I(q, Y, K) - \lambda K.$$

Equations (7)–(9) constitute the dynamics of this model.

### 9.1.4 Long-Run Equilibrium

Recall our discussion in Section 1.3: The long-run reference path must be compatible with relations implied by logarithmic differentiation of (2) and (3). We choose as our reference path a growth path characterized by constant prices $\dot{E}/E = 0$, $\dot{P}/P = 0$, $\dot{r} = 0$, and the growth rates $\dot{M}/M = \dot{F}/F = \dot{K}/K = \dot{Y}/Y = \dot{A}/A$. We assume that $R_1 K/R = -R_2 Y/R$, so that $q$ is constant on the reference path as well.

---

[2] The government holding of the international bonds remains fixed.

These relations imply that the model admits a balanced growth path, in which all stocks $K$, $F$, and $M$ grow at the same exogenous rate $n$, and all flow variables $Y$, $G$, $T$, $X$, and $I_m$ also grow at the same rate.[3] Although the labor population is implicit in the model, $n$ may be considered to be equal to the growth of technical progress plus labor population. In other words, the reference path of the economy is defined by a set of time paths given by $K(t) = K_0 e^{nt}$, $F(t) = F_0 e^{nt}$, $M(t) = M_0 e^{nt}$, $Y(t) = Y_0 e^{nt}$, $G(t) = G_0 e^{nt}$, $X(t) = X_0 e^{nt}$ and $I_m(t) = I_{m_0} e^{nt}$, $E = \bar{E}$, $P = \bar{P}$, $r = \bar{r}$, and $q = \bar{q}$. The coefficients are related by the following equalities: From (2), $\bar{E}F_0/M_0 = \phi(\bar{r}, \bar{P}Y_0/A_0)$, where $A_0 = M_0 + \bar{E}F_0 + \bar{q}K_0$. From (3), $\bar{q}K_0/\bar{E}F_0 = \psi(\bar{r}, \bar{P}Y_0/A_0)$. From (7), $nM_0 = \bar{P}(G_0 - T_0)$. From (8), $(n - i^*)F_0 = \bar{P}X_0/\bar{E} - P^*I_{m_0}$. From (9), $nK_0 = I(\bar{r}, Y_0 K_0) - \lambda K_0$.

### 9.1.5 Variational Equations

We now turn to the derivation of the variational equations governing dynamics of this small open economy in a neighborhood of the reference path given by the balanced growth path just defined. When the economy deviates from the reference path by exogenous shocks or changes in some of the instruments, $E$, $F$, and $M$ deviate from their respective reference time paths. Their relative deviations are related by the variational equations of (2), and (3):

(10) $$e + f - m = \tilde{\phi}(p + y - a),$$

where $\tilde{\phi} = (\phi_2/\phi)(PY/A)$ is evaluated along the reference path hence is a constant. Here we use our simplifying assumption that $\alpha_1/\alpha$ equals $\beta_1/\beta$. Variation of (3) yields the following relation

$$\delta q/q + k - e - f = \tilde{\psi}\delta r,$$

where

$$\tilde{\psi} = \psi_1/\psi = \gamma_1/\gamma - \beta_1/\beta > 0.$$

Here our simplifying assumption $\beta_2/\beta = \gamma_2/\gamma$ allows us to eliminate terms depending on $(p + y - a)$ from the above. Noting that $\delta q/q$ equals $-\delta r/r + \tilde{\rho}(y - k)$, where $\tilde{\rho} = R_1 K/R = -R_2 Y/R < 1$, by assumption we can relate the relative variation in the yield of capital as

(11) $$\delta r/r = -\rho_1(e + f) + \rho_2 y + (\rho_1 - \rho_2)k,$$

---

[3] We assume that the world income grows at the same rate $n$. It is possible to assume, as Knight and Wymer (1978) do, that the world income grows at a different rate.
The wage rate growth is determined by setting $\dot{Y}_s/Y_s$ to the common rate of growth, i.e., from $(1 - (Y_2/Y)K)n = (Y_1/Y)(\dot{w}/P)w/w$. We set $\bar{E}$ and $\bar{q}$ to one. There are six equations to determine $M_0$, $F_0$, $K_0$, $\bar{r}$, $\bar{P}$, and $Y_0$.

## 9.1 The Model

where

$$\rho_1 = (1 + \hat{\psi}r)^{-1} < 1, \qquad \rho_2 = \tilde{\rho}\rho_1.$$

Since the variation of $A$ is $a = \alpha m + \beta(e + f) + \gamma k + \gamma\{-\delta r/r + \tilde{\rho}(y - k)\}$, (10) can be solved for $e$ as

(12) $$e = -f + \varepsilon_1 m + \varepsilon_2 p + \varepsilon_3 y - \varepsilon_4 k,$$

where

$$\varepsilon_0 = 1 + (\beta + \gamma\rho_1)\tilde{\phi} > 0, \qquad \varepsilon_1 = (1 - \alpha\tilde{\phi})/\varepsilon_0 > 0, \qquad \varepsilon_2 = \tilde{\phi}/\varepsilon_0,$$
$$\varepsilon_3 = \varepsilon_2\{1 - \gamma(1 - \rho_1)\tilde{\rho}\} < 0, \qquad \varepsilon_4 = \gamma(1 - \rho_1)(1 - \tilde{\rho})\varepsilon_2 > 0.$$

Note that the coefficients $\varepsilon_3$ and $\varepsilon_4$ are less than $\varepsilon_2$.

Equations (11) and (12) describe equilibria of the variational variables in the asset sector. To derive the momentary equilibrium condition in the real sector, we equate the expression for the relative variation of the supply equation (4) with that of the demand relation (5). The former is

(13) $$y = \sigma_0 k + \sigma_1 p,$$

where

$$\sigma_0 = Y_2 K/Y \qquad \text{and} \qquad \sigma_1 = -(Y_1/Y)(w/P) > 0,$$

and the latter is

(14) $$y = -\eta_1 k + \eta_2(e + f) + \eta_3 g + \eta_4 \, \delta r/r,$$

where

$$\eta_0 = \{1 - C'(1 - \tau) - I_2\}Y, \qquad \eta_1 = (\lambda C' - I_3)K/\eta_0,$$
$$\eta_2 = i^*(1 - \tau)C'EF/\eta_0, \qquad \eta_3 = G/\eta_0, \qquad \eta_4 = I_1 r/\eta_0.$$

Equations (11)–(14) jointly determine the monetary deviations of the economy about the reference growth path.

These four equations can be solved for $\delta r$, $e$, $y$, and $p$: The solution process can be facilitated by expressing $e + f$ and $\delta r/r$ in terms of $m$, $k$, $p$, and $y$; and $y$ and $p$ in terms of $k$, $g$, $e + f$, and $\delta r/r$. These two two-dimensional relations are then solved simultaneously. The solution expresses $e + f$ and $\delta r/r$ as linear combinations of $m$, $k$, and $g$, and $p$ and $y$ in terms of $m$, $k$, and $g$. Thus we readily see that $f$ appears only in the expression for $e$ in (15), which gives the reduced form expressions for these four variables.

In the solution we note that $\eta_2$ and $\eta_4$ in (14) serve as "feedback" couplings between the real and asset sector.

$$\delta r/r = -\rho_m m + \rho_k k - \rho_0 g,$$

(15)
$$e = \varepsilon_m m - f - \varepsilon_k k - \varepsilon_0 g, \qquad \varepsilon_0 > 0,$$
$$\sigma_1 p = \eta_m m - \rho_k k + \eta_0 g, \qquad \eta_0 > 0,$$
$$y = \eta_m m + \eta_k k + \eta_0 g,$$

where $\rho_k = \sigma_0 - \eta_k$, and these coefficients are some complicated algebraic combinations of the coefficients in (11)–(14).[4] (Their exact expressions are not needed in our analysis.)

Note that the variation $f$ appears only in $e$ and does not affect $p$ nor $y$. This is because dependence of $C'$ and $X$ on the terms of trade has been omitted. When this dependence is recognized, $f$ influences $p$ and $y$. We return to this later.

### 9.1.6 Variational Dynamics

Deviations of the stocks of the financial assets and capital from the reference paths are governed by the variational equations of (7), (8), and (9)[5]

$$\delta \dot{M} = P(G - T)p + P(Gg - Y\tau),$$

where we assume that $\delta T = Y\tau y$,

$$\delta \dot{F} = \delta B_T + i^* \, \delta F,$$

where from its definition given below (8) and from (6),

$$\delta B_T/F = v_p(p - e) - (P^* I'_m/F) \, \delta Y' = v_p(p - e) - v_y y - v_k k,$$

where

$$v_p = PX/EF, \qquad v_k = \lambda P^* I'_m K/F,$$
$$v_y = (1 - \tau)P^* I'_m Y/F, \qquad v_f = P^* I'_m (1 - \tau) i^* E,$$

---

[4] Note that the combined effects of $g$ on $e$ through $p$, $y$, and $\delta r$ are such that $\varepsilon_0$ is positive. Let

$$\gamma_1 = \rho_1\{-\tilde{p} + \varepsilon_3 + \varepsilon_2/\sigma_1\} \qquad \text{and} \qquad \gamma_2 = \varepsilon_2 \gamma(1 - \rho_1)\tilde{p} > 0.$$

Then

$$\rho_0 = \eta_3 \gamma_1/(1 + \gamma_2 \eta_2 + \gamma_1 \eta_4) \qquad \text{and} \qquad \varepsilon_0 = \eta_3 \gamma_2/(1 + \gamma_2 \eta_2 + \gamma_1 \eta_4).$$

The sign of $\rho_0$ is ambiguous. If the effect of $K$ on $q$ is smaller than the effect of $r$ on $\phi$ in the sense that $(R_1 K/R) < \varepsilon_2/\sigma_1 + \varepsilon_3$, then $\rho_0$ is positive. We take $\eta_0 = \eta_3 - \rho_0 \eta_3 - \varepsilon_0 \eta_2$ to be positive.

[5] These expressions are derived by our usual procedure for deriving variational equations.

## 9.1 The Model

and

$$\delta\dot{K} = (-\kappa_k k + \kappa_y y - \kappa_r \,\delta r/r)K,$$

where

$$\kappa_k = I_1 R_1/R - I_3 + \lambda > 0, \qquad \kappa_y = I_1 R_1/r + I_2 Y/K > 0,$$

and

$$\kappa_r = I_1 q/K > 0.$$

These variational relations are substituted into the following equations:

$$\dot{m} = \delta \dot{M}/M - mn, \qquad \dot{f} = \delta \dot{F}/F - fn, \qquad \text{and} \qquad \dot{k} = \delta \dot{K}/K - kn,$$

since $\dot{M}/M$, $\dot{F}/F$ and $\dot{K}/K$ are all equal to $n$ along the reference path. The differential equations for $m$, $f$, and $k$ therefore become[6]

(16) $$\frac{d}{dt}\begin{bmatrix} f \\ m \\ k \end{bmatrix} = \tilde{\Phi}\begin{bmatrix} f \\ m \\ k \end{bmatrix} + \begin{bmatrix} v_p \\ \mu_p \\ 0 \end{bmatrix}p + \begin{bmatrix} -v_y \\ -\mu_y \\ \kappa_y \end{bmatrix}y$$

$$- v_e\begin{bmatrix} 1 \\ 0 \\ 0 \end{bmatrix}e + \mu_g\begin{bmatrix} 0 \\ 1 \\ 0 \end{bmatrix}g - \kappa_r\begin{bmatrix} 0 \\ 0 \\ 1 \end{bmatrix}\frac{\delta r}{r},$$

where

$$\tilde{\Phi} = \begin{bmatrix} i^* - (v_f + n) & 0 & v_k \\ 0 & -n & 0 \\ 0 & 0 & -(\kappa_k + n) \end{bmatrix},$$

where

$$\mu_p = P(G - T)/M, \quad \mu_g = PG/M > 0, \quad \mu_y = \tau PY/M > 0, \quad v_e = v_p + v_f.$$

Note that $\mu_p$ is positive if and only if the government budget is in deficit. This equation is not yet in the state-space representation, because $p$, $y$, and $e$ are not state variables. When (15) is used to substitute $p$, $y$, $e$, and $\delta r/r$ out, (16) is converted into state-space form. Equation (16) is useful because it explicitly shows the influence of variations in the price level, output, and the exchange rate on the dynamics. For example, if the price level is rigid the influence of $p$ on the dynamics disappears. If the output is growing smoothly at the rate $n$, the dynamics due to variations in output disappear. Similarly, if the exchange rate is fixed its effect on the dynamics disappear.

---

[6] Note that the variation of the export is zero because $X$ is assumed to be a function of a constant foreign income.

The dynamic equation in the state space form is

(17) $$\frac{d}{dt}\begin{bmatrix} f \\ m \\ k \end{bmatrix} = \Phi \begin{bmatrix} f \\ m \\ g \end{bmatrix} + \psi g,$$

where

$$\Phi = \tilde{\Phi} + \begin{bmatrix} v_p \\ \mu_p \\ 0 \end{bmatrix} [0 \quad \eta_m \quad -\rho_k]/\sigma_1 + \begin{bmatrix} -v_y \\ -\mu_y \\ \kappa_y \end{bmatrix} [0 \quad \eta_m \quad \eta_k]$$

$$- v_e \begin{bmatrix} 1 \\ 0 \\ 0 \end{bmatrix} [-1 \quad \varepsilon_m \quad -\varepsilon_k] - \kappa_r \begin{bmatrix} 0 \\ 0 \\ 1 \end{bmatrix} [0 \quad -\rho_m \quad \rho_k]$$

and where

$$\psi = \mu_g \begin{bmatrix} 0 \\ 1 \\ 0 \end{bmatrix} + \frac{\eta_0}{\sigma_1} \begin{bmatrix} v_p \\ \mu_p \\ 0 \end{bmatrix} + \eta_0 \begin{bmatrix} -v_y \\ -\mu_y \\ \kappa_y \end{bmatrix} + v_e \varepsilon_0 \begin{bmatrix} 1 \\ 0 \\ 0 \end{bmatrix} + \kappa_r \rho_0 \begin{bmatrix} 0 \\ 0 \\ 1 \end{bmatrix}.$$

Examination of the dynamic matrix $\Phi$ of (17) reveals that the differential equations for $m$ and $k$ separate from the differential equation for $f$, i.e., the dynamics are recursive. This is due to our assumption that consumption and exports are insensitive to the terms-of-trade changes. The exchange rate variations provide the only linkage between the dynamics for $f$ and those for $m$ and $k$. The dynamics for $m$ and $k$ act on the dynamics for $f$, but the converse does not occur. The make-up of the dynamic matrix in (17) reveals that variation of the money stock affects the variation of the capital stock growth through variations of output and the rate of return, and that $k$ in turn affect $m$ through $p$ and $y$. The recursiveness of the dynamics is reflected by the block triangular form of the dynamic matrix $\Phi$

$$\Phi = \begin{bmatrix} -n + \chi_f & \chi_m & \chi_k \\ 0 & & \\ 0 & & H \end{bmatrix},$$

where

$$\chi_f = i^* + v_p, \quad \chi_m = (v_p/\sigma_1 - v_y)\eta_m - v_e \varepsilon_m,$$

$$\chi_k = v_k - v_p \rho_k/\sigma_1 - v_y \eta_k + v_e \varepsilon_k,$$

(18) $H_{11} = -n - v_e \varepsilon_m - (\mu_y - \mu_p/\sigma_1)\eta_m, \quad H_{12} = -\mu_p \rho_k/\sigma_1 - \mu_y \eta_k,$

$H_{21} = \eta_m(\kappa_y + \kappa_r/\sigma_1), \quad H_{22} = -n - \kappa_k + \kappa_y \eta_k - \kappa_r \rho_k.$

## 9.2 Fiscal Multipliers

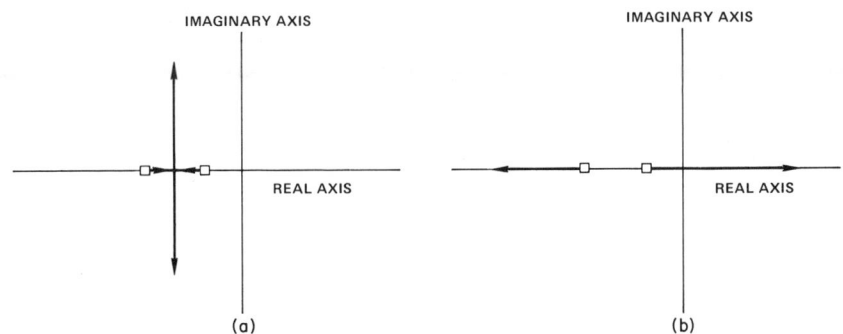

*Figure 1* Sign of $H_{12}$ affects the root-locus plots. (a) $H_{12} < 0$; (b) $H_{12} > 0$.

Because $H_{21}$ is likely to be positive (because $\kappa_y + \kappa_r/\sigma_1$ is positive and $\eta_m$ is likely to be positive) the sign of $H_{12}$ is an important determinant of the eigenvalues of $H$. With sufficiently negative $H_{12}$ the eigenvalues become complex conjugate giving rise to damped oscillatory behavior of the fiscal multiplier. (When $H_{12}$ is positive, no oscillation can occur.) The root-locus plot of the characteristic polynomial associated with the matrix $H$ is shown in Fig. 1.

On the reference path $\mu_p$ equals $n$. If the production function is a Cobb–Douglas constant $K^\alpha L^{1-\alpha}$ (where $L$ is labor), then $\sigma_0/\sigma_1$ equals $\alpha/(1-\alpha)$. Thus noting that $\rho_k$ equals $\sigma_0 - \eta_k$,

$$H_{12} = -\frac{n\alpha}{1-\alpha}(1-\eta_k) - \eta_k\mu_y$$

showing that $H_{12}$ is likely to be negative.

### 9.2 Fiscal Multipliers

We now follow the procedure of Chapter 4 to calculate the fiscal dynamic multipliers. To provide a simple illustration that the dynamic multipliers can behave qualitatively differently when the $k$-dynamics are included, we consider a temporary increase in $G$ over a short period of time on the assumption that $H_{12}$ is negative, and show that the fiscal multiplier for the money stock deviation oscillates. We consider the fiscal instrument variation given by

$$g(t) = \begin{cases} \bar{g}, & 0 \le t \le T, \\ 0, & \text{otherwise.} \end{cases}$$

When the dynamics of capital accumulation are ignored, the variational equation for $m$ in (18) reduces to

(19) $$\dot{m} = -n_2 m + \psi_2 g,$$

where $n_2$ is $H_{11}$ and $\psi_2$ is the second component of $\psi$. Variation in money stock caused by temporary deviation of the fiscal expenditure $G$ from its reference path, i.e., nonzero $g(t)$, is obtained by integrating this equation. Without capital growth, $m$ changes with time according to

(20) $$\frac{m_t}{(\psi_2 \bar{g})} = \begin{cases} (e^{-n_2 t}/n_2)(e^{n_2 t} - 1) & \text{for } t \leq T, \\ (e^{-n_2 t}/n_2)(e^{n_2 T} - 1) & \text{for } t \geq T. \end{cases}$$

In other words, the multiplier behaves monotonically with time. With growing capital stock, the differential equations governing $m$ are derived from (17) and (18) as

(21) $$\frac{d}{dt}\begin{bmatrix} m \\ k \end{bmatrix} = H \begin{bmatrix} m \\ k \end{bmatrix} + \begin{bmatrix} \psi_2 \\ \psi_3 \end{bmatrix} g,$$

where we write the elements of $H$ as

$$H = \begin{bmatrix} -n_2 & -h_2 \\ h_3 & -n_3 \end{bmatrix}, \quad n_i, h_i > 0, \quad i = 2, 3.$$

Equation (18) defines $n$s and $h$s.

Suppose that $(n_2 - n_3)^2 < 4h_2 h_3$. Then $H$ has a pair of complex eigenvalues. Denote them as $-\sigma \pm j\omega$, where $\sigma = (n_2 + n_3)/2 > 0$ and $\omega = \sqrt{-(n_2 - n_3)^2 + 4h_2 h_3}/2$. As we have derived in Chapter 4, the multiplier is

$$\frac{m_t}{(\psi_2 \bar{g})} = [1 \ 0] H^{-1} (e^{Ht} - I) \begin{bmatrix} 1 \\ \psi_3/\psi_2 \end{bmatrix} \quad \text{for } t < T$$

and

$$\frac{m_t}{(\bar{g}\psi_2)} = [1 \ 0] H^{-1} e^{Ht} (I - e^{-HT}) \begin{bmatrix} 1 \\ \psi_3/\psi_2 \end{bmatrix} \quad \text{for } t > T.$$

It is expressible as an exponentially damped sinusoidal function of time

$$m_t/(\bar{g}\psi_2) = e^{-\sigma t}(A_1 \sin \omega t + A_2 \cos \omega t)$$
$$= e^{-\sigma t}\sqrt{A_1^2 + A_2^2} \sin(\omega t + \mu),$$

where

$$\tan \mu = A_2/A_1.$$

## 9.3 Numerical Example

To exhibit a possibility of oscillation, let us consider a numerical example with $n_2 = 0.08$, $n_3 = 0.1$, $h_2 = 0.401$, and $h_3 = 0.1$. Take $T$ to be 0.1. The dynamic multiplier for $m$ without growth in capital is

$$\frac{m_t}{(\psi_2 \bar{g} T)} = \begin{cases} (1 - e^{-0.08t})/0.08, & t \leq 0.1, \\ 1.004 e^{-0.08t}, & t \geq 0.1. \end{cases}$$

This is plotted in Fig. 2. Note its monotone behavior. When growth in capital is incorporated, the same multiplier becomes

$$\frac{m_t}{(\psi_2 \bar{g} T)} = \begin{cases} [1 \ 0] H^{-1} \dfrac{(e^{Ht} - I)}{0.1} \begin{bmatrix} 1 \\ \psi_3/\psi_2 \end{bmatrix}, & t \leq 0.1, \\ [1 \ 0] H^{-1} e^{HT} \dfrac{(I - e^{-0.1H})}{0.1} \begin{bmatrix} 1 \\ \psi_3/\psi_2 \end{bmatrix}, & t > 0.1 \end{cases}$$

The matrix exponential function is

$$e^{Ht} = e^{-0.09t} \begin{bmatrix} \cos 0.2t + 0.05 \sin 0.2t & -2.005 \sin 0.2t \\ 0.5 \sin 0.2t & \cos 0.2t - 0.05 \sin 0.2t \end{bmatrix}.$$

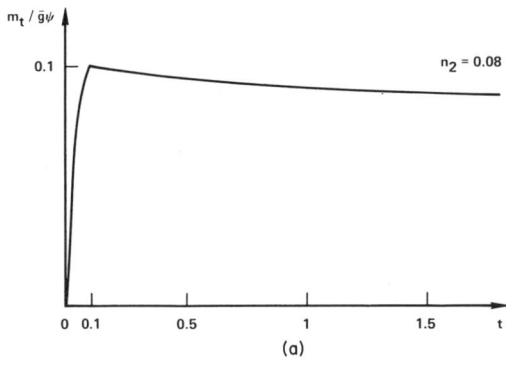

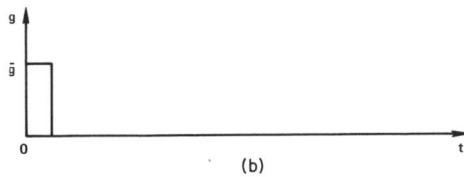

Figure 2   Time profile of a dynamic multiplier.

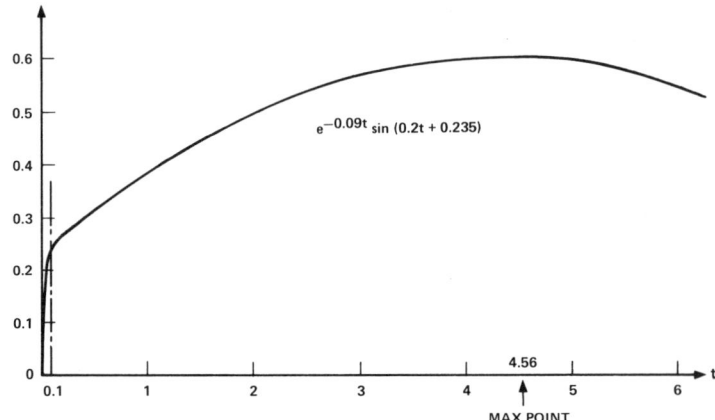

*Figure 3* The multiplier reaches its peak in a finite time.

Suppose $\psi_3/\psi_2 = 0.1$. Then the multiplier for $t \geq 0.1$ becomes $3.34 e^{-0.09t} \sin(0.2t + 0.235)$. This is plotted in Fig. 3. It reaches its first maximum approximately at $t = 4.56$.

The reason for the oscillation is easily found. The government fiscal expenditure crowds out the capital formation, at least initially, causing $k_t$ to become negative. This has two effects on the time path for $m$ through its effects on $p$ and $y$. With $H_{12} < 0$, as we have assumed, the net effect is to increase $m$. Price increase effect overwhelms the increase in tax receipt through increased output.

Initially, then, $m$ keeps increasing. Eventually the stabilizing effect through $-n_2$ takes over causing $m_t$ to peak some time after $g$ is reduced to zero.

### 9.4 Discussions and Summaries

With no growth in capital, the money stock deviation from its reference path values is described by the variation of the government budget constraint equation alone, i.e., by (19).

This differential equation for $m$ is not coupled to any other differential equation. Thus, in response to temporary deviations in the fiscal expenditure, $m$ changes according to an exponentially decaying function of time when $g$ ceases to be nonzero. This is (20). With growing capital stock, however, $m$ is no longer describable by (19) but is governed as a part of two-dimensional differential equation (21), i.e., influences of $k$ on $p$ and $y$ introduce dependence of $m$ in the government budget constraint variation equation on $k$. This second-order differential equation can produce oscillatory behavior of $m$ in

## 9.4 Discussions and Summaries

response to temporary deviation of $G$ from its reference time path. This was discussed at the end of Section 9.3.

To the first order of approximation, the effect of the changes in the terms of trade is felt more in $p$ than in $y$. We can show that $p$ in (15) is modified into

$$p = (\eta_m m - \rho_f f - \rho_k k + \eta_0 g)/\sigma_1,$$

where $\rho_f$ is expected to be small. The expressions for $e$ and $y$ remain the same as in (15).

The dynamic matrix $\Phi$ becomes

$$\Phi = \begin{bmatrix} -n + i^* + v_p(1 - \rho_f) & \chi_m & \chi_h \\ -\mu_p \rho_f/\sigma_1 & H & \\ 0 & & \end{bmatrix}.$$

The terms-of-trade, therefore, produces two-way dynamic coupling between $f$ and $m$ variables. Note that this coupling vanishes under a balanced budget, since $\mu_p$ is zero then.

With the terms-of-trade effects included in the model description, interactions between $m$ and $f$ exist. There is a possibility of $m$ and $f$ oscillating in response to a temporary change in $G$ even without capital growth. The root-locus method can be used to investigate this possibility.[7] The original third-order system always possesses an oscillatory dynamic multiplier provided $H_{12}$ is sufficiently negative. The detail is left for the interested reader.

---

[7] If $\chi_m \mu_p \rho_f$ is negative, however, this does not occur.

# 10 Stabilization Policies in a Small Open Economy

Policy reaction functions can stabilize otherwise unstable dynamics of open economies. Let us call them stabilization policies or stabilizing reaction functions. Their existence is guaranteed for controllable dynamic systems, as discussed in Chapter 6. In this chapter, we convey the basic idea of evaluating the effects of stabilization policies on a simple model of a small open economy.

First, a reference path of the economy is determined by the long-run policy objectives of the government. Since the short-run dynamics governing deviations of the economy about the reference path are determined by values of the endogenous variables on the reference path, the long-run policy instruments effectively determine the stability behavior of the short-run deviations. We show that long-run policy variables (marginal tax rate, the rate of the government budget deficit or surplus, and the rate of the current account surplus or deficit on the reference time path) are *interdependent* determinants of the short-run stability. Thus we demonstrate the existence of joint constraints on the long-run policy variables for the short-run deviations to behave stably. The joint constraints can not generally be stated separately for the current account and the government budget imbalances.

Then, effects of a particular policy reaction function are examined by the root-locus method of Section 2.4, by parametrizing the eigenvalue loci by coefficients of the policy reaction function.

If policy reaction functions are derived by explicit intertemporal optimization of quadratic objective (social welfare) functions, then the eigenvalue loci of resulting dynamic systems may sometimes be examined as functions of weights in the objective functions, such as relative weights assigned to inflation loss and unemployment loss. See Stein (1979) and Livesey (1980) for some results in this area.

## 10.1 The Model

The model produces a single traded good which is the same as the world traded good. The domestic money is nontraded. There is one type of international bond. Consequently, we impose on the model the purchasing power and the interest rate parity conditions. The basic expectational variable in the model is the expected rate of change of the exchange rate $\varepsilon$, which is generated adaptively. Because of the purchasing power parity condition, the expected rate of inflation must satisfy the consistency condition $\pi = \pi^* + \varepsilon$, where $\pi$ is the domestic inflation, and $\pi^*$ the world inflation rate, which we take to be zero. The model is summarized by the following set of structural equations and assumptions:

*Asset sector:*[1]

(1) $\qquad M = \alpha(i^* + \varepsilon)A, \qquad M = D + ER;$

(2) $\qquad V = \beta(i^* + \varepsilon)A,$

where

$$V = B + EB^* \quad \text{and} \quad \alpha + \beta = 1.$$

In (1), $D$ stands for the domestic component of the money stock $M$, and $R$ stands for the stock of international reserves. In (2), $B$ is the stock of domestic government bonds which is a perfect substitute for international bonds $B^*$ (in foreign currency).

This abbreviated asset sector specification is used to simplify our illustration of policy reaction functions, and is abandoned in Chapter 11.

*Real sector:*

(3) $\qquad Y = C(Y') + I(i - \pi) + \rho K + G + X(Y^*),$

where

$\qquad Y' = Y - T(Y) + Tr \qquad$ disposable income,

(4) $\qquad X = X(Y^*) \qquad$ exports,

(5) $\qquad I_m = I_m(Y') \qquad$ imports.

In the definitional relation of the disposable income $Tr$ stands for real transfer. In (3), $\rho$ is the rate at which capital stock depreciates per unit of capital stock. Because of the assumed purchasing power parity condition the terms-of-trade variable does not appear in the specifications of export or import

---

[1] To simplify analysis, the asset demand functions are assumed to depend only on $i^* + \varepsilon$ and not on a scale variable such as $Y/A$.

functions. Real investment is assumed to depend on real interest rate because output price inflation is thought to affect the cost of capital.

*Dynamics:*

(6) $\dot{D} + \dot{B} = P(G - T(Y)) + iB$      budget constraint,

(7) $\dot{R} + \dot{B}^* = PX/E - P^*I_m + i^*(B^* + R)$      current account in foreign currency.

We assume that the world real income $Y^*$ grows at an exogenous rate $l^*$. In addition, we assume:

(8)    $i = i^* + \varepsilon$      interest-rate–parity assumption,

(9)    $P = EP^*$      purchasing-power–parity assumption,

(10)   $\varepsilon = \mu(\bar{E} - E)/\bar{E}$,    $\mu \geq 0$,    expectations,

(11)   $\pi = \varepsilon + \pi^*$      consistency.

Note that the real interest rates at home and abroad equalize, i.e., $i - \pi = i^* - \pi^*$ from (8) and (11). The real flow of investment at home is thus exogenously fixed. Hence $I$ in (3) is treated as exogenous growing at the rate $l^*$.

## 10.2 Long-Run Equilibrium

Along the reference path, the asset sector must continuously be in equilibrium. Logarithmic differentiation of the ratio of (1) over (2) reveals that the growth rates

(12)      $\dot{D}/D = \dot{R}/R = \dot{B}/B = \dot{B}^*/B^* = l$,      $\dot{E}/E = 0$,    $\dot{\bar{\varepsilon}} = 0$,

are compatible with the asset sector equilibrium for any $l$. The rate $l$ can vary with time. There are many other reference paths which are compatible with the asset sector equilibrium, but this one produces simple and clean-cut results.

Equation (6) determines the ratio $B/D$ on the reference path as a function of a government long-run policy variable. To see this divide (6) by $D$, and use (12). Solving this relation for $B/D$ we obtain[2]

(13)      $(\overline{B/D}) = (l - \Delta)/(i^* - l)$,

where

$$\Delta = \overline{EP^*}(\bar{G} - \bar{T})/\bar{D}$$

[2] We assume that $B/D$ is positive. Hence either $\Delta < l < i^*$ or $i^* < l < \Delta$ must hold.

## 10.2 Long-Run Equilibrium

and where all these variables are evaluated along the reference path. The variable $\Delta$ is the government budget deficit (surplus) expressed as a ratio of the domestic component of the money stock on the reference path, hence can be regarded as a long-run government policy variable. An overbar denote values on the reference path.

Similarly, (7) determines the ratio $R/B^*$ which must hold on the reference path. Divide (7) by $B^*$, use (12), and solve the result for $R/B^*$,

(14) $\qquad (\overline{R/B^*}) = -1 - \overline{U}/(i^* - l),$

where

$$U = P^*(X - I_m)/B^*.$$

The variable $U$ is the trade balance on the reference path expressed as a ratio of the domestic private holding of international bonds.[3] This variable is influenced by $G$ since it affects the trade balance. We treat $U$ as another long-run policy variable of the government.

Differentiate (3) with respect to time to see that the real sector equilibrium along the reference path requires that

$$\{1 - C'(1 - T')\}\dot{Y} = C'\dot{T}r + \rho\dot{K} + \dot{G} + X'(Y^*)\dot{Y}^*,$$

where

$\dot{Y}^*/Y^* = l^*$ by assumption and $\dot{K}/K = I(i^* - \pi^*) - \rho.$

To simplify, assume that

$$\dot{Y}/Y = \dot{K}/K = \dot{I} = \dot{G}/G = \dot{T}r/Tr = l^* = l.$$

On the reference time path, we require that $Tr$ and $G$ also grow at the same rate $l$. Then the initial conditions on the reference path must satisfy[4]

$$\{1 - C'(1 - T')\}Y_0 = C'Tr_0 + \rho K_0 + G_0 + X'(Y^*)Y_0^*,$$

where the subscript zero denotes initial conditions and we assume that $C'$, $T'$, and $X'$ are constant along the reference path.

Equations (13) and (14) require that along the reference path the initial conditions $B_0$, $D_0$, $R_0$, and $B_0^*$ satisfy

$$B_0/D_0 = (l - \Delta_0)/(i^* - l) \quad \text{and} \quad R_0/B_0^* = -1 - U_0/(i^* - l),$$

where

$$\Delta_0 = P_0(G_0 - T_0)/D_0 \quad \text{and} \quad U_0 = P^*(X_0 - I_{m0})/B_0^*.$$

---

[3] Equations (7) and (9) imply that $l \geq i^*$ if and only if $\overline{U} \geq 0$ when $\overline{R/B^*}$ is positive.

[4] Differentiating the expression for the transfer in Appendix 2 at the end of this chapter, we establish $\overline{E}P^*Tr_0 = i^*(B_0 + \overline{E}B_0^*) - \rho K_0$ since $\overline{\pi} = 0$ and $\dot{\overline{\varepsilon}} = 0$ on the reference path.

We assume that these initial conditions are compatibly selected. These initial conditions jointly determined the balanced growth path which is used as the reference path in this chapter. From the footnotes 2 and 3, we note that on the assumption that $B/D$ is positive, there are two possibilities on the reference path: Either $\Delta \leq l < i^*$ and $U \leq 0$ or $i^* < l \leq \Delta$ and $U \geq 0$. (When $l$ equals $i^*$, the $\Delta$ must equal $l$ and $U$ must be zero.)

If we ignore the autonomous investment, and assume that $l^* = 0$, then we can simplify the analysis by choosing the stationary state as the long-run equilibrium. This is accomplished by setting $l$ to zero. Alternatively, we can complicate the analysis by choosing reference paths on which the growth rates of the financial assets are varying with time, such as reference paths that asymptotically approach the balanced growth path mentioned above.

## 10.3 Variational Differential Equations

We now derive dynamic equations which govern the adjustment process of the variational variables back to the reference path, after they have left the reference paths due to exogenous changes in the instrument time paths or some disturbances. The dynamics we derive are similar to those of Chapter 8. Slight differences arise from different specifications of the asset demand functions and of the government budget constraint equation. We did not consider policy reaction functions there. Here we explicitly consider policy reaction functions and show that they modify the dynamics of the variational variables.

### 10.3.1 The Budget Constraint

We develop our equation for the case of 100% money financing of the unexpected portion of the government budget deficit for simplicity. (The 100% bond financing or some mixture of the two modes of financing can be treated.) In other words, we assume $\delta B = 0$, i.e., $B(t)$ is assumed to grow along the reference time paths and is not used to finance unplanned budget deficit or absorb unplanned surplus.

Taking the variation of (6) and denoting $\delta D/D$ by $d$, we derive the differential equation for $d$, noting that $\delta i = \delta \varepsilon$,

(15) $$\dot{d} = -ld + le - m_1 y + m_2\, \delta\varepsilon,$$

where $m_1 = PT\tau/D > 0$, $m_2 = B/D$, and where $\tau = T'Y/T$ is the income elasticity of the real tax receipt. The coefficients are evaluated on the reference path and hence are constant. This parameter $\tau$ is important in signing the

## 10.3  Variational Differential Equations

coefficients to determine stability later in this chapter. Recall that (13) defines the dependence of $m_2$ on one of the long-run policy variables $\Delta$.

If we had chosen a reference path along which $l$ is varying with time, then $l(t) \to \bar{l}$ where $\bar{l}$ is the growth rate associated with the balanced growth reference path. If a stationary state is chosen as a reference path of the model, then $l = 0$ for all $t$, hence $d$ and $p$ effects disappear from $\dot{d}$ in (15). McGrath (1977) treats a similar problem.

### 10.3.2  The Current Account

Let $F = R + B^*$ in foreign currency in (7). In percentage terms, we have $f = (R/F)r + (B^*/F)b^*$, or solving it for $b^*$ we express $b^*$ as a function of $f$ and $r$ as

(16) $$b^* = \phi_1 f - \phi r,$$

where

$$\phi_1 = F/B^* \quad \text{and} \quad \phi = R/B^* \quad \text{and} \quad \phi_1 = 1 + \phi.$$

We treat $r$ as an exogenous instrument of the foreign exchange authorities (the central bank). Taking the variation of (7), we derive the differential equation for $f$, where we use $y' = (Y/Y')(1 - T')y$ from (3),

(17) $$\hat{f} = -\hat{l}f - \rho_1 y,$$

where

$$\hat{l} = l - i^*, \qquad \rho_1 = \frac{P^* I_m}{F} \frac{I'_m}{I_m} Y(1 - T') > 0.$$

Equations (15) and (17) constitute the dynamics describing interactions between the domestic and foreign assets. Putting them together, and recalling that $p = e$ due to the purchasing power parity assumption, we obtain a two-dimensional time-varying linear differential equation

(18) $$\frac{d}{dt}\begin{bmatrix} d \\ f \end{bmatrix} = \begin{bmatrix} -l & 0 \\ 0 & -\hat{l} \end{bmatrix}\begin{bmatrix} d \\ f \end{bmatrix} - \begin{bmatrix} m_1 \\ \rho_1 \end{bmatrix} y + \begin{bmatrix} 1 - m_2\mu \\ 0 \end{bmatrix} e,$$

where from (10)

(10') $$\delta\varepsilon = -\mu e$$

is used.

To describe the dynamic process fully we need variational expressions which relate $y$, $e$, and $\delta\varepsilon$ to $d$ and $f$ (and variations in the instruments). These are obtained by taking variations of the reduced form expressions for them.

Even before we proceed to their derivation, (18) already reveals interesting facts about dynamics of interaction of the internal and external balances.

If $l$ and $\mu$ are both zero, then $e$ has no effect on $d$ or $f$ as can be seen from (18).

An adaptive expectation mechanism for $\varepsilon$ does not introduce additional dynamics, and we can use (18) to discuss long-run and short-run stability of the model. Other expectation mechanisms, such as perfect foresight or an expectation augmented Phillips curve, require that (18) be augmented by an additional differential equation for $e$ in order to completely describe the dynamics. Some examples are found in footnote 18 of Chapter 8 and Appendix C.

### 10.3.3 Reduced Forms for Variational Variables

From our discussion of the interactions between various sources of dynamics in Chapter 8, we know that the (reduced form) expressions for $y$ and $e$ are crucial in embodying various transmission paths in the economy into the dynamics. Put another way, (18) clearly shows that deviation in the real gross national product (GNP) from its reference time path affects many important variables in the economy. The reduced form expression for $y$ will display the sources of deviations being reflected on $y$ and therefore establish feedback or transmission paths of the disturbances in the economy when substituted into (18).

Thus, before we return to the dynamics, we derive the reduced forms for $y$ and $e$. Assuming that portfolio balances are maintained always in the asset sector, the variational expression of one of the two Eqs. (1) and (2) or their ratio (since only one is independent) yields a relation between $e$ and $\delta\varepsilon$ and variations in the stocks of assets and $Y$. This is the variational version of the LM curve of the closed economy generalized to an open economy. A similar variational relation for $\delta y$ obtained in the real sector is a generalized IS curve. Together, they yield the reduced forms which give momentary equilibrium values for the perturbed variables and which we can use in conjunction with (18) or the more general differential equations we derive later.

Deviations in the stocks of the assets from their reference time paths for whatever reasons induce changes in $\varepsilon$ and the exchange rate from their respective reference time paths. The deviational variables $e$ and $\delta\varepsilon$ are related by a variational expression which is obtained by taking variation of the reduced form expression of $E$.

The perturbations on $E$ and $\varepsilon$, $e$, and $\delta\varepsilon$, are related by (recalling that $b = 0$)

(19)  $$e = \theta_1 \hat{m} - \theta_2 b^* + \theta_3 \, \delta\varepsilon,$$

## 10.3 Variational Differential Equations

where

$$\hat{m} = (D/M)d + (ER/M)r.$$

This equation is derived in Appendix 1 at the end of this chapter.

Since the domestic real interest rate equals the foreign interest rates in this model, the time path of the real domestic investment is exogenously fixed and so is the time path for real domestic export, since the terms of trade are fixed at one by the assumption of the purchasing power parity. These special conditions imply that the variational IS curve, which relates the perturbed (variational) variables in the real sector, is particularly simple. As we discuss the details of derivation in Appendix 2, the relative variation of the income is

$$y = -\eta_1 \delta\varepsilon - \eta_2 e + \eta_3 b^* - \eta_0 g.$$

The coefficients $\eta_2$ and $\eta_3$ are expected to be much smaller than $\eta_1$. From (10′) and the above, letting $g$ zero,

(20) $$y = -(\eta_2 - \mu\eta_1)e + \eta_3 b^*.$$

Solving (19) and (20) together, we determine the momentary equilibrium values for the variational variables (they can be equivalently derived by taking the variation of the reduced forms for $E$, $\varepsilon$, and $Y$):[5]

(21a) $$e = f_1 \hat{m} - f_2 b^*$$

and

(21b) $$y = -\tau_1 \hat{m} + \tau_2 b^*,$$

where

$$\bar{f} = 1 + \mu\theta_3 > 0, \qquad f_i = \theta_i/\bar{f}, \quad i = 1, 2,$$
$$\tau_1 = \theta_1(\eta_2 - \mu\eta_1)/\bar{f}, \qquad \tau_2 = \eta_3 + \theta_2(\eta_2 - \mu\eta_1)/\bar{f}.$$

Note that for $\mu$ large, $\tau_1$ and $\tau_2$ may become negative.

Since we assume the 100% money financing of the deviational government deficit, we set $b$ to zero in the above. Since $b = 0$, we can express $e$ and $y$, in view of (16) and (19), as functions of the state variables $d$ and $f$, and the instrument $r$. These are the reduced forms:

(22a) $$e = f_d d - f_f f + f_r r$$

and

(22b) $$y = -\tau_d d + \tau_f f - \tau_r r,$$

---

[5] Note the similarity of (21a) and (21b) with (25) and (27), respectively, of Chapter 8. What we denote by $B^*$ here corresponds to $F$ of Chapter 8.

where

$$f_d = f_1 D/M \quad \text{and} \quad \tau_d = \tau_1 D/M, \quad f_f = f_2\phi_1 \quad \text{and} \quad \tau_f = \tau_2\phi_1,$$
$$f_r = f_1 ER/M + f_2\phi \quad \text{and} \quad \tau_r = \tau_1 ER/M + \tau_2\phi.$$

Substitution of (22a) and (22b) into (18) yields the differential equation for the adjustment paths of $d$ and $f$, which is the state-space representation of the dynamics of this economy:

(23)
$$\frac{d}{dt}\begin{bmatrix} d \\ f \end{bmatrix} = \Phi \begin{bmatrix} d \\ f \end{bmatrix} + \psi_r r,$$

where

$$\Phi = \begin{bmatrix} -l & 0 \\ 0 & -\hat{\imath} \end{bmatrix} + \begin{bmatrix} m_1 \\ \rho_1 \end{bmatrix}[\tau_d \;\; -\tau_f] + \begin{bmatrix} l - m_2\mu \\ 0 \end{bmatrix}[f_d \;\; -f_f],$$
$$\psi_r = \tau_r \begin{bmatrix} m_1 \\ \rho_1 \end{bmatrix} + f_r \begin{bmatrix} l - m_2\mu \\ 0 \end{bmatrix}.$$

## 10.4 Short-Run Stability of the Variational Dynamics

Equation (23) governs short-run dynamic behavior of the model about the reference path under 100% money financing of the unplanned budget imbalance path. Because $m_2$ and $\phi$, which appear in the dynamic matrix $\Phi$, are functions of the government budget imbalance variable $\Delta$ and the current account variable $U$ on the reference path, respectively as seen from (13)–(14), the long-run policy variables affect short-run stability behavior of (23). We can make this dependence explicit by calculating the eigenvalues of $\Phi$ or more simply by examining restrictions imposed on the long-run policy variables by short-run stability conditions that the trace of $\Phi$ is negative and the determinant of $\Phi$ positive. This type of analysis has been illustrated in Chapter 8. Therefore we shall be brief here.

A major finding of this type of analysis is that the stability conditions are interdependent. We cannot in general impose separate, i.e., independent constraints on $\Delta$ and $U$ except in some special cases. The trace condition can be stated as an inequality for $\phi$ and $\Delta$:

(24)
$$\rho_1\tau_2\phi - \mu f_d(i^* - l)^{-1}\Delta + N > 0,$$

where

$$N = (2 - f_d)l - i^* - m_1\tau_d + \mu f_d l(i^* - l)^{-1}.$$

## 10.4 Short-Run Stability of the Variational Dynamics

The determinant condition defines a region for $\phi$ and $\Delta$ bounded by hyperbolic curves:

$$S\phi\Delta - T\phi - V\Delta + Z < 0,$$

where

$$S = \frac{\mu \rho_1 f_d}{i^* - l}\left[\tau_1\left(\frac{\theta_2}{\theta_1} - \frac{D}{M}\right) + \eta_2\right],$$

where we calculate in Appendix 1 that

$$\theta_2/\theta_1 = EB^*/(B + EB^*),$$

$$T = \rho_1 l\left\{\eta_3\left(1 - f_d + \frac{\mu f_d}{i^* - l}\right) + \tau_1 \frac{\theta_2}{\theta_1}\right\},$$

$$V = \mu f_d,$$

and

$$Z = (i^* - l)\{(1 - f_d)l - m_1 \tau_d\} + \mu f_d l.$$

Change the variables to

$$\xi = \phi - V/S \quad \text{and} \quad \eta = \Delta - T/S.$$

The inequality simplifies to

(25) $$S\xi\eta < (VT - SZ)/S,$$

where

$$VT - SZ = \mu f_d \rho_1 (m_1 \tau_d \eta_3 + \zeta \tau_1),$$

where

$$\zeta = (lf_d + m_1 \tau_d)\theta_2/\theta_1 - \mu f_d l(i^* - l)^{-1}$$
$$+ [\{1 - f_d + \mu f_d(i^* - l)^{-1}\}l - m_1 \tau_d]D/M.$$

Equations (24) and (25) impose joint constraint on $\Delta$ and $\phi$. These equations produce separate constraint if $\mu = 0$ (static expectations on the exchange rate): (24) reduces to

$$\phi > \{i^* + m_1 \tau_d - (2 - f_d)l\}/\rho_1 \tau_2$$

and (25) to

$$\phi > (i^* - l)\{(1 - f_d)l - m_1 \tau_d\}/[\rho_1 l\{\eta_3(1 - f_d) + \tau_1 \theta_2/\theta_1\}],$$

i.e., $\phi$ must be greater than the larger of these two lower bounds. In view of (14), these two lower bounds on $\phi$ impose a lower bound on $U$ for short-run stability, i.e., $U$ must be larger than some value for short-run dynamics to be stable if $\Delta > l$.

When $\mu > 0$, the constraints do not separate. Consider a benchmark case:

$l = 0$. From (13) $\Delta$ reduces to $-i^*\overline{B/D}$. Substituting this into (24) and simplifying it,

$$(24') \qquad \rho_1\tau_2\phi > i^* + m_1\tau_d - \mu f_d(\overline{B/D})$$

and (25) reduces to

$$(25') \qquad S\phi - \mu f_d < -m_1\tau_d/(\overline{B/D}).$$

Suppose $S$ is positive (this follows if $\theta_2/\theta_1 > \frac{1}{2}$ because $\theta_2/\theta_1 = EB^*/V > ER/M$ and $D/M = 1 - DR/M$). Equations (24') and (25') define a region in $\phi$ (or equivalently in $\overline{U}$) and $\overline{B/D}$ which simultaneously satisfies these two inequalities as constraints on the long-run policy objectives that are compatible with short-run stability. For example, suppose $\overline{U} = 0$ is chosen. Then $\overline{B/D}$ must satisfy

$$m_1\tau_d(S + \mu f_d)^{-1} < \overline{B/D} < (i^* + m_1\tau_d + \rho_1\tau_2)/(\mu f_d).$$

(The right-hand side is greater than the left-hand side if $S$ is positive.)

## 10.5 Policy Reaction Functions

In (23), the instrument $r$ is exogenous. Policy reaction functions endogenize $r$ by expressing it as a function (linear combination) of some variables in the model. The dynamic matrix $\Phi$ is consequently modified. Reaction functions are designed to stabilize otherwise unstable dynamics or improve model dynamic performance such as increased margin for stability or better transient responses.

As an example, we evaluate a reaction function which ties $r$ to $e$ by

$$r = \sigma e, \qquad \sigma > 0.$$

From (22a), this relates $r$ to the state vector components by

$$r = \hat{\sigma}(f_d d - f_f f),$$

where

$$\hat{\sigma} = \sigma(1 - \sigma f_r)^{-1}.$$

This reaction function modifies the dynamic matrix $\Phi$ into

$$\Phi' = \Phi + \hat{\sigma}\tau_r \begin{bmatrix} \tilde{m}_1 \\ \rho_1 \end{bmatrix} [f_d \ -f_f], \qquad \text{where} \quad \tilde{m}_1 = m_1 + \frac{f_r(l - m_2\mu)}{\tau_r}.$$

*Appendix 1  Deviation of the Expression for e*

The eigenvalues of $\Phi'$ are the roots of[6]

$$0 = |\lambda I - \Phi'|$$

$$= |\lambda I - \Phi| \left\{ 1 - \hat{\sigma}\tau_r(f_d \ -f_r)(\lambda I - \Phi)^{-1} \begin{bmatrix} \tilde{m}_1 \\ \rho_1 \end{bmatrix} \right\}$$

$$= q(\lambda) - \hat{\sigma}\tau_r(\kappa_1 \lambda - \kappa_0),$$

where $q(\lambda) = |\lambda I - \Phi|$, $\kappa_1 = \tilde{m}_1 f_d - \rho_1 f_f$, and $\kappa_0$ is a constant.

Then the eigenvalues of $\Phi'$ will be stable for sufficiently large $\sigma > 0$ regardless of the eigenvalue of $\Phi$. Four patterns of the root-locus plots are possible when $\kappa_1 < 0$. If $\kappa_1$ is positive, we must use $r = -\sigma e$ to stabilize $\Phi'$.

## Appendix 1    Deviation of the Expression for *e*

The variation of (1) yields

(26) $$m = (\alpha'/\alpha)\delta\varepsilon + a.$$

We define a shorthand notation $\hat{m}$ for the portion of the percentage variation of the money stock excluding the effect of $\delta e$ by

(27) $$\hat{m} = (D/M)d + \rho r,$$

where

$$\rho = ER/M.$$

Then $m = \hat{m} + \rho e$. Since $A$ can be written as $M + V = D + B + EF$, where $F = R + B^*$, the percentage variation of the domestic nonhuman wealth can be expressed as

(28) $$a = \alpha m + \beta v,$$

where, recalling that $V$ equals $B + EB^*$, the relative variation of $V$ is

$$v = (B/V)b + (EB^*/V)(e + b^*).$$

From (26)–(28), $e$ is expressible as

$$e = \theta_1 \hat{m} - \theta_2 b^* + \theta_3 \delta\varepsilon - \theta_4 b,$$

where

$$\theta = (EB^*/V - \rho), \quad \theta_1 = 1/\theta, \quad \theta_2 = (EB^*/V)/\theta,$$

$$\theta_3 = (-\alpha'/\alpha)/\theta\beta, \quad \theta_4 = (B/V)/\theta.$$

[6] The matrix $\Phi'$ is related to $\Phi$ by a rank one matrix. In such cases, the eigenvalues of $\Phi'$ can be computed by a formula in Aoki (1976, p. 390).

We assume that $EB^*/V > \rho$, i.e., the proportion foreign securities occupy in the domestic residents' portfolio is larger than the proportion reserves occupy in the domestic money stock. This condition can be equivalently stated as $D/B > R/B^*$. From the definitions of (13) and (14), we note that this inequality constrains the government budget deficit and current account jointly by $(l - i^*)/(l - \Delta) + \bar{U}/(l - i^*) < 1$. Footnotes 2 and 3 showed that $l \gtreqless i^*$ if and only if $\bar{U} \gtreqless 0$.

## Appendix 2  Variational IS Curve

On the assumption $P = EP^*$, we have $P_I = P$; the disposable income $Y'$ equals

$$Y' = Y - T(Y) + Tr,$$

where

$$PTr = iB + i^*EB^* - \pi A - \rho K.$$

Since $i = i^* + \varepsilon$, we can rewrite the transfer term as

$$PTr = i^*(B + EB^*) + \varepsilon B - \pi A - \rho K.$$

Assume that $P^* = \bar{P}^*$; hence $\pi^* \equiv 0$ and $\varepsilon = 0$; hence $\pi = 0$. The variables on perturbed time paths satisfy the relationship

(29)  $$\delta Y' = (1 - T')\delta Y + \delta Tr.$$

From the home GNP identity $Y = C + I + \rho K + X + G$, we have $\delta Y = C'(Y')\delta Y' + \delta G$, where $\delta I = 0$ and $\delta K = 0$ because $I$ is fixed exogenously and $K$ grows according to plan. The relative variational variable of $Y$, $y$ is governed by

(30)  $$Y[1 - C'(1 - T')]y = \delta G + C'\delta Tr.$$

Consider a reference path on which $\pi^* = 0$ and $\varepsilon = 0$. Then $\pi = 0$ follows from (11). Relative to this path, the variational $\delta Tr$ is given by

(31)  $$\delta Tr = \{i^*EB^*(e + b^*) - \delta\varepsilon(M + EB^*)\}/P - (Tr)e,$$

where we use $\delta\pi = \delta\varepsilon$, $\delta K = 0$, and $\delta B = 0$.

The term $\delta e$ affects $\delta Tr$ in two ways. One is by changing the interest receipt on $EB^*$, and the other is by changing the value of the international bonds.

Solve (30) for $y$ after substituting $\delta Tr$ out by (31) as

$$y = \eta_0 g - \eta_1 \delta\varepsilon - \eta_2 e + \eta_3 b^*,$$

## Appendix 2 Variational IS Curve

where

$$\eta = \{1 - C'(1 - T')\}Y, \quad \eta_0 = G/\eta, \quad \eta_1 = C'(M + EB^*)/(P\eta),$$
$$\eta_2 = -C'(i^*EB^*/P - Tr)/\eta = C'(i^*B - \rho K)/(P\eta),$$

and

$$\eta_3 = C'i^*EB^*/(P\eta).$$

These coefficients are all evaluated on the reference path. The coefficients $\eta_2$ and $\eta_3$ are expected to be smaller than $\eta_1$.

# 11 | Short-Run Comparative Dynamic Analysis of a Small Open Economy with Variable Wage Rates[1]

This chapter carries out a detailed comparative dynamic analysis of a model of a small open economy with two domestic financial assets and one foreign financial asset, producing a single good at variable output prices and wage rates.

Our analysis treats the domestic financial assets and domestic good as imperfect substitutes for the international bonds and the world goods.[2] In Chapter 8, we have discussed the sources of dynamics which arise from the two flow constraint equations, i.e., the domestic government budget constraint and the current account equation. To them we now add the wage rate

---

[1] An earlier version of this chapter was presented in Aoki (1978).

[2] Domestic residents normally would hold foreign currencies as well. Kouri (1976) examined a model of a small open economy in which domestic residents hold foreign money. He assumed that the purchasing power parity relation holds for the price of domestically produced goods. There are no bonds in the models. The expected rate of inflation (which is the same as the expected rate of exchange rate depreciation because of the assumed purchasing power parity) is the only variable that determines the ratio of the domestic and foreign money stocks held by the domestic residents. No essential change is introduced into the analysis when the menu of the available financial assets is changed to that of domestic money and international bonds. Calvo and Rodriguez (1977) analyzed a small open economy model with traded and nontraded goods in which domestic residents hold domestic and foreign money stocks. Their analysis can be adapted to discuss a small open economy with domestic money and international bonds as the menu of the financial assets. Their analysis can be further extended to that with domestic money, foreign money, and international bonds. None of these works includes wage rate dynamics.

In Mundell's model (1968), expectations on exchange rate changes are static. Ingram (1978) discusses that this assumption is incompatible with that of nontraded national monies, i.e., residents in each country hold only their own national money, if domestic and foreign securities are assumed to be perfect substitutes. Ingram goes on to argue that if national monies are tradeable assets, then they are perfect substitutes under the assumption that expectations are static and national securities are perfect substitutes. Thus, the assumption of perfect substitutability is generally too strong an assumption in modeling small open economies. He states that Dornbusch's model (1976) also suffers from similar logical inconsistency.

## 11.1 The Model

dynamics and the supply schedule. We use this model to perform various comparative dynamic analyses.

As an illustration of our procedure, we explore the consequences of different degrees of supply responsiveness and variable wage rates on output price inflation rates.[3] We examine the effects on the output price inflation rate of a fiscal instrument as a comparative dynamic problem of a small open economy. We shall compare the changes in the output price inflation rate time paths with rigid wage rate and variable wage rates for the same temporary change in the fiscal instrument time path and apply the perturbation or structural sensitivity analysis method of Section 5.2 to examine under what conditions, if any, positive $\mu$ in the wage rate adjustment equation implies higher inflation under suitable assumptions on the model parameters.

The model exhibits a wide range of dynamic behavior depending on particular values of its parameters. A shock elicits different responses from small open economies if they differ in some structural parameters. The same dosage of policy instrument change differently affects these economies, e.g., dynamic policy multipliers are different because the multipliers generally are functions of these model structure characteristics.

Without being exhaustively taxonomic several benchmark assumptions are used to illustrate dependence of model behavior on structural characteristics: One such assumption is on the portfolio behavior of domestic residents. Equal percentage changes in their holdings of domestic money and foreign bond stocks are induced by changes in the domestic interest rate. This assumption implies that the parameter $\phi_1$ defined in (10) below, is zero. Although none of the results is qualitatively affected, this assumption does simplify some of the calculations. So, we adopt it from time to time. A second benchmark assumption is made on the output supply responsiveness of the real sector to changes in real wage rates. The supply responsiveness is one of the key structural characteristics we examine in this chapter. We investigate how deviations of the time paths of the output price inflation rates and the wage rates depend on the parameter $\kappa$ in (17) below. In particular we consider two extreme cases of the economies with small $\kappa$ and large $\kappa$. We analytically prove, for example, that a temporary increase in the government expenditure is not inflationary for small open economies with small $\kappa$. Although the result

---

[3] Purvis (1979) suggests that West Germany succeeded in combating inflation because they controlled nominal wages in conjunction with their flexible exchange rate, while the Canadians experienced inflation under flexible rates because wage rates expanded excessively underwritten by a permissive monetary policy. Purvis did not establish these claims. He merely suggested the above interpretation because he did not conduct truly dynamic analysis but only partial analysis on models with two alternative assets.

Although Purvis' question should be addressed in a multiple-country model of the world, we do not directly address his question here.

may be hardly surprising, our analysis shows precisely why and where the assumption matters. A third and the final benchmark assumption is on the adjustment parameter of the nominal wage rate changes in (18).

More generally, our procedure for conducting comparative dynamic analysis is outlined in this chapter. Briefly it is as follows: Three sets of variational relations are developed which jointly characterize the model's short-run dynamic behavior about a reference time path. One set describes the relationship between changes in financial sector variables and variations of the policy instruments, exogenous variables, and real sector variables. The second set of variational variables shows how changes in the domestic real sector variables are related to changes in the asset sector variables and exogenous variables. The third relates variation in the aggregate supply to variations in wage rates, the consumer price index, and inflation rate expectations.

Joint solutions of these sets of variational equations yield reduced form relations of the variations of the domestic interest rate, the exchange rate, the domestic output, its price, and variations of the current account expression in terms of the state variables. Variations of the stocks of the domestic money, domestically held international bonds, and the nominal wage rate serve as the state variables in short-run dynamics. When endogenous variables are expressed by the state variables, a five-dimensional differential equation determines the time paths of the model endogenous variables in response to changes in the instruments from their respective reference paths, or to changes in exogenous variables.

Dynamic policy multipliers and (impulse) responses of the endogenous variables to exogenous variable changes can now be calculated following the procedure of Section 2.3.4 and Section 4.1.

In this chapter we assume that unplanned budget deficit (i.e., budget deficit not associated with the reference time path) is monetized 100%, because this assumption reduces the dimension of the differential equation to three.

In our analysis, we identify a set of elasticities as determinants of the "strength" of dynamic interaction (i.e., feedbacks) between the asset and real sectors, and define relations or restrictions that must exist between various counteracting influences in order for the economy to behave "normally." Both current account and the public debt are important linkages of these sectors. Together with various combinations of instruments, they affect the dynamics of the interest rate, the price level, wage rate and the exchange rate. In this way, we can assess the nature of the approximation of dynamic analysis which ignores the real sector.

Viotti (1978) carried out general equilibrium analysis of a small open economy. His analysis shares our concern that the models commonly used

## 11.1 The Model

in the portfolio balance approach are either partial or have only a vague general equilibrium structure. They are not very well suited for comparison with the general equilibrium treatment of models with fixed exchange rates nor do they particularly well illustrate effects of traditional demand management policy. Our analytical technique, however, is significantly different from Viotti's. In particular, the short-run dynamics for the economy are explicitly derived and macroeconomic policy implications explored in more detail. Also, both the current account and the rate at which the public debt grows are shown to be important ingredients for short-run dynamics for variational variables.

After the model specification in Section 11.1 and the statement of the reference time path characteristics in Section 11.2, the variational model dynamics are derived and analyzed in Section 11.3. As mentioned earlier, several benchmark models are used to illustrate the possible range of endogenous variable behavior in this section to elucidate algebraically messier general model analysis. Influences of rigid and variable wage rates are compared in Section 11.4. Section 11.5 is devoted to a numerical example. This chapter concludes with Section 11.6, where consequences of various elaborations on the basic models are discussed.

### 11.1 The Model

The economy produces a single (composite) domestic good which may be consumed, traded, or used as capital. Its domestic currency price is $P$. There are four financial assets which are gross substitutes: foreign bonds, domestic money, domestic government bonds, and domestic equities. The latter two assets are assumed to be perfect substitutes.

We assume that firms own all of the capital stock. Private equities reflect ownership of the firms; thus the value of private equities is the value of the existing capital stock $K$, which can deviate from its replacement cost $P$ since there is assumed to be no direct market for capital. The market value of the domestic private equities is $B/i$ in domestic currency, where $B = (F_K - \lambda)KP$, $i$ is the domestic interest rate, $F_K$ the marginal product of capital, and $\lambda$ capital depreciation rate per unit capital stock. We show later that variation of $B$ due to changes in output, domestic price, and $i$ forms an important linkage between the asset and the real sectors.

The government issues bonds, which are perfect substitutes for private equities. The government bonds are treated also as consols. There are $B_g$ of them each paying unit domestic currency interest per period. The market value (in domestic currency) of the total domestic bonds and equities held by

138    *11   Short-Run Comparative Dynamic Analysis of a Small Open Economy*

the domestic private sector is therefore $V/i$, where $V = B + B_g$. International bonds are also treated as consols. The value of domestic private holdings of international bonds in domestic currency is denoted by $EF/i^*$, where $E$ is the exchange rate (domestic money price of the unit of foreign currency). The home government holds the foreign bonds as international reserves,[4] the number of which is denoted by $R$.

The demands for these assets depend on expected interest rate differentials and scale variables, as shown below. The government can engage in open market operation in domestic securities as well as in foreign security operations.

### 11.1.1  The Asset Sector

We continue to use asset demand functions which are unit elastic with respect to real wealth so that we can derive our results without too much algebra. (More general asset demand functions introduce additional linkages between the asset and the real sectors in the short-run dynamics. [Aoki (1978) discusses them.]

Domestic residents hold three assets. In domestic currency they are

(1a) $$M = \alpha(i, i^* + \varepsilon)A,$$

(1b) $$V/i = \beta(i, i^* + \varepsilon)A,$$

(1c) $$EF/i^* = \gamma(i, i^* + \varepsilon)A,$$

where $A$ is the nonhuman nominal wealth of the domestic private sector, $M$ the stock of domestic money, $V$ the number of the domestic bond-equities treated as consols, and $F$ the number of international bond-equities held by the domestic residents, $Y$ is the domestic real output, $\varepsilon$ is the expected rate of change of $E$, i.e., $\dot{E}/E$. These asset demand functions are the same as those used by Girton and Henderson (1977).[5]

---

[4] Alternatively, international reserves may be held in foreign (key) currency. A key currency as an asset is treated in Chapter 14.

[5] In Aoki (1978) asset demand functions additionally depend on $PY/A$ as a third argument. This specification is similar to the one used by Clark and Kwack (1976).

The asset structures are sometimes specified as

$$M/P = L(i, i^* + \varepsilon, Y),$$
$$B/P = \beta(i, i^* + \varepsilon, Y)(A - M)/P,$$
$$EF/P = \gamma(i, i^* + \varepsilon, Y)(A - M)/P,$$

where $\beta$ and $\gamma$ sums up to one. The argument $Y$ in $\gamma$ may sometimes be omitted. Then the matrix relating $\delta i$ and $e$ to variations of the asset stocks become triangular. Aside from the effects of $p$

## 11.1 The Model

From the wealth constraint on the asset demand functions we have

(1d)
$$\alpha + \beta + \gamma = 1, \quad \gamma > 0,$$
$$\alpha_i + \beta_i + \gamma_i = 0, \quad i = 1, 2.$$

Of the three equations, Eqs. (1a–1c), only two are independent. We can use any two of them, or two ratios of these three equations, as two independent asset demand equations in our analysis. These two equations are solved out for two variables. We use the ratios of (1a) over (1b), and (1a) over (1c) to solve out $i$ and $\varepsilon$. (These variables can be solved out at least locally because the Jacobian is nonzero.) We assume that $\beta_1 > 0$, $\gamma_2 > 0$, and that the signs of all other partial derivatives are nonpositive. These signs follow from the assumption of wealth normality and gross substitutability of the financial assets. In words, an increase in the domestic interest rate induces a shift out of domestic money and foreign securities into domestic bonds. (One benchmark assumption posits $\alpha_1/\alpha$ equals $\gamma_1/\gamma$, as mentioned in the introductory remarks of this chapter.)

When the wealth elasticity is assumed to be one as in (1), the domestic price level $P_1$ (however defined) disappears from the asset equation and the direct effect of the change in the exchange rate is felt through valuation effect in the asset sector only if $\gamma > 0$. We assume $\gamma > 0$. Otherwise, the analysis of open market operations in the asset sector is ambiguous when the asset demand functions are unit elastic with respect to real wealth. The change in $P_1$ due to change $E$ is captured in the real sector as we shall see later. In order to facilitate our presentation, we derive all the formulas assuming that $i^*$ and $\pi^*$ are constants, where $\pi^*$ is the foreign rate of inflation. We set $\pi^*$ to zero.

### 11.1.2 The Real Sector

The aggregate real demand $Y^D$ is expressed by the GNP identity by purchasers

(2)
$$Y^D = \dot{K} + \lambda K + C + X + G.$$

---

and $y$, $\delta i$ is determined by $m$ alone, holding $\varepsilon$ constant,

$$\begin{pmatrix} L_1/L & 0 \\ \beta_1/\beta & \gamma \end{pmatrix} \begin{pmatrix} \delta i \\ e \end{pmatrix} = \begin{bmatrix} 1 & 0 & 0 \\ 0 & \gamma & -\gamma \end{bmatrix} \begin{bmatrix} m \\ b \\ f \end{bmatrix} + \text{(terms depending on } p \text{ and } y\text{)},$$

where $EF/(B + EF)$ equals $\gamma$. The variation $\delta i$ is now independent of changes in $B$ and $EF$. This eliminates one of the transmission links.

If $\varepsilon$ is variable, then $\delta \varepsilon$ is dependent on variations of $B$ and $EF$; hence $\delta i$ is no longer independent of them.

Here $C$ is the real demand for domestic output by the domestic residents, i.e., consumption less imports and $X$ represents the real exports, respectively specified by

(3)  $\qquad C = C(Y', v), \qquad C_1 > 0, \qquad C_2 < 0,$

(4)  $\qquad X = X(v), \qquad X' < 0,$

where $v = P/EP^*$, and $Y'$ is the real disposable income. We take it to be approximately given by (ignoring capital gains and losses due to changes in $i$)

(5)  $\quad P_1 Y' = P(Y - \lambda K - T) + (B_g + EF) - (M + B_g/i + EF/i^*)\pi_i + \varepsilon EF/i^*,$

where $T$ is the real tax receipt, $\lambda$ is the depreciation rate of capital stock per unit stock, $P_1$ is the price index which is the weighted geometric average of home and foreign prices $p^\chi(EP^*)^{1-\chi}$, and $\pi_i$ is the expected rate of inflation of the price index. Equation (5) is derived in exactly the same way that the disposable income is derived in Appendix B. The second term is the interest receipt. The third term is inflation loss of wealth. The last term represents the expected gain due to the exchange rate depreciation. The aggregate supply function is assumed to be specified by

(6)  $\qquad\qquad\qquad Y^S = H(K, W/P),$

where $W$ is the nominal wage rate and $P$ is the output price.

### 11.1.3 Dynamics

We have stated earlier that a momentary equilibrium of the economy shifts with time because of the changing stocks of assets. In this model, the stocks of domestic money, domestic bonds, and foreign bonds are governed by the government budget constraint equation, and stocks of the international bonds held by the domestic private sector and the domestic government are influenced by the current account equation: The former is described by

(7)  $\qquad\qquad\qquad \dot{M} + \dot{B}_g/i - E\dot{R}/i^* = D_f,$

where $D_f = P(G - T) + B_g - ER$ is the budget deficit when $D_f > 0$. It states that the government deficit (in the domestic currency) must be financed either by issuing money, issuing the government bonds, or by selling the international bonds. Because of the assumption that the bonds are perpetuities, $B_g$ and $ER^*$ are the interest on the government bonds and on the international reserves. The latter is described by

(8)  $\qquad\qquad (\dot{R} + \dot{F})/i^* = U, \qquad$ in foreign currency,

## 11.2 Long-Run Equilibrium

where $U$ is the current account,

$$U = B_T + F + R, \quad \text{in foreign currency,}$$

where the trade balance is

$$B_T = PX/E - P^* I_m,$$

where $X$ represents the exports and $I_m$ the imports.

We are already familiar with these two sources of dynamics because of our discussion of them in Chapter 8. In addition to these two sources of dynamics, changing wage rates and expectations contribute dynamics to the model. A wage rate adjustment equation similar to the one in Aoki and Canzoneri (1979) is adopted here. Suppose that the nominal wage rates adjust in proportion with the gap between the current and target real wage rate. Then $\dot{W}$ is a function of real wage rate $W/P_I$ and the inflationary expectation of the price index $\pi_i$, which enters into the target real wage rate determination:

$$(9) \qquad \dot{W} = N(W/P_I, \pi_i).$$

Note that the consumer price index $P_I$ is used in calculating the real wage rate. Finally, capital growth is governed by

$$\dot{K} = I(F_K - \lambda - i + \pi), \qquad I' > 0.$$

Dynamics due to expectational variables shall be discussed later.

### 11.2  Long-Run Equilibrium

We choose a reference path of the economy along which growth rates of the stocks of financial assets and prices are compatible with equilibrium in the asset and real sectors. These points have already been discussed in Chapters 1 and 2. Our reference path is characterized by the following:

$$\dot{M}/M = \dot{F}/F = \dot{B}/B = \dot{V}/V = \dot{R}/R = \dot{B}_g/B_g = n,$$
$$\dot{E}/E = 0, \qquad \dot{P}/P = 0, \qquad \bar{\varepsilon} = 0, \qquad i = \bar{i}, \qquad \bar{\pi} = 0,$$
$$\dot{Y}/Y = \dot{K}/K = \dot{G}/G = \dot{T}/T = n,$$

where an overbar denotes a reference path value.

From our definition of the price index, its inflation rate on the reference path is zero[6] because of the assumed zero inflation rate abroad and zero expectation of the exchange rate changes.

---

[6] This simplifies the expression for the deviational disposable income given by (13).

## 11.3  Short-Run Analysis

### 11.3.1  Asset Sector Variations

We obtain the first set of variational equations from the portfolio balance equations in the asset sector. This part of analysis shows how changes in the real sector variables and instruments cause $i$ and $E$ to change to maintain the momentary equilibrium in the asset sector treating $p$ and $y$ as exogenous. In the variational analysis of the real sector which follows next, we derive a variational aggregate demand curve. We then solve this equation together with an aggregate supply equation to derive the change in the domestic price level and real output. In this process we treat variations of $i$ and $E$ as given. This part of the analysis takes the place of the more usual IS–LM analysis. To convey the main idea simply, we neglect variations in capital stock. Note that this is not the same as neglecting the growth of capital. We merely assume that capital stock is growing along the reference path and that deviations from the reference path are negligible.[7]

Putting these two sets of equations together, we can deduce the effects of feedback between the two sectors. In this way, we can also distinguish primary effects that some policy instruments, such as the government expenditures, have on the endogenous variables and their secondary (or feedback) effects.

Take the ratios of (1a) over (1b) and (1a) over (1c) as the two independent equations determining the momentary equilibrium in the asset sector. Their variations are two equations in $\delta i$ and $e$:

$$(10) \quad \begin{aligned} \phi_1 \, \delta i - e &= -m + f - (\gamma, \alpha)_2 \, \delta\varepsilon, \\ \phi_3 \, \delta i &= -m + v + (\alpha, \beta)_2 \, \delta\varepsilon, \end{aligned}$$

where

$$(\gamma, \alpha)_2 = \gamma_2/\gamma - \alpha_2/\alpha > 0, \qquad (\alpha, \beta)_2 = \alpha_2/\alpha - \beta_2/\beta,$$

$$\phi_1 = -\alpha_1/\alpha + \gamma_1/\gamma = -(\alpha, \gamma)_1, \qquad \phi_3 = -\alpha_1/\alpha + \beta_1/\beta + 1/i > 0.$$

The sign of the parameter $\phi_1$ is ambiguous. It is positive if and only if the magnitude of the interest rate elasticity of demand for money is greater than that for foreign bonds.

The variations $\delta i$ and $e$ which maintain the momentary equilibrium in the asset sector in response to variations in the stocks of the assets and variations

---

[7] Because of the linearity of the variational dynamics, the effects of nonzero relative variation of the capital stock can be separately evaluated and superimposed on the results of our analysis. See Section 2.3.3.

## 11.3  Short-Run Analysis

in the expectational variable are obtained by solving (10):[8]

(11) $$\begin{bmatrix} \delta i \\ e \end{bmatrix} = \begin{bmatrix} -\sigma_1 \\ \theta_1 \end{bmatrix} m - \begin{bmatrix} 0 \\ 1 \end{bmatrix} f + \begin{bmatrix} \sigma_1 \\ 1 - \theta_1 \end{bmatrix} v + \begin{bmatrix} \sigma_\varepsilon \\ \theta_\varepsilon \end{bmatrix} \delta\varepsilon,$$

where the coefficients are given by

$$\sigma_1 = \phi_3^{-1} > 0, \qquad \theta_1 = (\phi_3 - \phi_1)\phi_3^{-1},$$
$$\sigma_\varepsilon = \phi_3^{-1}(\alpha, \beta)_2, \qquad \theta_\varepsilon = \phi_3^{-1}\phi_1(\alpha, \beta)_2 - (\alpha, \gamma)_2.$$

We note that $\theta_1$ is greater or less than one if and only if $\phi_1$ is negative or positive. The latter parameter is zero if and only if $\alpha_1/\alpha$ equals $\gamma_1/\gamma$. As mentioned in the introductory remarks of this chapter, this is our benchmark assumption one.

Since $V = B + B_g$, its variation is related to $b$ and $b_g$ by $v = \beta_p b + (1 - \beta_p)b_g$, where $\beta_p = B/V$. Since $B = (F_K - \lambda)KP$, the variation of $B$ is expressible in terms of $y$ and $p$ as $b = hy + p$, where $h = F_K/(F_K - \lambda)$, where we assume a Cobb–Douglas production function in calculating the marginal product of capital.[9] Incorporating these into (11), we rewrite (11) as

(12) $$\begin{bmatrix} \delta i \\ e \end{bmatrix} = \begin{bmatrix} -\sigma_1 \\ \theta_1 \end{bmatrix} m - \begin{bmatrix} 0 \\ 1 \end{bmatrix} f + \begin{bmatrix} \sigma_1 \\ 1 - \theta_1 \end{bmatrix}(1 - \beta_p)b_g$$
$$+ \begin{bmatrix} \sigma_\varepsilon \\ \theta_\varepsilon \end{bmatrix} \delta\varepsilon + \Sigma \begin{bmatrix} p \\ y \end{bmatrix},$$

---

[8] Alternatively, any two equations, (1a) and (1b) say, can be used. Then

$$\delta M = \alpha_1 A \, \delta i + \alpha \, \delta A,$$
$$V = \beta_1 A \, \delta i + \beta \, \delta A,$$

where

$$\delta A = \delta M + \delta V + e(EF) + E \, \delta F.$$

Hence $\delta i$ and $e$ are determined as the solution of

$$\begin{bmatrix} \alpha_1 A & \alpha EF \\ \beta_1 A & \beta EF \end{bmatrix} \begin{bmatrix} \delta i \\ e \end{bmatrix} = -\begin{bmatrix} -(1-\alpha) & \alpha & \alpha \\ \beta & -(1-\beta) & \beta \end{bmatrix} \begin{bmatrix} \delta M \\ \delta V \\ E \, \delta F \end{bmatrix}.$$

Upon solving it,

$$\begin{bmatrix} \delta i \\ e \end{bmatrix} = \frac{1}{\Delta} \begin{bmatrix} \beta & -\alpha \\ -\beta_1 & \alpha_1 \end{bmatrix} \begin{bmatrix} -(1-\alpha) & \alpha & \alpha \\ \beta & -(1-\beta) & \beta \end{bmatrix} \begin{bmatrix} \delta M \\ \delta V \\ E \, \delta F \end{bmatrix},$$

where $\Delta$ equals $-\alpha_1\beta + \beta_1\alpha$, a positive number. This equation is equivalent to (11), (which can be easily put in terms of $m$, $v$ and $f$, if so desired) and can be used to examine consequences of open market operations.

[9] By assumption, $k$ is zero identically.

where

$$\Sigma = \beta_p \begin{bmatrix} \sigma_1 \\ 1 - \theta_1 \end{bmatrix} [1 \ h] = \beta_p \sigma_1 \begin{bmatrix} 1 \\ \phi_1 \end{bmatrix} [1 \ h].$$

The last term shows how deviations of the real sector variables affect those of the asset sector. It is due to changes of the market valuation of the domestic bonds induced by changes in domestic output and its price level.[10] As $\phi_3$ becomes larger, the coefficients $\sigma_1$ and $\sigma_\varepsilon$ in (12) get closer to zero. Thus the domestic interest rate does not much respond to changes in expectations $\varepsilon$, $M$, $B_g$, $P$, or $Y$. Also the coefficient $\theta_1$ approaches one, hence the variation of the exchange rate $e$ nearly equals $m - f$, except for the effect of the expectation term $\delta\varepsilon$.

When domestic bonds and foreign bonds are perfect substitutes, $i$ equals $i^* + \varepsilon$. Expanding the asset demand ratio function $\beta$ (or $\gamma$) about $i^* + \varepsilon$, $\beta(i, i^* + \varepsilon) = \beta(i^* + \varepsilon, i^* + \varepsilon) + \beta_1(i^* + \varepsilon, i^* + \varepsilon)(i - i^* - \varepsilon) + \cdots$, we may interpret a large magnitude of the partial derivative as an indication of nearly perfect substitutability of domestic and foreign bonds.

---

[10] Under benchmark assumption one, $p$ and $y$ do not affect $e$, i.e., the feedback path between the asset and the real sector is severed. See Section 11.3.3.

Equation (12) can cover a wide range of behavior of the domestic interest rate deviations and the exchange rate changes. One extreme result can be simply obtained by letting $M$, $P$, and $B_g$ be constant. Then (12) reduces to $\delta i = \sigma_\varepsilon \delta\varepsilon + \sigma_1 p$ and $e = \theta_\varepsilon \delta\varepsilon$, where we approximate $\beta_p$ by one and set $\phi_1$ to zero for simplicity of illustration. We also assume that $y$ is zero. Now suppose that $\delta\varepsilon$ equals $\delta\pi$. (This would follow, for example, if $P = EP^*$ is posited. The logarithmic differentiation of this relation yields $\pi = \varepsilon + \pi^*$, from which its variational version follows because the foreign inflation rate is constant by assumption.) Suppose further that the real sector response is such that $p$ equals $e$. This would be a special case of (16) below and is compatible with the assumed zero for $y$. Then the expressions for $\delta i$ and $e$ are respectively given by $(\sigma_\varepsilon + \sigma_1\theta_\varepsilon) \delta\pi$ and $\theta_\varepsilon \delta\pi$ where the coefficient $\sigma_\varepsilon + \sigma_1\theta_\varepsilon$ equals $\sigma_1(\gamma, \beta)_2$, which is assumed to be positive, and the second coefficient $\theta_\varepsilon$ is positive with zero $\phi_1$, as can be seen from (10) and (11). Note that $\delta i$ and $e$ move in the same direction in this case. This case is therefore analogous to the one by the "Chicago" theory approach as described by Frankel (1979): Under the flexible price assumption, the nominal interest rate changes reflect the expected inflation rate changes. A rise in the domestic interest rate causes demand for the domestic currency to fall which in turn causes the exchange rate to depreciate.

To obtain another type of behavior, analogous to the one described as "Keynesian" theory by Frankel, set $p$ and $\delta\varepsilon$ equal to zero in (12). The domestic interest rate and the exchange rate respond to a change in $M$: $\delta i = -\sigma_1 m$, and $e = m$, where $\phi_1$ is zero as before. Note that $\delta i$ and $e$ move in the opposite direction in this case. Here, domestic money stock expansion relative to domestic money demand without a matching increase in price causes the domestic interest rate to fall, which in turn causes the exchange rate to depreciate because the lower interest rate at home induces capital outflow.

Note that interactions between the asset and the real sector variables are ignored in these cases because $\phi_1$ is assumed to be zero. Later in this chapter we adopt less extreme assumptions and re-evaluate movements in the domestic interest rate and the exchange rate by incorporating feedback effects.

### 11.3.2 Real Sector

In the previous section, we discussed how deviation in the real-sector variables such as $y$ or $p$ affect $\delta i$ and $e$ without specifying how these deviations are brought about. We now relate deviations of the real variables to deviations of the financial variables, thus completing the loops in the feedback paths. The main results of this section are the expressions for $p$ and $y$ in terms of the assumed deviations in $i$ and $E$. These, coupled with (12), complete the loops in the transmission paths between the asset and real sector.

In taking the variation of $P_1$ in (5), we can treat the weight $\chi$ and the foreign price as constant. On our reference path the inflation rate of the price index is zero as noted at the end of Section 11.2. Hence loss of wealth due to inflation is zero. To simplify our exposition without loss of essential linkages, we neglect capital stock depreciation, interest receipts, and expected gain due to the valuation effect of the assets denominated in foreign currency in the variational expression for disposable income. We retain only changes in the output, its price, and the inflationary expectation in the relative deviation of the disposable income:

(13) $$y' = l_1(p - e) + l_2 y - l_3 \, \delta\pi,$$

where

(14) $$\begin{aligned} l_1 &\simeq (1 - \chi)P(Y - T - \lambda K)/(P_1 Y'), \\ l_2 &= P(Y - \tau T)/(P_1 Y'), \\ l_3 &= \chi(M + B_g/i + EF/i^*)/(P_1 Y'). \end{aligned}$$

Here we assume that $\delta T/T = \tau y$, where $\tau$ is defined to equal $T'(Y)Y/T$. See the Appendix at the end of this chapter for the exact expression for $y'$.

To relate $y$ to $y'$, we take the variation of (2) to obtain another relation between $y$ and $y'$

(15) $$y^D = d_0 g + d_1 y' - d_2(\delta i - \delta \pi) - d_3(p - e),$$

where

$$d = Y - I'F_K, \qquad d_0 = G/d, \qquad d_1 = C_1 Y'/d,$$
$$d_2 = I'/d, \qquad d_3 = -(X' + C_2)v/d.$$

These coefficients are all assumed to be positive.

Eliminate $y'$ from (13) and (15). The result is the expression for $y^D$ and $p$ in terms of $\delta i$, $e$, and the instruments

(16) $$\mu_y y^D + \mu_p p = \mu_0 g + \mu_e e - \mu_i \, \delta i + \mu_\pi \, \delta \pi,$$

where

$$\mu_0 = d_0 > 0, \quad \mu_i = d_2, \quad \mu_y = 1 - d_1 l_2,$$
$$\mu_e = \mu_p, \quad \mu_p = d_3 - d_1 l_1, \quad \mu_\pi = d_2 - d_1 l_3.$$

This is the variational expression for the aggregate demand schedule in the short-run, a "generalized variational" IS curve. The slope of (16) is given by

$$p/y^D = -\mu_p/\mu_y.$$

The aggregate demand is downward sloping, therefore, if $d_3 - d_1 l_1$ and $1 - d_1 l_2$ are both positive.[11] If we assume $d_1 < 1$, then $1 - d_1 l_2 > 0$ since $l_2 < 1$. Roughly speaking, if the total demand of the domestic output is more responsive to direct price effect than to change in the disposable income due to the exchange rate change, then the aggregate demand is downward sloping.

Equation (16) shows that an expansionary fiscal policy $g > 0$ shifts the variational curve out directly. An expansionary monetary policy $m > 0$ does not have a direct effect but has a secondary expansionary effect which works through $\delta i$ and $e$. The expansionary effect can be calculated from (12) by $-\mu_i \delta i + \mu_e e = (\mu_i \sigma_1 + \mu_e \theta_1)m > 0$. This is positive for $m > 0$ if $\mu_i$ and $\mu_e$ are positive since $\sigma_1$ and $\theta_1$ are positive.

The above description of the effects of $m$ and $g$ is at best a partial analysis. For example, secondary effects on $\delta i$ and $e$ are ignored, and the effects of the current account are not incorporated. These effects are incorporated in our analysis of the next section where we examine these feedback effects directly. Equation (16) only gives us a relation between $y$ and $p$. To obtain $p$ and $y$ separately we need another relation. We could postulate a pricing equation or we could specify an aggregate supply schedule. We follow the latter option and assume that flow equilibrium is (re-)established between variations of the aggregate supply and demand schedules to separately determine $y$ and $p$. We take as the variational expression for our aggregate supply curve

(17) $$y^S = -\kappa(w - p), \quad \kappa > 0,$$

where $w$ is the variation of the nominal wage rate governed by [see (9)]

(18) $$\dot{w} = -\mu(w - p_i) + \delta \pi_i, \quad \mu > 0,$$

---

[11] When we incorporate a regressive expectation on the rate of domestic output price inflation, $\delta\pi = -v_p p$, the "effective" $\mu_p$ changes into $\mu_p + v_p \mu_\pi$ and makes the slope more (less) steeply downward sloping if $\mu_\pi$ is positive (negative).

The coefficient $d_3$ represents the direct effect of the terms-of-trade changes on the aggregate demand. The quantity $d_1 l_1$ expresses the indirect effect of the terms-of-trade changes on aggregate demand coming from changes in disposable income caused by changed terms-of-trade. We take this income effect to be smaller than the direct effect of relative price changes.

## 11.3 Short-Run Analysis

where variation of the price index inflationary expectation equals $\delta \pi_i = \chi \, \delta \pi + (1 - \chi) \, \delta \varepsilon$ since it is an estimate of the rate of change of $p_i$, i.e., $\dot{p}_i = \chi \dot{p} + (1 - \chi) \dot{e}$ by the domestic residents.

Equation (17) is the variational form of the aggregate supply schedule (6) which states that the domestic output deviates from the reference path in response to deviations in the real wage rate from its reference path. For firms, the real wage rate is the nominal wage divided by the output price. Wages change to close a gap between the target and the actual real wage. In variational forms $\dot{w} - \delta \pi_i$ is the estimate of the real wage changes for consumers. Equation (18) is a special case of the more general wage indexation schemes which can range from keeping the nominal wage rate constant to keeping the real wage rate constant.

### 11.3.3 Feedback Path

To be brief in our analysis, this section neglects changes in investment due to $\delta i$ in describing feedback paths between the real and asset sectors. This drops $\delta i$ from (15) and causes $\delta i$ to vanish in (16). This simplified version of the real sector momentary equilibrium condition is

(16')
$$\mu_y y^D + \mu_p p = \mu_e e + \zeta,$$

where

$$\zeta = \mu_g g + \mu_\pi \, \delta \pi.$$

Consequences of not making this simplifying assumption are outlined in Section 11.6.4 at the end of this chapter. When we equate $y^D$ to $y^S$ and drop $D$ and $S$ from $y$, we obtain from (16') and (17) deviations in the output and its price to equilibrate the real sector

(19)
$$p = (\kappa \mu_y w + \mu_e e + \zeta) \rho_c,$$
$$y = (-\mu_p w + \mu_e e + \zeta) \kappa \rho_c, \qquad \text{where} \qquad \rho_c^{-1} = \kappa \mu_y + \mu_p.$$

Since (12) and (19) jointly determine the momentary equilibrium in the asset and the real sector, their solutions express shifts of the interest rate, the exchange rate, the output, and its price that must occur to keep these two sectors in the momentary equilibrium state in response to changes in the stocks of the financial assets, the fiscal instrument, and the expectational variables.

Equation (19) states that $p$ is a weighted average of $w$, $e$, $g$ and $\delta \pi$ (the last two appearing in a fixed combination as $\zeta$). Since $\mu_p$ equals $\mu_e$ under static inflationary expectation as shown in (16), the weights assigned to $e$ and $w$ sum to one in the deviational expression for $p$. With a small $\kappa$, nearly all the weight is on $e + \zeta/\mu_e$, while more weight is given to $w$ as $\kappa$ becomes larger in determining $p$.

These observations on the weights assigned to $e$ and $w$, or more generally the manner by which $p$ is determined, can be made precise by parameter sensitivity analysis of the reduced form expressions of $\delta i$, $e$, $p$, and $y$, and consequently of the variational dynamic equation of the model with respect to $\kappa$. We introduce two benchmark assumptions on $\kappa$ to illustrate such sensitivity analysis simply: We treat models with a small $\kappa$ and a small $1/\kappa$.[12]

**Small $\kappa$.** Write $\rho_c$ as $(1/\mu_e)(1 - \kappa\mu_y/\mu_e) + o(\kappa)$, and $\kappa\rho_c$ as $\kappa/\mu_e + o(\kappa)$ where $o(\kappa)$ stands for terms with $\kappa^2$ or higher. Expanding (19) in powers of $\kappa$ and retaining only terms up to the first order in $\kappa$ we rewrite (19) as

(19-1)
$$p = e + \zeta/\mu_e + (\kappa\mu_y/\mu_e)(w - e - \zeta/\mu_e) + o(\kappa),$$
$$y = -\kappa(w - e - \zeta/\mu_e) + o(\kappa).$$

To the first order in $\kappa$, $p$ fully reflects changes in the exchange rate. Deviations in the wage rate appears in the combination $w - e - \zeta/\mu_e$ as a term of the first order of smallness in $\kappa$. Now jointly solve (12) and (19-1) to obtain the reduced forms of $\delta i$, $e$, $p$, and $y$. For example the exchange rate deviation is given as[13]

(20-1) $$e = \rho(\theta_1 m - f + Q + \gamma\zeta/\mu_e) + O(\kappa),$$

where

$$\gamma = \sigma_1\phi_1\beta_p, \qquad \rho = (1 - \gamma)^{-1}, \quad \text{and} \quad Q = (1 - \theta_1)(1 - \beta_p)b_g + \theta_\varepsilon\delta\varepsilon.$$

The notation $O(\kappa)$ stands for terms linear in $\kappa$.[14] Comparing (19-1) with (12), we note that the parameters $\gamma$ and $\rho$ embody two effects of feedback: The parameter $\rho$ expresses the magnification of the effects of the financial sector variable $\theta_1 m - f + Q$ on $e$; the parameter $\gamma\rho$ embodies the spill-over of the effects of the fiscal instrument onto $e$. Both effects are larger, the larger is $\gamma$.

In particular, if $\phi_1$ is zero (our benchmark assumption one), then there are no feedback effects. The parameter $\gamma$ vanishes and the parameter $\rho$

---

[12] For any other value of $\kappa$, $\bar{\kappa}$ say, one can expand about $\bar{\kappa}$. For example, $\rho_c^{-1} = \bar{\kappa}\mu_y + \mu_e + (\kappa - \bar{\kappa})\mu_y$. Define $\bar{\mu}_e$ by $\bar{\kappa}\mu_y + \mu_e$. Then $\rho_c$ equals $1/\bar{\mu}_e$ times $1 - (\kappa - \bar{\kappa})\mu_y/\bar{\mu}_e$. With these and other minor changes the analysis for models with small $\kappa$ apply to models with $\kappa$ near $\bar{\kappa}$.

[13] We do not exhibit the solution for $\delta i$ here because it is not used until Section 11.6.5.

[14] The exact expression is not important for our purpose here. It is

$$\kappa\gamma\rho(\mu_y/\mu_e - h)\{w - \zeta/\mu_e - \rho(\theta_1 m - f + Q + \gamma\zeta/\mu_e)\}.$$

Note that $w$ does not appear in the term independent of $\kappa$.

## 11.3 Short-Run Analysis

becomes one; no spill-over and magnification effects are present. The reduced forms specialize to those shown in (20-2)

(20-2)
$$e = m - f + \theta_\varepsilon \, \delta\varepsilon,$$
$$p = e + \zeta/\mu_e = m - f + \zeta/\mu_e + \theta_\varepsilon \, \delta\varepsilon + O(\kappa),$$
$$y = O(\kappa).$$

**Small $1/\kappa$.** When $\kappa$ is large in (17), it is convenient to expand the reduced form expression in terms of $1/\kappa$. Equation (19) is rewritten as

(19-2)
$$p = w - \mu_e(\kappa\mu_y)^{-1}(w - e - \zeta/\mu_e) + O(1/\kappa),$$
$$y = -(\mu_e/\mu_y)(w - e - \zeta/\mu_e) + (\mu_e/\mu_y)\mu_e(\kappa\mu_y)^{-1}(w - e - \zeta/\mu_e) + o(1/\kappa).$$

Now price deviations certainly behave differently from that of (19-1). $p$ equals $w$ to the zeroth order approximation. The reduced form expression for $e$ now becomes

(20-3)
$$e = \tilde{\rho}\{\theta_1 m - f + Q + \tilde{\gamma}\zeta/\mu_e + \omega w\} + O(1/\kappa),$$

where $\tilde{\rho}$ is now defined by

$$\tilde{\rho}^{-1} = 1 - \tilde{\gamma}, \qquad \tilde{\gamma} = \gamma h \mu_e/\mu_y, \qquad \omega = \gamma - \tilde{\gamma} = \gamma(1 - h\mu_e/\mu_y).$$

The feedback has a slightly different magnification factor. The spill-over effect of $\zeta$ is also slightly different. The major effect of feedback, however, is to introduce $w$ into the expression for $e$. With zero $\phi_1$, all these effects disappear.

From now on for simpler exposition we drop terms of the order $O(\kappa)$ or $O(1/\kappa)$ in our equations. Their inclusions are simple enough. The reader is invited to refine the analysis of this section by carrying these terms along.

The general expressions of the reduced forms of $e$ and $p$ are

(20)
$$e = \rho(\theta_1 m - f + Q + \gamma\zeta/\mu_e + \omega w),$$
$$\begin{bmatrix} p \\ y \end{bmatrix} = \rho_c \left\{ \begin{bmatrix} \kappa\mu_y + \rho\mu_e\omega \\ \kappa(-\mu_p + \mu_e\rho\omega) \end{bmatrix} w + \mu_e \begin{bmatrix} 1 \\ \kappa \end{bmatrix} \rho\{\theta_1 m - f + Q + (1 + \rho\gamma)\zeta/\mu_e\} \right\},$$

where

$$\rho = (1 - \gamma)^{-1}, \qquad \gamma = \sigma_1\phi_1\beta_p\rho_c(1 + \kappa h)\mu_e,$$
$$Q = (1 - \theta_1)(1 - \beta_p)b_g + \theta_\varepsilon \, \delta\varepsilon, \qquad \omega = \sigma_1\phi_1\kappa_p\rho_c(\mu_y - h\mu_p).$$

Comparing the expression for $e$ in (20) with that in (12), we recognize that the feedback effects between the asset and the real sector modify (12) in two ways: by magnifying the effects of the asset stock variations $m, f, b_g$ by $\rho$, and by introducing the term depending on $w$ and $\zeta$ into $e$. As $\gamma$ increases from zero, $\rho$ becomes greater than one. The larger $\rho$, the stronger the effects of interaction between the asset and the real sector. When the effects of $\delta i$ are included in (16'), more complex feedback effects are observed. For example, the effects $m$ and $f$ are magnified not by the same factor $\rho$ but by two different factors both of which are larger than $\rho$. Exact expressions are found at the end of this chapter.

### 11.3.4 Policy Reaction Functions

Equation (20) suggests various policy reaction functions. To maintain $y = 0$, for example, we must set the expression for $y$ to zero and solve it for $g$. [Note from (16') that $\zeta$ is a function of $g$.] The result will be the policy reaction function of $g$ for maintaining the output along the planned path. To illustrate, suppose $y$ is to be kept at zero in economies with large $\kappa$. Setting the right-hand side of $y$ in (19-2) to zero, and substituting $e$ out by (20-3), we obtain an equation containing $g$, $m$, and $w$

$$\theta_1 m + (1 + \tilde{\rho}\tilde{\gamma})(\mu_0/\mu_e)g = \tilde{\rho}(f - Q) + (1 - \tilde{\rho}\omega)w.$$

Under benchmark assumption 1, this simplifies to

$$m + (\mu_0/\mu_e)g = f + w.$$

If the stocks of $M$ and $F$ are held fixed, then $g$ must simply equal $(\mu_e/\mu_0)w$ to keep $y$ at zero in this benchmark case.

We later show that $m, f$, and $w$ are the state variables of the variational dynamic equations under 100% monetization of the unplanned budget deficit. Thus the above equation can be solved for $g$ in terms of the state variables, hence it is a policy reaction function for $g$ to keep $y$ at zero: Deviations of the state variables are multiplied by constants shown above to generate automatic changes in the fiscal instrument.

For economies with small $\kappa$, the reaction function to keep $e$ at zero becomes independent of $w$. Assuming zero $\delta\pi$, (20–1) gives

$$\theta_1 m + \gamma(\mu_0/\mu_e)g = f - Q.$$

In economies with large $\kappa$, however, the reaction function to keep $e$ at zero depends on $w$. Under the same assumption as above, (20–3) yields

$$\theta_1 m + \gamma h(\mu_0/\mu_y)g = f - Q - \omega w.$$

## 11.3 Short-Run Analysis

Under assumption one, $\gamma$ is zero in the above two reaction functions and $\theta_1$ becomes one, i.e., they both collapse into the same reaction function, $m = f$, i.e., $g$ cannot be used to keep the exchange rate fixed in economies with no feedbacks between the asset and the real sector, regardless of supply responsiveness of the output to real wage changes.

### 11.3.5 Variational Dynamics

We are now ready to derive the differential equations for the variational time paths of the economy about the reference path chosen in Section 11.2.

The variation of the budget constraint yields

(21) $$\delta \dot{M} + \delta \dot{B}_g/i - E\,\delta \dot{R}/i^* = \delta D_f.$$

Off the reference path, the international bonds are being accumulated at the rate

(22) $$\delta \dot{R} + \delta \dot{F} = i^*\,\delta U.$$

The government policy decides how the total shown on the right of (21) and (22) are allocated to the individual terms on the left, respectively. For example, let $\theta$ be the extent of the variation in the government budget deficit to be monetized. Then

(23) $$\delta \dot{M} = \theta\,\delta D_f, \qquad 0 \le \theta \le 1,$$

and the remainder becomes

(24) $$\delta \dot{B}_g/i - E\,\delta \dot{R}/i = (1 - \theta)\,\delta D_f.$$

If $\sigma \%$ of the current account deviation from the reference is planned to be added to the reserve, we can write this as

(25) $$\delta \dot{R} = \sigma i^*\,\delta U, \qquad 0 \le \sigma \le 1.$$

Then from (22) and (25), we deduce that

$$\delta \dot{B}_g/i = (1-\theta)\,\delta D_f + \sigma E\,\delta U, \quad \text{and} \quad \delta \dot{F} = (1-\sigma)i^*\,\delta U.$$

The total variational dynamics are obtained by collecting these individual variational differential equations including (18):

$$\dot{w} = -\mu w + \mu\{\chi p + (1-\chi)e\} + \delta\pi_i,$$
$$\dot{m} = -nm + \theta\,\delta D_f/M,$$
$$\dot{b}_g = -nb_g + i(1-\theta)\,\delta D_f/B_g + \sigma E\,\delta U/B_g,$$
$$\dot{r} = -nr + i^*\sigma\,\delta U/R,$$

and

$$\dot{f} = -nf + (1 - \sigma)i^* \, \delta U/F.$$

Having derived these general fifth-dimensional dynamics, we specialize $\theta$ to one and $\sigma$ to zero, i.e., we assume that the unplanned budget deficit is monetized 100% and that the government adheres to the planned rate of accumulation of the international bonds. Unplanned fluctuation in the current account is fully absorbed by the private sector. In this case, the dynamics separate into two subdynamics:

(26)
$$\dot{b}_g = -nb_g,$$
$$\dot{r} = -nr.$$

(27)
$$\dot{w} = -\mu w + \mu\{\chi p + (1 - \chi)e\} + \delta\pi_i,$$
$$\dot{m} = -nm + \delta D_f/M,$$
$$\dot{f} = -nf + (i^* \, \delta U/F).$$

Since (26) is self-contained, we concentrate on (27). In (27), $\delta D_f$, and $\delta U$ are changes in the budget deficit and in the current account, respectively. Taking the variation of the government budget deficit,

(28) $\quad \delta D_f/M = m_0 g + m_1 p - m_2 y + m_3 b_g - m_4(e + r).$

Here we define

$$m_0 = PG/M, \quad m_1 = P(G - T)/M \quad m_2 = PT(Y)\tau/M,$$

where $\tau = T'(Y)Y/T(Y)$,

$$m_3 = B_g/M, \quad m_4 = ER/M.$$

Along the reference path, if financial stocks grow at the rate equal to that of the long-run equilibrium, then we can write the government budget equation as $n(M + B_g/i - ER/i^*) = P(G - T) + B_g - ER$. Furthermore, $i = i^*$ because $\bar{\varepsilon} = 0$ in the long-run equilibrium. Hence $n + n(m_3 - m_4)/i^* = m_1 + (m_3 - m_4)$ or $n - m_1 = (m_3 - m_4)(1 - n/i^*)$. Money stock deviations and consequently the dynamics of this economy are strongly influenced by the parameters in (28). In particular, the sign of $m_1$ matters. With $n = 0$, $m_1 \gtrless 0$ if and only if $ER \gtrless B_g$. Having thus expressed $\delta D_f$ in terms of more basic variational variables, do likewise for $\delta U$. The variation in the current account is

(29) $\quad \delta U = \delta R + \delta F + \delta B_T,$

## 11.3 Short-Run Analysis

where the balance of trade varies according to

(30) $$\delta B_T = (PX/E)(p - e + x) - P^* I_m i_m,$$

where $x$ is the relative variation of the exports and $i_m$ is the relative variation of imports.

Since we have specified the export to depend only on the terms of trade in (4), its variation depends only on $p - e$,

(31) $$x = (X'/X)(P/EP^*)(p - e).$$

The imports have been specified to depend on the terms of trade and a scale variable which we take to be $Y'$. With this specification, we can write

(32) $$i_m = c_1(p - e) + c_2 y',$$

where

$$c_1 = \frac{\partial I_m}{\partial v} \frac{v}{I_m} > 0 \quad \text{and} \quad c_2 = \frac{\partial I_m}{\partial Y'} \frac{Y'}{I_m} > 0.$$

When (31) and (32) are substituted into (30), the balance of trade is seen to vary with changes in the exchange rate, output, and the output price level according to

(33) $$\delta B_T = \Omega_e(e - p) - \Omega_y y',$$

where

$$\Omega_e = -(PX/E)\{1 + (X'/X)(P/EP^*)\} + P^* I_m c_1, \quad \Omega_y = P^* I_m c_2 > 0.$$

We assume that $\Omega_e$ and $\Omega_y$ are positive, so that devaluation leads to improvement in trade balance. Since $P^* I_m = (PX/E) + F + R - U$, we can rewrite $\Omega_e$ as

$$\Omega_e = (PX/E)\{c_1 - (X'/X)(P/EP^*) - 1\} - c_1 B_T.$$

In this form we see that the Marshall–Lerner condition implies that the first term is positive. In the long-run equilibrium state, the current account equation can be written as $n(R + F) = B_T + i^*(F + R)$; hence $B_T = (n - i^*)(F + R)$. We see then that if $i^* > n$, then $\Omega_e$ is larger, the larger is the holding of $F + R > 0$. Substitute (33) into (29) to write $\delta U$ as

$$\delta U = Rr + Ff + \Omega_e(e - p) - \Omega_y y'.$$

The state representation of the dynamics for $w$, $m$, and $f$ is reached when first the expressions for $\delta D_f$ and $\delta U$ are substituted out and then $e$, $p$, and $y$

are replaced by their respective reduced forms given in (20). After the first step is carried out, the dynamics are expressed as

$$(34) \quad \frac{d}{dt}\begin{bmatrix} w \\ m \\ f \end{bmatrix} = \begin{bmatrix} -\mu & 0 & 0 \\ 0 & -n & 0 \\ 0 & 0 & -n+i^* \end{bmatrix}\begin{bmatrix} w \\ m \\ f \end{bmatrix} + \begin{bmatrix} \mu(1-\chi) \\ -m_4 \\ \Omega_1 \end{bmatrix} e + \begin{bmatrix} \mu\chi \\ m_1 \\ -\Omega_1 \end{bmatrix} p - \begin{bmatrix} 0 \\ m_2 \\ \Omega_2 \end{bmatrix} y$$

$$+ \begin{bmatrix} 0 \\ m_0 \\ 0 \end{bmatrix} g + \text{terms due to } b_g, r, \delta\pi, \text{ and } \delta\varepsilon,$$

where

$$\Omega_1 = i^*(\Omega_e + l_1\Omega_y)/F, \qquad \Omega_2 = i^*l_2\Omega_y/F.$$

In this form influences of deviations of the output, its price level, and the exchange rate are explicitly shown. For example, this equation shows that if the price level is rigid, the term

$$\begin{bmatrix} \mu\chi \\ m_1 \\ -\Omega_1 \end{bmatrix}$$

is absent from (34).

## Static Expectations

Assume static expectations on the exchange rate changes and inflation rates for the time being. When $e$, $p$, and $y$ are substituted out by (20), the state-space representation of the dynamic equation of the economy results. Let $\Phi$ be the dynamic matrix. In economies with small $\kappa$ it is obtained by substituting (19-1) and (20-1) into (34). Substitute (19-2) and (20-3) to obtain the dynamic matrix corresponding to economies with large $\kappa$. (Recall that under static expectations $\zeta$ equals $\mu_0 g$.) Denote the former by $\Phi(\kappa)$ and the latter by $\Phi(1/\kappa)$:

$$(34\text{-}1) \quad \Phi(\kappa) = \begin{bmatrix} -\mu & 0 & 0 \\ 0 & -n & 0 \\ 0 & 0 & -n+i^* \end{bmatrix} + \rho\begin{bmatrix} \mu \\ m_1 - m_4 \\ 0 \end{bmatrix}\begin{bmatrix} 0 & \theta_1 & 1 \end{bmatrix}$$

and

$$(34\text{-}2) \quad \Phi(1/\kappa) = \begin{bmatrix} -\mu(1-\chi) & 0 & 0 \\ \phi_{21} & -n & 0 \\ -\phi_{31} & 0 & -n+i^* \end{bmatrix} + \rho\begin{bmatrix} \mu(1-\chi) \\ -\phi_4 \\ -\phi_{31} \end{bmatrix}\begin{bmatrix} \omega & \theta_1 & -1 \end{bmatrix},$$

## 11.3  Short-Run Analysis

where
$$\phi_{21} = m_1 + m_2 \mu_e/\mu_y, \qquad \phi_{31} = \Omega_1 - \Omega_2 \mu_e/\mu_y, \qquad \phi_4 = m_2 \mu_e/\mu_y + m_4.$$

The general expression of the dynamic matrix is

$$(34\text{-}3) \quad \Phi = \begin{bmatrix} -\mu(1-\phi_{11}) & 0 & 0 \\ \phi_{21} & -n & 0 \\ -\phi_{31} & 0 & -n+i^* \end{bmatrix} + \begin{bmatrix} \mu\psi_1 \\ \psi_2 \\ \psi_3 \end{bmatrix} [\omega \quad \theta_1 \quad -1],$$

where
$$\phi_{11} = \kappa\chi\rho_c\mu_y, \qquad \phi_{21} = (m_1\mu_y + m_2\mu_p)\kappa\rho_c, \qquad \phi_{31} = (\Omega_1\mu_y - \Omega_2\mu_p)\kappa\rho_c,$$
$$\psi_1 = \{\chi\mu_e\rho_c + 1 - \chi\}\rho, \qquad \psi_2 = \{(m_1 - \kappa m_2)\mu_e\rho_c - m_4\}\rho,$$
$$\psi_3 = \{\Omega_1 - (\Omega_1 + \kappa\Omega_2)\mu_e\rho_c\}\rho.$$

To evaluate the fiscal policy multiplier we need the column vector multiplying $g$. The complete dynamic equation adds this to the homogeneous part of the dynamic equation by collecting terms dependent on $g$ from (34). Denoting the three-dimensional vector in (34) by s, (34) is rendered as

$$(35) \qquad \frac{ds}{dt} = \Phi s + \begin{bmatrix} \Gamma_1 \\ \Gamma_2 \\ \Gamma_3 \end{bmatrix} g.$$

For use in Section 11.4 we give the expressions for these gammas. For small $\kappa$

$$(35\text{-}1) \quad \begin{aligned} \Gamma_1 &= (\mu_0/\mu_e)\mu(\rho\gamma + \chi), \\ \Gamma_2 &= m_0 + (\mu_0/\mu_e)\{\rho\gamma(m_1 - m_4) + m_1\}, \\ \Gamma_3 &= -(\mu_0/\mu_e)\Omega_1. \end{aligned}$$

With large $\kappa$, gammas are given by

$$(35\text{-}2) \quad \begin{aligned} \Gamma_1 &= \mu(1-\chi), \\ \Gamma_2 &= m_0 - (\mu_0/\mu_y)(m_2 + \tilde{\rho}\tilde{\gamma}\phi_4), \\ \Gamma_3 &= (\mu_0/\mu_e)\{\tilde{\rho}\tilde{\gamma}\phi_{31} - (\mu_e/\mu_y)\Omega_2\}. \end{aligned}$$

Note that the elasticity of balance of trade with respect to disposable income does not appear in the expressions for gammas in economies with small $\kappa$ because $\Omega_2$ is proportional to $\Omega_y$.

Also for later use we give the expression for gammas valid for any value of $\kappa$

$$(35\text{-}3) \quad \begin{aligned} \Gamma_1 &= \mu(1-\chi)\gamma\mu_0/\mu_e + (\mu - v_p)\chi\rho_c\mu_0(1+\gamma\rho), \\ \Gamma_2 &= -m_4\gamma\mu_0/\mu_e + m_1\rho_c\mu_0(1+\gamma\rho) - m_2\kappa\rho_c\mu_0(1+\gamma\rho) + m_0, \\ \Gamma_3 &= \Omega_1\{\gamma\rho\mu_0/\mu_e - \mu_0\rho_c(1+\gamma\rho)\} - \Omega_2\kappa\rho_c\mu_0(1+\gamma\rho). \end{aligned}$$

In $\Gamma_2$, $m_0$ represents the direct expansionary effect of $g > 0$ on the budget deficit, while the remainder of $\Gamma_2$ expresses the indirect effects working through the effects of $g$ on changes in the exchange rate, price, and output level. When $\Gamma_2$ is positive, the impact effect of $g > 0$ is to increase the money stock to finance the excess fiscal expenditure. (If $\Gamma_2$ is negative, then the effects of $g > 0$ on the exchange rate depreciation and expansionary effects of $g > 0$ on $y$ outweighs the direct effect, and $\dot{m}$ becomes negative.)

## Stability Analysis

**Economies with small $\kappa$.** The characteristic polynomial of the dynamic matrix of (34-1) is easily calculated to be

$$|\lambda I - \Phi(\kappa)| = (\lambda + \mu)(\lambda + n - i^*)\{\lambda + n - \rho\theta_1(m_1 - m_4)\}.$$

Hence the dynamics are stable if and only if the following two inequalities are met:

$$\mu \geq 0, \quad n \geq \max\{i^*, \rho\theta_1(m_1 - m_4)\},$$

where from (28) the second condition can be put as a constraint on the budget deficit if $n > i^*$;

$$P(G - T) \leq ER + (n/\rho\theta_1)M.$$

A smaller $\beta_p$ implies a larger upper bound on $P(G - T)$ because $1/\rho$ is larger from (20-1). A larger $ER$ means a larger upper bound.

**Economies with large $\kappa$.** The stability conditions are a bit more involved. The characteristic polynomial now becomes

$$|\lambda I - \Phi(1/\kappa)|$$

$$= \begin{vmatrix} \lambda + \mu(1-\chi)(1-\rho\omega) & -\mu(1-\chi)\rho\theta_1 & \mu(1-\chi)\rho \\ -A & \lambda + n + \rho\theta_1\phi_4 & -\rho\theta_4 \\ B & -\rho\phi_{31}\theta_1 & \lambda + n - i^* + \rho\phi_{31} \end{vmatrix},$$

where

$$A = \phi_{21} - \rho\omega\phi_4, \quad B = (1 - \rho\omega)\phi_{31}.$$

When rendered in the root-locus form the characteristic polynomial assumes the expression

$$N(\lambda)/D(\lambda) = -1/(\rho\theta_1\phi_{31}),$$

where

$$N(\lambda) = \lambda(\lambda + n),$$

$$D(\lambda) = (\lambda + n - i^*)[\lambda^2 + \{n + \rho\theta_1\phi_4 + \mu(1-\chi)(1-\rho\omega)\}\lambda$$
$$+ \mu(1-\chi)\{(1-\rho\omega)n + \rho\theta_1(\phi_4 - \phi_{21})\}].$$

## 11.3 Short-Run Analysis

Therefore, economies with large $\kappa$ are stable for all positive values assumed by $\phi_{31}$ if and only if (i) $n + \rho\theta_1\phi_4 + \mu(1 - \chi)(1 - \rho\omega)$ and (ii) $(1 - \rho\omega)n + \rho\theta_1(\phi_4 - \phi_{21})$ are both positive. From their definitions given below (34-2), we see that $\phi_4 - \phi_{21} = -(m_1 - m_4)$. Because $\phi_4$ is positive, (i) is automatically positive if $\rho\omega$ is less than one, i.e., if $(1 - \gamma)/(1 - \gamma h\mu_e/\mu_y)$ is positive. This is normally satisfied. Thus (ii) is the only real binding condition: It constrains $P(G - T)$ to be less than or equal to $ER + n(1 - \rho\omega)M/(\rho\theta_1)$. This condition is almost the same as the one for the stability of the dynamic matrix $\Phi(\kappa)$, except for $n$ being replaced with a smaller $n(1 - \rho\omega)$. A positive parameter $\phi_{31}$ obtains if and only if

$$\Omega_e + \{(l_1 - (\mu_e/\mu_y)l_2\}\Omega_y > 0.$$

Provided that $l_1$ is greater than $(\mu_e/\mu_y)l_2$, this is always met. Even if the coefficient multiplying $\Omega_y$ is negative, it will be satisfied if $\Omega_e$ and $\Omega_y$ are of the same order of magnitude.

**General case.** The characteristic polynomial can be written as

(34-4) $$0 = |\lambda I - \Phi| = \lambda q_1(\lambda) + \mu q_2(\lambda),$$

where

$$q_1(\lambda) = \begin{vmatrix} \lambda + n - \psi_2\theta_1 & -\psi_2 \\ -\psi_3\theta_1 & \lambda + n - i^* - \psi_3 \end{vmatrix}$$
$$= (\lambda + n - i^*)(\lambda + n - \psi_2\theta_1) + \psi_3(\lambda + n)$$

and

$$q_2(\lambda) = (1 - \phi_{11} - \psi_1\omega)q_1(\lambda) - \psi_1\theta_1(\phi_{21} + \psi_2\omega)(\lambda + n - i^*)$$
$$- \psi_1(\phi_{31} + \psi_3\omega)(\lambda + n).$$

When $\mu$ is zero in (18), $\dot{w}$ responds only to $\delta\pi_i$. Under static expectation on $\pi$ and $\varepsilon$, $\delta\pi_i = 0$. Hence, $w = $ const under $\mu = 0$. The matrix $\Phi$ has one zero eigenvalue. The other two are determined as the roots of $q_1(\lambda)$. If $\psi_2$ is too negative, then $q_1(\lambda)$ will have one unstable root. From its definition, $\psi_2$ takes a large negative value for large $\kappa\mu_e\rho_c$ and large $\rho_2$, i.e., either when the aggregate supply vigorously responds to changes in the real wage [see (18)] or when the feedback couplings between the asset and the real sectors become too tight, i.e., when $\mu_e\rho_c$ and $\rho_2$ become large. A large negative $\psi_3$ helps in stabilizing $q_1(\lambda)$. A negative $m_1$ (budget surplus) also helps stabilize the dynamics since it makes $\psi_2$ less negative. If $q_2(\lambda)$ is stable, then the dynamics are stable even for $\mu > 0$.

Even when the dynamics are unstable under static expectations, the dynamics can be stabilized in several ways: We can introduce a stabilization policy as a reaction function for $g$. This approach has been illustrated in Chapter 10. Another way to stabilize dynamics is discussed next.

### Stabilizing Expectations

Here, we discuss expectations as a stabilizing factor of dynamics. Let us discuss a regressive output price expectation, i.e., $\delta\pi = -v_p p$ while keeping a static expectation hypothesis on $\varepsilon$. Consequences of introducing regressive expectations on $\varepsilon$ are explored at the end of the chapter.

The regressive expectation on the home output price level has two effects. The first is to change "effective" value of $\mu_p$ in (16'). To see this, we rewrite (16') as $\mu_y y + \hat{\mu}_p p = \mu_e e + \hat{\zeta}$, where

$$\hat{\mu}_p = \mu_p + v\mu_\pi \quad \text{and} \quad \hat{\zeta} = \mu_0 g.$$

Then, Eq. (19) changes into

$$p = (\kappa\mu_y w + \mu_e e + \hat{\zeta})\hat{\rho}_c, \quad y = (-\hat{\mu}_p w + \mu_e e + \hat{\zeta})\kappa\hat{\rho}_c,$$

where

$$\hat{\rho}_c^{-1} = \kappa\mu_y + \hat{\mu}_p.$$

The expressions of (20) remain valid when $\rho_c$ is replaced by $\hat{\rho}_c$, and $\mu_p$ by $\hat{\mu}_p$.

The second effect is to introduce the $\delta\pi_i$ term into the dynamics of (34). To the right-hand side of (34), we must add

$$\begin{bmatrix} 1 \\ 0 \\ 0 \end{bmatrix} \delta\pi_i = -\chi v_p \begin{bmatrix} 1 \\ 0 \\ 0 \end{bmatrix} p.$$

The column vector multiplying the $p$ variation is therefore modified. The parameter $\mu$ is now replaced by $\mu - v_p$. The dynamic matrix (34-3) changes into

$$\Phi = \begin{bmatrix} -\mu + (\mu - v_p)\phi_{11} & 0 & 0 \\ \phi_{21} & -n & 0 \\ -\phi_{31} & 0 & -n + i^* \end{bmatrix} + \begin{bmatrix} (\mu - v_p)\psi_1 \\ \psi_2 \\ \psi_3 \end{bmatrix} [\omega \quad \theta_1 \quad -1].$$

The presence of a regressive inflationary expectation is neutral or stabilizing. For economies with small $\kappa$, the expectation does not alter the dynamic characteristics at all. Because of the upper triangular structure of the dynamic matrix, it has exactly the same characteristic polynomial. For economies with large $\kappa$, the characteristic polynomial does change. The numerator polynomial $N(\lambda)$ now is given by $(\lambda + n)(\lambda + v_p)$. The denominator polynomial

## 11.4 Are Variable Wage Rates More Inflationary?

$D(\lambda)$ also changes slightly with roots slightly more negative. The main difference is then due to the presence of the factor $(\lambda + v_p)$ which replaces $\lambda$. This implies that the dynamics are stable even for some slightly negative value of $\phi_{31}$, while the matrix (34-2) is unstable for negative $\phi_{31}$. In the general case, the characteristic equation changes into

$$0 = (\lambda + \mu)q_1(\lambda) - (\mu - v_p)q_3(\lambda),$$

where

$$q_3(\lambda) = (\phi_{11} + \psi_1\omega_2)q_1(\lambda) + \psi_1\theta_1(\phi_{21} + \psi_2\omega_2)(\lambda + n - i^*)$$
$$+ \psi_1(\phi_{31} + \psi_3\omega_2)(\lambda + n).$$

Now, primarily due to the effect of $\delta\pi_i$ on $\dot{w}$, the dynamics (34) can be made stable for a certain range of values of $\mu - v_p$. The adjustment coefficients on inflationary expectations must be sufficiently fast to stabilize (34). Numerical examples illustrate some of the points raised above.

### 11.4 Are Variable Wage Rates More Inflationary? An Example of Structural Perturbation Analysis

First we note that the variational expression for the output price inflation approximately is given by $\dot{p}$.[15]

Now we can precisely formulate and answer the question loosely posed in Section 11.1. Consider a temporary change in the government fiscal expenditure

(36)
$$g(t) = \begin{cases} \bar{g}, & 0 < t < T \\ 0, & t > T \end{cases}$$

of some positive duration $T$. Calculate the time path of $\dot{p}(t)$ with zero $\mu$ and positive $\mu$. Denote the inflation time path of an economy with a positive $\mu$ by $\dot{p}^{\mu}(t)$. The difference $\dot{p}^{\mu}(t) - \dot{p}(t)$ is denoted by $\delta\dot{p}(t)$. Then we ask: Is $\delta\dot{p}(t)$ positive for all $t$? Does the answer depend on the value of $\kappa$; i.e., is the answer qualified by the nature of the supply responsiveness?

We answer these questions both for economies under stationary expectations and regressive expectations.

---

[15] The domestic output price inflation, by definition, equals $\dot{P}/P$ where $P$ is the output price. The inflation rate on the reference path then is $\dot{P}^0/P^0$, where $P^0$ is the price of the output on the reference path. Recall that $P$ and $P^0$ are related by $P = P^0(1 + p)$ by definition of the lower case variable $p$. Taking the logarithmic derivative of this with respect to time, $\dot{P}/P$ equals $\dot{P}^0/P^0$ plus $\dot{p}/(1 + p)$. Thus, the inflation rate deviation, $\dot{P}/P$ minus $\dot{P}^0/P^0$, approximates $\dot{p}$.

### 11.4.1 Stationary Expectations

***Economies with small $\kappa$.*** When supply schedules are not very responsive, i.e., in economies with small $\kappa$, $p$ is given by (19-1); hence $\delta p$ equals $\delta e$ because the common term $\zeta$ disappears from $\delta p$.

From (20-1)

$$\delta p = \delta e = \rho[\theta_1 \ -1]\, \delta z.$$

where $\delta z$ is defined to be the two-dimensional vector composed of $\delta m$ and $\delta f$, i.e., $z$ consists of $m$ and $f$. Differentiate the above. Substitute out the derivative $\delta \dot{z}$ by the variational differential equation (35) with the dynamic matrix given by (34-1). The result is

$$\delta \dot{p} = \rho[\theta_1 \ -1]\, \delta \dot{z} = \rho[\theta_1 \ -1] H(\kappa)\, \delta z,$$

where the two-by-two matrix $H(\kappa)$ is defined to be

$$H(\kappa) = \begin{bmatrix} -n + \rho\theta_1(m_1 - m_4) & -\rho(m_1 - m_4) \\ 0 & -n + i^* \end{bmatrix},$$

and $\delta z(0) = 0$. The instrument variation $g$ does not appear in the above because $H(\kappa)$ nor $\Gamma_2$ and $\Gamma_3$ in (35-1) depend on the parameter $\mu$. Because the initial condition for $\delta z$ is zero, $\delta \dot{p}$ remains at zero for all $t$. This can be summarized as

***Proposition.*** Under stationary expectations on inflation, economies with variable nominal wage rate are no more inflationary than economies with rigid nominal wage rate if the supply responsiveness is low.

***Economies with large $\kappa$.*** The inflation rate difference behaves more complexly in economies with large $\kappa$. Equation (19-2) reveals that $\delta \dot{p}$ now equals $\delta \dot{w}$. From (34-2), (35), and (35-2) the variational differential equations are

(37)
$$\dot{w} = 0,$$
$$\dot{z} = H(1/\kappa)z + \phi w + Jg, \qquad J = [\Gamma_2 \ \Gamma_3]$$

for the economy with rigid nominal wage rate, and

(38)
$$\dot{w}^\mu = -\mu(1-\chi)(1-\rho\omega)w^\mu + \rho\mu(1-\chi)(\theta_1 - 1)z + \mu(1-\chi)g,$$
$$\dot{z}^\mu = H(1/\kappa)z + \phi w^\mu + Jg,$$

for the economy with variable nominal wage rate. Take the difference of these two sets of differential equations:

(39)
$$\delta \dot{w} = \mu v_1\, \delta w + \mu[v_2 \ v_3]z + \mu\gamma_1 g,$$

## 11.4 Are Variable Wage Rates More Inflationary?

where

$$v_1 = -\gamma_1(1-\rho\omega), \qquad [v_2 \quad v_3] = \gamma_1\rho[\theta_1 \quad -1], \qquad \gamma_1 = 1-\chi.$$

In (39), **z** is obtained by integrating (37). In our notation, **z** is expressed as $(Z, Jg)$, where $Z$ is $e^{Ht}$. (We drop $1/\kappa$ from the argument of $H$ for simpler notation.) The first term of (39) is of second order of smallness and is negligible. Hence the difference of the inflation rates is given by

$$(40) \quad \delta\dot{p} = \delta\dot{w} \doteq \mu\{[v_2 \quad v_3](Z, Jg) + \gamma_1 g\} = \left\{\gamma_1 g + \int_0^t S_0(t-u)g(u)\,du\right\},$$

where

$$S_0(u) = [v_2 \quad v_3]e^{Hu}J$$

and

$$[v_2 \quad v_3]e^{Hu}J = (L_1 e^{s_1 u} - L_2 e^{s_2 u})/(s_1 - s_2)$$

with

$$L_i = (\theta_1\Gamma_2 - \Gamma_3)s_i - \Gamma_2(h_{21} + \theta_1 h_{22}) + \Gamma_3(\theta_1 h_{12} + h_{11}), \qquad i = 1, 2.$$

As an example, suppose $t < T$. Then, carrying out the integration in (40) and noting (36), we rewrite (40) as

$$(41) \quad \delta\dot{p}(t) = \mu\bar{g}\left\{\gamma_1 + \int_0^t [L_1 e^{s_1(t-u)} - L_2 e^{s_2(t-u)}](s_1 - s_2)^{-1}\,du\right\}$$

$$= \mu\bar{g}\{\gamma_1 + [(L_1/s_1)(e^{s_1 t} - 1) - (L_2/s_2)(e^{s_2 t} - 1)](s_1 - s_2)^{-1}\}$$

$$\simeq \mu\bar{g}\gamma_1 > 0 \quad \text{for small } t.$$

For $t > T$ we obtain also from (36) and (40)

$$(42) \quad \delta\dot{p}(t) = \mu\bar{g}(s_1 - s_2)^{-1}[(L/s_1)(e^{s_1 t} - e^{s_1(t-T)}) - (L/s_2)(e^{s_2 t} - e^{s_2(t-T)})].$$

To summarize, the inflation rate difference jumps to $\mu\bar{g}\gamma_1$ at $t = 0$. It increases initially with time if $(L_1 - L_2)(s_1 - s_2)^{-1}$ is positive, i.e., if $\theta_1\Gamma_2 - \Gamma_3$ is positive. Otherwise, the difference decreases with time. Depending on the parameter values, the difference may reach a peak before $T$ or after $T$.

### 11.4.2 Regressive Expectations

Now assume that $\delta\pi$ equals $-v_p p$.

***Economies with small $\kappa$.*** The semireduced for expression for $P$ changes into

$$p = (1 + \tilde{v})^{-1}\{e + (\mu_0/\mu_e)g\},$$

where
$$\tilde{v} = \mu_\pi v_p/\mu_e.$$
Then the reduced form expression for $e$ becomes
$$e = \tilde{\rho}[\theta_1 m - f + \tilde{\gamma}(\mu_0/\mu_e)g],$$
where
$$\tilde{\gamma} = \sigma_1\phi_1\beta_p/(1+\tilde{v}) \quad\text{and}\quad \tilde{\rho} = (1-\tilde{\gamma})^{-1}.$$
From the above we see that
$$\delta p = \tilde{\rho}[\theta_1 \ -1]\,\delta\mathbf{z}.$$
The dynamic equation for $\delta\mathbf{z}$ is exactly as before; the parameter $v_p$ does not appear in the dynamics for $\delta\mathbf{z}$. Hence
$$\delta\dot{p} = \tilde{\rho}[\theta_1 \ -1]\,\delta\dot{\mathbf{z}} = \tilde{\rho}[\theta_1 \ -1]H\,\delta\mathbf{z} = 0.$$
We state this as

**Proposition.** Under regressive inflationary expectations, the inflation rate is independent of the parameter $\mu$ in economies with small $\kappa$.

**Economies with large $\kappa$.** From (19-2),
$$\delta\dot{p} = \delta\dot{w},$$
where

(43) $$\delta\dot{w} = -\mu w + (\mu - v_p)\rho[\theta_1 \ -1]\mathbf{z} + \mu\gamma_1 g$$

and $w$ and $\mathbf{z}$ are determined as the solution of the differential equations
$$\dot{w} = -v_p[\theta_1 \ -1]\mathbf{z} \quad\text{and}\quad \dot{\mathbf{z}} = \phi w + H\mathbf{z} + Jg.$$
Integrating these out and substituting them into (43), we obtain
$$\delta\dot{p} = \{-\mu,\ (\mu - v_p)\rho[\theta_1 \ -1]\}\left(S,\begin{bmatrix}0\\J\end{bmatrix}g\right) + \mu\gamma_1 g,$$
where the matrix $S(u)$ stands for
$$\exp\begin{bmatrix}0 & -v_p[\theta_1-1]\\ \phi & H\end{bmatrix}(u).$$

Immediately we see that a positive $\mu$ makes $\delta\dot{p}$ positive at least for small $t$. As time progresses, the path of $\delta\dot{p}$ depends on various other model parameters. The second term definitely increases the inflation rate of the variable wage rate economy more than that of the economy with rigid wage rate. There is a range of parameter values for which the contribution from this second term dominates that of the first.

## 11.5 Numerical Examples

Dynamics of this economy are mainly influenced by three sets of system parameters: The first set of parameters determine the "strength" of feedback couplings between the asset and the real sector which is captured by the magnitude of $\rho$ in (20). The larger $\rho$, the stronger the interactions between the asset and the real sectors; the second set of parameters are those in (28) and (33), affecting the dynamic behavior of the internal and external balances. They are $ms$ in (28) and $\Omega_1$ and $\Omega_2$ in (34); the third set contains $\mu$, $n$, and $i^*$.

Dynamic responses of some key endogenous variables are numerically calculated to illustrate how these system parameters affect dynamic behavior of this economy. Calculations are conducted by choosing portfolio parameters which produce $\theta_1 < 1$ in (11). We also keep $\chi$ at 0.7 in the definition of $P_1$ in (5), and $\kappa$ at 0.1 in (17) of all the numerical experiments. Influences of the feedbacks between the asset and the real sectors are examined by varying the value of $\rho$, i.e., by changing $\mu_e \rho_c$, while keeping all the other parameters the same. (Note that $\sigma_1 \phi_1$ in $\rho$ is determined as $1 - \theta_1$ once $\theta_1$ is chosen.) We also vary $ms$ in (28) and $\Omega s$ in (33). The balanced budget case corresponds to the value $m_1 = 0$. Positive $m_1$ corresponds to $ER$ being larger than $B_g$, i.e., net excess interest receipt by the domestic government finances the budget deficit if $i > n$. Negative values of $m_1$ result from $B_g$ being larger than $ER$.

### *Common Parameter Values*

The asset sector parameter: $\alpha = 0.3$, $\beta = 0.36$, $\gamma = 0.34$; $-(\alpha_1/\alpha)i = 0.06$, $(\beta_i/\beta)i = 0.07$, $-(\gamma_i/\gamma)i = 0.02$. These values produce $\theta_1 = 0.965$ and $\sigma_1 \phi_1 = 0.035$ in (11). We set

$n = 0.03$,   $i^* = 0.05$;

$\chi = 0.7$   in (5);   $\kappa = 0.1$   in (17);

$l_1 \simeq 0.3$   $l_2 \simeq 0.6$,   $l_3 \simeq 3$;   in (13);

$m_0 = 0.1$,   $m_2 = 0.02$,   $m_3 = (1 - \beta_p)\beta/\alpha = 0.24$   in (28);

$\mu_p = \mu_e$: static expectations,   $\hat{\mu}_p = 1.2\mu_p = 1.2\mu_e$: regressive expectations.

### *Variable Parameters*

In (28) we consider three subcases: From $n - m_1 = m_3 - m_4$, we set

(i) $m_1 = 0$; hence $m_4 = 0.21$;
(ii) $m_1 = 0.1$; hence $m_4 = 0.31$;
(iii) $m_1 = -0.1$; hence $m_4 = 0.11$.

In (20) we consider two possibilities:

(A) weak feedback case $\mu_e \hat{\rho}_c = 0.2$; hence $\rho \simeq 1.006$;
(B) strong feedback case $\mu_e \hat{\rho}_c = 0.6$; hence $\rho \simeq 1.019$.

Under static expectations, $\hat{\rho}_c = \rho_c$ and $\kappa\mu_y\hat{\rho}_c = 1 - \mu_e\rho_c$; that is, 0.8 and 0.4 for (A) and (B). Under regressive expectations, $\kappa\mu_y\hat{\rho}_c = 0.684$ in (A) and is 0.280 in (B).

In (34), we consider two categories:

(a) $\Omega_e/F = 2.93$ and $\Omega_y/F = 0.1$, producing $\Omega_1 = 3i^*$ and $\Omega_2 = 0.06i^*$;
(b) $\Omega_e/F = 9.7$ and $\Omega_y/F = 1$, producing $\Omega_1 = 10i^*$ and $\Omega_2 = 0.6i^*$.

We have in total $3 \times 2 \times 2 = 12$ cases, each of which can further be subdivided by the type of expectations used. Rather than discuss them all, we discuss three representative cases. Each case is specified by referring to these indices. For example, the case $(i, A, b)$, under static expectation, is a case with balanced budget, weak feedback, and large terms-of-trade effects on the balance of trade. The case $(i, B, b)$ is run with $\mu = 0.1$, $v_p = 0.15$ and with $\mu = 0.1$, $v_p = 0.09$.

In calculating the fiscal multiplier, we let $\mu_0$ in (16') equal $4\mu_e$ in all cases. In $(i, A, b)$, under static expectation, $\phi_{11} = 0.56$, $\phi_{21} = 0.0004$, $\phi_{31} = 0.399$, $\psi_1 = 0.443$, $\psi_2 = -0.212$, $\psi_3 = -0.402$, and $\omega = 0.022$.

The polynomial $q_1(\lambda)$ is $\lambda^2 + 0.664\lambda + 0.008$. Hence (34-4) is stable under static expectation, for $\mu = 0$. Because $q_2(\lambda)$ becomes $0.43\lambda^2 + 0.114\lambda - 0.002$, (34-4) is unstable for $\mu > 0$. We consider a regressive expectation with $\hat{\mu}_p = 1.2\mu_p$. Under $(i, A, b)$, $\phi_{11} = 0.479$, $\phi_{21} = 0.0004$, $\phi_{31} = 0.341$, $\psi_1 = 0.443$, $\psi_2 = -0.212$, $\psi_3 = -0.402$, and $\omega = 0.018$. The polynomial $q_1(\lambda)$ becomes $\lambda^2 + 0.617\lambda + 0.007$ and $q_3(\lambda)$ equals $0.487\lambda^2 + 0.447\lambda + 0.008$. The dynamics are stable only if $v_p > \mu - 7/8$; that is, even for some positive $\mu - v_p$, provided that $\dot{w}$ does not increase too rapidly with $p > 0$. With $(i, B, b)$, $\phi_{11} = 0.196$, $\phi_{21} = 0.0014$, $\phi_{31} = 0.138$, $\psi_1 = 0.734$, $\psi_2 = -0.215$, $\psi_3 = -0.202$, and $\omega_2 = 0.006$. The polynomials are $q_1(\lambda) = \lambda^2 + 0.420\lambda + 0.001$ and $q_3(\lambda) = 0.2\lambda^2 + 0.184\lambda + 0.003$. The dynamics are stable for all $\mu$, $v_p$ pairs satisfying the inequality $v_p \geq 2\mu/3$. We tabulate the dynamic responses for a temporary change in $G$:

$$g = \begin{cases} 1, & 0 \leq t \leq 0.1, \\ 0, & \text{otherwise.} \end{cases}$$

See Tables 1–3 for comparison of the time paths of $w$, $m$, $f$, $e$, and $p$ of the three cases.

## 11.5 Numerical Examples

### Table 1

*Static Expectation Case (i, A, b) with Balanced Budget, Weak Feedback, Large Terms-of-Trade Effects on Balance of Trade, for $\mu = 0^a$*

| t | w | m | f | p | y | e |
|---|---|---|---|---|---|---|
| 0.1 | 0 | 0.89 | −3.89 | 81.52 | 8.15 | 7.62 |
| 0.4 | 0 | 0.53 | −3.55 | 0.82 | 0.08 | 4.09 |
| 1.2 | 0 | 0.00 | −2.57 | 0.50 | 0.05 | 2.49 |
| 2.0 | 0 | −0.05 | −1.98 | 0.31 | 0.03 | 1.53 |
| 3.2 | 0 | −0.78 | −1.49 | 0.15 | 0.02 | 0.76 |
| 9.2 | 0 | −0.96 | −1.02 | 0.02 | 0.00 | 0.09 |

[a] All in %.

### Table 2

*Regressive Expectation Case (i, B, b) for $\mu = 0.1$, $v_p = 0.15^a$*

| t | w | m | f | e | y | p |
|---|---|---|---|---|---|---|
| 0.4 | −2.34 | 35.78 | −26.70 | 62.35 | 3.91 | 36.75 |
| 1.2 | −2.77 | 26.11 | −18.39 | 44.38 | 2.86 | 25.85 |
| 2.0 | −2.96 | 19.22 | −12.36 | 31.46 | 2.10 | 18.05 |
| 3.2 | −2.97 | 12.45 | −6.25 | 18.59 | 1.33 | 10.32 |
| 4.0 | −2.85 | 9.55 | −3.53 | 12.96 | 0.98 | 6.98 |
| 9.2 | −1.47 | 3.59 | 2.88 | 0.59 | 0.14 | 0.00 |
| 20. | 0.38 | 3.26 | 3.50 | −0.36 | 0.00 | −0.11 |
| 40. | 0.80 | 2.15 | 2.08 | 0.00 | 0.00 | 0.23 |

[a] All in %.

### Table 3

*Regressive Expectation Case (i, B, b) for $\mu = 0.1$, $v_p = 0.09^a$*

| t | w | m | f | e | y | p |
|---|---|---|---|---|---|---|
| 0.4 | −2.04 | 35.78 | −26.70 | 62.36 | 3.89 | 36.84 |
| 1.2 | −1.76 | 26.11 | −18.46 | 44.45 | 2.79 | 26.18 |
| 2.0 | −1.54 | 19.20 | −12.55 | 31.64 | 2.01 | 18.55 |
| 3.2 | −1.29 | 12.36 | −6.65 | 18.92 | 1.23 | 10.99 |
| 4.0 | −1.17 | 9.40 | −4.07 | 13.38 | 0.89 | 7.70 |
| 9.2 | −0.70 | 2.98 | 1.84 | 1.05 | 1.13 | 0.43 |
| 20. | −0.37 | 2.49 | 2.83 | −0.44 | 0.00 | −0.37 |
| 40. | −0.25 | 2.75 | 3.08 | −0.44 | 0.00 | −0.33 |

[a] All in %.

## 11.6 Elaborations

### 11.6.1 Wealth Effects

Adding a scale variable $PY/A$ as an additional argument of the asset demand functions in (1) does not modify (12) substantially. Coefficients in (11) are slightly modified by the presence of this scale variable. No new variables are introduced into (11), however.

Adding wealth as an additional argument in the specification of the consumption function (3) produces two kinds of changes in the previous analysis. To the right-hand side of (16), we must now add $\mu_f f + \mu_b b_g + \mu_m m$; i.e., relative variations of the asset stocks, $f$, $b_g$, and $m$, now appear in the equilibrium equation for the real sector. The magnitudes of these coefficients depend on the wealth elasticity of the consumption, for example, $\mu_b = d_4 \beta (1 - \beta_p)/(1 - d_4 \beta \beta_p h)$, where $d_4 = C_3(A/P_1)/d$, and where $C_3$ is the wealth elasticity of consumption.

Subsequent analysis remains the same if we reinterpret $\zeta$ in (16′) to equal $\mu_0 g + \mu_\pi \delta\pi + \mu_f f + \mu_b b_g + \mu_m m$. Because $p$ and $y$ now additionally depends on $b_g$, as we can see from (19), this additional source of dependence introduces additional dynamic coupling between two sets of variables, $\{b_g, r\}$ and $\{w, m, f\}$. The net effect is to add a dyad

$$\mu_b \rho_c (1 - \gamma\mu_e) \begin{bmatrix} \mu\chi \\ m_1 - \kappa m_2 \\ -\Omega_1 + \kappa\Omega_2 \end{bmatrix} \begin{bmatrix} 1 & 0 \end{bmatrix}$$

in the dynamics (27) as the coupling term of $\{b_g, r\}$ on $\{w, m, f\}$. This additional source of dynamic coupling does not affect the fiscal policy multiplier. They do affect the policy multipliers of $b_g$ and $r$, however.

### 11.6.2 Expectations

#### Regressive Expectations on Exchange Rate Changes

Previously, we examined the consequence of a regressive expectations mechanism for $\delta\pi$. We can equally discuss a regressive expectation mechanism $\delta\varepsilon = -v_e e$ as a stabilizing element of dynamics. This also introduces two effects. A regressive scheme $\delta\varepsilon = -v_e e$ reduces by $(1 + v_e \theta_\varepsilon)^{-1}$ the coefficients in the variational equation for $e$, i.e.

$$e = \{\theta_1 - f + (1 - \theta_1)(1 - \beta_p)b_g + \beta_p \sigma_1 \phi_1(p + hy)\}/(1 + v_e \theta_\varepsilon).$$

Therefore, by redefining $\rho$ as

$$\rho^{-1} = 1 + v_e \theta_\varepsilon - \sigma_1 \phi_1 \beta_p (1 + h\kappa)\mu_e \rho_c,$$

## 11.6 Elaborations

the equations following (19) remain valid. The coefficient $v_e$ tends to reduce the effects of feedback.

More important for stabilization is the effect introduced by $\delta\pi_i = -(1 - \chi)v_e e$. The matrix $\Phi$ in (34-4) is modified into

$$\Phi = \begin{bmatrix} -\mu(1 - \phi_{11}) & 0 & 0 \\ \phi_{21} & -n & 0 \\ -\phi_{31} & 0 & -n + i^* \end{bmatrix} + \begin{bmatrix} \mu\psi_1 - v_e(1 - \chi) \\ \psi_2 \\ -\psi_3 \end{bmatrix} [\omega \quad \theta_1 \quad -1].$$

### Nonstatic Expectations

Under perfect foresight, $\delta\pi$ equals $\dot{p}$ and $\delta\varepsilon$ equals $\dot{e}$. When $\delta\pi$ and $\delta\varepsilon$ are replaced by $\dot{p}$ and $\dot{e}$, respectively, in (34), we derive the dynamic equation of the model under perfect foresight. Alternatively we may approximately assume that

$$\delta\varepsilon = \tilde{\varepsilon}_1 w - \tilde{\varepsilon}_2 m - \tilde{\varepsilon}_3 f + \tilde{\varepsilon}_0 g \quad \text{and} \quad \delta\pi = v_w w + v_m m + v_f f + v_g g$$

can serve as expectations equations for suitably chosen coefficients. The magnitudes of these coefficients determine how strongly the dynamics are affected by the expectational variables. See the numerical experiments for some indications.

### 11.6.3 Asset Sector Respecifications

The set of asset demand equations as given in (1) is a simplification of a more complex set of portfolio balance equations such as

$$M/P_1 = L(i, i^* + \varepsilon, Y', A/P_1),$$
$$V/(iP_1) = H(i, i^* + \varepsilon, Y', A/P_1),$$
$$EF/(i^*P_1) = J(i, i^* + \varepsilon, Y', A/P_1).$$

In this form, $L$, $H$ and, $J$ depend on $E$ through $A/P_1$ even if $F$ is zero.

If we assume that the asset demand functions are homogeneous of degree one in real wealth and if $Y'$ is approximated by $PY/P_1$, then we have $L(i, i^* + \varepsilon, Y', A/P_1) = L(i, i^* + \varepsilon, PY/A)A/P_1$, etc. [see Girton and Henderson (1973)].

### 11.6.4 Effects of $\delta i$ Terms

When the $\delta i$ term is retained in (16'), the reduced form expressions of $e$, $p$, and $y$ given by (20) become more complex. Feedbacks between the asset and the real sector now amplify the effects of $m$ and $f$ on $e$ not with the common factor $\rho$, but with different magnification factors, for example.

With the $\delta i$ term included, (19) is modified into

$$(19') \qquad \begin{bmatrix} p \\ y \end{bmatrix} = \begin{bmatrix} \mu_y \\ -\mu_e \end{bmatrix} \kappa \rho_c w + \begin{bmatrix} 1 \\ \kappa \end{bmatrix} (\mu_e e - \mu_i \, \delta i + \zeta) \rho_c.$$

To show the exact expressions, we rederive (20) using (12) and (16) rather than (12) and (16′) on the assumption that expectations are static. The reduced form expressions result by solving a set of simultaneous equations for $\delta i$, $e$, $p$, and $y$:

$$\begin{bmatrix} I & S \\ T & I \end{bmatrix} \begin{bmatrix} \delta i \\ e \\ p \\ y \end{bmatrix} = \begin{bmatrix} \begin{bmatrix} -\sigma_1 \\ \theta_1 \end{bmatrix} m - \begin{bmatrix} 0 \\ 1 \end{bmatrix} f + (1 - \beta_p) \begin{bmatrix} \sigma \\ 1 - \theta_1 \end{bmatrix} b_g \\ \begin{bmatrix} \mu_y \\ -\mu_e \end{bmatrix} \kappa \rho_c w + \rho_c \begin{bmatrix} 1 \\ \kappa \end{bmatrix} \zeta \end{bmatrix},$$

where

$$S = -\sigma_1 \beta_p \begin{bmatrix} 1 \\ \theta_1 \end{bmatrix} [1 \quad h], \quad T = \rho_c \begin{bmatrix} 1 \\ \kappa \end{bmatrix} [\mu_y \quad -\mu_e].$$

To invert the matrix on the left, note that

$$\begin{bmatrix} I & S \\ T & I \end{bmatrix}^{-1} = \begin{bmatrix} C_{11} & C_{12} \\ C_{21} & C_{22} \end{bmatrix},$$

where

$$C_{11} = I - \tilde{\rho} \sigma_1 \beta_p \rho_c (1 + \kappa h) \begin{bmatrix} 1 \\ \phi_1 \end{bmatrix} [\mu_i \quad -\mu_e],$$

$$C_{12} = \tilde{\rho} \sigma_1 \beta_p \begin{bmatrix} 1 \\ \phi_1 \end{bmatrix} [1 \quad h],$$

$$C_{21} = -\tilde{\rho} \rho_c \begin{bmatrix} 1 \\ \kappa \end{bmatrix} [\mu_i \quad -\mu_e],$$

$$C_{22} = I - \tilde{\rho} \sigma_1 \beta_p \rho_c (\mu_i - \mu_e \phi_1) \begin{bmatrix} 1 \\ \kappa \end{bmatrix} [1 \quad h],$$

and

$$\tilde{\rho} = (1 - \tilde{\Delta})^{-1} \quad \text{with} \quad \tilde{\Delta} = \sigma_1 \beta_p \rho_c (1 + \kappa h)(\mu_e \phi_1 - \mu_i).$$

*Appendix The Variational Disposable Income Expression*

For example, the reduced form $e$ is given by

$$e = \tilde{\rho}[[\{1 + \sigma_1\beta_p\rho_c(1 + \kappa h)\mu_i\}\theta_1 + \sigma_1\beta_p\rho_c(1 + \kappa h)\mu_i\sigma_1\phi_1]m$$
$$- \{1 + \sigma_1\beta_p\rho_c(1 + \kappa h)\mu_i\}f + (1 - \beta_p)(1 - \theta_1)\{1 + \sigma_1\beta_p\rho_c$$
$$\times (1 + \kappa h)\mu_i\}b_g + \sigma_1\beta_p\phi_1\rho_c\{(\mu_y - \mu_e h)\kappa w + (1 + \kappa h)\zeta\}].$$

The expressions for $p$ and $y$ are similarly obtained.

We conclude that the inclusion of the $\delta i$ effects does not introduce any new transmission mechanism, although the coefficients in the dynamic matrix $\Phi$ of (35) become slightly different.

## Appendix  The Variational Disposable Income Expression

The disposable income is given by (5). Taking variation of (5), the exact expression for the variation of the disposable income is given by

$$y' = l_p P - l_e e + l_y y - l_\pi \delta\pi - l_K k - l_m m + l_b b_g + l_F f - l_\varepsilon \delta\varepsilon + l_i \delta i/i,$$

where

$$P_I Y' l_p = (1 - \chi)P(Y - \lambda K - T) - \chi\{Bg + EF - W\pi_i + \varepsilon EF/i^*\},$$
$$P_I Y' l_e = -P_I Y' l_p - B_g + (M + Bg/i)\pi_i,$$
$$P_I Y' l_y = P(Y - \tau T),\ P_I Y' l_\pi = \chi W,\ P_I Y' l_K = \lambda PK,$$
$$P_I Y' l_m = M\pi_i,$$
$$P_I Y' l_b = B_g(1 - \pi_i/i),\ P_I Y' l_F = EF(1 - \pi_i/i^* + \varepsilon/i^*),$$
$$P_I Y' l_i = \pi_i B_g/i.$$

When we neglect the interest receipt term, $Bg + EF$, loss of wealth due to inflation, $W\pi_i$, and the expected increase in the value of the foreign asset due to $\varepsilon$, $\varepsilon EF/i^*$, $l_p$ is approximated by $l_1$ in (13). To the same order of approximation, $l_e \approx l_p \approx l_1$, $l_m \approx 0$, $l_b \approx 0$, $l_F \approx 0$, and $l_i \approx 0$. Furthermore, $l_K \approx 0$ if capital stock depreciation is neglected compared with $P_I Y'$.

# Part Three | Multiple-Country Models of the World

Economies tied together through trade in goods and financial assets are interdependent. States of the domestic economy and decisions of the domestic policy maker affect not only the domestic economy but foreign economies as well. Conversely, the state of the domestic economy is influenced by states of the foreign economies and by actions of foreign policy makers. In other words, feedback effects generally exist among countries; i.e., changes in an economy will induce the rest of the world to change in response, and these induced changes in the rest of the world will further affect the original economy. These feedback effects may be reinforcing or in the opposite direction of the original change; feedback effects may be felt in markets other than the ones in which the initial changes or disturbances have originated.

Analysis of a small open economy treats the rest of the world as exogenous, hence, ignores feedback effects. Because feedback effects are important in assessing macroeconomic policy in many open economies, the rest of the world must be endogenized to properly account for interactions among countries. We are thus led to study world models composed of at least two countries.

In this part of the book, we drop the small country assumption, maintained in Part Two, and squarely face the problems of analyzing dynamic interdependence of national economies and instruments of national governments. Some of the techniques introduced in Part One are applied to several two- and three-country models of the world under flexible exchange rate regimes to study dynamic interdependence and cross-country dynamic policy multipliers. This introduction concludes with a brief and selective summary of recent works on interdependence and a brief description of our methods of analysis since we use some novel analytical methods to lighten our task.

Emphasis of our analysis also differs from the literature: We pay more attention to distributional aspects of national policies in the world and to implications of national characteristic differences on policy effectiveness or policy coordination questions. Chapter 12 provides simplified introductions to two aspects of analysis of two-country models as preparations for their more complete treatments later on. The first aspect deals with implications of national structural characteristic differences and is illustrated by a simple two-country model due to Henderson (1978) who used it to examine the effects of fiscal instruments of the two governments. We use this model to serve a different purpose of motivating and illustrating our structural sensitivity analysis procedure to be applied to more completely specified models later in this part of the book. With this simple model I make an important and general observation that dynamic transmission paths are eliminated or substantially modified in symmetrically specified models because of symmetry. That such symmetry may seriously limit analyses of dynamic interdependence is simply illustrated by our analysis of this model. For example, if two economies have the same propensity to consume out of the marginal increase in bond holding, then past history of the fiscal instruments of the two countries has no effect on the current exchange rate deviation. Exchange rate deviations are determined solely by the current deviations of the fiscal instruments of the two countries. Put differently, the relations among these variables become static, rather than dynamic, because past values of the instruments do not matter. I explicitly warn against overspecialized results obtainable from such symmetric specifications. The second aspect mentioned in Chapter 12, the distributional effects of policies, is taken up in Chapter 13 and 15.

In Chapter 13, we analyze a two-country model which is more fully specified than the one in Chapter 12. The collapse of some dynamic relations to static relations, as we point out in Chapter 12, persists in this model as well when two countries are symmetrically specified. The consequences of national characteristic differences in several markets are then examined and their policy implications derived. In Chapter 14, we assume that one country's currency serves as key currency in the world, thus breaking symmetrical treatment of two countries by imposing nonidentical asset holding specifications on the model. Chapter 15 is devoted to a three-country model. This model is used to consider some distributional questions not possible with earlier two-country models. For example, we show how differences in national characteristics interact with different values of national monetary instruments to determine worldwide distribution of real gains and losses among the three countries. Here as well as in Chapter 13, our variational and sensitivity analysis methods are crucial in simplifying otherwise messy analytical details.

## Some Previous Works on Interdependence and Distributions

Dynamic interactions among $n$ economic agents or countries, or distributional questions have been extensively analyzed in the economic literature. In the early 1950s, Metzler showed interdependence of incomes of $n$ regions or countries and demonstrated how exogenous disturbances, such as income transfer between two countries, affect not only these two countries but also the rest of the countries in the model as well (Metzler, 1950, 1951). He assumed fixed production capacities, prices, and costs and allowed only incomes and employments to vary. In a related two-country model of the world, he allowed the exchange rate to be flexible in addition to the incomes and employements, while assuming that wages and costs are fixed (Laursen and Metzler, 1950). Nothing much happened after Metzler's seminal work until Cooper (1968) considered interdependence through trade and financial flows due to interest rate differences. Several writers since have attempted analysis of interdependence: Roper (1971) focused on interlinkage of money stocks in the world as a source of interactions under a fixed exchange rate regime. De Grauwe (1975) examined the interaction of monetary policies of several countries via reserve flows. His model is composed of only the financial sectors of the countries, however, and is not of the general equilibrium framework. [De Grauwe's model has been also analyzed by Aoki (1977).] Aoki considered a stock-flow model of $n$ agents in Aoki (1976, Section 7.2).[1]

Restricting our attention to more recent analytical general equilibrium models, we find few explicitly specified three-country models.[2] There are several two-country models, for example, Dornbusch (1976), Henderson (1978a), and Phelps (1978). Dornbusch (1976) developed a two-country model with flexible exchange rates and capital mobility. He assumes full employment and price flexibility. In his model, there is one type of internationally traded bond, and the money of each country is a nontraded asset. There is only one traded good and the purchasing power parity is imposed. His model contains a wealth-saving relationship as well as portfolio balance behavior. There is a desired level of real wealth in each country and a saving function is hypothesized which partially closes the gap between the actual and desired level of wealth. There is no explicit account of growing capital nor investment. Although he explicitly recognizes the government budget constraint, his discussion of the dynamic implication of the budget constraint is incomplete. We shall discuss models similar to that of Dornbusch, paying more attention to the dynamic consequences and dropping the assumption of the purchasing power parity relation. A simple two-country Keynesian

---

[1] This model is unusual because of the dynamics which do not stay the same but change as the patterns of excess demands and supplies change among the agents as time progresses.

[2] See Marston (1980) and Krugman (1980), however.

model with one good and two monies has been outlined by Henderson (1978) to analyze effects of fiscal shocks in open economies. In his analysis. he takes the output of each country to be maintained at full employment level. Henderson does not analyze dynamic behavior of the model but focuses his analysis on the momentary and long-run equilibrium. Fiscal shocks propagate through the system via changes in the interest rates and the output price levels.

The problem of distributions of financial assets and capital stocks arises in a model containing two or more countries. For example, the distribution of the world money stock was discussed under the fixed exchange rate regime by Roper (1971). In a flexible exchange rate regime, several definitions of the world stocks of financial assets can be made in terms of generalized purchasing power as is done in Kouri and Macedo (1978). In Dornbusch's two-country model, a fixed world stock of permanent real income streams (a fixed number of real income claims) is to be divided between the two countries to simplify analysis. Policy effects on distributions have not received much analytical attention either.[3]

Argy and Salop (1979) stress the importance of the specification of the labor market in effectiveness of monetary and fiscal policies in a two-country world model. They use two benchmark assumptions about the degree of wage indexation or money illusion in two-country models; constant real wage rates and constant nominal wage rates. They show that (i) with rigid real wages in the expanding country, monetary expansion has no real effects in either country; (ii) with money illusion in the expanding country, and constant real wage in the other country, both countries outputs expand with the larger output increase occurring in the expanding country; and (iii) under similar circumstances, fiscal expansion may cause its partner's output to fall. They suggest that the most successful cases as well as those least likely to create conflict between countries and retaliation are: monetary expansion by the country with the lesser degree of wage indexation and fiscal expansion by the country with the greater degree of wage indexation. Their conclusions and recommendations are based on largely static analysis, however.

In Chapter 13, we analyze distributional effects of monetary expansions in one or both countries of a two-country model of the world with variable wages and output prices. (The wage rate equation we use can encompass constant nominal wage rates and constant expected real wage rates as extreme cases. Argy and Salop's model does not contain any expectational variables.) Our dynamic analysis reveals that expressions and conditions for output

---

[3] See Johnson and Salop (1980) and the references they cite for examples of nonanalytical discussions of some aspects of distributional questions.

increases that result from monetary expansion by one or both of the two governments are more involved and contain cumulative effects of past monetary instruments.

## *Variational and Structural Perturbation Methods for Multiple-Country Models*

Although the models that we analyze in this part of the book tend to be more fully specified than the ones used by the previous writers because the models incorporate some features not found in these previous models, our claim of novelty and the usefulness of our analysis lies elsewhere and not in the models we employ to illustrate our analysis. We significantly differ from the previous writers in our mode of analysis: We use variational and structural sensitivity or perturbations analysis procedures. These procedures enable us to treat models too complex or too messy to be analyzed by the usual approach. Because of our methods, we can narrow the gap between the small analytical models and large econometric models by analyzing models that do not leave out some important features just for analytical convenience.

Put briefly, our procedure is the following: We first posit a benchmark or reference model of the world, e.g., a world composed of countries with identical "key" characteristics. Then we analyze models with different characteristics by treating the differences as structural perturbation on the reference model. This amounts to applying the variational analysis, not by examining neighboring time paths of some reference time path as we have done so far in this book, but by applying the variational analysis to models related to the reference model by structural perturbation. This distinction may be clarified by introducing the following notations. Denote the reference model by $\mathcal{M}_0$. Let $\mathcal{M}$ denote a model related to $\mathcal{M}_0$ by some structural changes. Let $\mathcal{VM}_0$ be the variational dynamic model of $\mathcal{M}_0$; i.e., $\mathcal{VM}_0$ describes deviations of $\mathcal{M}_0$ from its reference (trend) path or stationary equilibrium states as the case may be. Thus $\mathcal{VM}_0$ is a (detrended) log-linear model as we have commented on in Section 2.3. The model $\mathcal{VM}$ is similarly defined. We analyze $\mathcal{VM}$ via our analysis of $\mathcal{VM}_0$ plus analysis of differences between the two variational models. We thus apply the variational approach twice: once to generate $\mathcal{VM}$ and $\mathcal{VM}_0$ from $\mathcal{M}$ and $\mathcal{M}_0$, respectively (or more conveniently $\mathcal{VM}_0$ may be generated from $\mathcal{VM}$ by specializing the latter to some standard or reference case), and once more to perform comparative dynamics on $\mathcal{VM}$, comparing its dynamic behavior with that of $\mathcal{VM}_0$.[4]

---

[4] Since the models $\mathcal{VM}$ and $\mathcal{VM}_0$ are log-linearly specified, such comparison can be conducted without error. This corresponds to the large parameter sensitivity analysis of Section 2.4.

In this way, we can better highlight natures of policy interdependence. Chapters 13 and 15 illustrate our approach. Before we launch into our analysis in full, we provide preliminary illustration of the notion of the reference model and its use in structural perturbation or sensitivity analysis in Chapter 12.

# 12 | Two-Country Model: A Preliminary Analysis

In Chapter 12 we analyze two benchmark models as a preliminary to the more detailed analysis in Chapters 13–15, so that we can more straightforwardly draw implications of structural characteristic differences and implications of wage rate dynamics on the distributional effects of monetary policy changes in a two-country model of the world. Each of these two aspects is later re-examined using considerably more elaborate models than the benchmark models of this chapter.

## 12.1 Implications of Structural Differences

One of the purposes of this chapter is to demonstrate that the policy effects in a world model rather sensitively depend on assumed values of model parameters by a simple two-country model. At the same time, we indicate how to address structural sensitivity question by using $\mathscr{VM}$ and $\mathscr{VM}_0$ mentioned at the end of the introduction to Part Three.

Henderson (1978) used a simple two-country model to illustrate workings of the fiscal instruments of the two governments under flexible exchange rate. We use his model to show the existence of a general phenomenon that some of the dynamic relations of world models collapse to static ones, i.e., some of the dynamic transmission or linkage mechanisms between the two countries disappear if some "key" parameters of the models happen to be the same in the countries involved. In Henderson's model, if certain consumption elasticities [$\gamma_2$ in (11) below] happen to be the same in the two countries (this defines the reference model), then all deviations of prices (interest rates, output prices, and the exchange rate) from their equilibrium values depend only on the current value of the sum of the two fiscal instruments. Their past values do not influence the deviations at all. Past histories become relevant only in the nonreference models and in the form of time integrals of past differences of the two fiscal instruments.

This chapter will motivate our more detailed discussions in the later chapters where implications of model construction and relations between the reference variational model $\mathscr{VM}_0$ and its structurally perturbed version $\mathscr{VM}$ are discussed. The collapse of some dynamic relations to static ones has important implications on analytical or simulation studies of interdependence by models with countries with same or similar characteristics in some sectors of economies.

It is important to realize that this pehomenon of (unintended) elimination of dynamic linkages is not limited to Henderson's model but is more general.

The models of this chapter do not contain explicit labor markets. More recent literature on wage rate indexation explicitly deals with wage rate changes. Our later analysis in Chapters 13-15 will include labor markets. In all these modified models, the same phenomenon exists: Some dynamics still collapse to static relations under some simple conditions.

### 12.1.1 The Model $\mathscr{M}$

In this section, we treat the real outputs as fixed at $\overline{Y}$ and $\overline{Y}^*$. To focus on the effects of the fiscal policy, stocks of monies in the two countries are also assumed constant at $\overline{M}$ and $\overline{M}^*$, respectively. There are two financial assets, money and bonds, in each country. Each country produces the same world good. We model government securities as perpetuities, each security paying one unit of the world good per period.[1] Therefore, we assume that the two government securities are perfect substitutes. Monies are assumed to be nontraded. In the home country, the demand function for real balances is given by

(1) $$\overline{M}/P = L(\overline{Y}, i).$$

The demand for bonds is residually determined and not explicitly modeled. The disposable income is $\overline{Y} + B - T$, where $T$ is real tax receipt and $B$ is the number of the securities held by the domestic private sector. The expenditure is assumed to depend on the real wealth $M/P + B/i$, where $B/i$ is the present

---

[1] Henderson (1979) also examines the consequences of assuming that securities are nontraded assets. Since securities of the two governments pay the same world good, Henderson attributes the unwillingness of residents of each country to hold foreign securities to risk averseness, i.e., residents must regard foreign securities to be more unreliable. (Even when the residents hold the opinion that the foreign government is more unreliable, some degree of portfolio diversification generally occurs. For now, we merely assume that securities of both governments are perfect substitutes.)

## 12.1 Implications of Structural Differences

discounted real value of the government security holding by the domestic private sector, since zero inflation is expected in this model. The balanced budget condition is expressible as

$$G + \bar{B}_g = T,$$

where $\bar{B}_g$ is the interest payments by the home government. The number of the home government bonds is constant by assumption of the balanced budget. The balance of trade is equal to[2]

(2) $\qquad B_T = \bar{Y} - C(\bar{Y} + B - T, i, \bar{M}/P + B/i) - G.$

A set of similar equations holds for the foreign country:

(3) $\qquad \bar{M}^*/P^* = L^*(\bar{Y}^*, i^*),$

(4) $\qquad G^* + \bar{B}_g^* = T^*,$

(5) $\qquad B_T^* = \bar{Y}^* - C^*(\bar{Y}^* + B^* - T^*, i^*, \bar{M}^*/P^* + B^*/i^*) - G^*.$

The two countries are tied together by the world markets for the good and the securities. These conditions are stated as the interest rate parity condition

$$i = i^*,$$

where zero expectations on the exchange rate changes are assumed, and the good arbitrage condition, assuming zero transportation cost of goods,

(6) $\qquad\qquad P = EP^*.$

The momentary market clearing conditions are

(7) $\qquad\qquad B + B^* = \bar{B}_g + \bar{B}_g^*$

in the security market, where the right-hand side gives the total supply of the bonds, and

(8) $\qquad\qquad B_T = -B_T^*$

in the good market.

We use (7) to express $B^*$ as a function of $B$. The foreign disposable income then can be written as $Y^* + \bar{B}_g^* - B - G^*$. Since the money stock is constant, the asset accumulation by the home country is equal to $\dot{B}$, which is the excess of disposable income over expenditure

$$\dot{B} = \bar{Y} + B - T - C.$$

---

[2] Here we follow Henderson and assume that consumption negatively depends on the interest rate $i$.

Using the government budget condition to substitute out $T$, we write this equation as

(9)  $$\dot{B} = \bar{Y} - C - G + B - \bar{B}_g = B_T + (B - \bar{B}_g),$$

where the second term is the net interest receipt of the home country, i.e., $\dot{B}$ is equal to the current account. Saving in the home country is $\bar{Y} + B - T - C$ which is equal to $B_T + (B - \bar{B}_g)$.

In the long-run equilibrium, $\dot{B}$ is zero. From (9), the long-run equilibrium condition is given by $B_T + (B - \bar{B}_g) = 0$. This equation, (7), and (8) yield $B_T^* = B - \bar{B}_g = -(B^* - \bar{B}_g^*)$ or $B_T^* + (B^* - \bar{B}_g^*) = 0$, i.e., the saving is zero in the foreign country. (Note that we assume investment is zero since we do not treat capital growth.)

The long-run equilibrium is characterized by the two zero saving conditions

$$\bar{Y} + B - \bar{B}_g - C - G = 0, \quad \bar{Y}^* + B^* - \bar{B}_g^* - C^* - G^* = 0$$

and two equilibrium conditions of the money demand functions

$$\bar{M}/P = L(\bar{Y}, i), \quad \bar{M}^*/P^* = L^*(\bar{Y}^*, i),$$

and the purchasing power parity condition (6).

These five equations determine the long-run values of $B$, $P$, $E$, $P^*$, and $i$ for fixed levels of $\bar{G}$ and $\bar{G}^*$.

### 12.1.2 Variational Model

When $G$ is changed by $\delta G$ over some time interval, the economy's momentary equilibrium state shifts. We use variational equations to show that increases in either $G$ or $G^*$ create an excess demand for the good which can be removed only by a rise in $i$. Because of the constant money stocks in the two countries and fixed outputs, a rise in the interest rate causes $P$ and $P^*$ to rise as well. An increase in $G$ or $G^*$ has inflationary effects in both countries.

From variation of (1) and (3), deviations in the interest rate and prices are related by

(10)  $$p = -(L_i/L)\,\delta i$$

and

(10′)  $$p^* = -(L_i^*/L^*)\,\delta i.$$

Utilizing the above relations, the variation of the balance of trade is expressible as

(11)  $$\delta B_T = -\gamma_0\,\delta G + \gamma_1\,\delta i - \gamma_2\,\delta B,$$

## 12.1 Implications of Structural Differences

where

$$\gamma_0 = 1 - C_1 > 0, \qquad \gamma_1 = -C_2 + C_3\{b/i^2 + (\overline{M}/P)(-L_i/L)\} > 0,$$
$$\gamma_2 = C_1 + C_3/i > 0.$$

Then the variation of the momentary equilibrium condition in the goods market can be solved for the deviation of the interest rate.[3]

(12) $$\delta i = (\gamma_1 + \gamma_1^*)^{-1}\{(\gamma_2 - \gamma_2^*)\,\delta B + \gamma_0\,\delta G + \gamma_0^*\,\delta G^*\},$$

where $\gamma_i^*$, $i = 1, 2, 3$ are defined analogously to $\gamma$s.

Variation of the current account equation (9) yields the differential equation for deviation of the number of the bonds held in the domestic private sector. From (9) and (11),

(13) $$\delta \dot{B} = -\gamma_0\,\delta G + \gamma_1\,\delta i + (1 - \gamma_2)\,\delta B.$$

The deviation $\delta B$ affects real saving via its effects on the disposable income and the real wealth effect, we assume that $1 - C_1 < C_3/i$; i.e., the latter effect dominates the former. Substituting out the deviation of the interest rate in (12) and (13), the state-space representation of the differential equation for $\delta B$ becomes

(14) $$\delta \dot{B} = (1 - \beta_1)\,\delta B - \beta_0\,\delta G + \beta_0^*\,\delta G^*,$$

where

$$\beta_0^* = \gamma_0\gamma_1^*(\gamma_1 + \gamma_1^*)^{-1}, \qquad \beta_0^* = \gamma_0^*\gamma_1(\gamma_1 + \gamma_1^*)^{-1},$$
$$\beta_1 = (\gamma_1^*\gamma_2 + \gamma_1\gamma_2^*)(\gamma_1 + \gamma_1^*)^{-1}.$$

### 12.1.3 Benchmark Model $\mathcal{VM}_0$

Equations (10), (10′), (11), (12), and (14) together with

(15) $$e = p - p^*, \qquad \delta i^* = \delta i,$$

constitute the (variational) two-country model of the world, $\mathcal{VM}$.

Although this model is simple enough to be analyzed by itself, we define the reference variational model $\mathcal{VM}_0$ and analyze $\mathcal{VM}$ as structural perturbation on $\mathcal{VM}_0$ to illustrate our general procedure.

---
[3] Note that $\delta i$ depends on both $\delta G$ and $\delta G^*$.

We define the benchmark or reference model to be the one in which gammas in (11) are the same in the two countries. The benchmark model $\mathscr{V}\mathscr{M}_0$ thus consists of the following structural equations:

(10*) $\qquad p = -(L_i/L)\,\delta i, \qquad p^* = -(L_i^*/L^*)\,\delta i,$

(11*) $\qquad \delta B_T = -\gamma_2\,\delta B - (\gamma_0/2)(\delta G - \delta G^*),$

(12*) $\qquad \delta i = \delta i^* = (\gamma_0/2\gamma_1)(\delta G + \delta G^*),$

(13*) $\qquad \delta \dot{B} = (1 - \gamma_2)\,\delta B - (\gamma_0/2)(\delta G - \delta G^*),$

(15*) $\qquad e = (-L_i/L + L_i^*/L^*)(\gamma_0/\gamma_1)(\delta G + \delta G^*).$[4]

Note in particular that the state variable $\delta B$ appears only in the variational balance-of-trade expression (11*). All other variables are determined by the sum of the current values of the fiscal instruments; past histories of their values do not matter in the expressions for variational interest rates, (12*), and hence in output prices, (10*), and exchange rate, (15*).

### 12.1.4 Implications of Model Differences

Past histories of the fiscal instruments of the two governments affect the interest rate, prices, and the exchange rate when we leave the benchmark model and assume that the gammas in (11) are different in the two countries. The past histories of the instruments enter, however, only as time integrals of difference as shall be shown below. The current values of the instruments enter as a sum. We next turn to demonstrate these facts. To provide an algebraically simple demonstration, suppose that $\mathscr{V}\mathscr{M}$ is such that the parameters $\gamma_2$ and $\gamma_2^*$ are unequal but all other $\gamma$s are equal to the corresponding $\gamma^*$s. Denote the variables of $\mathscr{V}\mathscr{M}_0$ by superscript zero. From (6), (10), and (10*), the reduced form expression for the deviation of the exchange rate is

(16) $\quad e = p - p^*$
$\qquad = (-L_i/L + L_i^*/L^*)(\gamma_1 + \gamma_1^*)^{-1}\{(\gamma_2 - \gamma_2^*)\,\delta B + \gamma_0\,\delta G + \gamma_0^*\,\delta G^*\}.$

Noting that $\gamma_0$ and $\gamma_1$ are equal to their respective counterparts with superscript *, (16) can be expressed as

$$e = e^0 + (-L_i/L + L_i^*/L)(\gamma_2 - \gamma_2^*)\,\delta B/2\gamma_1.$$

Since $\delta B$ is determined by past history of the fiscal instruments as can be seen from (14), the exchange rate deviations in $\mathscr{V}\mathscr{M}$ now reflect past values of the

---

[4] If we additionally assume that the interest elasticities of demands for real balances are the same in the two countries, then the exchange rate deviations remain at zero at all times.

## 12.1 Implications of Structural Differences

fiscal instruments and not just their current values. This dependence on past fiscal values can be made explicit by substituting the solution of (14) and (16)

$$e(t) = (-L_i/L + L_i^*/L^*)(2\gamma_1)^{-1}\gamma_0\{\delta G(t) + \delta G^*(t)\}$$
$$- (L_i/L + L_i^*/L^*)(\gamma_2 - \gamma_2^*)(2\gamma_1)^{-1}e^{(1-\beta_1)t}$$
$$\times \int_0^t e^{-(1-\beta_1)\tau}\beta_0\{\delta G(\tau) - \delta G^*(\tau)\}\,d\tau.$$

Therefore, even after $\delta G$ or $\delta G^*$ is zero, there will be the residual effects represented by the second term if $\gamma_2 \neq \gamma_2^*$. To illustrate, suppose that the difference of the two instruments is given by a nonzero constant, over a time interval from zero to $s$, and is zero otherwise. Then, at any time $t$ greater than $s$, the exchange rate deviation of the reference variational mode $\mathscr{VM}_0$ is zero, but the same variable of the model $\mathscr{VM}$ is nonzero and is given by

$$e(t) = \text{const}\, \exp[(1-\beta_1)t].$$

Except for the coefficients, the other variables, such as $\delta i - \delta i^0$ and $p - p^0$, behave exactly like the difference of the exchange rate deviations between the two models $\mathscr{VM}_0$ and $\mathscr{VM}$.

Comparing (13) with (13*), or equivalently with (14), we see that the difference of the variational variable of $B$ between $\mathscr{VM}$ and $\mathscr{VM}_0$, i.e., $\delta B - \delta B^0$, is governed by the differential equation

(17) $\quad \delta\dot{B} - \delta\dot{B}^0 = (1 - \beta_1)(\delta B - \delta B^0) + (\gamma_2 - \beta_1)\delta B^0,$

where the expression $\gamma_2 - \beta_1$ equals $(\gamma_2 - \gamma_2^*)\gamma_1(\gamma_1 + \gamma_1^*)^{-1}$.

Equation (17) is exact, involving no approximation. Since $\delta B^0$ is governed by (13*), it depends on the time integral of the difference of the two instruments, $\delta G - \delta G^*$.

Define the difference of $\delta B$ and $\delta B^0$ as $z$. Noting that its initial condition is zero because the initial conditions of $\delta B$ and $\delta B^0$ are the same, $z(t)$ depends on some time integral of past history of $\delta G - \delta G^*$. From the identity $\delta B = \delta B^0 + z$, we conclude that $\delta B$ depends only on the past history of the difference of the fiscal instruments.[5]

### 12.1.5 Elaborations

Now we keep fiscal expenditures of the two countries constant in order to examine the effects of monetary policies. We vary $M$ and $M^*$ keeping the

---

[5] In our notation, we can state this fact succinctly as follows: $\delta B^0 = -(\gamma_0/2)(\Phi, \delta G - \delta G^*)$, $z = (\gamma_2 - \beta_1)(\Psi, \delta B^0)$, where $\Phi$ stands for $\exp[(1-\gamma_2)t]$ and $\Psi$ for $\exp[(1-\beta_1)t]$. Substitute the former into the latter to write $z = (\gamma_2 - \beta_1)(\gamma_0/2)(\Phi*\Psi, \delta G^* - \delta G)$. Adding the expression for $z$ with that for $\delta B^0$, we show that $\delta B = -(\gamma_0/2)(\Phi + (\gamma_2 - \beta_1)\Phi*\Psi, \delta G - \delta G^*)$.

number of the bonds constant. We still assume that national outputs are constant at full employment levels and assume $i = i^*$. From variations of (1) and (3)

(18) $\qquad p = m - (L_i/L)\,\delta i \qquad$ and $\qquad p^* = m^* - (L_i^*/L^*)\,\delta i.$

After substituting $p$ out by the above, we can derive the trade balance changes from (2). We note that some of the effects of price changes are canceled out by the term depending on $m$ leaving

$$\delta B_T = \gamma_1 \,\delta i - \gamma_2 \,\delta B,$$

where $\gamma_1$ and $\gamma_2$ are as defined earlier in connection with (11) with $\overline{M}$ now replaced by $M$. Similarly, the trade balance of the foreign country varies according to

$$\delta B_T^* = \gamma_1^* \,\delta i - \gamma_2^* \,\delta B^*.$$

Since $\delta B^* = -\delta B$, we write the preceding as

$$\delta B_T^* = \gamma_1^* \,\delta i + \gamma_2^* \,\delta B.$$

The momentary equilibrium condition in the world good market can be used to solve for $\delta i$ as

(19) $\qquad \delta i = (\gamma_1 + \gamma_1^*)^{-1}(\gamma_2 - \gamma_2^*)\,\delta B.$

Note that $m$ disappears from the variational expression for the interest rate. Equation (9) still describes the change in the number of international bonds held in the home country. Its variational equation becomes

$$\delta \dot{B} = (1 - \gamma_2)\,\delta B + \gamma_1 \,\delta i = (1 - \beta_1)\,\delta B.$$

This equation corresponds to (14). We note the absence of the monetary instruments $m$ or $m^*$ from the equation. From (18) and (19) the price levels change according to

$$p = m - (L_i/L)(\gamma_2 - \gamma_2^*)(\gamma_1 + \gamma_1^*)^{-1}\,\delta B$$

and

$$p^* = m^* - (L_i^*/L^*)(\gamma_2 - \gamma_2^*)(\gamma_1 + \gamma_1^*)^{-1}\,\delta B.$$

In the context of this model, the proposition that the exchange rate deviation equals the difference of the relative deviations of the money stocks in the two countries, i.e., $e$ equals $m \pm m^*$, holds if and only if $\gamma_2 = \gamma_2^*$, i.e., holds only in the reference variational model $\mathcal{V}\mathcal{M}_0$. In all other variational models past history of $\delta B$ [nonzero initial disturbance $\delta B(0)$, for example] will affect the current value of $e$.

## 12.2 Distributional Effects of Monetary Policies

This section provides a simple illustration of how wage rate dynamics affect distribution of the effects of monetary instruments between the two countries.

### 12.2.1 The Model

There is one bundle of goods produced by two countries and there is one type of international bond. Each country's private sector also holds (non-traded) money of its own. The model is a simplified version of that discussed in Chapter 13 when two countries produce the same (bundle of) goods, so that the variational purchasing power parity $p = e + p^*$ holds. The log-linear model about steady state is specified assuming stationary expectations. Country A's model is specified by a set of equations:

(20) $\quad y_a = -a(w - p) \quad$ (supply),

(21) $\quad y_d = -\sigma i + \xi y^* \quad$ (demand for home good),

(22) $\quad m - p = m_1 y - m_2 i \quad$ (demand for real balances),

(23) $\quad \dot{w} = \eta y \quad$ (wage rate dynamics).

The fiscal instrument is adjusted to keep the money stock constant in the reference state. The variable $m$ is therefore the instrument of the home government.

The other country is similarly specified. The interest rates of the two countries are equal; $i = i^*$ because the expected depreciation of the exchange rate is zero. The expected rate of inflation is also taken to be zero.

### 12.2.2 Monetary Policy Effects

Equating (20) to (21) and substituting $-a^*(w^* - p^*)$ for $y^*$ in country $A$ and replicating the similar condition for country $B$, the real sector equilibrium conditions are

$$-a(w - p) = -\sigma i + \xi a^*(w^* - p^*),$$
$$-a^*(w^* - p^*) = -\sigma^* i - \xi^* a(w - p),$$

where $i^*$ is set to $i$. Solve it for $\mathbf{p}' = (p, p^*)$ as

$$\mathbf{p} = \mathbf{w} - \rho i,$$

where we define

$$\boldsymbol{\rho} = \begin{bmatrix} \rho \\ \rho^* \end{bmatrix} = \begin{bmatrix} a & -\zeta a^* \\ -\zeta^* a & a^* \end{bmatrix}^{-1} \begin{bmatrix} \sigma \\ \sigma^* \end{bmatrix}.$$

The output deviations are then related to $i$ by

(24) $$\mathbf{y} = -\boldsymbol{\zeta} i,$$

where

$$\boldsymbol{\zeta} = \begin{bmatrix} a & 0 \\ 0 & a^* \end{bmatrix} \boldsymbol{\rho}.$$

From (22) and its counterpart in country $B$

$$\begin{bmatrix} m_2 \\ m_2^* \end{bmatrix} i = -\mathbf{m} + \mathbf{p} + M_1 \mathbf{y},$$

where

$$M_1 = \operatorname{diag}(m_1 \quad m_1^*).$$

Upon substituting $\mathbf{p}$ and $\mathbf{y}$ out, the equation for $i$ becomes, after defining $\mathbf{m}_2' = (m_2, m_2^*)$,

$$\{\mathbf{m}_2 + (I + M_1 A)\boldsymbol{\rho}\} i = -\mathbf{m} + \mathbf{w}.$$

Equating $i$ to $i_a$ (here $i_\delta$ is identically zero),

(25) $$i = i_a = \mu(w_a - m_a),$$

where

$$\mu^{-1} = m_2 + m_2^* + (1 + m_1 a)\rho + (1 + m_1^* a^*)\rho^*.$$

Combining (24) with (25), the reduced form expression for $\mathbf{y}$ becomes

(26) $$\mathbf{y} = -\mu(w_a - m_a)\boldsymbol{\zeta}.$$

Thus, from (23) and its counterpart in country $B$, Eq. (26) shows that $m$ and $m^*$ always acts together as $m + m^*$ in influencing $\mathbf{y}$, i.e., it does not matter which country deviates in its money stock from steady state (i.e., incurs budget deficit on surplus). Its effects distribute or divide into the two countries' real output according to the vector $\boldsymbol{\zeta}$.

Because the average wage rate $w_a$ is governed by the differential equation given by (27) below, it does not change instantaneously. The monetary impact multipliers are then

$$\Delta Y / \Delta M_a = (Y/M_a)\mu\zeta \quad \text{and} \quad \Delta Y^* / \Delta M_a = (Y^*/M_a)\mu\zeta^*.$$

## 12.2 Distributional Effects of Monetary Policies

Because the signs of $\zeta$ and $\zeta^*$ are positive, the multipliers are positive in both countries. Analysis in Chapter 13 reveals that this result becomes less clear-cut when we leave this benchmark case.

To evaluate dynamic multipliers we must account for the dynamics of the model. The only dynamics of this model are by wage rate changes of (23) and its counterpart in country $B$:

$$\dot{\mathbf{w}} = \begin{bmatrix} \eta & 0 \\ 0 & \eta^* \end{bmatrix} \mathbf{y} = -\mu \begin{bmatrix} \eta & 0 \\ 0 & \eta^* \end{bmatrix} \zeta(w_a - m_a).$$

Hence

(27) $$\dot{w}_a = \mathbf{u}'\dot{\mathbf{w}} = -\lambda(w_a - m_a),$$

where $\lambda = \mu(\eta\zeta + \eta^*\zeta^*) > 0$.

Again, (26) shows that the wage rate changes act in the same direction in both countries. Integrating (27),

$$w_a(t) = w_a(0)e^{-\lambda t} + \lambda \int_0^t e^{-\lambda(t-u)} m_a(u) \, du.$$

Substitute this into (26):

$$\mathbf{y}(t) = -\mu\zeta \left\{ w_a(0)e^{-\lambda t} + \lambda \int_0^t e^{-\lambda(t-u)} m_a(u) \, du \right\} + \mu\zeta m_a(t).$$

To illustrate, suppose that $w_a(0)$ is zero and $m_a(u) = \bar{m}_a$ for $0 \le u \le T$. Then

$$\mathbf{y}(t)/\bar{m}_a = \mu\zeta e^{-\lambda t}, \qquad t < T,$$

$$\mathbf{y}(t)/\bar{m}_a = -\mu\zeta(e^{\lambda T} - 1)e^{-\lambda t}, \qquad t \ge T,$$

showing that after the monetary stimulus ceases, the wage rate deviations cause the real outputs of the two countries to become negative unless of course $\mu$ is zero. Then $\mathbf{y}$ remains at zero.[6] Again this clear-cut result become less clear-cut in more complex models. The output difference $y(t) - y^*(t)$ is proportional to $\sigma(1 - \xi^*) - \sigma^*(1 - \xi)$. Because $e^{\lambda T}$ is greater than one for any positive $T$, the sign of the output difference reverses when $m_a$ becomes zero.

---

[6] The case of zero $\mu$ may be regarded as the case in which real wage rates are rigid because we later modify (23) into $\dot{\mathbf{w}} = \eta \mathbf{y} + \mathbf{\rho}_i$, where $\mathbf{\rho}_i$ is the vector of the price index inflation expectations. See Branson and Rotenberg (1980) for an impact analysis of fiscal expansion in a two-country world model under alternate assumptions on wage rates. They do not perform dynamic analysis, however.

# 13 Monetary Policies in a Two-Country Model of the World

## 13.1 Introduction

This chapter analyzes interdependence of national monetary policies and their distributional effects in a two-country world model and shall serve as an introduction to a similar study on a three-country model of the world in Chapter 15.

One of the objectives of this chapter is to provide a general procedure for evaluating dynamic effects of national macroeconomic policies, such as a coordinated expansion of monetary instruments by the two governments or a unilateral expansion by one of the governments in a multiple country model of the world.[1] Our procedure can also be used to assess the relative importance of various transmission paths and calculate various cross-country policy multipliers, i.e., dynamically analyze effects of one country's instruments spilling over to the other country.

We conduct such policy evaluations first on a (variational) world model composed of countries of same characteristics, $\mathcal{VM}_0$, and then of different characteristics,[2] $\mathcal{VM}$. These comparative dynamic analyses of effects of monetary instruments on two or more different models meet a second

---

[1] Although we illustrate the procedure on monetary policies, we can just as well analyze interdependent effects of national fiscal policies or of a common exogenous shock to some sectors of individual economies by the same procedure.

[2] Effects of economic interdependence are sometimes studied by computer simulation of a world model composed of two econometric models symmetrically specified with respect to the two countries (with possible exceptions for policy reaction functions). See Shafer (1976) and Fair (1979). Analytical studies of interdependence are also conducted sometimes using world models consisting of two economically identical countries. Reference models need not, however, be composed of two similar countries. For example, we can take one country to have rigid nominal wages and the other rigid real wages as a reference model. We have discussed these more general cases in Chapter 5.

## 13.1 Introduction

objective of this chapter, which is to conduct a sensitivity study of policy effects: How well does a policy perform in a world composed of two different countries when its design is based on analysis of a world of two identical countries? Can better policies be designed if some country-specific characteristics are explicitly utilized in designing policies? We also ask other sensitivity questions that may be regarded as comparative dynamics questions: Can we sign deviations of the time paths of endogenous variables when two countries are known to differ in some specific way, indicated by differences in some elasticities appearing in structural equations?

The world model composed of two countries of same characteristics is simpler to analyze and generally produces stronger conclusions than models with two different countries. Thus the "sameness" assumption is convenient and seems useful. We take this as our reference model in this chapter.[3] We need to assess, however, if the conclusions drawn from such models are robust; e.g., we must calculate (secondary) policy effects due to national differences and see how large they are and if they are in the same or opposite direction from (primary) policy effects exhibited by the simpler model consisting of two identical countries. Sometimes, differences of national characteristics produce effects not encountered in the symmetrically specified world, because some transmission paths could be entirely eliminated rather than be merely modified by the sameness assumption. In such cases, results may differ qualitatively from those predicted by models without the sameness assumption. Earlier in Chapter 12 we pointed out this possibility, using Henderson's model. Without such sensitivity analysis, results obtained from a two-identical country model of the world may be special and may not be indicative of more generally valid results and hence cannot be relied on in policy analysis.

A third and final objective of this chapter is to provide and illustrate usefulness of a novel framework in which the first two objectives can be carried out. This framework is the one that has already been mentioned in Chapter 5: Let $z$ and $z^*$ be the state vectors of the two countries in the variational model $\mathscr{VM}$. We then choose $(z_a, z_\delta)$, where $z_a$ equals $(z + z^*)/2$, and $z_\delta$ equals $(z - z^*)/2$, as the state vector of the world, rather than $(z, z^*)$, because this choice of the state vector of the world model simplifies the representation of the dynamics.[4]

---

[3] See, however, footnote 2.

[4] When the world is modeled as consisting of two countries, these two countries are usually presumed to be roughly of equal size. In such cases the variable $z_a$ may be interpreted as the world average of $z$ and $z^*$.

When two countries which considerably differ in their economic size are modeled as a two-country model, $z_a$ may not be properly interpretable as the world average. In such cases, we

(*Footnote continued on page* 190)

This choice is based on two observations: First, some variables, such as the exchange rate, are (primarily) affected by the differences of national macroeconomics instruments, while some other variables seem to respond (primarily) to changes in the average of the instruments rather than to their differences. We have seen one example of this in Chapter 12. In a similar vein some disturbances affect the world averages while leaving the national differences the same, i.e., affect each country in the same direction, while others affect the national differences but leave the world averages intact, i.e., affect each country in opposite directions. These two types of effects are better distinguished by the averages and differences of the endogenous variables of the two economies following the procedure of Chapter 5. Second, policy coordination questions can be better phrased in terms of the averages and the differences of policy instruments. We return to this point a little later.

These observations are borne out by our analysis of this chapter. One of our strong results for the two symmetric country model is that our choice of the state vector separates the equation governing the deviational time behavior of the average variables from that governing the difference variables; i.e., these two sets of dynamic equations are independent, responding only to the average and the differences of the instruments, respectively. The differential equations (to be derived in Section 13.6) of our reference variational model $\mathscr{VM}_0$ become[5]

$$(1) \qquad \dot{z}_a = \phi_a z_a + \psi_a x_a, \qquad \dot{z}_\delta = \phi_\delta z_\delta + \psi_\delta x_\delta.$$

Equation (1) states that $z_a$ is affected only by $x_a$, and $z_\delta$ only by $x_\delta$. The reason for this separation of the dynamics for the averages and the differences is simply that the reduced form of the average of any endogenous variable depends only on $z_a$, and the reduced form of the difference of any endogenous variable depends only on $z_\delta$. This fact will be made explicit later in Section 13.5. Although we do not analyze any explicit optimization of the national instruments, such an optimization problem may be more conveniently posed in terms of $z_a$ and $z_\delta$. For example, if policy makers are more concerned with narrowing the national differences of some variables such as

---

regard $z_a$ and $z_\delta$ as merely a choice of state vector which is mathematically equivalent to $z$ and $z^*$ and which simplifies representation of dynamics, since these two different choices of state vectors are equivalent (i.e., related by a nonsingular linear transformation). Our $z_a$ may or may not have interpretation as world averages. Our choice of the state vector should not be confused with an attempt to aggregate national economies into a single world economy. We do not need such aggregates. In fact we are interested in national differences and not in the aggregate variables.

With these cautionary comments, we refer to $z_a$ as the average and $z_\delta$ as the difference variables in this chapter.

[5] Refer to Chapter 5 for derivations.

## 13.1 Introduction

real wage rates or inflation rates than changing world average values, then the choice of $z_a$ and $z_\delta$ as the state vector of the world is more convenient in expressing an optimization criterion function.

A coordinated change in instruments or common shifts of some exogenous variables means that $x_\delta$ is zero in this mode of representation. A unilateral change $x \neq 0$, $x^* = 0$ produces $x_a = x_\delta = x/2$, and $x_a = -x_\delta = x^*/2$ when $x = 0$ and $x^* \neq 0$. Note also that convergence of national variables to the world averages is equivalent to some difference variables converging to zero. Take the inflation rates for example. The difference of national inflation rates converges to zero, if and only if national inflation rates converge to the same rate.[6] Our study of (1), to be carried out in Section 13.7, reveals some elasticities as key determinants of dynamic interactions. These facts are useful in designing simulation experiments to be run on a large econometric model. Another important fact about (1) is that the eigenvalues of $\phi_a$ and $\phi_\delta$ are often separated. When this is the case, then $z_a$ and $z_\delta$ will behave with a different time scale, a fact that can be used to advantage in some approximation analysis (although we do not exploit this fact in this chapter).

When we drop the sameness assumption, interaction terms are introduced into the differential equation (1) as off-diagonal submatrices as shown in (2).[7] Because of the superposition principle for linear systems discussed in Chapter 2 we can approximately study national characteristic differences in several markets one by one. We later show that these off-diagonal submatrices often have simple structures.

This chapter is organized as follows: After a general discussion of our method for deriving the primary and secondary policy effects in Section 13.2, our procedure for policy evaluations is outlined in Section 13.3. Then the remainder of this chapter illustrates the procedures on a particular model of the world.

After the model description in Section 13.4, we derive reduced forms for the averages and differences of endogenous variables separately in Section 13.5, then of dynamic equations in Section 13.6. As we asserted in Chapter 5, this procedure turns out to be algebraically simpler and the policy implications easier to draw than, alternatively, deriving dynamic equations for the two economies first and then examining the averages and differences of the solutions. In Section 13.7, the dynamics are examined when the two countries differ in some of their characteristics. We examine three cases as specific examples: Two countries adjust their inflation expectation with different speeds; they have nonidentical interest elasticities of demands for money, and

---

[6] Branson (1975) analyzed convergence of inflation rates in a small country model, taking the world rate as exogenously given. In multiple-country world models, the world (i.e., some weighted average of individual countries') rate is endogenous.

[7] Diagonal submatrices may also be modified. See Chapter 5 for these more general cases.

their wage rates respond to excess demands with different speeds.[8] Analysis of policy effects is conducted in Section 13.8. Section 13.9 discusses some elaborations of the basic model. Numerical examples are presented to help visualize time paths of some endogenous variables in Section 13.10. The difference dynamics introduced in Section 13.4 are also an ideal vehicle to examine "convergence" questions such as whether national rates of inflation converge to the world rate in some sense. This topic is further pursued in Chapter 15.

## 13.2  Structural Perturbation Analysis

We apply the procedure of Chapter 5 to examine consequences of structural differences. When two countries differ, interaction terms between the average state vector $z_a$ and the difference state vector $z_\delta$ are generally introduced. Equation (1) must be replaced by the differential equation (2) for $\mathcal{VM}$

(2) $$\frac{d}{dt}\begin{bmatrix} z_a \\ z_\delta \end{bmatrix} = \begin{bmatrix} \phi_a & \phi_{a\delta} \\ \phi_{\delta a} & \phi_\delta \end{bmatrix}\begin{bmatrix} z_a \\ z_\delta \end{bmatrix} + \begin{bmatrix} \psi_a \\ \psi_{\delta a} \end{bmatrix} x_a + \begin{bmatrix} \psi_{a\delta} \\ \psi_\delta \end{bmatrix} x_\delta.$$

Here all submatrices are treated as constants. Time varying submatrices can equally easily be examined. The submatrices introduced into (2) which are absent in (1) all reflect the effects of non-sameness of the characteristics of the two countries.[9] Derivations of their specific expressions are postponed to Section 7 where a specific model is discussed. We need not restrict these submatrices in any way for the purpose of this section.

The nonzero submatrix $\phi_{\delta a}$ in the dynamic equation (2) implies the existence of transmission paths from the average variables to the difference variables. This means, in turn, that $x_a$, which primarily affects $z_a$, also influences $z_\delta$ as its secondary effect. The presence of the submatrix $\phi_{a\delta}$ has a similar implication on dynamics and on the effects of the instrument $x_\delta$.

Let superscript zero distinguish the solution of (1) from that of (2). The solution of (1) with zero initial conditions is, in our notation, simply written

(3) $$z_a^0 = (\Phi_a \psi_a, x_a)$$

---

[8] Argy and Salop (1979) also examined this question albeit in a static model. They examined effects of fiscal instruments as well as monetary instruments.

[9] Particular forms of these off-diagonal submatrices depend on specific differences that exist between the two countries. We illustrate some of them in Section 13.7. In some examples $\phi_\delta$ also changes in going from $\mathcal{VM}_0$ to $\mathcal{VM}$. We can analyze this case by the same method, as discussed in Chapter 5.

## 13.2 Structural Perturbation Analysis

and

(4) $$z_\delta^0 = (\Phi_\delta \psi_\delta, x_\delta),$$

where $\Phi_a$ and $\Phi_\delta$ are the transition matrices for $z_a$ and $z_\delta$.

The initial conditions are set to zero in the above to focus on the effects of the instruments. Nonzero initial conditions merely introduce terms which are independent of the instruments into the solution of (2) as parts of the secondary effects.

Now, we define their variational variables by[10]

$$\delta z_a = z_a - z_a^0 \quad \text{and} \quad \delta z_\delta = z_\delta - z_\delta^0.$$

Treating various submatrices in (2) that are absent in (1) as being small,[11] the differential equations governing the variational variables are derived from (1) and (2):

(5) $$\delta \dot{z}_a = \phi_a \delta z_a + \phi_{a\delta} z_\delta^0 + \psi_{a\delta} x_\delta, \quad \delta z_a(0) = 0,$$

(6) $$\delta \dot{z}_\delta = \phi_\delta \delta z_\delta + \phi_{\delta a} z_a^0 + \psi_{\delta a} x_a, \quad \delta z_\delta(0) = 0.$$

Since $x_\delta$ affects $z_\delta^0$ as can be seen from (4), (6) shows that $x_\delta$ affects $\delta z_a$. This is the secondary effect on $z_a$, the primary effect being that of $x_a$ on $z_a^0$ given by (3). This cross dependence can be made more explicit by substituting (4) into the solution of (5):

$$\delta z_a = (\Phi_a, \phi_{a\delta} z_\delta^0 + \psi_{a\delta} x_\delta)$$
$$= (\Phi_a \phi_{a\delta}, z_\delta^0) + (\Phi_a \psi_{a\delta}, x_\delta)$$
$$= (\Phi_a \phi_{a\delta}, (\Phi_\delta \psi_\delta, x_\delta)) + (\Phi_a \psi_{a\delta}, x_\delta).$$

Here the first term of the above can be written as $((\Phi_\delta \psi_\delta)^* \Phi_a \phi_{a\delta}, x_\delta)$ in our notation. Combining these two terms we can succinctly express the effects of $x_\delta$ on $\delta z_a$ as

(7) $$\delta z_a = (S_{a\delta}, x_\delta) = \int_0^t S_{a\delta}(t, s) x_\delta(s)\, ds,$$

where $S_{a\delta}$ is defined to equal $\Phi_a \psi_{a\delta} + (\Phi_\delta \psi_\delta)^* \Phi_a \phi_{a\delta}$, i.e.,

$$S_{a\delta}(t, s) = \Phi_a(t, s) \psi_{a\delta} + \left[\int_s^t \Phi_a(t, \tau) \phi_{a\delta} \Phi_\delta(\tau, s)\, d\tau\right] \psi_\delta.$$

---

[10] Unlike the earlier variational variables, which refer to deviation of given endogenous variables from their reference path values, i.e., to values on two different time paths of the same model, the variational variables here refer to values of endogenous variables on the time paths generated by two different models. The model consisting of two countries of same characteristics is taken to be the one which generates the reference time path. This is our reference model $\mathcal{VM}_0$. The superscript 0 refers to this model variables.

[11] More specifically expressions such as $\phi_{a\delta} \delta z_\delta$ and $\phi_{\delta a} \delta z_a$ are ignored as being small.

This equation shows that the secondary effects due to $x_\delta$ are introduced by the nonzero elements of $\phi_{a\delta}$ and $\psi_{a\delta}$, where the latter represents the direct impact effects of $x_\delta$ on $z_a$ in $\mathscr{VM}$. The secondary effects are absent if $\phi_{a\delta}$ and $\psi_{a\delta}$ are both zero.

We can similarly express the effects of $x_a$ on $z_\delta$. Solving (6) and substituting (3) into $z_a^0$, we can write

$$\delta z_\delta = (\Phi_\delta \phi_{\delta a}, z_a^0) + (\Phi_\delta \psi_{\delta a}, x_a) = (\Phi_\delta \phi_{\delta a}, (\Phi_a \psi_a, x_a)) + (\Phi_\delta \psi_{\delta a}, x_a).$$

Rewriting the first term as $((\Phi_a \psi_a)^* \Phi_\delta \phi_{\delta a}, x_a)$, we can combine the two terms to state that $\delta z_\delta$ is affected by $x_a$ by

(8) $$\delta z_\delta = (S_{\delta a}, x_a),$$

where

$$S_{\delta a}(t, s) = \Phi_\delta(t, s) \psi_{\delta a} + \left[ \int_s^t \Phi_\delta(t, \tau) \phi_{\delta a} \Phi_a(\tau, s) \, d\tau \right] \psi_a.$$

This secondary effect due to $x_a$ is absent if $\psi_{\delta a}$ and $\phi_{\delta a}$ are both zero.

Equations (3), (4), (7), and (8) summarize the effects of the instruments in $\mathscr{VM}$ and $\mathscr{VM}_0$. As an illustration of potential use of these expressions, consider the exchange rate deviation $e(t)$ in $\mathscr{VM}$. By definition, $e(t)$ equals $e^0(t)$ prevailing in $\mathscr{VM}_0$ plus $\delta e(t)$. We later show that $e^0(t)$ depends on $z_\delta^0$ and $\delta e(t)$ depends on $\delta z_\delta$. Equation (4) shows that $z_\delta^0$ is determined by $x_\delta$. The variable $\delta e(t)$, however, is influenced by $x_a$ as (8) shows. Thus, we can write

$$e(t) = e^0(t) + \delta e(t) = f^0(x_\delta) + f^1(x_a),$$

where $f^1(\cdot)$ is the secondary effect of $x_a$. Put differently, the exchange rate in the reference model $\mathscr{VM}_0$ is influenced by the current value of $x_\delta$ only. Between the two countries of different characteristics, the exchange rate has a component responding to $x_a$ as well.

We illustrate this and more by examining a model of Section 13.4. Before we get involved in detailed expressions specific to the model we choose, we next discuss how policy effects can be calculated in the two-country world model and evaluate sensitivity of our results on the assumed sameness or difference of the characteristics of the two countries.

## 13.3 Policy Sensitivity and Distributional Effects

The framework provided in Section 13.2 is now applied to evaluate consequences of (unilateral or coordinated changes of) monetary instruments by one or two governments. First, we analyze this policy on the reference model.

## 13.3 Policy Sensitivity and Distributional Effects

Later we examine modifications introduced when two countries are not exactly alike.

From (1) we know that $x_a$ affects only $z_a^0$ and that $x_\delta$ affects only $z_\delta^0$: These effects are given by (3) and (4) under zero initial conditions. In our model of Section 13.4, $\psi_a$ and $\psi_\delta$ turn out to be the same and are given by (dropping the subscripts) the two dimensional vector

$$\psi = \begin{bmatrix} 0 \\ 1 \end{bmatrix}.$$

Real output deviations from the equilibrium are linearly related to deviations of the state vectors which are two dimensional by

$$y = [a \ \ b]z, \qquad y^* = [a \ \ b]z^*$$

for some coefficients $a$ and $b$; their averages and the differences are also related by the same linear relation

$$y_a^0 = [a \ \ b]z_a^0 \qquad \text{and} \qquad y_\delta^0 = [a \ \ b]z_\delta^0.$$

### 13.3.1 Synchronized Changes in x and x*

A synchronized change in $x$ and $x^*$ of the same magnitude implies then that $x_\delta$ is zero. Hence $z_\delta^0$ is zero from (4), which in turn means that $y_\delta^0$ is zero. In terms of the individual country output, noting that $y^0$ and $y^{*0}$ equal $y_a^0$ plus $y_\delta^0$ and $y_a^0$ minus $y_\delta^0$, respectively, it follows that

$$y(t) = y^*(t) = [a \ \ b](\Phi_a, \psi x_a)(t)$$
$$= \int_0^t h(t - s)x_a(s) \, ds,$$

where

$$h(t - s) = [a \ \ b]\Phi_a(t - s)\begin{bmatrix} 0 \\ 1 \end{bmatrix}.$$

A synchronized change in $x$ and $x^*$ of the same magnitude changes the outputs in the two countries by the same amount, unless the function $h(\cdot)$ is identically zero. A positive value of $h(u), 0 \le u \le t$ means that real outputs at time $t$ in both countries expand by the same amount in response to an expansion of the monetary instruments. This function $h(\cdot)$, therefore, serves as the dynamic multiplier of $x_a$.

Since this function $h$ often appears in our subsequent discussions, we calculate it explicitly by defining

(9) $\quad h_a(t; a, b) = [a \ \ b] \Phi_a(t) \begin{bmatrix} 0 \\ 1 \end{bmatrix} = \zeta_a(t; \lambda_1; a, b) - \zeta_a(t; \lambda_2; a, b),$

where

$$\zeta_a(t; \lambda; a, b) = (\lambda_2 - \lambda_1)^{-1} \{a\phi_a^{12} - b(\lambda + \phi_a^{11})\} e^{-\lambda t},$$

$0 < \lambda_1 < \lambda_2$ are the negatives of the eigenvalues of the matrix $\phi_a$, and $\phi_a^{ij}$ is the $(i,j)$th element of the matrix $\phi_a$. See Appendix E for details of calculations. At least for small positive time, the sign of $h_a(t; a, b)$ is that of $b$. In the model we introduce in the next section, $b$ turns out to be positive. We can state

**Proposition 1.** A coordinated expansion of the monetary instruments by the two governments increases real outputs of the two-country model by the same amount at least initially in the reference model, if $b$ is positive.

How are the real outputs affected if two countries differ in some macroeconomic characteristics? Does coordinated expansion of the instruments still result in equal increase in $y$ and $y^*$? To answer this question, we note that

$$y = y_a + y_\delta \quad \text{and} \quad y^* = y_a - y_\delta,$$

where

$$y_a = y_a^0 + \delta y_a \quad \text{and} \quad y_\delta = y_\delta^0 + \delta y_\delta.$$

With the coordinated expansion implying that $\mathbf{x}_\delta$ is identically zero, $y_\delta^0$ is zero; hence

$$y = y_a^0 + \delta y_a + \delta y_\delta \quad \text{and} \quad y^* = y_a^0 + \delta y_a - \delta y_\delta.$$

From (7) with zero $\mathbf{x}_\delta$, $\delta \mathbf{z}_a$ is zero; hence

$$\delta y_a = [a \ \ b] \, \delta \mathbf{z}_a = 0.$$

The expression for $\delta y_\delta$ is given by

$$\delta y_\delta = [a \ \ b] \, \delta \mathbf{z}_\delta,$$

where $\delta \mathbf{z}_\delta$ is given by (8).

We see that $y$ and $y^*$ are now affected differently because

$$y = y_a^0 + \delta y_\delta \quad \text{and} \quad y^* = y_a^0 - \delta y_\delta$$

and $\delta y_\delta$ is generally nonzero.

In our model to be described in the next section, the dynamics are governed by (2) where $\psi_{\delta a}$ and $\psi_{a\delta}$ are both zero.

## 13.3 Policy Sensitivity and Distributional Effects

We can express the effects of $\mathbf{x}_a$ on $\delta y_\delta$ as

$$\delta y_\delta = (\theta_\delta, \mathbf{x}_a),$$

where

(10) $$\theta_\delta(t - s) = \int_s^t [a \ \ b] \Phi_\delta(t - \tau) \phi_{\delta a} \Phi_a(\tau - s) \begin{bmatrix} 0 \\ 1 \end{bmatrix} d\tau.$$

If the submatrix $\phi_{\delta a}$ is zero, or if the expression $\phi_{\delta a} \Phi_a \begin{bmatrix} 0 \\ 1 \end{bmatrix}$ is zero, then $\delta y_\delta$ vanishes, and differences in national economic characteristics do not matter for the coordinated expansion. Otherwise, the outputs of the two countries are differently affected. If the function $\theta_\delta(\cdot)$ is positive over $[0, t)$, then $\delta y_\delta(t)$ is positive implying that $y(t)$ is greater than $y^*(t)$. If $\theta_\delta(\cdot)$ changes its sign over the time interval $[0, t)$, then we need to examine the expression $(\theta_\delta, \mathbf{x}_a)$ in detail before we can say which country benefits more from the coordinated expansion.

Note that, with $\mathbf{x}_\delta$ zero, $y$ and $y^*$ become positive if and only if

$$[a \ \ b]\left(\Phi_a \pm \Phi_a^* \Phi_\delta \phi_{\delta a}, \begin{bmatrix} 0 \\ 1 \end{bmatrix} \mathbf{x}_a\right) > 0.$$

This inequality will be examined for the model of the next section. In the case where $\phi_{\delta a} \Phi_a \begin{bmatrix} 0 \\ 1 \end{bmatrix}$ is identically zero, the inequality reduces to that of the reference model. We state this as

**Proposition 2.** *If national characteristics differences are such that $\phi_{\delta a} \Phi_a(t) \begin{bmatrix} 0 \\ 1 \end{bmatrix}$ is zero for all positive time, then the real outputs of the two countries behave the same as in the reference model, $\mathcal{VM}_0$. The equal expansion $\mathbf{x} = \mathbf{x}^*$ results in $y = y^*$. If $\phi_{\delta a} \Phi_a \begin{bmatrix} 0 \\ 1 \end{bmatrix}$ is nonzero, $\mathbf{x} = \mathbf{x}^*$ results in $y \neq y^*$.*

### 13.3.2 Unilateral Changes in $\mathbf{x} \neq 0$, $\mathbf{x}^* = 0$

Next, consider $\mathbf{x} \neq 0$, $\mathbf{x}^* = 0$. This produces $\mathbf{x}_a = \mathbf{x}_\delta = \mathbf{x}/2$. No longer is $\mathbf{z}_\delta^0$ zero. From (3), (4), and the definitional relation

$$y^0 = [a \ \ b](\mathbf{z}_a^0 + \mathbf{z}_\delta^0) = \int_0^t h_+^0(t - \tau) \frac{\mathbf{x}(\tau)}{2} d\tau,$$

where

$$h_+^0(u) = [a \ \ b](\Phi_a + \Phi_\delta) \begin{bmatrix} 0 \\ 1 \end{bmatrix} = h_a(u; a, b) + h_\delta(u; a, b),$$

where $h_\delta(\ )$ is defined analogously to $h_a(\ )$ of (9) by substituting $\phi_\delta$ for $\phi_a$,

(11) $$h_\delta(t; a, b) = [a \ \ b]\Phi_\delta(t)\begin{bmatrix}0\\1\end{bmatrix} = \zeta_\delta(t; \mu_1; a, b) - \zeta_\delta(t; \mu_2; a, b),$$

where

$$\zeta_\delta(t; \mu; a, b) = (\mu_2 - \mu_1)^{-1}\{a\phi_\delta^{12} - b(\mu + \phi_\delta^{11})\}e^{-\mu t},$$

where $0 < \mu_1 < \mu_2$ are the negatives of the eigenvalues of the matrix $\phi_\delta$. Near $t$ zero, the sign of $\zeta_\delta$ is that of $b$ as before.

Similarly

$$y^{*0} = [a \ \ b](\mathbf{z}_a^0 - \mathbf{z}_\delta^0) = \int_0^t h_-^0(t - \tau)\frac{\mathbf{x}(\tau)}{2} d\tau,$$

where

$$h_-^0(u; a, b) = h_a(u; a, b) - h_\delta(u; a, b).$$

Generally $y^0 \neq y^{*0}$ when $h_\delta(\cdot) \neq 0$. When $\mathbf{x} = 0$ but $\mathbf{x}^* \neq 0$, $\mathbf{x}_a = -\mathbf{x}_\delta = \mathbf{x}/2$, implying that only the roles of $y^0$ and $y^{*0}$ are reversed. A sufficient condition for the nonexpanding country's output, $y^{*0}(t)$ to be increased by $\mathbf{x} \neq 0$ is[12]

(12) $$h_a(u) \geq h_\delta(u) \quad \text{for} \quad 0 \leq u \leq t.$$

### 13.3.3  Better Policies

To take advantage of the differences in national characteristics, $\mathbf{x}$ and $\mathbf{x}^*$ should not be the same. How should they be chosen if two countries are to benefit equally? The difference of the instruments $\mathbf{x}_\delta$ affects $\mathbf{z}_\delta^0$ and $\delta\mathbf{z}_a$. We next trace out the implications of these terms in order to answer the question.

---

[12] When written out this inequality becomes $(\lambda_2 - \lambda_1)^{-1}[\{a\phi_a^{12} - b(\lambda_1 + \phi_a^{11})\}e^{-\lambda_1 u} - \{a\phi_a^{12} - b(\lambda_2 + \phi_a^{11})\}e^{-\lambda_2 u}] \geq (\mu_2 - \mu_1)^{-1}[\{a\phi_\delta^{12} - b(\lambda_1 + \phi_\delta^{11})\}e^{-\mu_1 u} - \{a\phi_\delta^{12} - b(\mu_2 + \phi_\delta^{11})\}e^{-\mu_2 u}]$, where $-\mu_1$ and $-\mu_2$ are the eigenvalues of $\phi_\delta$. For small $u$, this inequality reduces to (to the first order in $u$) $a\phi_a^{12} - b\phi_a^{11} - b(\lambda_1 + \lambda_2) \geq a\phi_\delta^{12} - b\phi_\delta^{11} - b(\mu_1 + \mu_2)$. This is a sufficient condition that $y^{*0}(u)$ be positive for small $u > 0$. In the model of Section 13.5 [see (39)], the parameters are $a = -\eta_1 < 0$, $b = \eta_2 > 0$, $\phi_a^{11} = -v$, $\phi_a^{12} = -\mu_3$, $\lambda_1 + \lambda_2 = v + \mu_3$, $\phi_\delta^{11} = -(\eta\eta_1 + v\omega_1)$, $\phi_\delta^{12} = \eta\eta_2 - v\omega_2$, and $\mu_1 + \mu_2 = \eta\eta_1 + \omega_4$. [See (39) for their definitions.] With constant nominal wage rates in the two countries, $v$ and $\eta$ are both zero and the sufficient condition reduces to $\eta_2 \omega_4 \geq \mu_3 2 \, dm_2 D_\delta$. One of the ways this inequality can be satisfied is to have the two governments run budget deficits since this causes $\omega_4$ to be a large positive number. See Section 13.5 for detail.

## 13.3 Policy Sensitivity and Distributional Effects

Rewriting the identities for $y$ and $y^*$ in terms of $y_a^0$, $y_\delta^0$, $\delta y_a$, and $\delta y_\delta$, we can express the dependence of the real outputs on $\mathbf{x}$ and $\mathbf{x}^*$ by the following two equations:

$$y = y_a^0 + y_\delta^0 + \delta y_a + \delta y_\delta,$$

and

(13)  $$y^* = y_a^0 - y_\delta^0 + \delta y_a - \delta y_\delta.$$

For $y$ and $y^*$ to be equal, $\mathbf{x}_a$ and $\mathbf{x}_\delta$ must be chosen to satisfy the relation which is obtained by equating the right-hand sides of the above equations. Equating $y$ with $y^*$ in (13) results in

(14)  $$(h_\delta, \mathbf{x}_\delta) = -(\theta_\delta, \mathbf{x}_a),$$

where $\theta_\delta$ is as defined by (10) and $h_\delta$ by (11).

Note that when the submatrix $\phi_{\delta a}$ is zero, $\theta_\delta$ vanishes, leaving

$$0 = (h_\delta, \mathbf{x}_\delta)$$

as the necessary and sufficient condition for the instruments $\mathbf{x}$ and $\mathbf{x}^*$ which equally affect outputs of the two countries.

This shows that equal monetary expansions in the two countries, i.e., $\mathbf{x}_\delta \equiv 0$, results in equal expansion of $y$ and $y^*$ if and only if $\phi_{\delta a}$ is zero. In terms of $\mathbf{x}$ and $\mathbf{x}^*$, (14) may be written as

(14')  $$(h_\delta + \theta_\delta, \mathbf{x}) = (h_\delta - \theta_\delta, \mathbf{x}^*).$$

This equation defines the relation between the time paths of $\mathbf{x}$ and $\mathbf{x}^*$. Since $(\ ,\ )$ is a convolution, we can take the Laplace transforms of both sides of (14') to relate the transform of $\mathbf{x}^*$ to that of $\mathbf{x}$, and take the inverse Laplace transform to evaluate how these time paths must be related to achieve equality of output deviations. We return to this point in Section 13.8 after the model is described.

The effects of $\mathbf{x}$ and $\mathbf{x}^*$ on $y$ and $y^*$ can be summarized by the following distribution matrices [which are also evident from (11') and (12) of Chapter 5]:

$$\begin{bmatrix} y \\ y^* \end{bmatrix} = (H_1 + H_2) \begin{bmatrix} \mathbf{x} \\ \mathbf{x}^* \end{bmatrix},$$

where the first matrix $H_1$ captures the effects of $\mathbf{x}$ and $\mathbf{x}^*$ in $\mathcal{VM}_0$ and is given by

$$H_1 = \begin{bmatrix} h_a + h_\delta & h_a - h_\delta \\ h_a - h_\delta & h_a + h_\delta \end{bmatrix}.$$

This matrix states that $y$ and $y^*$ are affected symmetrically by the changes in $\mathbf{x}$ and $\mathbf{x}^*$ from their respective control time paths. The second matrix is antisymmetric and is given by

$$H_2 = \begin{bmatrix} \theta_a + \theta_\delta & -\theta_a + \theta_\delta \\ \theta_a - \theta_\delta & -\theta_a - \theta_\delta \end{bmatrix}.$$

Note that this matrix vanishes in $\mathscr{VM}_0$. We close this section by pointing out that the procedure can be applied to evaluate policy effects on any other endogenous variable. The coefficients $a$ and $b$ merely change. The general procedure remains the same. [Interchange $\delta$ and a in (10) to define $\theta_a$.]

## 13.4 The Model

Having outlined our procedures for sensitivity and policy analyses, we now apply them to a two-country model of the world, which has a more fully specified structure than the one discussed in Chapter 12 and yet is a relatively simple general equilibrium monetary macroeconomic model. We examine dynamic interaction and policy effects with and without symmetric specifications of the two countries; i.e., the two economies are described by the same structural relationships possibly with different coefficient values. In order to focus on the interaction of the monetary policies of the two countries in the short run, we assume that the fiscal policies are fixed,[13] and abstract from growth considerations. Briefly, each country produces a different good (a different composite bundle of goods), demands some of both goods, holds its own money, and trades in a perfect world capital market in which one international bond is traded. Expectations of rates of change of some "key" variables are assumed to be regressive and proportional to the deviations of the variables from their long-run equilibrium values. Dynamics arise from changes in money supply via the government budget constraints, and from changes in nominal wage rates.

The structural relations of the model are already expressed in relative deviational form from a stationary equilibrium,[14] i.e., the equations in the following tabulation describe $\mathscr{VM}$.

The price indices of the two countries are given by (15),[15] and are used to define the real money stocks in the money demand equations (19). Their expectations appear in the wage rate dynamic equations (18) where the expected rate of changes in the price index is denoted by $\rho_i$. Nominal wage rates are assumed to respond to excess demands, $\eta$ being the adjustment

---

[13] Interdependent effects of fiscal policies can be similarly examined.

[14] A simplified version of this model with zero $\chi$ has been used earlier in Section 12.2.

[15] Equation (15) is the variational expression for the consumer price index when $\chi$ of the total consumption is on the imported goods. Because (15) is the variational expression, $\chi$ can be regarded to be constant.

## 13.4 The Model

|  | Country A | Country B |
|---|---|---|

**Price indices:**

(15) $\quad p_i = (1 - \chi)p + \chi(p^* + e), \chi \geq 0 \qquad p_i^* = (1 - \chi^*)p^* + \chi^*(p - e), \chi^* \geq 0$

**Supply:**

(16) $\quad y_s = -a(w - p) \qquad\qquad y_s^* = -a^*(w^* - p^*)$

**Demand:**

(17) $\quad y_d = \hat{d}(p^* + e - p) - \sigma(i - \rho) + \xi y^* \qquad y_d^* = \hat{d}^*(p - e - p^*) - \sigma^*(i^* - \rho^*) + \xi^* y$

**Wage rate dynamics:**

(18) $\quad \dot{w} = \eta y + \rho_i, \eta \geq 0 \qquad \dot{w}^* = \eta^* y^* + \rho_i^*, \eta^* \geq 0$

(19) $\quad m - p_i = m_1 y - m_2 i \qquad m^* - p_i^* = m_1^* y^* - m_2^* i^*$

**Interest rate parity:**

(20) $\qquad\qquad\qquad i = i^* + \varepsilon$

**Government budget constraint:**

(21) $\quad \dot{m} = -\mu_1 y + \mu_2 p + \mu_3 i + x \qquad \dot{m}^* = -\mu_1^* y^* + \mu_2^* p^* + \mu_3^* i^* + x^*$

**Price index expectations (rationality assumptions):**

(22) $\quad \rho_i = (1 - \chi)\rho + \chi(\varepsilon + \rho^*) \qquad \rho_i^* = (1 - \chi^*)\rho^* + \chi^*(\rho - \varepsilon)$

**Regressive expectations on the exchange rate changes:**

(23) $\qquad\qquad\qquad \varepsilon = -\theta e, \theta > 0$

**Regressive expectations on the price index inflation:**

(24) $\quad \rho_i = -\nu p_i, \nu \geq 0 \qquad \rho_i^* = -\nu^* p_i^*, \nu^* \geq 0$

speed coefficient, and to inflationary expectations of the price indices in (15). More complicated dynamics than those under analysis here result if we assume that nominal wage rates respond to deviations in the real wage rates from their desired levels in the two countries, e.g., when we replace (18) with

$$\dot{w} = -\eta(w - p_i) + \rho_i.$$

We later explore implications of this alternate specification and show that no fundamental changes are introduced by it.

Firms of the two countries supply two distinct bundles of outputs. The supply schedules respond to the changes in real wage rate measured by the output price as specified by (16). Demands for the outputs are functions of the terms of trade and real output of the other country, as well as of the real rate of interest prevailing in each country. To simplify our algebra and to simply exhibit implications of the sameness on dynamics, an interest-elastic term in (17) is initially dropped. Effects of this term are discussed later in Section 13.9. The interest-elastic term complicates the exact expressions but will not materially alter our qualitative conclusions.[16] The demand equations in (17) may be regarded as being in a partially reduced form in which $y_d$ is already solved out.

By assumption, there is only one type of international bond in the world. So we impose the interest rate parity condition (20), where $\varepsilon$ is the expected rate of change of the exchange rate. We assume that the government budgets of the two countries are in balance in equilibrium. Deviation of the outputs from the "full" employment output levels then causes the budget imbalance which is assumed to be monetized 100% in both countries. This gives rise to (21).[17] The first three terms are the policy reaction part of the money stock changes. The variables $x$ and $x^*$ are the policy instruments.

---

[16] A usual explanation for separating out a term which is responsive to the real interest rate is that investment is interest elastic and that only a country's own goods are used in investment in that country. Alternatively, $i - \rho$ may be thought to represent real cost of capital. When the aggregate demand is interest inelastic, the arithmetic average of two output deviations, $y$ and $y^*$, is shown to be zero, because the arithmetic average of the price deviations fully reflects the average wage rate deviation. See (32) below. With interest-elastic aggregate demand, however, the average price does not fully reflect average wage rate changes, hence the average output deviations is not zero. Rather than treating the latter, more complicated case, first, we develop this chapter for the simpler former case, then later indicate the nature of modifications brought about by including interest-elastic aggregate demand terms.

[17] The variational government budget constraint simplifies to $\delta \dot{M} = \delta\{P(G - T)\} + B_g \delta i$, when the government does not intervene in the foreign exchange market, and the budget deficit (or surplus) is monetized 100%. In the first term of the variational expression above, we assume that $\delta T$ equals $\tau Y y$. Because $\dot{M}/M$ is zero at the equilibrium by assumption, we can write the above in terms of relative variations as $\dot{m} = -\mu_1 y + \mu_2 p + \mu_3 i + x$, where we write $i$ for $\delta i$, $\mu_1$ for $\tau PT/M$, $\mu_2$ for $P(G - T)/M$, and $\mu_3$ for $B_g/M$. The first three terms represent the automatic part of the money stock changes and $x$ is the exogenous part of the money stock changes. Part of $x$ can also be thought of as being generated automatically by a policy reaction function, which is linear in $p$, $y$, and $i$. Note that the balanced budget in the reference state implies that $\mu_2$ equals $-i^*\mu_3$, because $\dot{M}$ is zero in the reference state. (As we show later, a negative $\mu_2$ is one of the sufficient conditions for stable dynamics for the difference variables.) Both governments are assumed not to intervene in the international securities markets to correct variational changes in the budget deficits or surpluses. The analysis of this chapter considerably simplify if the government budget deficits are treated as exogenous, i.e., as $\dot{m} = x$, where $x$ is an instrument (or equivalently if $m$ is treated as an instrument). The coefficients $\mu_1 - \mu_3$ become zero in (21). Assume the same for the other country. The dynamics (39) simplify to a two-dimensional dynamics consisting of $\dot{w}_a = -vw_a$, and $\dot{w}_\delta = -(\eta\eta_1 + v\omega_1)w_{\delta^t} + (\eta\eta_2 - v\omega_2)m_\delta$. The reader may wish to carry through the parallel development of this chapter for this simpler version first. This simplification may be reasonable if deviation of $M$ from its equilibrium is treated as random. (A similar comment applies in Chapter 15 as well.)

13.5 Reduced Form Equations of the Reference Variational Model $\mathscr{V\!M}_0$

Inflation expectations on the output prices, $p$ and $p^*$ in home and abroad, on price indices, $p_i$ and $p_i^*$, and on the exchange rate expectations, $\varepsilon$, are not arbitrary, but must satisfy rationality or consistency assumptions which is implied by (15). Equation (22) is such a consistency relation. We assume that residents of both countries have access to an identical set of information on the conditions of the asset markets and that the asset sectors of the two economies are sufficiently similar. Hence we assume that the same adjustment speed coefficient, $\theta$, in the regressive expectations equation for the exchange rate changes (23).

An alternate and more complete specification of the exchange rate change expectation would be

$$\varepsilon = -\theta_1 e - \theta_2(p - p^*) - \theta_3(y - y^*),$$

which states that the expectations are additionally influenced by the inflation rate differential $p - p^*$ and by balance of trade which is captured by the relative deviations of outputs $y - y^*$. The presence of these additional terms modifies the reduced form expressions but will not introduce any new transmission mechanism. These points are substantiated in Section 13.9. Also see Appendix C. In addition to the exchange rate expectations, we assume that the residents of each country form a regressive expectation on the price index inflation given in (24). Here the adjustment speed coefficients $v$ and $v^*$ may or may not be equal to each other because the expectations are about two different variables. Besides, the same information set on the goods markets may not be reasonably assumed to be available to the residents of the two countries, and the dynamics of the goods sectors may not be similar. Even if the information sets are the same, this does not necessarily imply identical adjustment behavior if residents of the two countries use different objective functions in their intertemporal optimizations. Initially we assume that $v$ and $v^*$ are equal to each other, but drop this assumption in Section 13.7.

## 13.5 Reduced Form Equations of the Reference Variational Model $\mathscr{V\!M}_0$

We derive the momentary equilibrium conditions of the model and express the output, output price, and interest rate variations in terms of variations of the wage rates and money stocks. Wage rate and money stock variations serve as the state variables. In this section, all the parameters are the same in the two countries. The reduced form expressions we derive here are those of $\mathscr{V\!M}_0$. We form vectors of like variables of the two economies such as $\mathbf{p} = (p, p^*)'$, where the prime denotes the transpose and where the boldface type denotes a vector.

The endogenous variables $e$ and $i - i^*$ are simply related in this model. We eliminate $e$ from (20) and (23) by

(25) $\quad e = -\theta^{-1}(i - i^*) = -\theta^{-1}\mathbf{v}'\mathbf{i}, \quad$ where $\quad \mathbf{v}' = [1\ -1]$.

The asset market momentary equilibrium is maintained when $e$ and $i$ are related by (25). Equation (25) shows that the assumption of the interest rate parity, (20), and that of regressive expectations, (23), imply that of the exchange rate being proportional to the interest rate difference.

Demand (17) with zero $\sigma$s is equated with supply (16) in each country to obtain the goods markets clearing relation. The interest rates and output prices of the two economies must satisfy an equation which is a generalization of the conventional IS schedule to clear the goods markets of the two economies. Using (25), the equilibrium condition in the real sector is expressed as

(26) $\quad\quad\quad\quad\quad A\mathbf{p} + B\mathbf{i} = a\mathbf{w} + \Gamma \mathbf{y},$

where

$$A = \hat{d}\mathbf{v}\mathbf{v}' + aI, \quad\quad B = \hat{d}\theta^{-1}\mathbf{v}\mathbf{v}',$$

and

$$\Gamma = \xi \begin{bmatrix} 0 & 1 \\ 1 & 0 \end{bmatrix}.$$

The expression for the real outputs of the two economies, written as a vector $\mathbf{y}$ (because we equate supply with demand, we drop the distinction of the supply and demand), is given from (16) as

(27) $\quad\quad\quad\quad\quad \mathbf{y} = -a(\mathbf{w} - \mathbf{p}).$

Substituting this expression of $\mathbf{y}$ into (26), we can rewrite the goods market equilibrium condition as

(28) $\quad\quad (I + a^{-1}d\mathbf{v}\mathbf{v}')\mathbf{p} + a^{-1}d\theta^{-1}\mathbf{v}\mathbf{v}'\mathbf{i} = \mathbf{w},$

where $d = \hat{d}/(1 - \xi)$.

Using (15) and (25), $\mathbf{p}_i$ is expressible as

(29) $\quad\quad\quad\quad \mathbf{p}_i = (I - \chi\mathbf{v}\mathbf{v}')\mathbf{p} - \chi\theta^{-1}\mathbf{v}\mathbf{v}'\mathbf{i}.$

From (27) and the above expression for $\mathbf{p}_i$, we rewrite (19) to obtain the momentary equilibrium condition in the asset sector, i.e., a generalized LM relation

(30) $\quad \{(1 + am_1)I - \chi\mathbf{v}\mathbf{v}'\}\mathbf{p} - (m_2 I + \chi\theta^{-1}\mathbf{v}\mathbf{v}')\mathbf{i} = \mathbf{m} + am_1\mathbf{w}.$

## 13.5 Reduced Form Equations of the Reference Variational Model $\mathscr{V}\mathscr{M}_0$

The two equations (28) and (30) determine deviations in the interest rates and output prices in the two countries which maintain momentary equilibrium in the asset and the goods sectors.

The differences of the pattern of dynamic interactions are most clearly shown by choosing the averages and the differences of endogenous variables as our basic modes of representation which are introduced in Chapter 5. For this and other reasons outlined in Sections 13.1 and 13.2, we use averages and differences denoted by subscripts $a$ and $\delta$, respectively. Thus, we write $\mathbf{p} = p_a \mathbf{u} + p_\delta \mathbf{v}$, where $p_a = \mathbf{u}'\mathbf{p}/2$, $p_\delta = \mathbf{v}'\mathbf{p}/2$, and where $\mathbf{u} = [1 \ \ 1]'$ and $\mathbf{v} = [1 \ \ -1]'$. From (27) we immediately can write

$$(27') \qquad y_a = -a(w_a - p_a), \qquad y_\delta = -a(w_\delta - p_\delta).$$

Equations (28) and (30) can be separately written for the averages and the differences as

$$(31a) \qquad R_a \begin{bmatrix} i_a \\ p_a \end{bmatrix} = \begin{bmatrix} 1 & 0 \\ am_1 & 1 \end{bmatrix} \begin{bmatrix} w_a \\ m_a \end{bmatrix},$$

where

$$R_a = \begin{bmatrix} 0 & 1 \\ -m_2 & 1 + am_1 \end{bmatrix},$$

and

$$(31b) \qquad R_\delta \begin{bmatrix} i_\delta \\ p_\delta \end{bmatrix} = \begin{bmatrix} 1 & 0 \\ am_1 & 1 \end{bmatrix} \begin{bmatrix} w_\delta \\ m_\delta \end{bmatrix},$$

where

$$R_\delta = \begin{bmatrix} \alpha & \beta \\ -(m_2 + 2\chi\theta^{-1}) & 1 + am_1 - 2\chi \end{bmatrix},$$

where $\alpha = 2\gamma\theta^{-1}$, $\beta = 1 + 2\gamma$, and $\gamma = d/a$.

Equations for the averages separate from those for the differences. We solve (31a) to derive reduced form expressions for the average price deviation and the deviation in interest rate:

$$(32) \qquad \begin{aligned} i_a &= D_a\{w_a - m_a\}, \\ p_a &= w_a, \end{aligned}$$

where $D_a^{-1} = m_2 > 0$.

Similarly from (31b), we can express $p_\delta$ and $i_\delta$ as functions of $w_\delta$ and $m_\delta$ alone as

(33)
$$i_\delta = D_\delta\{(1 - 2\tilde{\chi})w_\delta - \beta m_\delta\},$$
$$p_\delta = D_\delta\{(m_2 + 2\tilde{\chi}\theta^{-1})w_\delta + \alpha m_\delta\},$$
$$\tilde{\chi} = \chi + dm_1,$$

where $D_\delta^{-1} = 2\gamma(m_2 + \theta^{-1}) + m_2 + 2\tilde{\chi}\theta^{-1} > 0$.

Substituting (32) and (33) into (27'), the reduced form expressions for $y_a$ and $y_\delta$ are derived as[18]

(34) $$y_a = 0, \qquad y_\delta = -\eta_1 w_\delta + \eta_2 m_\delta,$$

where $\eta_1 = D_\delta 2d(m_2 + \theta^{-1}) > 0$ and $\eta_2 = D_\delta 2 d\theta^{-1} > 0$.

Later we need the reduced form expressions for $p_{ia}$ and $\rho_{i\delta}$ which are used to derive the dynamics for the wages rate. From (22), $\rho_i$s are related to $\rho$ and $\rho^*$. Hence we must also calculate $\rho_a$ and $\rho_\delta$.

Since we treat $\varepsilon$, $\rho_i$, and $\rho_i^*$ as the primary variables for expectations, the expectations on the output price inflations, $\rho$ and $\rho^*$, which are needed above, are implied by (23) and (24). The expressions which relate $\rho_a$ and $\rho_\delta$ to the averages and differences of the prices and interest rate can be deduced from (23) and (24) after solving (22) for them on the assumption that residents of both countries form the same expectations on the home output inflation and the foreign output inflation. In other words, we assume that $\rho$ is the commonly held inflation expectation on the domestic output price changes, and likewise for $\rho^*$. Since we assume that $\chi = \chi^*$ and $v = v^*$ in the reference model, (22) can be put as

$$(I - \chi \mathbf{v}\mathbf{v}')\boldsymbol{\rho} = \boldsymbol{\rho}_i - \chi\varepsilon\mathbf{v}.$$

Solving the above for $\boldsymbol{\rho}$, we can write $\rho$ and $\rho^*$ as

(35)
$$\rho = \{(1 - \chi)\rho_i - \chi\rho_i^* - \chi\varepsilon\}/(1 - 2\chi)$$
$$= \{-v(1 - \chi)p_i + \chi v p_i^* + \chi\theta e\}/(1 - 2\chi)$$
$$= -vp + \chi(\theta - v)e/(1 - 2\chi),$$

(36)
$$\rho^* = \{-\chi\rho_i + (1 - \chi)\rho_i^* + \chi\varepsilon\}/(1 - 2\chi)$$
$$= \{\chi v p_i - v(1 - \chi)p_i^* - \chi\theta\varepsilon\}/(1 - 2\chi)$$
$$= -vp^* + \chi(v - \theta)e/(1 - 2\chi),$$

where (24) is used.

Because $e_a$ is zero, we have $\rho_a = -vp_a$. The difference is given by $\rho_\delta = -vp_\delta - 2\chi(1 - 2\chi)^{-1}(1 - v\theta^{-1})i_\delta$.

---

[18] The variable $y_a$ becomes nonzero when the interest-elastic term in aggregate demand (17) is retained. See later sections.

## 13.5 Reduced Form Equations of the Reference Variational Model $VM_0$

### 13.5.1 A Simple Special Case

When we set the coefficients $\eta$ and $\eta^*$ in (18) and those in (24), i.e., $v$ and $v^*$, to zero, we reduce this model to the one in which nominal wage rates are constant in the two countries. This model is especially simple because the model becomes static if we take money stock deviations $m$ and $m^*$ rather than $x$ and $x^*$ as instruments. [Mundell (1964) assumes constant nominal wage rates and prices. Argy and Salop's case 2 (1979) assumes constant nominal wage rates in the home country.] We derive consequences of monetary expansion at home, i.e., $m > 0$ and $m^* = 0$ for this static model for later comparison. When aggregate demands are interest inelastic [i.e., $\sigma$ and $\sigma^*$ in (17) are zero], the foreign price and output always decrease in response to home money expansion. When aggregate demands are interest elastic ($\sigma$ and $\sigma^*$ are positive), the domestic as well as foreign outputs can increase under certain conditions on $\sigma$ and the coefficient of regressive expectation $\theta$ in (23). Because the model is static, the condition for an output increase abroad turns out to be algebraic. Later we show that corresponding conditions for our dynamics model involve integrals of past instrument values.

Noting that $w = w^* = 0$ by assumption of constant nominal wages, (32) shows that the average interest rate drops:

$$i_a = -D_a m_a < 0 \quad \text{and} \quad p_a = 0.$$

From (33), the differences of the interest rates and prices become

$$i_\delta = -D_\delta \beta m_\delta < 0 \quad \text{and} \quad p_\delta = \alpha D_\delta m_\delta > 0.$$

From (25) then the exchange rate depreciates:

(25') $$e = -2\theta^{-1} i_\delta > 0.$$

From (34), the output difference becomes positive:

$$y_\delta = \eta_2 m_\delta > 0.$$

In terms of individual country variables, home monetary expansion results in price and output increases at home, price and output decreases abroad, and a decrease in interest rates in both countries.

The terms of trade improve because the exchange rate sufficiently depreciates:

$$p = p_a + p_\delta = \alpha D_\delta m_\delta > 0, \qquad p^* = p_a - p_\delta = -\alpha D_\delta m_\delta < 0,$$
$$y = y_a + y_\delta = \eta_2 m_\delta > 0, \qquad y^* = y_a - y_\delta = -\eta_2 m_\delta < 0,$$
$$i = i_a + i_\delta = (-D_a - D_\delta \beta)m/2 < 0,$$
$$i^* = i_a - i_\delta = (-D_a + D_\delta \beta)m/2 < 0,$$

and from (25') and the above expressions for $p$ and $p^*$, we can write

$$p - e - p^* = 2p_\delta + 2\theta^{-1}i_\delta = -2\theta^{-1}\tilde{D}_\delta m_\delta < 0.$$

where the definitions of $\alpha$ and $\beta$ given below (31b) are substituted out. Except for the price effects, the effects are similar to the Mundell model.

When we include the interest-elastic demand term, still under the assumption of rigid nominal wage rates, the output of the foreign country also expands under certain conditions on $\sigma$ and $\theta$. The interest rates are likely to still be negative in both countries; $i < i^* < 0$, and the terms-of-trade expression remains negative for a certain range of $\sigma$ and $\theta$ values.[19]

## 13.6 Dynamics of the Reference Model

We are now ready to describe the dynamics governing the averages and differences of the endogenous variables of the model and derive (1) of Section 13.1. The dynamics are described by (18) and (21). Written together for the two countries, they are

$$\dot{\mathbf{w}} = \eta \mathbf{y} + \boldsymbol{\rho}_i, \qquad \dot{\mathbf{m}} = -\mu_1 \mathbf{y} + \mu_2 \mathbf{p} + \mu_3 \mathbf{i} + \mathbf{x},$$

where $\mathbf{x}$ is the vector of the exogenous instruments for controlling the money stocks of the two countries. Define the state vector by $\mathbf{z}_j = (w_j, m_j)', j = a, \delta$.

---

[19] Noting that $y_i = ap_i$, $i = a, \delta$, and from (51) and (52) below after some algebra, $p_a = (\sigma_1/a)m_a \tilde{D}_a$, where $\tilde{D}_a^{-1} = (\sigma_1/a)(1 + am_1) + m_2$ and $p_\delta = [2\gamma\theta^{-1} + \sigma_2/(1 - 2\chi)]\tilde{D}_\delta m_\delta$, $\sigma_1 = \sigma/(1 - \xi)$, $\sigma_2 = \sigma/(1 + \xi)$, where $\tilde{D}_\delta^{-1} = [2\gamma\theta^{-1} + \sigma_2/(1 - 2\chi)](1 - 2\chi + am_1) + (1 + 2\gamma) \times (m_2 + 2\chi\theta^{-1})$.

From $y = y_a + y_\delta = a(p_a + p_\delta)$ and $y^* = a(p_a - p_\delta)$, the output in the foreign country also expands in response to $m > 0$ and $m^* = 0$ if and only if $p_a - p_\delta$ is positive. After some algebra this inequality can be put as

$$\frac{m_2 d(1 - \xi)}{\sigma} + \left\{\frac{2\chi}{1 - 2\chi}\frac{\sigma}{1 + \xi} + m_2\left(\frac{a}{1 - 2\chi}\frac{1 - \xi}{1 + \xi} - 1 - \frac{2d}{a}\right)\right\}\theta < 2\chi,$$

which states that if $\sigma$ is not too small, then $y > y^* > 0$ (and $p > p^* > 0$) will result while the terms-of-trade changes are negative $p - e - p^* = -2\{\theta^{-1} - [\sigma/(1 - 2\chi)(1 + \xi)]\}m_\delta < 0$, if and only if $2\chi > [2\chi/(1 - 2\chi)][\sigma\theta/(1 + \xi)]$. These two inequalities are simultaneously satisfied if

$$d(1 - \xi) < \left(1 + 2\frac{d}{a} - \frac{a}{1 - 2\chi}\frac{1 - \xi}{1 + \xi}\right)\sigma\theta,$$

i.e., if $1 + 2d/a - [a/(1 - 2\chi)][(1 - \xi)/(1 + \xi)] > 0$ and if $d(1 - \xi)/\{1 + 2d/a - [a/(1 - 2\chi)] \times [(1 - \xi)/(1 + \xi)]\} < \sigma\theta < (1 - 2\chi)(1 + \xi)$.

## 13.6 Dynamics of the Reference Model

When written separately for the averages and the differences, the dynamics become separated as

(37)
$$\frac{d}{dt} \mathbf{z}_a = \mu_2 \begin{bmatrix} 0 \\ 1 \end{bmatrix} p_a + \mu_3 \begin{bmatrix} 0 \\ 1 \end{bmatrix} i_a + \begin{bmatrix} 0 \\ 1 \end{bmatrix} x_a + \begin{bmatrix} 1 \\ 0 \end{bmatrix} \rho_{ia},$$

$$\frac{d}{dt} \mathbf{z}_\delta = \begin{bmatrix} \eta \\ -\mu_1 \end{bmatrix} y_\delta + \mu_2 \begin{bmatrix} 0 \\ 1 \end{bmatrix} p_\delta + \mu_3 \begin{bmatrix} 0 \\ 1 \end{bmatrix} i_\delta + \begin{bmatrix} 1 \\ 0 \end{bmatrix} \rho_{i\delta} + \begin{bmatrix} 0 \\ 1 \end{bmatrix} x_\delta.$$

From (34) and noting that $p_{ia}$ equals $p_a$ and that $p_{i\delta}$ equals $(1 - 2\chi)p_\delta - 2\chi\theta^{-1}i_\delta$ from (29), we can express the expectational variables as

(38)
$$\rho_{ia} = -\nu p_a,$$
$$\rho_{i\delta} = -\nu p_{i\delta} = -\nu(1 - 2\chi)p_\delta + 2\chi\nu\theta^{-1}i_\delta = -\nu(\omega_1 w_\delta + \omega_2 m_\delta),$$

where we define

$$[\omega_1 \ \omega_2] = -[2\chi\theta^{-1} \ -(1 - 2\chi)]R_\delta^{-1} \begin{bmatrix} 1 & 0 \\ am_1 & 1 \end{bmatrix},$$

i.e.,

$$\omega_1 = D_\delta\{(1 - 2\chi)m_2 + 2\,dm_1\theta^{-1}\}, \qquad \omega_2 = 2D_\delta(\chi + \gamma)\theta^{-1}.$$

When $p_a$, $i_a$, $p_\delta$, $i_\delta$ and $y_\delta$ are substituted out by (32), (33), and (34), the dynamics are put in the state-space representation.

As we have already mentioned, the averages depend only on $w_a$ and $m_a$ and the differences only on $w_\delta$ and $m_\delta$. Therefore, the dynamics for the average state vector $\mathbf{z}_a$ and the dynamics for the difference vector $\mathbf{z}_\delta$ are independent, i.e., decoupled from each other. Written jointly they become (39) in which the dynamic matrix is block diagonal. This is what we claimed for (1) in Section 13.1.

(39)
$$\frac{d}{dt} \begin{bmatrix} \mathbf{z}_a \\ \mathbf{z}_\delta \end{bmatrix} = \begin{bmatrix} \phi_a & 0 \\ 0 & \phi_\delta \end{bmatrix} \begin{bmatrix} \mathbf{z}_a \\ \mathbf{z}_\delta \end{bmatrix} + \begin{bmatrix} 0 \\ 1 \\ 0 \\ 0 \end{bmatrix} x_a + \begin{bmatrix} 0 \\ 0 \\ 0 \\ 1 \end{bmatrix} x_\delta,$$

where

$$\phi_a = D_a\left[ \begin{bmatrix} -\nu \\ \mu_2 \end{bmatrix}[m_2 \ 0] + \begin{bmatrix} 0 \\ \mu_3 \end{bmatrix}[1 \ -1] \right] = \begin{bmatrix} -\nu & 0 \\ \mu_2 + \mu_3/m_2 & -\mu_3/m_2 \end{bmatrix},$$

$$\phi_\delta = \begin{bmatrix} \eta \\ -\mu_1 \end{bmatrix}[-\eta_1 \ \eta_2] + \begin{bmatrix} -\nu\omega_1 & -\nu\omega_2 \\ \omega_3 & \omega_4 \end{bmatrix},$$

and where

$$\omega_3 = \{\mu_2(m_2 + 2\tilde{\chi}\theta^{-1}) + \mu_3(1 - 2\tilde{\chi})\}D_\delta, \qquad \omega_4 = (\mu_2\alpha - \mu_3\beta)D_\delta.$$

The (1, 2) element of $\phi_\delta$, $\eta\eta_2 - v\omega_2$, indicating the effects of $m_\delta$ on $w_\delta$ dynamics, is one of the key determinants of the dynamic behavior of the model. We illustrate this later by numerical examples. Also, this same expression largely influences the pattern of distributional effects of the money stock deviations on wage rate time paths in the two countries. We return to this point later when we discuss the effects of the instruments.

The matrix $\phi_a$ in (39) is lower triangular. This indicates that the dynamics for $m_a$ can be separated from (39), i.e., the average dynamics become recursive.

The average money stock deviation is governed by

(39a) $$\dot{m}_a = -(\mu_3/m_2)m_a + \phi_a^{21}w_a + x_a,$$

where $\phi_a^{21} = \mu_2 + \mu_3/m_2$. The average of the monetary instrument, $x_a$, affects only $m_a$. Its effect does not spill over to $z_\delta$. Conversely, $x_\delta$'s effect does not spill over to $z_a$, either. Relative deviations of the exchange rate are uniquely determined by the difference of the interest rate deviation in the two countries. The variable $i_\delta$ is a function of $z_\delta$ alone for this model. Since only the difference of the monetary instruments acts on $z_\delta$, $e$ is determined solely by the time history of $x_\delta$.

The matrix $\phi_a$ is stable if and only if $v$ is positive because $\mu_3$ is positive. A sufficient condition for stable $\phi_\delta$ is $\mu_2 < 0$ and $\eta > v(1 + \chi/\gamma)$ because the trace becomes negative and the determinant positive under these inequalities.[20] This does not preclude stability for some $\mu_2 \geq 0$, however. (If both $\mu_2$ and $\mu_3$ are zero, then the dimension of the average dynamics reduces by one.)

### Dynamic Behavior of the Reference Model

For later use we record here the solutions of $w_a$ and $z_\delta$:

(40a) $$w_a = e^{-vt}w_a(0),$$

(40b) $$z_\delta = \left(\Phi_\delta \begin{bmatrix} 0 \\ 1 \end{bmatrix}, x_\delta\right) + \Phi_\delta z_\delta(0),$$

where $\Phi_\delta$ is the transition matrix of $z_\delta$.

We note that the time behavior of the average wage rate deviation is independent of the instruments. With positive $v$, $w_a$ approaches zero asymptotically. From (39), $m_a$ is affected by $x_a$:

$$m_a(t) = e^{-(\mu_3/m_2)t}m_a(0) + (\mu_3/m_2 - v)^{-1}\phi_a^{21}w_a(0)(e^{-vt} - e^{-(\mu_3/m_2)t})$$
$$+ \int_0^t e^{-(\mu_3/m_2)(t-\tau)}x_a(\tau)\,d\tau.$$

---

[20] Note that $\mu_2$ is negative if the reference state is characterized by balanced budget.

## 13.7 Dynamics of VM

In the case where $\sigma$ and $\sigma^*$ are zero, $y_a$ is identically zero, $p_a$ being equal to $w_a$, i.e., the price fully reflects changes in the wage rate.

A synchronized expansion in the instruments, such that $x_\delta = 0$, implies that $z_\delta \equiv 0$. It merely increases $m_a$; hence $p_a$ and $w_a$ remain zero if $w_a(0)$ is zero, and from (32), $i_a$ decreases by

$$i_a = -D_a \int_0^t e^{-(\mu_3/m_2)(t-\tau)} x_a(\tau) \, d\tau < 0.$$

### 13.7 Dynamics of VM

In this section we examine models composed of two different countries. First we compute the variational state variables $\delta w = w - w^0$ and $\delta m = m - m^0$, where the superscript zero refers to the state vector of the reference model consisting of two countries of the same characteristics. Then we explore implications of different country characteristics on policy effects. As we mentioned earlier, we examine three separate instances of different characteristics: wage rate adjustment behavior, inflation expectations behavior, and demands for real balances.

### 13.7.1 Nonidentical Wage Rate Adjustment Coefficients

#### Modification of Dynamic Equations

This section derives consequences of wage rates adjusting with different speeds in the otherwise identical countries, i.e., $\eta \neq \eta^*$ in (18). Let $\eta_a = (\eta + \eta^*)/2$ and $\eta_\delta = (\eta - \eta^*)/2$. Then the wage rate dynamics become from (18)

$$\dot{w}_a = \eta_a y_a + \eta_\delta y_\delta + p_{ia} = \eta_\delta y_\delta + p_{ia}$$

and

$$\dot{w}_\delta = \eta_\delta y_a + \eta_a y_\delta + p_{i\delta} = \eta_a y_\delta + p_{i\delta},$$

because $y_a$ still remains at zero as in (34). Hence the dynamics (39) are now replaced with

$$(39') \quad \frac{d}{dt}\begin{bmatrix} z_a \\ z_\delta \end{bmatrix} = \left\{ \phi_a \; \eta_\delta \begin{bmatrix} 1 \\ 0 \end{bmatrix} [-\eta_1 \; \eta_2] \atop 0 \quad \overline{\phi_\delta} \right\} \begin{bmatrix} z_a \\ z_\delta \end{bmatrix} + \begin{bmatrix} 0 \\ 1 \\ 0 \\ 0 \end{bmatrix} x_a + \begin{bmatrix} 0 \\ 0 \\ 0 \\ 1 \end{bmatrix} x_\delta,$$

where $\bar{\phi}_\delta$ is the same as $\phi_\delta$ of (39) with $\eta$ replaced by $\eta_a$. Compared with (39), the dynamics of $\mathscr{VM}$ have the one-way coupling term from $z_\delta$ to $z_a$.

Equation (39′) shows that the dynamics for $m_a$ are not affected by unequal $\eta$ and can be separated from the rest. They remain the same as in $\mathscr{VM}_0$. Now $w_a$ and $z_\delta$ are governed by

$$(41) \qquad \frac{d}{dt}\begin{bmatrix} w_a \\ z_\delta \end{bmatrix} = \begin{bmatrix} -v & \bar{\phi}_{a\delta} \\ 0 & \bar{\phi}_\delta \end{bmatrix}\begin{bmatrix} w_a \\ z_\delta \end{bmatrix} + \begin{bmatrix} 0 \\ 0 \\ 1 \end{bmatrix} x_\delta,$$

where $\bar{\phi}_{a\delta} = \eta_\delta[-\eta_1 \quad \eta_2]$.

The difference of dynamic behavior of this model and that of the reference model is captured then by $\delta w_a = w_a - w_a^0$, $\delta m_a = m_a - m_a^0$, and by $\delta z_\delta = z_\delta - z_\delta^0$. Following our procedure of Section 13.2, the dynamics for these deviational variables are

$$(42) \qquad \delta\dot{w}_a = -v\delta w_a + \bar{\phi}_{a\delta} z_\delta^0, \qquad \delta w_a(0) = 0,$$
$$\delta\dot{m}_a = -(\mu_3/m_2)\delta m_a + \phi_a^{21}\delta w_a, \qquad \delta m_a(0) = 0,$$

and

$$\delta\dot{z}_\delta = 0, \qquad \delta z_\delta(0) = 0,$$

where we let $\eta$ in (39) assume the value $\eta_a$. The important result implied by (42) is that $\delta z_\delta$ remains zero.

### Modifications of Endogenous Variables

Because $\delta z_\delta$ remains zero for all $t$, endogenous variables depending on $\delta z_\delta$ do not change, i.e., the time paths for $y_\delta$, $p_\delta$, $i_\delta$, hence $e$ are the same as the ones generated by the reference model (39). Only the time paths for $i_a$ and $p_a$ become different. In terms of variables of the individual countries, we note that

$$\delta p = \delta p_a + \delta p_\delta = \delta w_a, \qquad \delta p^* = \delta p_a - \delta p_\delta = \delta w_a.$$

Therefore, each country's variables shift by the same amount when $\eta$ and $\eta^*$ are unequal.

Since $\delta w_a$ depends on $x_\delta$ via $z_\delta^0$, as can be seen in (42), $\delta w_a$ is zero only if $x_\delta$ is zero. Policy effects are discussed later in Section 13.8.

### 13.7.2  $v \neq v^*$: Nonidentical Adjustment Speeds of the Expectational Variables

Because the variable $v$ does not affect the reduced forms for $i$, $y$, and $p$ and because $v$ affects only the expectational variables, which have direct effects only on $w_a$ and $w_\delta$, the dynamics for $m_a$ remain the same as in (39).

## 13.7 Dynamics of VM

A major difference from previous analysis lies in the different expressions for $\rho$ and $\rho_i$. Compared with (38), the average and the difference variables become interdependent:

$$\rho_{ia} = -v_a p_a - (1 - 2\chi)v_\delta p_\delta + 2\chi\theta^{-1} v_\delta i_\delta,$$
$$\rho_{i\delta} = -v_\delta p_a - (1 - 2\chi)v_a p_\delta + 2\chi\theta^{-1} v_a i_\delta,$$

and

$$\rho_a = -v_a p_a - v_\delta\{(1 - 2\chi)p_\delta - 2\chi\theta^{-1} i_\delta\},$$
$$\rho_\delta = -v_a p_\delta - 2\chi(1 - 2\chi)^{-1}(1 - v_a\theta^{-1})i_\delta - v_\delta(1 - 2\chi)^{-1} p_a.$$

From (18), (33), and the above, $w_a$ is governed by

$$\dot{w}_a = -v_a w_a - v_\delta[\omega_1 \quad \omega_2]\mathbf{z}_\delta,$$

where $\omega_1$ and $\omega_2$ are as defined in (38), and $v_a = (v + v^*)/2$ and $v_\delta = (v - v^*)/2$.

The dynamics for $\mathbf{z}_\delta$ are given by

$$\dot{\mathbf{z}}_\delta = \hat{\phi}_\delta \mathbf{z}_\delta - v_\delta \begin{bmatrix} 1 \\ 0 \end{bmatrix} w_a + \begin{bmatrix} 0 \\ 1 \end{bmatrix} x_\delta,$$

where $\hat{\phi}_\delta$ is $\phi_\delta$ as defined in (39) with $v$ replaced by $v_a$. Hence, the dynamics governing $w_a$ and $\mathbf{z}_\delta$ become

$$(43) \qquad \frac{d}{dt}\begin{bmatrix} w_a \\ \mathbf{z}_\delta \end{bmatrix} = \Phi \begin{bmatrix} w_a \\ \mathbf{z}_\delta \end{bmatrix} + \begin{bmatrix} 0 \\ 0 \\ 1 \end{bmatrix} x_\delta,$$

where the elements of the dynamic matrix $\Phi$ are

$$\phi_{aa} = -v_a, \quad \phi_{a\delta} = -v_\delta[\omega_1 \quad \omega_2], \quad \phi_{\delta a} = -v_\delta \begin{bmatrix} 1 \\ 0 \end{bmatrix}, \quad \phi_{\delta\delta} = \hat{\phi}_\delta.$$

To the first order in $v_\delta$, $\delta w_a$ and $\delta \mathbf{z}_\delta$ change with time according to

$$(43') \qquad \begin{aligned} \delta \dot{w}_a &= -v_a \delta w_a + \phi_a \delta \mathbf{z}_\delta^0, & \delta w_a(0) &= 0, \\ \delta \dot{m}_a &= -(\mu_3/m_2) \delta m_a + \phi_a^{21} \delta w_a, & \delta m_a(0) &= 0, \\ \delta \dot{\mathbf{z}}_\delta &= \phi_{\delta a} w_a^0 + \hat{\phi}_\delta \delta \mathbf{z}_\delta, & \delta \mathbf{z}_\delta(0) &= 0. \end{aligned}$$

The variable $\delta \mathbf{z}_\delta$ remains at zero because $w_a^0$ remains at zero if $w_a^0(0)$ is zero.

The variables $\delta i_\delta$, $\delta p_\delta$, and $\delta y_\delta$ and consequently $\delta e$ are all zero, i.e., $i$, $i^*$ and $p$, $p^*$ change by the same amount in the two countries from their respective reference model time paths. The amount of shift depends on $x_\delta$. In this sense, the case with different $v$ is similar to that with different $\eta$. The exact amount of shift differs in these two cases, however.

### 13.7.3 $m_2 \neq m_2^*$: Nonidentical Interest Elasticities of Demands for Real Balances

In the Appendix at the end of this chapter, we show that the average and the difference variables no longer separate. Instead of (32) and (33), the reduced forms are now given by

(44)
$$\begin{bmatrix} i_a \\ p_a \end{bmatrix} = \bar{R}_a^{-1} \mathbf{z}_a + \zeta D_a D_\delta \begin{bmatrix} -1 \\ 0 \end{bmatrix} [1 - 2\tilde{\chi} - \beta] \mathbf{z}_\delta + O(\zeta^2),$$

$$\begin{bmatrix} i_\delta \\ p_\delta \end{bmatrix} = \bar{R}_\delta^{-1} \mathbf{z}_\delta + \zeta D_a D_\delta \begin{bmatrix} -\beta \\ \alpha \end{bmatrix} [1 - 1] \mathbf{z}_a,$$

where $\bar{R}_a$ and $\bar{R}_\delta$ are the same as $R_a$ and $R_\delta$ of (31a) and (31b) when $(m_2 + m_2^*)/2$ replaces $m_2$. We use $\zeta$ for $(m_2 - m_2^*)/2$.

#### Modifications of Dynamics

Equation (39) is replaced by

(45)
$$\frac{d}{dt} \begin{bmatrix} \mathbf{z}_a \\ \mathbf{z}_\delta \end{bmatrix} = \begin{bmatrix} \phi_a & \phi_{a\delta} \\ \phi_{\delta a} & A \end{bmatrix} \begin{bmatrix} \mathbf{z}_a \\ \mathbf{z}_\delta \end{bmatrix} + \begin{bmatrix} 0 \\ 0 \\ 1 \end{bmatrix} x_\delta,$$

where

$$\phi_{a\delta} = \zeta D_a D_\delta \begin{bmatrix} v \\ -\mu_3 \end{bmatrix} [1 - 2\tilde{\chi} - \beta], \quad \phi_{\delta a} = D_a D_\delta \begin{bmatrix} -\beta \\ \alpha \end{bmatrix} [1 - 1],$$

and where $A$ is the same as $\phi_\delta$ in (39) with $m_2$ replaced by $\bar{m}_2$. See this chapter's Appendix for deviation of these equations.

The dynamics for the variational variable become

(46)
$$\delta \dot{m}_a = -(\mu_3/\bar{m}_2) \delta m_a + \phi_a^{21} \delta w_a + \psi_\delta \mathbf{z}_\delta^0, \quad \delta m_a(0) = 0,$$

$$\psi_\delta = -\zeta(\mu_3/\bar{m}_2) D_\delta [1 - 2\tilde{\chi} - \beta], \quad \bar{m}_2 = (m_2 + m_2^*)/2,$$

$$\delta \dot{w}_a = -v \delta w_a + \bar{\phi}_{a\delta} \mathbf{z}_\delta^0, \quad \delta w_a(0) = 0,$$

$$\bar{\phi}_{a\delta} = \zeta v D_a D_\delta [1 - 2\tilde{\chi} - \beta],$$

$$\delta \dot{\mathbf{z}}_\delta = \phi_{\delta a} \mathbf{z}_a^0 + A \delta \mathbf{z}_\delta, \quad \delta \mathbf{z}_\delta(0) = 0.$$

#### Modification of the State Vector

On the assumption that $w_a^0(0) = 0$ and $\mathbf{z}_\delta^0(0) = 0$, the solutions are essentially the same ones derived in earlier sections. The variable $\delta \mathbf{z}_\delta$ still remains at zero. Now, however, $\delta i_\delta$ depends on $x_a$ through its influence on

$m_a^0$. For example, even though $w_a^0$ remains at zero, $m_a^0$ will change with non-zero $x_a$ which will cause $e$ to deviate from its time path of the reference model according to

$$\delta e = -2\theta^{-1}\zeta D_a D_\delta \beta m_a^0.$$

Thus, even when $x_\delta$ is zero, the exchange rate appreciates if $m_2 > m_2^*$ when $x_a$ is positive.

## 13.8  Policy Effects

Policy effects are discussed in this section. We first dispose of qualitative questions of whether certain endogenous variables are controllable by one or both of the governments in the model before we turn to more quantitative questions.

### 13.8.1  Path Controllability

Generally, both instruments $x$ and $x^*$ act on any endogenous variable in the model. One type of policy coordination question asks: If home country policy makers are informed of the (intended) future time path of $x^*$, can they guide the endogenous variables of the home economy, such as $w$ or $y$, along any time path they choose? The other type of coordination question asks: If chosen jointly, can $x$ and $x^*$ guide endogenous variables of both countries, such as $w$ and $w^*$ or $p$ and $p^*$, along mutually agreed on time paths? Put differently, are the average and the difference of a given endogenous variable path controllable by $x$ and $x^*$? Is the difference of a given endogenous variable path controllable by the difference of the instrument $x_\delta$?

We can use (39) to answer these controllability questions for the reference model.[21] We can verify path controllability of any endogenous variable with respect to a specified instrument by appealing to one of the sufficient conditions given in Chapter 6, sufficient condition (iii) of Section 6.2.1 being the most convenient for the present model.

#### ($w$, $w^*$)-Path Controllability

To verify that $w$ and $w^*$ are path controllable by $x$ and $x^*$ if they are jointly chosen, we identify the matrix $C$ in the sufficient condition (iii) from

$$\begin{bmatrix} w \\ w^* \end{bmatrix} = \begin{bmatrix} 1 & 0 & 1 & 0 \\ 1 & 0 & -1 & 0 \end{bmatrix} \begin{bmatrix} z_a \\ z_\delta \end{bmatrix},$$

---

[21] For nonreference models appropriate dynamics derived in Section 13.7 must be used instead of (39). Here we use the reference model as an illustration.

and rewrite the last two terms of (39) as

$$\begin{bmatrix}0\\1\\0\\0\end{bmatrix}x_a + \begin{bmatrix}0\\0\\0\\1\end{bmatrix}x_\delta = \frac{1}{2}\begin{bmatrix}0 & 0\\1 & 1\\0 & 0\\1 & -1\end{bmatrix}\begin{bmatrix}x\\x^*\end{bmatrix}$$

to identify $B$. We can omit $\frac{1}{2}$ with no harm and we use the matrices $B$ and $C$ given by

$$B = \begin{bmatrix}0 & 0\\1 & 1\\0 & 0\\1 & -1\end{bmatrix} \quad \text{and} \quad C = \begin{bmatrix}1 & 0 & 1 & 0\\1 & 0 & -1 & 0\end{bmatrix}.$$

Sufficient condition (iii) is satisfied if

$$0 \neq \det\left\{C\begin{bmatrix}\phi_a^{-1} & 0\\0 & \phi_\delta^{-1}\end{bmatrix}B\right\}.$$

This expression is equivalent to $(\phi_a)_{12}(\phi_\delta)_{12} \neq 0$. Now, the (1, 2) element of the matrix $\phi_a$ is zero in (39) if the interest-elastic term is neglected from the aggregate demand equation (17). However, when the term depending on $\sigma$ is retained in (17), then the (1, 2) element of $\phi_a$ is nonzero. In the latter case, then both $w$ and $w^*$ are jointly path controllable by $x$ and $x^*$. This means, of course, that these instruments are chosen by both policy makers by mutual consent.

If policy makers are merely interested in reducing the wage rate differences to zero over a path which is mutually chosen, then they may ask Is $w_\delta$ path controllable by $x_\delta$? The answer is affirmative by sufficient condition (iii) again since

$$w_\delta = [1 \ 0]z_\delta \quad \text{and} \quad [1 \ 0]\phi_\delta^{-1}\begin{bmatrix}0\\1\end{bmatrix} \neq 0.$$

This is because $(\phi_\delta)_{12} \neq 0$. Note that this condition holds even if the aggregate demand is interest inelastic.

### $y_\delta$-Path Controllability

The difference of the outputs is path controllable if

$$0 = [-\eta_1 \ \eta_2]\phi_\delta^{-1}\begin{bmatrix}0\\1\end{bmatrix} = -v(\eta_1 w_2 + \eta_2 w_1)$$

## 13.8 Policy Effects

by sufficient condition (iii). This indicates that if the adjustment coefficient for the inflationary expectation, $v$, is not zero, then $y_\delta$ is path controllable with $x_\delta$.

### Exchange Rate-Path Controllability

From (25) and (33), the exchange rate deviation is expressible as $e = \text{const}[1 - 2\tilde{\chi} \ -1 - 2\gamma]z_\delta$. The exchange rate deviation is path controllable since

$$0 \neq [1 - 2\tilde{\chi} \ -1 - 2\gamma]\phi_\delta^{-1}\begin{bmatrix}0\\1\end{bmatrix}.$$

Other variables can be similarly tested for path controllability.

### 13.8.2 Quantitative Policy Effects

We now apply the procedure developed in Section 13.3 to the model of Section 13.4 to evaluate consequences of two countries differing in some economic characteristics. In particular we analyze the differences in their wage rate adjustment behavior, expectational behavior, and demand for real balances.

### $\eta \neq \eta^*$

The variable $\delta y_\delta$ vanishes when the coefficient $\eta$ is unequal in the two countries, because $\delta z_\delta$ is zero due to the vanishing of the submatrix $\phi_{\delta a}$ and $\psi_{\delta a}$ in (2) and (8) as can be seen from (39'). Changes in the outputs are given by

$$y = y_a^0 + y_\delta^0 + \delta y_a \quad \text{and} \quad y^* = y_a^0 - y_\delta^0 + \delta y_a.$$

The condition of equal increase in the two countries' outputs imposes a constraint that $y_\delta^0$ be zero. This holds if and only if

$$0 = [-\eta_1 \ \ \eta_2]\left(\Phi_\delta\begin{bmatrix}0\\1\end{bmatrix}, x_\delta\right) = (h_\delta, x_\delta) \quad \text{for all } t,$$

i.e., $x_\delta \equiv 0$. (The coefficient $a$ and $b$ in (11) are $-\eta_1$ and $\eta_2$ here.)

Thus, two countries equally benefit only from the coordinated expansion $x = x^*$. A unilateral monetary expansion increases foreign output if and only if $y_a^0 - y_\delta^0 + \delta y_a > 0$, or $y_a^0 + \delta y_a > y_\delta^0$. When the aggregate demand is interest inelastic, $y_a^0$ is zero. Thus $y^*$ is positive if and only if

$$\delta y_a > y_\delta^0, \quad \text{where} \quad x_a = x_\delta = x/2 > 0.$$

Recalling that $\phi_{a\delta}$ equals $\eta_\delta[{}^1_0][-\eta_1 \quad \eta_2]$ in (39′) and that

$$\delta y_a = [-\eta_1 \quad \eta_2] \delta z_a = (\theta_a, x_\delta) \quad \text{and} \quad y^0_\delta = (h_\delta, x_\delta),$$

where from (7), after substituting $\phi_{a\delta}$ out,

$$\theta_a(t-s) = [-\eta_1 \quad \eta_2] S_{a\delta} = \eta_\delta \int_s^t g_a(t-\tau; -\eta_1, \eta_2) h_\delta(\tau - s; -\eta_1, \eta_2) \, d\tau,$$

where

$$g_a(u; a, b) = [a \quad b]\Phi_a(u)\begin{bmatrix}1\\0\end{bmatrix}.$$

The inequality can equivalently be put as

$$(\theta_a - h_\delta, x_\delta) = \tfrac{1}{2}(\theta_a - h_\delta, x) > 0 \quad \text{for} \quad x > 0.$$

This follows if $\theta_a - h_\delta$ is positive for all $t \geq 0$, i.e., if

$$\eta_\delta \int_0^t g_a(t-\tau; -\eta_1, \eta_2) h_\delta(\tau; -\eta_1, \eta_2) \, d\tau > h_\delta(t).$$

As $t$ becomes larger, $g_a$ and $h_\delta$ both approach zero exponentially. This implies that for a given $\eta_\delta$, $y^*$ becomes negative for $t$ large. For small $t$, $g_a$ is approximately equal to $-\eta_1$ and $h_\delta$ to $\eta_2$. Thus for $t$ small, $y^*$ is also negative. There is an intermediate $t$ value for which $y^*$ can be positive if $\eta_1 \phi_\delta^{12} - \eta_2 \phi_\delta^{22} - \eta_\delta \eta_1 \eta_2$ is positive. Because $\eta_1 \phi_\delta^{12} - \eta_2 \phi_\delta^{22}$ is likely to be positive, $y^* > 0$ follows even when $\eta_\delta > 0$. However, with negative $\eta_\delta$, $y^*$ becomes positive sooner.[22]

**Proposition.** With $\eta < \eta^*$, $y^*$ can become positive for some intermediate range of $t$ values sooner than the case with $\eta > \eta^*$, in response to $x > 0$ and $x^* = 0$, under the condition that aggregate demands are interest inelastic.

When aggregate demands are interest elastic, $y_a^0$ is not zero. $y^*$ becomes positive if and only if $y_a^0 + \delta y_a > y_\delta^0$ or if and only if

$$(h_a, x_a) + (-h_\delta + \theta_a, x_\delta) > 0.$$

---

[22] For small $t$, we can approximate these functions by the Taylor series expansion in $t$: $g_a(t; a, b) \simeq a + (b\phi_a^{21} - a\phi_a^{22})t - a(\lambda_1 + \lambda_2)t + o(t)$, and $h_\delta(t; a, b) \simeq b + (a\phi_\delta^{12} - b\phi_\delta^{11})t - b(\mu_1 + \mu_2)t + o(t)$.

This inequality approximately becomes $\eta_\delta(-\eta_1)\eta_2 t > \eta_2 - (\eta_1 \phi_\delta^{12} + \eta_2 \phi_\delta^{22})t - \eta_2(\mu_1 + \mu_2)t$.

Thus, initially $y$ is negative. If $\eta_1 \phi_\delta^{12} - \eta_2 \phi_\delta^{22} - \eta_\delta \eta_1 \eta_2 > 0$, however, $y^*$ increases and becomes positive for $t > \underline{t} = \eta_2/(\eta_1 \phi_\delta^{12} - \eta_2 \phi_\delta^{22} - \eta_\delta \eta_1 \eta_2) > 0$.

## 13.8 Policy Effects

With the unilateral expansion at home, $x_a = x_\delta = x/2 > 0$. This condition becomes

$$(h_a - h_\delta + \theta_a, x) > 0,$$

where

$$h_a(t; a, b) = [a \quad b]\Phi_a(t)\begin{bmatrix}0\\1\end{bmatrix},$$

with

$$a = -\sigma_1 \tilde{D}_a(1 + m_2 v)$$

and

$$b = \sigma_1 \tilde{D}_a$$

[see (51) later in Section 13.9]. For small $t$, $h_a(t; a, b) \approx b$. Therefore, if $\sigma_1 \tilde{D}_a$ is greater than $\eta_2$ then $y^*$ can be initially positive. For large $t$, $y^*$ approaches zero. As before, for negative $\eta_\delta$, i.e., $\eta < \eta^*$, $y^*$ can remain positive over a larger interval.

### $v \neq v^*$

Now $\delta y_\delta$ is nonzero because $\phi_{\delta a}$ is nonzero. In this case, we need to assume $\sigma$ is nonzero to obtain nontrivial results.[23] Changes in the outputs are expressible as

$$y = y_a^0 + y_\delta^0 + \delta y_a + \delta y_\delta \quad \text{and} \quad y^* = y_a^0 - y_\delta^0 + \delta y_a - \delta y_\delta.$$

The condition that two countries equally benefit from monetary expansion becomes

$$0 = y_\delta^0 + \delta y_\delta.$$

We can relate these relations to $x_a$ and $x_\delta$ as follows: Noting that

$$y_\delta^0 = [-\eta_1 \quad \eta_2]z_\delta^0 = (h_\delta, x_\delta)$$

and

$$\delta y_\delta = [-\eta_1 \quad \eta_2]\delta z_\delta = [-\eta_1 \quad \eta_2](S_{\delta a}, x_a) = (\theta_\delta, x_a),$$

---

[23] The condition $y = y^*$ implies vanishing of $y_\delta^0 + \delta y_\delta$. With zero $\sigma$, $\delta y_\delta$ is zero because $[1 \quad 0]\Phi_a[^0_1]$ in $S_{\delta a}$ of (8), is identically zero implying that $x = x^*$ is the only way to achieve equality of $y$ and $y^*$, which in turn implies that $\delta y_a$ is zero; i.e., $y = y^* = 0$ is the only possibility.

where

$$\theta_\delta(t - s) = [-\eta_1 \quad \eta_2] S_{\delta a}(t - s)$$
$$= -v_\delta \int_s^t g_\delta(t - \tau; -\eta_1, \eta_2) h_a(\tau - s; 1, 0) \, d\tau,$$

the condition can be written as

(47) $$0 = (h_\delta, x_\delta) + (\theta_\delta, x_a).$$

Two countries equally benefit, then, if and only if $x$ and $x^*$ are such that

(47') $$(h_\delta + \theta_\delta, x) = (h_\delta - \theta_\delta, x^*).$$

Taking the Laplace transforms of both sides, the time paths of $x$ and $x^*$ must be such that their Laplace transforms satisfy

(48) $$\frac{\hat{x}}{\hat{x}^*} = \frac{(H_\delta - \Theta_\delta)}{(H_\delta + \Theta_\delta)} = \frac{H_\delta + v_\delta G_\delta H_a}{H_\delta - v_\delta G_\delta H_a},$$

where $H_\delta$ and $G_\delta$ are the Laplace transforms of $h_\delta$ and $g_\delta$, respectively,[24] and we use $\wedge$ to denote the transform. This equality states that $x$ and $x^*$ must be coordinated to satisfy[25]

$$\hat{x}^* = \frac{H_\delta - v_\delta G_\delta H_a}{H_\delta + v_\delta G_\delta H_a} \hat{x} = \frac{(s + \lambda_1)(s + \lambda_2) + v_\delta(\eta_1 s - \eta_3)}{(s + \lambda_1)(s + \lambda_2) - v_\delta(\eta_1 s - \eta_3)} \hat{x},$$

where $\eta_3 = \eta_1 \phi_\delta^{22} + \eta_2 \phi_\delta^{21}$.

For example, let

$$\hat{x} = 1/s,$$

i.e., once-and-for-all change of 1% in the rate of money stock growth. Then $x^*$ to the first order in $v_\delta$ should be $(1 - 2v_\delta)\eta_3/\lambda_1\lambda_2$ plus some transient terms decaying to zero exponentially.[26] We state this as

**Proposition.** The increase in the monetary instruments must be greater in a country with larger $v$ in order for the two countries to benefit equally in terms of the increased real output.

[24] From

$$\theta_\delta(t) = -v_\delta \int_0^t g_\delta(t - \tau) h_a(\tau - s)) \, d\tau,$$

we have $\Theta_\delta = -v_\delta G_\delta H_a$.

[25] Using $s$ to denote the Laplace transform variable, $H_\delta = (\eta_2 s - \eta_1 \phi_a^{12} - \eta_2 \phi_a^{11})/(s + \mu_1)(s + \mu_2)$, $H_a = (\eta_s s - \eta_1 \phi_a^{12} - \eta_2 \phi_a^{11})/(s + \lambda_1)(s + \lambda_2)$, and $G_\delta = -(\eta_1 s - \eta_3)/(s + \mu_1)(s + \mu_2)$, where $\eta_3 = \eta_1 \phi_\delta^{22} + \eta_2 \phi_\delta^{21}$.

[26] $x^* \approx (1 - 2v_\delta \eta_3/\lambda_1\lambda_2) + [2v_\delta/(\lambda_2 - \lambda_1)]\{[(\eta_1 \lambda_1 + \eta_3)/\lambda_1]e^{-\lambda_1 t} - [(\eta_1 \lambda_2 + \eta_3)/\lambda_2]\}e^{-\lambda_2 t}$. Therefore, if $v_\delta > 0$ ($v > v^*$) and $\eta_3$ is negative, then it is necessary that $x^* > x$ for $t$ large.

## 13.9 Elaborations on the Basic Model

Larger $|\phi_a|$ implies smaller $\eta_3/\lambda_1\lambda_2$ since $\lambda_1\lambda_2$ equals $|\phi_a|$, hence the difference in $x$ and $x^*$ can be smaller to result in the same real output increase. Put differently, larger $|\phi_a|$ means that $y$ and $y^*$ are nearly the same in response to the same expansion $x = x^*$.

### $m_2 \neq m_2^*$

The condition for equal expansion of outputs of the two countries following changes in $x$ and $x^*$ is the same as in the previous case, and is given by (47) or (47'). The expression for the submatrix of interaction $\phi_{\delta a}$ now reads

$$\phi_{\delta a} = \zeta \tilde{D}_a \tilde{D}_\delta \begin{bmatrix} -\beta \\ \alpha \end{bmatrix} [1 \quad -1], \qquad \text{where} \quad \zeta = \frac{m_2 - m_2^*}{2}.$$

Hence, the expression for the Laplace transform of the function $\theta_\delta$ changes into

$$\Theta_\delta = \zeta \tilde{D}_a \tilde{D}_\delta (\alpha H_\delta - \beta G_\delta) \tilde{H}_a,$$

where $\tilde{H}_a$ is the Laplace transform of $h_a(t; 1, -1)$. With this change (48) is valid for this case as well. Analyzing this, we reach the following statement.

**Proposition.** *The increase in the monetary instrument should be greater in a country with smaller interest elasticity of demand for money for the two-country to benefit equally by increased real outputs.*

Following a step change in $x$, we derive from (48) that $x^*$ must be chosen to be

$$x^* = 1 - 2\zeta H + \text{two exponentially decaying terms},$$

where $H = \{\tilde{D}_a \tilde{D}_\delta/(\lambda_1\lambda_2)\}\{\alpha(\eta_1 \phi_\delta^{12} + \eta_2 \phi_\delta^{11}) + \beta \eta_2\}$.

Analysis of the dependence of this expression on various system parameters and their implications on the size of the difference $x$ are left for the interested reader.

### 13.9 Elaborations on the Basic Model

In this section we consider various factors which are not included in our basic model of Section 13.4 and assess changes in our analysis brought about by these omitted elements.

#### 13.9.1 Case $\sigma \neq 0$

Now that we have outlined behavior of the model and policy effects under the assumption of zero $\sigma$ and $\sigma^*$, we drop this assumption. The interest elastic components of the aggregate demands in the two countries introduce certain modifications to our results; the main ones being that $y_a$ is no longer zero and that the dynamics for $m_a$ can no longer be separated in (39). Otherwise our procedure remains the same and most of our conclusions still hold.

When the $\sigma$ term is retained in (17), the real sector equilibrium condition (26) changes into

(49)  $$A\mathbf{p} + \tilde{B}\mathbf{i} = a\mathbf{w} + \sigma\mathbf{\rho} + \Gamma\mathbf{y},$$

where $\tilde{B} = B + \sigma I$.

Solving (49) and (27) together, we need to replace (28) by

$$(aI + d\mathbf{vv'})\mathbf{p} + \{d\theta^{-1}\mathbf{vv'} + \hat{\sigma}(I + \Gamma)\}\mathbf{i} = a\mathbf{w} + \hat{\sigma}(I + \Gamma)\mathbf{\rho},$$

where $\hat{\sigma} = \sigma(1 - \xi^2)^{-1}$.

Equation (29) remains the same.

In terms of the average and the difference variables, the next two equations replace the first equations of (31a) and (31b):

$$\sigma_1 i_a + ap_a = aw_a + \sigma_1 \rho_a$$

and

$$(2\gamma\theta^{-1} + \sigma_2)i_\delta + (1 + 2\gamma)p_\delta = w_\delta + \sigma_2\rho_\delta,$$

where

$$\sigma_1 = \sigma(1 - \xi)^{-1} \quad \text{and} \quad \sigma_2 = \sigma(1 + \xi)^{-1}.$$

Thus the expression for $R_a$ in (31a) is replaced by

(50)  $$R_a = \begin{bmatrix} \sigma_1/a & 1 + \sigma_1 v/a \\ -m_2 & 1 \end{bmatrix},$$

and $\alpha$ and $\beta$ in $R_\delta$ of (31b) are replaced by

$$\tilde{\alpha} = \alpha + \sigma_2(1 - 2\chi\theta^{-1}v)(1 - 2\chi)^{-1}/a, \qquad \tilde{\beta} = \beta + \sigma_2 v/a.$$

Instead of (34), $y_a$ and $y_\delta$ are determined by

$$y_a = -\sigma_1(i_a - \rho_a) \quad \text{and} \quad y_\delta = -2d(p_\delta + \theta^{-1}i_\delta) - \sigma_2(i_\delta - \rho_\delta).$$

The expressions for $\rho_a$ and $\rho_\delta$ remain the same.

Consequently (34) is changed into

(51)  $$y_a = -\sigma_1 \tilde{D}_a\{(1 + m_2 v)w_a - m_a\},$$

where

$$\tilde{D}_a^{-1} = m_2 + \sigma_1(m_2 v + 1)/a,$$

and

(52) $$y_\delta = -\tilde{\eta}_1 w_\delta + \tilde{\eta}_2 m_\delta,$$

where $\tilde{\eta}_i$ is the same as $\eta_i$ with $\alpha$ and $\beta$ replaced with $\tilde{\alpha}$ and $\tilde{\beta}$.

We see that nonzero $\sigma$ mainly causes the dynamics for $z_a$ to differ from those of (37). A term $[-\frac{\eta}{\mu_1}] y_a$ is added to the right-hand side of $\dot{z}_a$. In (39), the vector $[m_2 \ 0]$ is replaced by $[m_2 \ \sigma_1/a]$. The vector $[1 \ -1]$ becomes $[1 \ -1 - \sigma_1 v/a]$. The dynamic matrix $\phi_a$ in (39) now becomes

$$\phi_a = \tilde{D}_a \begin{bmatrix} -vm_2(1 + \sigma_1\eta) - \sigma_1\eta & \sigma_1(\eta - v/a) \\ \mu_2 m_2 + \mu_3 + \sigma_1\mu_1(1 + m_1 v) & -\mu_3(1 + \sigma_1 v/a) - \sigma_1\mu_1 \end{bmatrix}.$$

The (1, 2) element of $\phi_a$ introduces coupling between $m_a$ and $w_a$ which, in turn, causes the perturbation calculation to become slightly more complicated. See Chapter 5 also. The reduced form expression of $y_a$ is for zero $v$

(53) $$y_a = -\sigma_1 \tilde{D}_a (w_a - m_a)$$

$$= -\sigma_1 \tilde{D}_a \left( (1 \ -1) \Phi_a \begin{bmatrix} 0 \\ 1 \end{bmatrix}, x_a \right) = \sigma_1 \tilde{D}_a (h_a, x_a).$$

*Alternate Wage Rate Dynamics*

We earlier mentioned an alternate wage rate adjustment equation $\dot{w} = -\eta(w - p_i) + \rho_i$. The dynamics for the averages remain the same. The expression for the dynamics matrix for the differences in (39) changes into

$$\phi_\delta = \begin{bmatrix} -\eta + (\eta - v)\omega_1 & (\eta - v)\omega_2 \\ \mu_1 \eta_1 + \omega_3 & -\mu_1 \eta_1 + \omega_4 \end{bmatrix}.$$

The changes consist of $\eta_1$ being replaced by $1 - \omega_1$ and $\eta_2$ by $\omega_2$. No fundamental changes in the dynamic behavior are therefore brought about by this alternate specification of wage rate dynamics.

## 13.10 Numerical Examples

The following numerical examples illustrate possible ranges of dynamic behavior of the model and changes in the model behavior due to non-identical economies. They also highlight the roles played by some of the more important transmission mechanisms in determining the overall model dynamic behavior.

First we examine the effects of initial state vector deviations, keeping the instruments at zero; then we evaluate the effects of instruments on the model in the equilibrium. Because of the linearity of the variational dynamic equations, these effects superimpose. We thus can examine these effects separately.

### *Effects of Initial Displacements*

We first focus on the effects of national differences in the state vector $z_\delta(0)$ by setting $w_a(0)$ and $m_a(0)$ to zero. The effects of initial displacement of the $w_a$ are later illustrated. On the assumption that $w_a(0) = 0$, $m_a(0) = 0$, and $x(t) = 0$, $x^*(t) = 0$ for all $t \geq 0$, (39) shows that $w_a(t) = 0$ and $m_a(t) = 0$ for all $t \geq 0$ when the two economies are the same. We then solve (39) for $z_\delta(t)$. Later these solutions are used to derive the dynamic behavior of nonidentical economies, i.e., two countries with different adjustment speeds in (24). Even with $w_a(0) = 0$ and $m_a(0) = 0$, $w_a(t)$ no longer remains at zero. Then the consequences of $m_2 \neq m_2^*$ are calculated.

### *Model Parameters*

Three types of system parameters are important: The parameters $\eta_1$ and $\eta_2$ in (34) show how much relative deviations in the wage rate and money stock differentials affect $y_\delta$; the vector $z_\delta$ affects $\rho_{i\delta}$ via its effects on $i_\delta$ and $p_\delta$. This transmission path is characterized by the parameter $\omega_1$ and $\omega_2$ in (38). These parameters also determine the "strength" of coupling between the difference and the average dynamics in (39); the $\mu$s in the government budget constraint equation (21) have a strong influence on the dynamics for $z_\delta$ because $z_\delta$ directly affects $i_\delta$ and $p_\delta$ in (33); the latter in turn affect $\dot{m}_\delta$. The parameter $\theta$ affects all the elements in the dynamic matrix by changing $D_\delta$ and $\eta$s.

The relative money stock difference $m_\delta$ affects the dynamics of the wage rate difference, i.e., $w_\delta$, via two opposing channels: $m_\delta$ tends to increase $w_\delta$ because $m_\delta$ increases $y_\delta$ as shown in (34) which in turn increases $\dot{w}_\delta$ by (18). $m_\delta > 0$ also causes the price index differential change $p_{i\delta}$ to increase, causing $\dot{w}_\delta < 0$ via the expectational variable $\rho_{i\delta}$ in (38). The sign of $\phi_\delta^{12}$, i.e., $\eta\eta_2 - \nu\omega_2$, shows which effects dominate.

Two sets of parameter values are used to generate quite different dynamic behavior. With the first, the dynamics for $w_\delta$ and for $m_\delta$ are both slow, and the net effects of $m_\delta > 0$ on $\dot{w}_\delta$ are negative, i.e., the contractionary influence of $m_\delta$ on $\dot{w}_\delta$ via $\rho_{i\delta}$ is stronger than the expansionary effect of $m_\delta$ on $\dot{w}_\delta$ via $y_\delta$. In the second set, the dynamics are much faster. The expansionary effect of $m_\delta$ on $\dot{w}_\delta$ via $y_\delta$ outweighs the contractionary effect via $\rho_{i\delta}$.

## 13.10 Numerical Examples

### The First Case

We set $\chi$ to 0.1 in (15) so that 10% of the bundle of the consumer goods are foreign goods; the supply response to changes of the real wage rate is set with $a = 0.2$ in (16); the demand is responsive to changes in the terms of trade with $d = 0.4$ in (28). By (31b), $\gamma = 2$ follows. The wage rate changes are responsive to the excess demand with $\eta = 0.1$ in (18); Dornbusch (1976) cites a value 0.05 for $m_2 i$. Taking $i = 0.05$, this implies $m_2 = 1$ in (19). As a small value of $\theta$ in (23), we take $\theta = 0.1$. In the other set we examine consequences of a much larger $\theta$. Throughout the numerical experiments, we use $\mu_1 = 0.1$, $\mu_2 = 0$, and $\mu_3 \theta = 1$. With $\theta = 0.1$, this implies $\mu_3 = 10$. The effects of nonzero $\mu_2$ are discussed at the end.

With these parameter values, the model is specified as having $\eta_1 = 0.187$ and $\eta_2 = 0.170$ in (34); $\omega_1 = 0.017$, $\omega_2 = 0.894$, $\omega_3 = 0.170$, and $\omega_4 = -1.064$ in (39). The eigenvalues of $\phi_\delta$ are $-0.147$ and $-0.961$.

### The Second Case

Here we choose a faster response in (23) by letting $\theta = 1$; hence, $m_2 \theta = 1$. We change $d$ to 0.5 and choose a faster supply response $a = 1$. These imply $\gamma = 0.5$. We choose $\mu_3 \theta$ to be 4 and $\eta = 0.8$. All other parameter values remain the same. They specify the model with $\eta_1 = 0.625$, $\eta_2 = 0.312$; $\omega_1 = 0.25$, $\omega_2 = 0.375$, $\omega_3 = 1.0$, and $\omega_4 = -2.5$. The eigenvalues of $\phi_\delta$ are $-0.591$ and $-2.565$. The coefficient $v$ is set at 0.5 in both cases. The parameter $m_1$ is set to zero in both cases.

### Dynamic Behavior: Identical Economies

With the first set of parameters, the dynamic matrix $\phi_\delta$ is

$$\phi_\delta = \begin{bmatrix} -0.027 & -0.430 \\ 0.260 & -1.081 \end{bmatrix}.$$

The wage rate and the money stock differentials change with time according to

(54) $$w_\delta(t) = (-0.147 e^{-0.961t} + 1.147 e^{-0.147t}) w_\delta(0) \\ - 0.528(e^{-0.147t} - e^{-0.961t}) m_\delta(0),$$

and

(55) $$m_\delta(t) = 0.319(e^{-0.147t} - e^{-0.961t}) w_\delta(0) \\ + (1.147 e^{-0.961t} - 0.147 e^{-0.147t}) m_\delta(0).$$

With the second parameter set, the dynamic matrix becomes

$$\phi_\delta = \begin{bmatrix} -0.625 & 0.062 \\ 1.0625 & -2.531 \end{bmatrix},$$

and $w_\delta(t)$ and $m_\delta(t)$ are now described by

(56) $$w_\delta(t) = (0.017e^{-2.565t} + 0.983e^{-0.591t})w_\delta(0) \\ + 0.031(e^{-0.591t} - e^{-2.565t})m_\delta(0)$$

and

(57) $$m_\delta(t) = 0.531(e^{-0.591t} - e^{-2.565})w_\delta(0) \\ + (0.983e^{-2.561t} + 0.017e^{-0.591t})m_\delta(0).$$

The effect of $w_\delta(0)$ spills over to $m_\delta(t)$, and $m_\delta(0)$ affects $w_\delta(t)$. As discussed earlier, these two cases differ in the sign of the effects of $m_\delta(0)$ on $w_\delta(t)$ as can be seen from (54) and (56). In (54)–(57), the cross-coupling (spill-over) effects of $m_\delta(0)$ on $w_\delta(t)$ and $w_\delta(0)$ on $m_\delta(t)$ have the same time profile except for the scalings. The initial condition $m_\delta(0)$ has negligible effects on $w_\delta(t)$ in (56).

The time paths of $w_\delta(t)/w_\delta(0)$ with zero $m_\delta(0)$, and $w_\delta(t)/m_\delta(0)$ and $m_\delta(t)/m_\delta(0)$ with zero $w_\delta(0)$ are plotted in Fig. 1. With the first set of parameters, all time

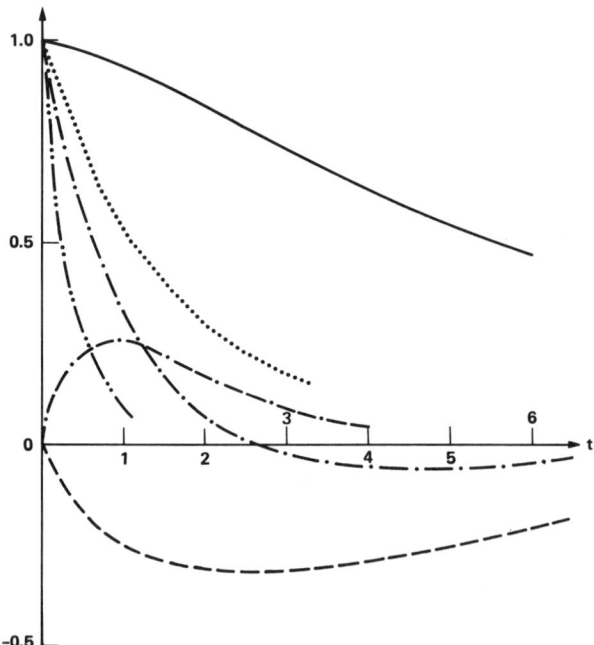

Figure 1  Time paths of differences in wage rate deviations and money stock deviations due to initial differences.
   Case 1:  ——, $w_\delta(t)/w_\delta(0)$; ---, $w_\delta(t)/m_\delta(0)$; –·–, $m_\delta(t)/m_\delta(0)$.
   Case 2:  ·····, $w_\delta(t)/w_\delta(0)$; –··–, $w_\delta(t)/m_\delta(0)$; –···–, $m_\delta(t)/m_\delta(0)$.

## 13.10 Numerical Examples

paths decay more slowly than with the second set of parameters; $m_\delta(t)/m_\delta(0)$ becomes negative before returning to zero; $m_\delta(0)$ causes $w_\delta(t)$ to become negative with the first set of parameters, while $w_\delta(t)$ is a small positive number with the second set. The relative magnitude of $\eta\eta_2$ and $vw_2$ are primarily responsible for these opposite behaviors.

### Dynamic Behavior: Nonidentical Economies $v \neq v^*$

The effects of nonzero $v_\delta$ is directly proportional to it. A larger $v_\delta$ value of course magnifies the effects of nonidentical $v$ values. Equation (42) shows that $z_\delta$ is the same as above to the first order in $v_\delta$, i.e., the same as the case of $v_\delta = 0$. Equation (43) also shows that $w_a$ no longer remains at zero. Integrating (43) and recalling that $w_a(0) = 0$, the average wage rate deviates according to

$$(58) \qquad w_a(t)/v_\delta = -e^{-0.5t} \int_0^t e^{0.5\tau}\{\omega_1 w_\delta(\tau) + \omega_2 m_\delta(\tau)\} \, d\tau.$$

With the first parameter set, $\omega_1 = 0.017$ and $\omega_2 = 0.894$. Substituting (54) and (55) into (58) we derive

$$(59) \quad w_a(t)/v_\delta = (0.397e^{-0.147t} - 2.64e^{-0.5t} + 2.244e^{-0.961t})m_\delta(0)$$
$$+ (-0.863e^{-0.147t} + 1.488e^{-0.5t} - 0.625e^{-0.961t})w_\delta(0).$$

With the second parameter set, $\omega_1 = 0.25$ and $\omega_2 = 0.375$. The time path is described by

$$(60) \quad w_a(t)/v_\delta = (-0.33e^{-0.5t} + 0.155e^{-0.591t} + 0.175e^{-2.565t})m_\delta(0)$$
$$+ (-4.796e^{-0.5t} + 4.89e^{-0.591t} - 0.094e^{-2.565t})w_\delta(0).$$

The average dynamics are much slower than the difference dynamics are for the second parameter set, while the opposite is true for the first parameter set. This is due to our choice of $v = 0.5$ which is greater than 0.147 but less than 0.591. The effect of $m_\delta(0)$ on $w_a$ peaks earlier than that of $w_\delta(0)$ for both sets of parameters, and they decay faster as well. With $v_\delta = 0.1$, $w_a/w_\delta(0)$ peaks at $-0.04$ for the first set and at $-0.01$ for the second set. See the plots in Fig. 2.

We calculate the effects of $w(0) = \bar{w}$, $w^*(0) = -\bar{w}$, by

$$w(t) = w_a(t) + w_\delta(t) \quad \text{and} \quad w^*(t) = w_a(t) - w_\delta(t),$$

$w_\delta(0) = \bar{w}$, and $m_\delta(0) = 0$ in Eqs. (54)–(60). With the first parameter set, we combine (54) with (59). When (56) is combined with (60), the wage rate time paths for the second case is obtained. Note that $w(t)$ and $w^*(t)$ both go to zero with time; i.e., with $x = 0$ and $x^* = 0$, no permanent effects remain of

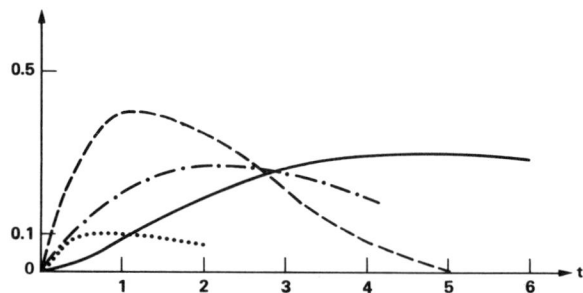

*Figure 2* Time paths of average wage rates when $v$ and $v^*$ are unequal.
Case 1: ———, $-w_a(t)/v_\delta w_\delta(0)$; ---, $-w_a(t)/v_\delta m_\delta(0)$.
Case 2: —·—, $-w_a(t)/v_\delta m_\delta(0)$; ......, $-w_a(t)/v_\delta w_\delta(0)$.

the initial wage rate differential. Figure 3 depicts $w(t)$ and $-w^*(t)$ for the second parameter set and with $\zeta = 0.3$. Note that $w^*(t)$ decays to zero slower than $w(t)$. In Figure 3 and below $\zeta$ stands for $v_\delta$.

**Instruments.** We now evaluate the effect of a nonzero instrument $x_\delta$ on $z_\delta$ and on $w_a$.[27] We assume that $x_\delta$ is nonzero only over $0 \leq t \leq 1$. One major difference is that $w_a(\infty)$ becomes nonzero with $\zeta \neq 0$, i.e., permanent effects exist on the average wage rate, although $z_\delta(\infty)$ is zero.

With the first parameter set, for $0 \leq t \leq 1$,

(61) $\quad w_\delta(t)/x_\delta = -7.093(0.43 - 0.508e^{-0.147t} + 0.078e^{-0.961t})$,

(62) $\quad m_\delta(t)/x_\delta = -7.093(-0.027 - 0.141e^{-0.147t} + 0.168e^{-0.961t})$

for $t \geq 1$,

(63) $\quad w_\delta(t)/x_\delta = -7.093(0.0804e^{-0.147t} - 0.125e^{-0.961t})$,

(64) $\quad m_\delta(t)/x_\delta = -7.093(0.023e^{-0.147t} - 0.272e^{-0.961t})$.

With two identical economies $w_a \equiv 0$ if $x_a \equiv 0$. With $v_\delta \neq 0$, however, $w_a$ becomes nonzero even if $x_a \equiv 0$. For $0 \leq t \leq 1$, the induced effects on $w_a$ are given by

(65)

$$w_a(t)/x_\delta = 7.093\zeta(-0.084 - 0.382e^{-0.147t} + 0.72e^{-0.5t} - 0.329e^{-0.961t}).$$

For $t > 1$, the average wage rate deviates from zero according to

(66) $\quad w_a(t)/x_\delta = w_a(1)/x_\delta + \zeta(0.0615e^{-0.147t} - 0.244e^{-0.5t} + 0.248e^{-0.961t})$.

---

[27] If home country changes $x$, while $x^*$ is still zero, then $x_a = x/2$ and $x_\delta = -x/2$. $w_a(t)$ is still all zero. However, $m_a$ deviates from zero. As (43) shows, $m_a$, however, does not affect $z_\delta$.

## 13.10 Numerical Examples

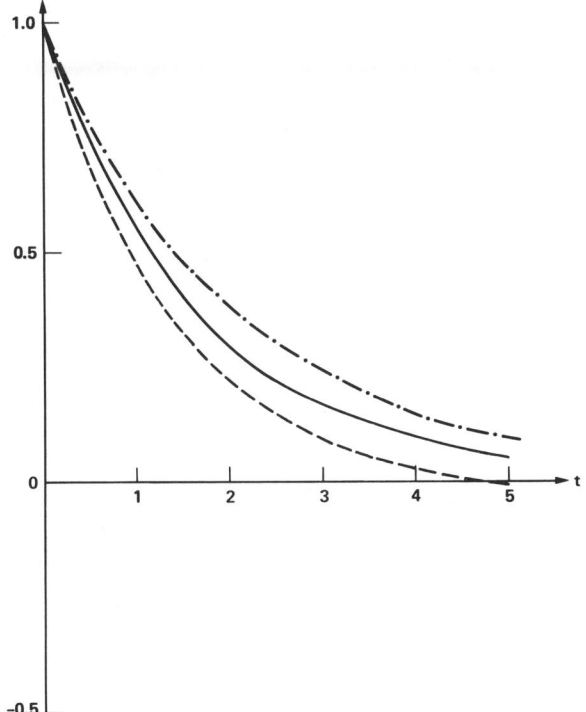

*Figure* 3  Initial discrepancies in the wage rates in the two countries disappear over time if the instruments remain at zero.
Case 2: $\zeta = 0$; —, $w(t)/\overline{w}$; $\zeta = 0.3$: ---, $w(t)\overline{w}$; —·—, $-w^*(t)/\overline{w}$.

Note that $w_a$ is permanently shifted from zero, $w_a(\infty)/x_\delta = -0.596v_\delta$, even though $x_\delta$ returns to zero after $t = 1$.

With the second parameter set; the next equations, (67)–(70), correspond to (61) through (64).

For $0 \le t \le 1$,

(67) $\quad w_\delta(t)/x_\delta = -0.660(-0.062 + 0.08e^{-0.591t} - 0.018e^{-2.561t})$,

(68) $\quad m_\delta(t)/x_\delta = -0.66(-0.625 + 0.44e^{-0.591t} + 0.582e^{-2.561})$;

for $t > 1$,

(69) $\quad w_\delta(t)/x_\delta = -0.66(-0.064e^{-0.591t} + 0.21e^{-2.561t})$,

(70) $\quad m_\delta(t)/x_\delta = -0.66(-0.035e^{-0.591t} - 6.948e^{-2.561t})$.

Equations (71) and (72) are the expressions corresponding to (65) and (66). For $t < 1$,

(71) $\quad w_a(t)/x_\delta = 0.66\zeta(-0.5 + 0.995e^{-0.5t} - 0.398e^{-0.591t} - 0.097e^{-2.561t})$.

For $t > 1$,

$$w_a(t)/x_\delta = w_a(1)/x_\delta + 0.66(-0.451e^{-0.5t} + 0.321e^{-0.591t} + 1.239e^{-2.561t}),$$
(72)

and the long-run effect equals

$$w_a(\infty)/x_\delta = -0.33\zeta.$$

We plot (61), (63) and (65), (66) in Fig. 4. The time path of $w_\delta/x_\delta$ for $v_\delta = 0.1$ is plotted for case 1 for comparison in Fig. 5, and translated into the plots for $w$ and $w^*$ in Fig. 6.

Treating next $m$ and $m^*$ as the instruments, we consider a one-and-for-all change in $m_\delta$, i.e., $m_\delta(t) = \bar{m}_\delta$, $t \geq 0$. With the parameter set 1, the pattern of interaction is determined by

$$D_1(t) = -0.311(1 - 0.050\zeta)e^{-0.158t} - 0.905\zeta e^{-0.5t},$$

$$D_2(t) = 0.311(1 + 0.05\zeta)e^{-0.158t} - 0.9095\zeta e^{-0.5t}.$$

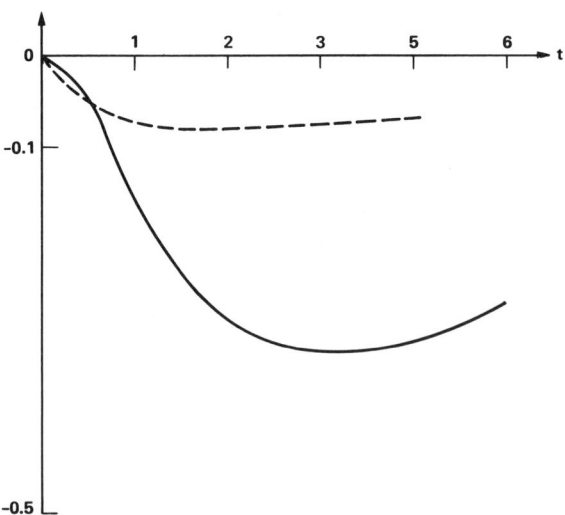

**Figure 4** Effects of temporary differences in the instruments on wage rate differences. Case 1: ———, $w_\delta/x_\delta$; ---, $w_a/x_\delta(v_\delta = 0.1)$.

## 13.10 Numerical Examples

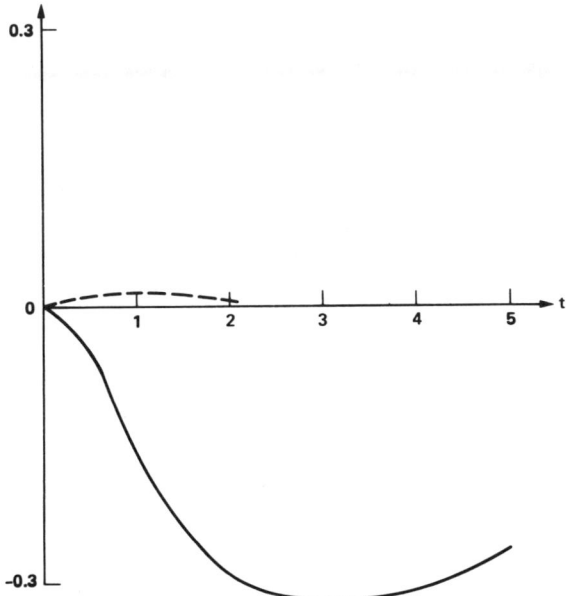

*Figure 5* Effects of temporary differences in the instruments on wage rate averages and difference.
Case 1: ——, $w_\delta(t)/x_\delta$.    Case 2: ---, $w_a(t)/x_\delta$.

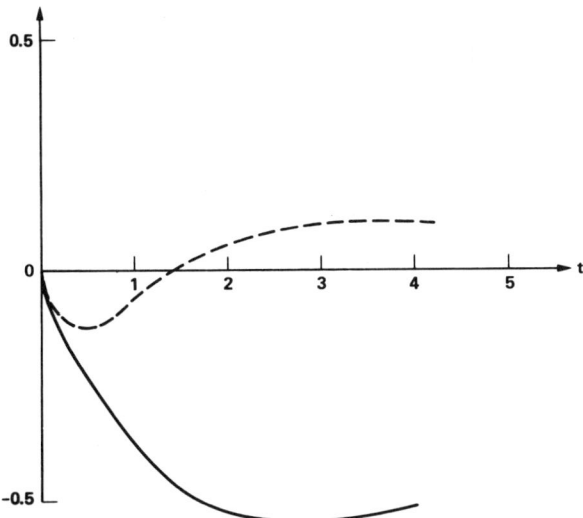

*Figure 6* Effects of temporary differences in the instruments on the wage rate deviations in the two countries.
Case 1: ——, $w/x_\delta$; ---, $w^*/x_\delta$.

With the second parameter set,

$$D_1(t) = 0.062(1 + 2\zeta)e^{-0.625t} - 0.499\zeta e^{-0.5t},$$
$$D_2(t) = -0.062(1 - 2\zeta)e^{-0.625t} - 0.499\zeta e^{-0.5t}.$$

With constant $\bar{m}_\delta$ and with the first parameter set,

(73) $$\begin{bmatrix} w(t) \\ w^*(t) \end{bmatrix} = \bar{m}_\delta \int_0^t \begin{bmatrix} D_1(t-s) \\ D_2(t-s) \end{bmatrix} ds = \bar{m}_\delta \left\{ l_1(t) \begin{bmatrix} 1 \\ 1 \end{bmatrix} + l_2(t) \begin{bmatrix} 1 \\ -1 \end{bmatrix} \right\},$$

where

$$l_1(t) = -1.721\zeta + 1.819\zeta e^{-0.5t} - 0.098\zeta e^{-0.158t}$$

and

$$l_2(t) = -1.968(1 - e^{-0.158t}).$$

Here $l_1(t)$ is the component of the effects of $m_\delta$ which affect $w$ and $w^*$ in the same way and $l_2(t)$ the opposite way.

With the second parameter set, the wage rates behave according to

(74) $$\begin{bmatrix} w(t) \\ w^*(t) \end{bmatrix} = \bar{m}_\delta \left\{ l_3(t) \begin{bmatrix} 1 \\ 1 \end{bmatrix} + l_4(t) \begin{bmatrix} 1 \\ -1 \end{bmatrix} \right\},$$

where

$$l_3(t) = -0.7996\zeta + 0.998\zeta e^{-0.5t} - 0.1984\zeta e^{-0.625t}$$

and

$$l_4(t) = 0.0992(1 - e^{-0.625t}).$$

Note that the long-run effects are opposite to each other in cases 1 and 2, due to the sign difference in $(\eta\eta_2 - v_a\omega_2)$. The functions $w(t)/\bar{m}_\delta$ and $w^*(t)/\bar{m}_\delta$ are plotted in Fig. 7.

**Effects of nonzero $w_a(0)$.** With nonzero $w_a(0)$, $w_a(t)$ becomes $w_a(0)e^{-v_a t}$. This causes $z_\delta$ to deviate from its time path of $\mathscr{V}\mathscr{M}_0$. From (43), we see that

$$z_\delta(t) - z_\delta^0(t) = -v_\delta w_a(0) \left[ \int_0^t e^{\hat{\phi}_\delta(t-\tau)} e^{-v_a \tau} d\tau \right] \begin{bmatrix} 1 \\ 0 \end{bmatrix}$$

$$= -v_\delta w_a(\hat{\phi}_\delta + v_a I)^{-1} \left\{ e^{\hat{\phi}_\delta t} \begin{bmatrix} 1 \\ 0 \end{bmatrix} - e^{-v_a t} \begin{bmatrix} 1 \\ 0 \end{bmatrix} \right\},$$

where the superscript zero denotes the reference time path.

## 13.10 Numerical Examples

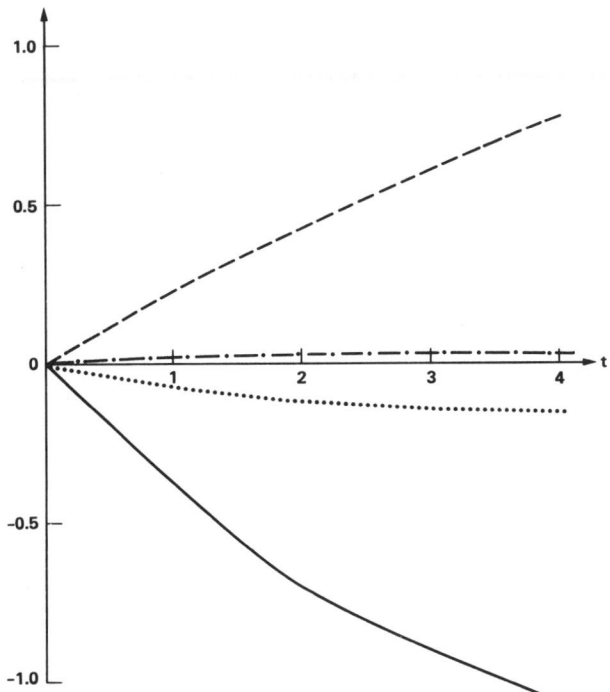

*Figure 7* Effects of once-and-for-all changes in money stocks on wage rate deviations in the two countries.
Case 1: $v_\delta = 0.1$: ———, $w(t)/\overline{m}_\delta$; ---, $w^*(t)/\overline{m}_\delta$.
Case 2: —·—, $w(t)/\overline{m}_\delta$; ......, $w^*(t)/\overline{m}_\delta$.

With the first parameter set, the difference variables equal the following:

(75) $\{w_\delta(t) - w_\delta^0(t)\}/\{v_\delta w_a(0)\}$
$= 6.1345(0.5292e^{-0.147t} - 0.581e^{-0.5t} + 0.0518e^{-0.961t})$
$= 3.2464e^{-0.147t} - 3.564e^{-0.5t} + 0.3178e^{-0.961t}$

and

(76) $\{m_\delta(t) - m_\delta^0(t)\}/\{v_\delta w_a(0)\}$
$= 6.1345(0.1473e^{-0.147t} + 0.1127e^{-0.961t} - 0.26e^{-0.5t})$
$= 0.9036e^{-0.147t} + 0.6914e^{-0.961t} - 1.595e^{-0.5t}.$

With the second parameter set, they are given by

(77) $\{w_\delta(t) - w_\delta^0(t)\}/\{v_\delta w_a(0)\}$
$= -5.318(2.0294e^{-0.591t} + 0.002e^{-2.565t} - 2.031e^{-0.5t})$
$= -10.7923e^{-0.591t} - 0.011e^{-2.565t} + 10.801e^{-0.5t}$

and

(78) $\{m_\delta(t) - m_\delta^o(t)\}/\{v_\delta w_a(0)\}$
$= -5.318(1.110e^{-0.591t} - 0.048e^{-2.565t} - 1.062e^{-0.5t})$
$= -5.903e^{-0.591t} + 0.2553e^{-2.565t} + 5.6477e^{-0.5t}.$

We can use the previous results to evaluate the change in the initial wage rate deviation at home, when $w^*(0) = 0$. This situation implies that $w_a(0) = w(0)/2$ and $w_\delta(0) = w(0)/2$. We evaluate $w_\delta(t)$ with $w_\delta(0) = w(0)/2$. Then add the correction factor calculated above.

With the first parameter set $w_\delta^o(t)$ is given by (54) by setting $m_\delta(0)$ to zero, and with $w_\delta(0) = w(0)/2$, the interaction term equals (59) with $w_a(0) = w(0)/2$.

With the second parameter set, $w_\delta^o(t)$ is given by (56) by setting $m_\delta(0)$ to zero, and the effect of interaction equals (60) with $w_a(0) = w(0)/2$.

The interaction terms (75)–(78) are plotted in Fig. 8.

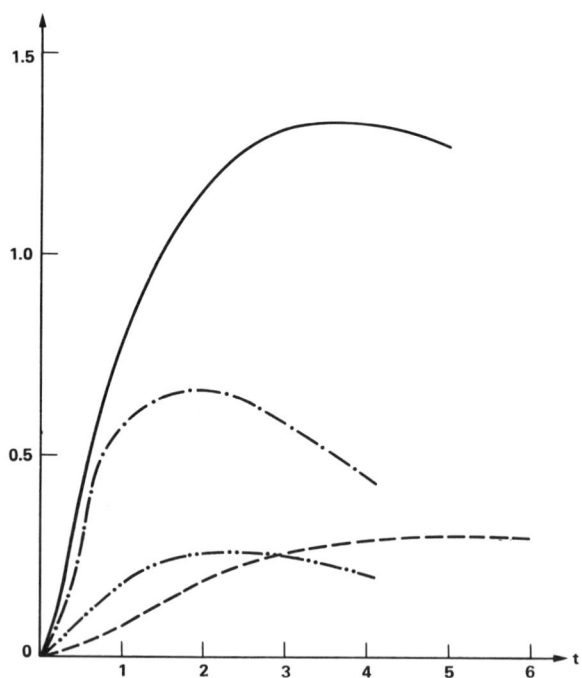

Figure 8  Time paths of the interaction term.
Case 1: ———, $w_\delta(t) - w_\delta^o(t)/v_\delta w_a(0)$; ---, $m_\delta(t) - m_\delta^o(t)/v_\delta w_a(0)$.
Case 2: —·—, $w_\delta(t) - w_\delta^o(t)/v_\delta w_a(0)$; —··—, $m_\delta(t) - m_\delta^o(t)/v_\delta w_a(0)$.

## 13.10 Numerical Examples

**Exchange Rate Behavior.** To the first order in $v_\delta$, if $w_a(0) = 0$, $e$-behavior is the same as in $\mathcal{V}\mathcal{M}_0$. From (25) and (33),

$$e = -2\theta^{-1}i_\delta = -2\theta^{-1}D_\delta\{(1 - 2\chi)w_\delta - \beta m_\delta\}.$$

**Effects of Initial Conditions.** With the first parameter set,

$$\begin{aligned}e &= -0.340 w_\delta + 2.1277 m_\delta \\ &= (0.317 e^{-0.147t} - 0.629 e^{-0.961t}) w_\delta(0) \\ &\quad - (0.133 e^{-0.147t} - 2.260 e^{-0.961t}) m_\delta(0).\end{aligned}$$

With the second set,

$$\begin{aligned}e &= -0.5 w_\delta + 1.25 m_\delta \\ &= (0.172 e^{-0.591t} - 0.672 e^{-2.565t}) w_\delta(0) \\ &\quad + (0.0370 e^{-0.591t} + 1.213 e^{-2.565}) m_\delta(0).\end{aligned}$$

When $w(0)$ shifts while $w^*(0) = 0$, it leads to $w_a(0) = w(0)/2$ and $w_\delta(0) = w(0)/2$ causing $w_\delta$ and $m_\delta$ to deviate from zero. The effects of nonidentical $v$ can be evaluated as

$$e - e^0 = \kappa_1(w_\delta - w_\delta^0) + \kappa_2(m_\delta - m_\delta^0),$$

where $w_\delta - w_\delta^0$ and $m_\delta - m_\delta^0$ are as given in (43').

With the first parameter set, the interactions between two different economies produce the correction term $(e - e^0)/(\zeta w_a(0)) = 3.069 e^{-0.147t} - 2.259 e^{-0.5t} + 1.397 e^{-0.961t}$. Large interactions in this example are quite striking. The effects of instruments on $e$ are evaluate by $e/x_\delta = -2\theta^{-1}D_\delta\{(1 - 2\chi)w_\delta/x_\delta - \beta m_\delta/x_\delta\}$. For example, with the first parameter set, from (61)–(64)

$$\frac{e}{x_\delta} = -0.034 \frac{w_\delta}{x_\delta} + 0.213 \frac{m_\delta}{x_\delta}$$

$$= \begin{cases} 0.1445 + 0.0905 e^{-0.147t} - 0.235 e^{-0.961t} & \text{for } t \leq 1, \\ -0.0154 e^{-0.147t} + 0.3808 e^{-0.961t} & \text{for } t \geq 1, \end{cases}$$

$$\frac{e}{x_\delta} = -0.5 \frac{w_\delta}{x_\delta} + 1.25 \frac{m_\delta}{x_\delta}$$

$$= \begin{cases} 0.4952 - 0.01 e^{-0.591t} - 0.486 e^{-2.561} & \text{for } t \leq 1, \\ 0.008 e^{-0.591t} + 5.801 e^{-2.561} & \text{for } t \geq 1. \end{cases}$$

These are plotted in Fig. 9.

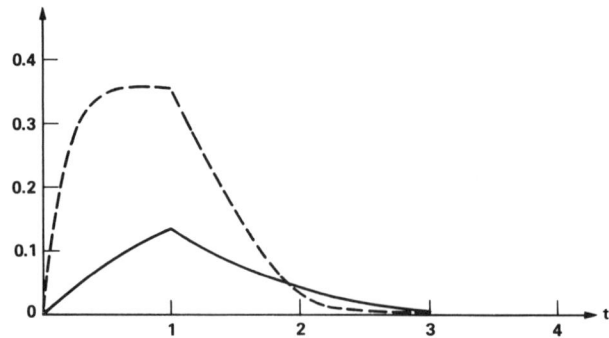

*Figure 9*  Exchange rate deviations caused by nonzero $x_\delta$.
Case 1: ———, $e/x_\delta$.
Case 2: ——— $e/x_\delta$.

## Case with $m_2 \neq m_2^*$

***Effects of Initial Conditions.***  When two economies differ in their interest elasticities of demands for money, the model behavior is determined by (45) and (46) of Section 13.7. Let the perturbation parameter $\zeta$ stands for $(m_2 - m_2^*)/2$. With zero $w_a(0)$, and $m_a(t)$ zero for all $t \geq 0$, the time paths of $w_\delta(t)$ and $m_\delta(t)$ are the same as in the model with identical economies. The time path for $w_a(t)$ is different. It is now given by

$$w_a(t) = \zeta e^{-0.5t} \int_0^t e^{a\tau} A_1 \mathbf{z}_\delta(\tau) \, d\tau.$$

To illustrate, take the case of the second parameter set and set $v$ to 0.5. The integrand becomes

$$A_1 \mathbf{z}_\delta(\tau) = 0.125 w_\delta(\tau) - 0.3125 m_\delta(\tau).$$

Substituting (56) and (57) into the above and integrating, we obtain

$$\frac{w_a(t)}{\zeta} = e^{-0.5t} \int_0^t e^{0.5\tau} \{(0.168 e^{-2.565\tau} - 0.043 e^{-0.591\tau}) w_\delta(0)$$
$$+ (0.002 e^{-0.591\tau} - 0.311 e^{-0.2565\tau}) m_\delta(0)\} \, d\tau$$
$$= -(0.391 e^{-0.5t} - 0.473 e^{-0.591t} + 0.081 e^{-2.565t}) w_\delta(0)$$
$$- (0.132 e^{-0.5t} + 0.019 e^{-0.591t} - 0.151 e^{-2.565t}) m_\delta(0).$$

This expression corresponds to (60). This differs from (60) in that the effects of $w_\delta(0)$ are about one order of magnitude smaller. For the model with the

## 13.10 Numerical Examples

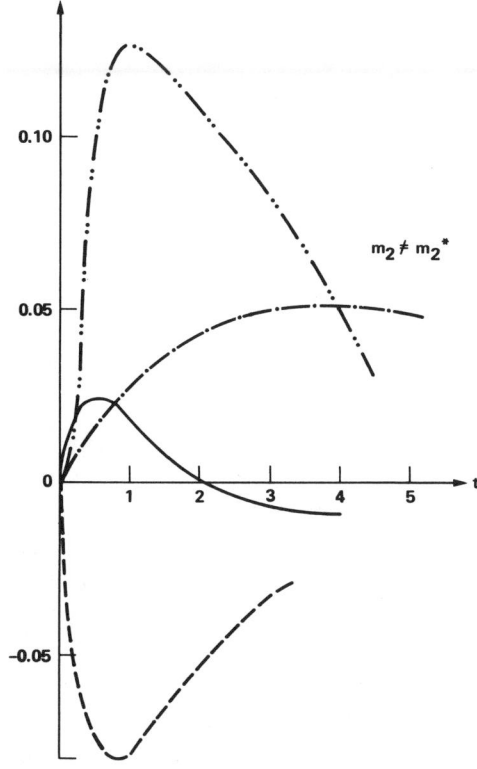

*Figure 10* Effects of unequal elasticity parameter $m_2$ on average wage rate deviation.
Case 1: —·—, $w_a(t)/\zeta w_\delta(0)$; ——, $w_a(t)/\zeta m_\delta(0)$.
Case 2: ———, $w_a(t)/\zeta w_\delta(0)$; - - -, $w_a(t)/\zeta m_\delta(0)$.

first parameter set, the time path expression corresponding to (59) now becomes

$$w_a(t)/\zeta = (0.124e^{-0.147t} - 0.142e^{-0.5t} + 0.018e^{-0.961t})w_\delta(0) \\ + (-0.057e^{-0.147t} + 0.691e^{-0.5t} - 0.634e^{-0.961t})m_\delta(0).$$

Here the effect of $m_\delta(0)$ is approximately one order of magnitude smaller.

Compare Fig. 10 with Fig. 8. With zero initial conditions, $w_a(t) = 0$ regardless of the value of $\zeta$.

**Effects of Instruments.** In the previous cases, $m_a$ has no effects of $\mathbf{z}_\delta$. Now, $m_a$ affects $\mathbf{z}_\delta$ through $(w_a - m_a)$ as can be seen from the matrix $\phi_{\delta a}$ in (45). Consider a temporary change in the instrument $x$ of the home country:

$$x = \begin{cases} 2\bar{x}, & 0 \le t \le 1, \\ 0, & t \ge 1. \end{cases}$$

With $x^* \equiv 0$, the average and the difference become

$$x_a = \begin{cases} \bar{x}, & 0 \leq t \leq 1, \\ 0, & t \geq 1, \end{cases} \quad \text{and} \quad x_\delta = \begin{cases} \bar{x}, & 0 \leq t \leq 1, \\ 0, & t \geq 1. \end{cases}$$

The time path of $m_a$ is obtained by integrating $\dot{m}_a = x_a$ as

$$m_a = \begin{cases} \bar{x}t, & 0 \leq t \leq 1, \\ \bar{x}, & t \geq 1. \end{cases}$$

Integrate (45) with $w_a(0), z_\delta(0) = 0$, noting that $w_a(t) \equiv 0$ for all $t$,

$$z_\delta(t) = e^{A^*t} \int_0^t e^{-A^*\tau} \begin{bmatrix} 0 \\ 1 \end{bmatrix} x_\delta(\tau) + \zeta e^{A^*t} \int_0^t e^{-A^*\tau} A_2(w_a(\tau) - m_a(\tau)) \, d\tau$$

$$= e^{A^*t} \int_0^t e^{-A^*\tau} \begin{bmatrix} 0 \\ 1 \end{bmatrix} x_\delta(\tau) \, d\tau - \zeta e^{A^*t} \int_0^t e^{-A^*\tau} A_2 m_a(\tau) \, d\tau.$$

The first term, denoted by $z_\delta^0(t)$, represents the behavior of the difference state vector with two identical economies, i.e., $z_\delta^0(t)$ is given by (61)–(64) with the first parameter set and by (65)–(68) with the second parameter set.

The time path for $w_a$ then obtained by integrating (46).

With the first parameter set,

$$A_1 z_\delta^0(t) = 0.0851 w_\delta^0(t) - 1.064 m_\delta^0(t).$$

With the second parameter set,

$$A_1 z_\delta^0(t) = 0.125 w_\delta^0(t) - 0.3125 m_\delta^0(t).$$

Substituting the (61)–(64) or (65)–(68) into the above, we deduce that, with the first parameter set,

$$\frac{w_a(t)}{(\zeta x_\delta)} = \int_0^t (-0.463 - 0.758 e^{-0.147\tau} + 1.221 e^{-0.961\tau}) \, d\tau$$

$$= -0.463t + 5.153 e^{-0.147t} - 1.27 e^{-0.961t} - 3.883 \quad \text{for} \quad t \leq 1;$$

$$\frac{w_a(t)}{(\zeta x_\delta)} = \frac{w_a(1)}{(\zeta x_\delta)} + \int_1^t (0.125 e^{-0.147\tau} - 0.868 e^{-0.961\tau}) \, d\tau$$

$$= w_a(1)/(\zeta x_\delta) - 0.849 e^{-0.147t} + 0.903 e^{-0.961t} + 0.387, \quad t > 1.$$

Note that

$$w_a(\infty)/(\zeta x_\delta) = w_a(1)/(\zeta x_\delta) + 0.387 = 0.0004.$$

Note that this is opposite of the previous example.

## 13.10 Numerical Examples

With the second parameter set,

$$\frac{w_a(t)}{(\zeta x_\delta)} = \int_0^t (-0.042 + 0.003 e^{-0.591\tau} + 0.122 e^{-2.561\tau}) \, d\tau$$

$$= -0.042 t - 0.004 e^{-0.591 t} - 0.047 e^{-2.561 t} + 0.0514, \qquad t \le 1,$$

and

$$\frac{w_a(t)}{(\zeta x_\delta)} = \frac{w_a(1)}{(\zeta x_\delta)} + \int_1^t (-0.002 e^{-0.591\tau} - 1.450 e^{-2.561\tau}) \, d\tau$$

$$= w_a(1)/(\zeta x_\delta) + 0.003 e^{-0.591 t} + 0.642 e^{-2.561 t} - 0.0513,$$

hence

$$\frac{w_a(x)}{(\zeta x_\delta)} = \frac{w_a(1)}{(\zeta x_\delta)} - 0.0513, \qquad t > 1,$$

$$= -0.0047.$$

Previously, $z_\delta^0(t)$ and $z_\delta(t)$ were the same if $w_a(0) = 0$. Now they are different:
For $0 \le t \le 1$,

$$z_\delta(t)/\bar{x} = z_\delta^0(t)/\bar{x} - \zeta\{-tI + A^{*-1}(e^{A^*t} - I)\} A^{*-1} A_2.$$

For $t \ge 1$,

$$z_\delta(t)/\bar{x} = z_\delta^0(t)/\bar{x} - \zeta\{-I + A^{*-1}(e^{A^*} - I) + e^{A^*(t-I)}\} - I\} A^{*-1} A_2.$$

To indicate the order of interaction terms, we note that

$$A^{*-1} A_2 = \begin{bmatrix} 7.408 \\ 0.033 \end{bmatrix},$$

and

$$-\zeta\{-I + A^{*-1}(e^{A^*} - I) A^{*-1} A_2\} = -\zeta 7.093 \begin{bmatrix} -0.244 \\ 0.010 \end{bmatrix} = \zeta \begin{bmatrix} 1.731 \\ -0.071 \end{bmatrix}$$

is the interaction term at $t = 1$ with the first parameter set. Recalling that $z_\delta^0(\infty) = 0$, the long-run effects of $\bar{x}$ are

$$\frac{z_\delta(\infty)}{\bar{x}} = -\zeta\{-I + A^{*-1}(e^{A^*} - I) - I\} A^{*-1} A_2 = \zeta \begin{bmatrix} 9.138 \\ -0.038 \end{bmatrix}.$$

***Effects of $\mu_2$.*** Write the characteristic equation of $\phi_\delta$, $|\lambda I - \phi_\delta|$ as

$$0 = q(\lambda) + \mu_2 D_\delta(\alpha\lambda + \tau),$$

where $\tau = \alpha(\eta\eta_1 + v\omega_1) + (m_2 + 2\tilde{\chi}\theta^{-1})(\eta\eta_2 - v\omega_2)$.

Two cases arise, depending on the sign of $\tau$. When it is positive, the difference dynamics are stable for all negative $\mu_2$. A sufficient condition is a positive $\eta\eta_2 - v\omega_2$, i.e., when the effects of $m_\delta$ on $\dot{w}_\delta$ via $y_\delta$ [recall (18) and (34)] are stronger than that on $w_\delta$ via $\rho_{i\delta}$ [recall (38)]. When the opposite is true, i.e., when $\eta\eta_2 - v\omega_2$ is sufficiently negative, it could cause $\tau$ to become negative. In this case, a large negative $\mu_2$ could render dynamics unstable.

When $-\tau/\alpha$ is positive, dynamic responses slow down with a negative $\mu_2$ (before dynamics become unstable). With a negative value for $-\tau/\alpha$, which is more positive than the eigenvalues of $\phi_\delta$, dynamic responses become slower with a negative $\mu_2$ than with a positive $\mu_2$. In all other cases, negative values of $-\tau/\alpha$ speed up dynamic responses.

## Appendix  Calculation of the Averages and the Differences

When $m_2$ and $m_2^*$ are different, it is no longer possible to solve for the differences in the interest rates and the output prices separately. Instead of (31a) and (31b), the averages and the differences are jointly determined from

$$S\begin{bmatrix} i_a \\ p_a \\ i_\delta \\ p_\delta \end{bmatrix} = \begin{bmatrix} z_a \\ z_\delta \end{bmatrix}, \quad \text{where} \quad S = \begin{bmatrix} \bar{R}_a & T \\ T & \bar{R}_\delta \end{bmatrix}, \quad T = \begin{bmatrix} 0 & 0 \\ -\zeta & 0 \end{bmatrix},$$

where

$$\bar{R}_a = \begin{bmatrix} 0 & 1 \\ -\bar{m}_2 & 1 \end{bmatrix}, \quad \bar{R}_\delta = \begin{bmatrix} \alpha & \beta \\ -(\bar{m}_2 + 2\chi\theta^{-1}) & 1 - 2\chi \end{bmatrix},$$

where $\bar{R}_a$ and $\bar{R}_\delta$ are the ones given by (31a) and by (31b) when $m_2$ is replaced with the average value of the two parameters, $\bar{m}_2$. Calculate the inverse of $S$ approximately by neglecting quadratic and higher order terms in $\zeta$ as

$$S^{-1} = \begin{bmatrix} \bar{R}_a^{-1} & -\bar{R}_a^{-1}T\bar{R}_\delta^{-1} \\ -\bar{R}_\delta^{-1}T\bar{R}_a^{-1} & \bar{R}_a^{-1} \end{bmatrix}.$$

We solve the above to replace (32) and (33) by

(79a) $\quad \begin{bmatrix} i_a \\ p_a \end{bmatrix} = \bar{R}_a^{-1}\mathbf{z}_a + \zeta D_a D_\delta \begin{bmatrix} -1 \\ 0 \end{bmatrix}[1 - 2\tilde{\chi} - \beta]\mathbf{z}_\delta + O(\zeta^2),$

(79b) $\quad \begin{bmatrix} i_\delta \\ p_\delta \end{bmatrix} = \bar{R}_\delta^{-1}\mathbf{z}_\delta + \zeta D_a D_\delta \begin{bmatrix} -\beta \\ \alpha \end{bmatrix}[1 \; -1]\mathbf{z}_a.$

# 14 | Two-Country Model of the World under Key Currency Regime[1]

## 14.1 Introduction

A government budget constraint equation provides one source of dynamics, hence, is a possible cause of instability in dynamic models of open economies. In determining stability of two-country models of the world, the budget status (deficit or surplus) of the two governments plays an equal or symmetric role if the two countries are identically specified.

Specifications of the two countries or reaction functions of the two governments, if they exist, must differ in some ways for the budget status of the two governments to have a different effect on the stability of the world model. We let the menus of financial assets be different in the two countries. This is a third way of imposing nonsymmetry in the two-country world models. The other ways have been examined in Chapter 13.

Two objectives motivate this chapter. The major objective is to examine implications on stability of a particular form of nonsymmetry in the asset sector, i.e., one country issuing key currency:[2] How differently does the budget status of each of the two governments affect stability? In what sense, if any, is the budget deficit of the key currency country a more crucial determinant of the overall stability of the world model? Subsidiary to this, we ask how wage rate flexibilities in the two countries modify the

---

[1] An earlier version was reported at the Econometric Society World Congress, Aix-en-Provence, France, August 1980.

[2] Girton and Henderson (1977) studied impact effects of a two-country model under a key-currency regime in which a central bank holds the other country's currency and bonds while the other central bank does not hold currency or bonds of the former. Kudoh (1978) performed a comparative statics study of a two-country model in which one country's currency is a traded asset while the others is not. He did not consider dynamics.

effects of budget deficits on stability. We answer these questions in this chapter.

Except in some extreme cases, answers to these questions are complex because several sector characteristics and many model parameters turn out to be interdependent determinants of overall stability of the model. Three extreme cases are examined as benchmark cases for which clear-cut answers can be provided.

In the first benchmark case, the output of nonkey-currency country does not change [the parameter $\sigma$ determining supply responses is zero in (17) below]. As we demonstrate below, relative deviations in the exchange rate are fully reflected on relative deviations of the output price of the nonkey-currency country, while the output price of the key-currency country as well as the outputs of the two countries remain unchanged. In this case stability is a function of only the budget deficit of the nonkey-currency government. In the second case, in which only the output price of the key currency country fully reflects changes in the exchange rate while the other three variables remain unchanged, the budget deficit of the key-currency government is the overall determinant of stability.

In the third case, which allows less extreme assumptions than the first two cases, both government budgets affect stability more or less symmetrically. In these three cases, wage rates are rigid in both countries. Flexible wage rates do not alter basic stability characteristics of the first two benchmark cases. Flexible wage rates do change stability behavior of the model in the third benchmark case. Budget deficits in the key-currency country turn out to be more crucial than budget deficits of the nonkey-currency country.

To keep this chapter to a reasonable length, we keep government instruments constant. (Policy effects can be analyzed following our procedure of Chapter 13 but are not examined here.) After the model is described in Section 14.2, basic variational dynamic equations governing deviations of endogenous variables from some reference state are derived in Section 14.3. Stability of benchmark models is discussed in Section 14.4. Section 14.5 examines consequences of flexible wage rates. Section 14.6 evaluates influences of some factors ignored in benchmark models, such as expectations and interest rate effects.

The results of this chapter are summarized as a series of propositions. Assumptions on the real sectors of the two countries sensitively influence the relative importance of the budget status of the two governments. Under rigid wage rates, both budget statuses appear more or less symmetrically in the stability conditions. Under flexible wage rates, however, the key-currency country's budget status is a more important determinant of stability.

## 14.2 The Model

### 14.2.1 Asset Sector

The world is composed of a key-currency country (country $K$ for short) and a nonkey-currency country (henceforth country $N$). We treat country $N$ as the home country and denote variables of country $K$ with superscript *. Some of country $K$'s money stock is held by the central bank and the private sector of country $N$. The total stock of the key currency held by country $N$ is denoted by $Z$, i.e., $Z = H^* + R$, where $H^*$ is the private holding of currency $K$, and $R$ is the stock held by the central bank of country $N$ as a reserve. See (3b) below. Total stock of country $K$'s government bonds is $B_g^*$, some of which are held by the private sector of country $K$ and country $N$. The latter is denoted by $F$. The central bank of country $K$ also holds some stocks of the country $K$ government bonds. This stock is denoted by $B_c^*$. See (1b) below. Table 1 summarizes the stocks of assets held by the private sectors and the governments (including central banks) of these two countries.

*Table 1*

*Sectoral Balance Sheets*[a]

| Country N | | Country K | |
|---|---|---|---|
| Government | Private | Government | Private |
| ER | EH* | $B_c^*$ | M* |
|  | EF | $B_c^*$  $B_g^*$ | B* |
| M | M |  |  |

[a] $Z = H^* + R$, $B^* = B_g^* - F - B_c^*$, $M^* = B_c^* - Z$.

The private sector of country $K$ holds $M^*$ and $B^*$ of the key currency and the government bonds. The asset demand functions in country $K$ are specified by

(1a) $$M^* = \mu(i^*)A^*, \qquad \mu' < 0,$$

(1b) $$B^* = v(i^*)A^*, \qquad v' > 0,$$

where $i^*$ is the rate of return of country $K$'s government bonds,

$$M^* = B_c^* - Z \quad \text{and} \quad B^* = B_g^* - F - B_c^*.$$

Note that $B^*$ is a function of $F$, country $N$'s private holdings of government $K$ bonds. There is only one independent equation due to the balance sheet constraint among (1a) and (1b). We use the ratio of the two as an independent equation

(2) $$B^*/M^* = v(i^*)/\mu(i^*).$$

The private sector of country $N$ also holds a stock of country $N$'s money denoted by $M$, in addition to country $K$'s government bond $F$ and money stock $H^*$. The real rate of return due to holding a stock of country $N$s money is the negative of the inflation rate of the price index in country $N$ (however defined). The real rate of return to holding (i) a stock of key currency and (ii) a stock of country $K$'s government bonds equals for (i) the expected rate of depreciation of the exchange rate minus the inflation rate of the price index in country $K$ plus the inflation rate in country $N$ and for (ii) $i^*$ plus the expected rate of depreciation of the exchange rate minus the price index inflation rate of country $K$ plus the inflation rate in country $N$, where the exchange rate is defined to be the country $N$'s currency price of the unit of the key currency. Denoting the expected rate of depreciation of the exchange rate by $\varepsilon$ and the expected difference of the inflation rates of the price indices of country $N$ and $K$ by $\chi$, the demand functions for the financial assets in country $N$ can be given as

(3a) $$M = l(\varepsilon + \chi, i^*)A, \quad l_1 < 0, \quad l_2 < 0,$$

(3b) $$EH^* = \alpha(\varepsilon + \chi, i^*)A, \quad \alpha_1 > 0, \quad \alpha_2 < 0,$$

(3c) $$EF = q(\varepsilon + \chi, i^*)A, \quad q_1 > 0, \quad q_2 > 0,$$

where $M = H + ER$, $H$ being the domestic component of $M$. In (3a) as well as in (1a), we drop scale variables which represent economic activity levels in the two countries for simplicity in the short-run analysis we conduct. Such scale variables introduce feedbacks between the asset sectors and the real sectors of the two countries. The effects of such feedbacks, however, are not enough to reverse the signs of various short-run multipliers and hence are ignored for simplicity of the asset demand equations in (1) and (3).

Only two equations in (3) are independent due to the balance sheet constraint. We use two ratios:

(4a) $$M/EH^* = l(\varepsilon + \chi, i^*)/\alpha(\varepsilon + \chi, i^*),$$

(4b) $$F/H^* = q(\varepsilon + \chi, i^*)/\alpha(\varepsilon + \chi, i^*).$$

### Equilibrium and (Semi-)Reduced Forms

We have three independent equilibrium conditions in the asset markets as (2), (4a), and (4b). The question of which of the three variables are solved out

## 14.2 The Model

from these three equations representing the asset sector equilibrium depends on our assumptions on the expectations variables. Here $i^*$, $E$, and $F$ are solved out by the implicit function theorem, at least in a local neighborhood of a (temporary or long-run) equilibrium state if the Jacobian of (2), (4a), and (4b), with respect to $i^*$, $E$, and $F$, is nonsingular:

$$i^* = \phi(B_g^*, B_c^*, Z, M, R; \varepsilon + \chi),$$
(5) $$E = \xi(B_g^*, B_c^*, Z, M, R; \varepsilon + \chi),$$
$$F = \eta(B_g^*, B_c^*, Z, M, R; \varepsilon + \chi).$$

We treat $\varepsilon$ and $\chi$ as given by some regressive expectations generation mechanisms to be specified later. The alternative case where $\varepsilon$ and $\chi$ are specified by a myopic perfect foresight equation is likely to produce a saddle point instability. For example, in the case where $\varepsilon = \dot{E}/E$, the expectations on the exchange rate can change discontinuously and then jump to the conditionally stable manifold. We do not treat this case here. (See Appendix C at the end of this book.) We make a key, but reasonable, simplifying assumption that $F/H^*$ depends only on $i^*$ and not on $\varepsilon + \chi$, i.e., we assume that $\alpha_1/\alpha$ equals $q_1/q$. This assumption simplifies algebra with no essential changes in transmission paths of the model.

### *Variational Equations*

Under this assumption, relative deviations of $E$ and $F$ and deviation of $i^*$ from their respective (temporary) equilibrium values can be expressed by taking variations of (5). Since our focus of analysis is stability and not asymmetrical effects of instruments of the two governments, we assume $b_c^*$ and $r$ are both zero, i.e., we assume that central banks of the two countries do not intervene when the economies deviate from a reference state.[3] Variation of (5) yields (see Appendix 1 at the end of this chapter for derivations):

$$e = \mu_h h - \mu_z z + s_2 \mu_g b_g^* + s_1 \delta(\varepsilon + \chi),$$
(6) $$f = v_z z - s_4 \mu_g b_g^*,$$
$$\delta i^* = -\theta_z z + \mu_g b_g^*,$$

where $\mu_h = H/M > 0$, $s_1 = -l_1/l + q_1/q > 0$, $s_2 = -l_2/l + q_2/q > 0$, $s_4 = -\alpha_2/\alpha + q_2/q > 0$, $s_5 = v'/v - \mu'/\mu > 0$. $D^{-1} = s_5 - (F/B^*)s_4$, $\mu_z = D(s_5/H^* + s_2/M^*)Z$, $\mu_g = DB_g^*/B^*$, $v_z = D(s_5/H^* - s_4/M^*)Z$, $\theta_z = D\{(F/B^*)H^{*-1} - M^{*-1}\}Z$. The coefficient $\mu_z$ is positive if and only if $D$ is

---

[3] The dynamic equation (25), however, can easily be amended to accommodate effects of nonzero $b_c^*$ and $r$ to examine policy effects. Interested readers are invited to calculate the dynamic multipliers.

positive. The sign of $D$ is positive if and only if $s_5$ is greater than $(F/B^*)s_4$. Since the latter inequality can be equivalently put as

$$\partial B^*/\partial i^* - \partial F/\partial i^* \geq (\partial M^*/\partial i^*)(B^*/M^*) - (\partial H^*/\partial i^*)(F/H^*),$$

we can roughly state that $D$ is positive if and only if "net" changes in country $K$'s bond holding (country $K$'s holding minus country $N$'s holding) in response to changes in $i^*$ are greater than certain "weighted net" changes in the key-currency holding.

With a positive $D$, the coefficient $\mu_z$ is positive, i.e., an increase of key currency holding in country $N$ leads to an appreciation of the exchange rate (country $N$ currency value of a unit of key currency). The sign of $\mu_z$ is the same as that of $\mu_g$. The coefficient $v_z$ is positive if and only if $s_5$ is greater than $(H^*/M^*)s_4$. Except for the weights, this inequality has a similar interpretation as that associated with $D$. On the assumption that $D$ is positive, the coefficient $\theta_z$ is positive if and only if $F/B^*$ is greater than $H^*/M^*$. If so, then a positive $\mu_z$ implies that $v_z$ is also positive because of the following inequality

$$s_5 \geq (F/B^*)s_4 \geq (H^*/M^*)s_4.$$

### 14.2.2 Dynamics

Country $K$'s government budget imbalance causes the stocks of key currency and the bonds of government $K$ to change according to

(7) $$\dot{M}^* + \dot{B}_g^* = P^*(G^* - T^*) + i^*(B_g^* - B_c^*),$$

while the corresponding budget restraint relation for country $N$ is

(8) $$\dot{H} = P(G - T)$$

since country $N$ is assumed not to issue any bonds of its own. Stocks of financial assets also change by the current account relations

$$\dot{M}^* = B_T^* - i^*F$$

in key currency in country $K$, and

(9) $$\dot{Z} + \dot{F} = B_T + i^*F,$$

in key currency in country $N$, where $Z = H^* + R$, and $B_T^* = -B_T$. Of these two relations we use (9) since only one of them is independent.

## 14.3 Variational Dynamics

### 14.3.1 Asset Sectors

Suppose that we abstract from growth, and that a steady state exists in the model so that all stock variables are constant.[4] Recalling that we keep $b_c^*$ and $r$ to zero, we obtain from (7), because $\delta M^*$ equals $-\delta Z$ when $\delta B_c^*$ is zero [see the relation below (1b)],

(10) $\quad \delta \dot{M}^* + \delta \dot{B}_g^* = \delta \dot{B}_g^* - \delta \dot{Z} = B_g^*(\omega_p^* p^* + \omega_g^* g^* - \tau^* \omega_g^* y^*)$
$\quad\quad\quad\quad\quad\quad\quad\quad\quad\quad + (B_g^* - B_c^*)\delta i^* + i^* \delta B_g^*,$

where $\omega_p^* = P^*(G^* - T^*)/B_g$, $\omega_g^* = P^*G^*/B_g^*$, and where we assume that $\delta T^* = \tau^* \, \delta Y^*$.

In terms of the relative deviational variables, the above becomes, after substituting $\delta i^*$ out by (6),

(11) $\quad \dot{b}_g^* - (Z/B_g^*)\dot{z} = \rho_g b_g^* - \rho_z z + \omega_p^* p + \omega_g^* g - \tau^* \omega_g^* y^*,$

where $\rho_g = i^* + \mu_g(1 - B_c^*/B_g^*)$, $\rho_z = \theta_z(1 - B_c^*/B_g^*)$.

From (8), relative variation of $H$ is related to $g$, $p$, and $y$ by

(12) $\quad\quad\quad\quad\quad\quad \dot{h} = \omega_p p + \omega_g g - \tau \omega_g y,$

where $\omega_p = P(G - T)/H$, $\omega_g = PG/H$, and where $\delta T = \tau \, \delta Y$ is assumed.

From (9),

(11') $\quad\quad\quad\quad \dot{z} + (F/Z)\dot{f} = \delta B_T/Z + (i^*f + \delta i^*)F/Z,$

where $f$ is as given by (6). Differentiating it with respect to time, $\dot{f}$ is expressible as $\dot{f} = v_z \dot{z} - s_4 \mu_g \dot{b}_g^*$ since $v_z$ and $s_4 \mu_g$ are constant. When $f$, $\dot{f}$, and $\delta i^*$ are substituted out from (11'), we see that $\dot{z}$ and $\dot{b}_g^*$ are related by

(13) $\quad\quad\quad\quad \chi_z \dot{z} - \chi_g \dot{b}_g^* = \delta B_T/Z - \zeta_z z + \zeta_g \mu_g b_g^*,$

where

$\chi_z = 1 + v_z F/Z$, $\chi_g = s_4 \mu_g F/Z$, $\zeta_z = (\theta_z - i^* v_z)F/Z$, $\zeta_g = (1 + s_4 i^*)F/Z$.

---

[4] Logarithmic differentiations of (2), (4a), and (4b) yield relations among the rates of changes that must hold in the long-run equilibrium state: $\dot{B}^*/B^* = \dot{M}^*/M^*$, $\dot{M}/M = \dot{E}/E + \dot{H}^*/H^*$, and $\dot{F}/F = \dot{H}^*/H^*$, because $i^*$, $\varepsilon$, and $\chi$ are assumed to be constant in the long-run equilibrium. These long-run relations are satisfied if $E$ is constant and all stocks are constant, or grow at the same rate.

Collecting (11)–(13), we can write the coupled differential equations representing the dynamics of the relative deviations of the stock variables

(14) $\quad \mathscr{H} \dfrac{d}{dt}\begin{bmatrix} h \\ b_g^* \\ z \end{bmatrix} = \mathscr{F}_0 \begin{bmatrix} h \\ b_g^* \\ z \end{bmatrix} + \begin{bmatrix} 0 \\ 0 \\ 1 \end{bmatrix}\dfrac{\delta B_T}{Z} + \mathscr{F}_1 \begin{bmatrix} p \\ y \end{bmatrix} + \mathscr{F}_2 \begin{bmatrix} p^* \\ y^* \end{bmatrix} + \zeta,$

where

$\mathscr{H} = \begin{bmatrix} 1 & 0 & 0 \\ 0 & & \\ 0 & & \mathscr{J} \end{bmatrix}, \quad \mathscr{J} = \begin{bmatrix} 1 & -Z/B_g^* \\ -\chi_g & \chi_z \end{bmatrix}, \quad \mathscr{F}_0 = \begin{bmatrix} 0 & 0 & 0 \\ 0 & & \\ 0 & & \mathscr{L} \end{bmatrix},$

$\mathscr{L} = \begin{bmatrix} \rho_g & -\rho_z \\ \zeta_g \mu_g & -\zeta_z \end{bmatrix}, \quad \mathscr{F}_1 = \begin{bmatrix} \omega_p & -\tau\omega_g \\ 0 & 0 \\ 0 & 0 \end{bmatrix}, \quad \mathscr{F}_2 = \begin{bmatrix} 0 & 0 \\ \omega_p^* & -\tau^*\omega_g^* \\ 0 & 0 \end{bmatrix},$

$$\zeta = \mathscr{I} g + \mathscr{I}^* g^*,$$

and where

$$\mathscr{I} = \begin{bmatrix} \omega_g \\ 0 \\ 0 \end{bmatrix}, \quad \mathscr{I}^* = \begin{bmatrix} 0 \\ \omega_g^* \\ 0 \end{bmatrix}.$$

### 14.3.2 Real Sectors

The effects of real sectors on the dynamic are expressed by deviations of the trade balance and deviations of prices and outputs in the two countries.

The real demands for the output of country $N$ are given by the GNP identity by the purchasers as $Y = C + I + \lambda K + X + G$, where $C$ is country $N$ residents' demand for country $N$ output and is assumed to depend on the terms-of-trade and activity level variables as $C = C(EP^*/P, Y - T)$, and where $X$ is the export, i.e., country $K$'s demand for output of country $N$, and is assumed to be given by $X = X(EP^*/P, Y^* - T^*)$.[5] The term $\lambda K$ represents capital stock depreciation. We treat the investment demand to be autonomous. This assumption effectively removes the interest rate as a connecting factor between asset and real sectors, and leaves only the relative prices as feedback paths between the sectors. This simplifies

---

[5] Eliminating $\dot{M}^*$ from (7) by the current account equation $\dot{M}^* = B_T^* - i^*F$, (7) becomes $\dot{B}_g^* = B_T + P^*(G^* - T^*) + i^*(B_g^* + F - B_c^*)$, where we use $B_T^* = -B_T$. This equation indicates that the balance-of-trade surplus by the home country contributes to the increase of the stock of $B_g^*$.

## 14.3 Variational Dynamics

analysis without causing any serious loss in generality. The variational expression of the demand is approximately taken to equal the following (semi-reduced form) expression:

(15) $$y = d(e + p^* - p) + \eta y^*.^6$$

The corresponding expression for the relative variation of the output of country $K$ has a similar form:

(16) $$y^* = d^*(p - e - p^*) + \eta^* y.$$

The variational expressions of the aggregate supply schedules of the two countries are assumed to be proportional to relative deviations of the price level, assuming that the wage rates are fixed in the short run in the two countries. (When wage rates are variable, another source of dynamics is introduced. This is discussed later in Section 14.5.)

(17) $$y = \sigma p, \qquad y^* = \sigma^* p^*.$$

Temporary equilibrium values of the output prices in the two countries can be obtained by equating (15) and (16) with (17). Jointly, they represent a kind of IS schedule in variational variables:

(18) $$\begin{bmatrix} p \\ p^* \end{bmatrix} = \begin{bmatrix} \rho \\ -\rho^* \end{bmatrix} e$$

and

(19) $$\begin{bmatrix} y \\ y^* \end{bmatrix} = \begin{bmatrix} \sigma\rho \\ -\sigma^*\rho^* \end{bmatrix} e,$$

where

$$\rho = \sigma^*(d - \eta d^*)/\{(1 - \eta\eta^*)\sigma\sigma^* + d(\sigma^* - \sigma\eta^*) + d^*(\sigma - \sigma^*\eta)\},$$

$$\rho^* = \sigma(d^* - \eta^* d)/\{(1 - \eta\eta^*)\sigma\sigma^* + d(\sigma^* - \sigma\eta^*) + d^*(\sigma - \sigma^*\eta)\}.$$

Zero $\sigma$ in (17) produces benchmark model $A$. Note that $\rho$ becomes one and $\rho^*$ zero. In benchmark $A$, (18) and (19) show that $p$ equals $e$, and $p^*$, $y$, and $y^*$ all are zero. Even though $\sigma^*$ is not zero, $y^*$ is zero because $p^*$ remains at zero when the exchange rate deviates from the reference value. Setting $\sigma^*$ to zero in (18) yields benchmark model $B$, where $\rho$ is now zero and $\rho^*$ equals

---

[6] More precisely, the disposable incomes in country $N$ and $K$ are $Y - T + i^*F$ and $Y^* - T^* + i^*B^*$, respectively. These changes cause $y = d(e + p^* - p) + d_2 f + d_3 b_g^* + d_4 \delta i^* + d_5 y^*$, where $d_0 = 1 - C_2(1 - T)Y/C$, $d_1 = (C_1 + X_1)(EP^*/P)/(d_0 Y)$, $d_2 = (C_2 - X_2)i^*F/(d_0 Y)$, $d_3 = X_2 i^* B_g^*/(d_0 Y)$, $d_4 = (C_2 F/Y + X_2 B^*)/(d_0 Y)$, $d_5 = X_2 Y^*(1 - \tau)/(d_0 Y)$. When we ignore $d_2$, $d_3$ and $d_4$ as being small, then (15) results. The effects of retaining $d_4$ are examined in Section 14.6.3.

one. Thus exchange rate deviations cause $p^*$ to equal $-e$, leaving $p$, $y$, and $y^*$ at zero. A third case, benchmark model C, is examined later where both $\sigma$ and $\sigma^*$ are nonzero. A fourth model is introduced in Section 14.5.

Effects of the output and price variations of the two countries on the dynamics in the right-hand side of (14) are summarized by substituting (18) and (19) into (14) as

$$(20) \qquad \mathscr{F}_1 \begin{bmatrix} p \\ y \end{bmatrix} + \mathscr{F}_2 \begin{bmatrix} p^* \\ y^* \end{bmatrix} = \begin{bmatrix} \omega\rho \\ -\omega^*\rho^* \\ 0 \end{bmatrix} e,$$

where we define

$$(20') \qquad \omega = \omega_p - \sigma\tau\omega_g, \qquad \omega^* = \omega_p^* - \sigma^*\tau^*\omega_g^*.$$

Referring to their definitions given below (12), we see that in country N, $\omega_p = 0$ when the budget is balanced, i.e., $\bar{\omega} = -\sigma\tau\bar{\omega}_g \leq 0$ where the overbar denotes the balanced budget value. This fact is later used in stability analysis. In country K, (7) vanishes in the steady state, i.e., $\bar{\omega}^* < 0$ since $\bar{\omega}_p^* = -i^*(1 - B_c^*/B_g^*) < 0$ from the definitions given below (10).

The balance of trade by definition is equal to

$$B_T = (P/E)X(EP^*/P, Y^* - T^*) - P^*X^*(EP^*/P, Y - T),$$

where $X$ and $X^*$ are the export functions of the two countries. Its variation then equals

$$\delta B_T = (PX/E)(p + p^* - e) - P^*X^*(p^* + x^*),$$

where

(21) $\quad x = \xi_1(e + p^* - p) + \xi_2 y^*$ and $x^* = -\xi_1^*(e + p^* - p) + \xi_2^* y,$

where, recalling that $\delta T = \tau\, \delta Y$ and $\delta T^* = \tau^*\, \delta Y$ by assumption,

$$\xi_1 = (X_1/X)(EP^*/P) > 0, \qquad \xi_2 = (1 - \tau^*)(X_2/X)Y^* > 0,$$
$$\xi_1^* = -(X_1^*/X^*)(EP^*/P) > 0, \qquad \xi_2^* = (1 - \tau)(X_2^*/X^*)Y > 0.$$

From (18), (19), and (21), we deduce that the variation of the trade balance is proportional to the variation of the exchange rate, just as the variations of the prices and outputs are; we can write $\delta B_T$ as

$$(22) \qquad \delta B_T = \Omega e,$$

where

$$\Omega = (PX/E)\{-(1 - \xi_1)(1 - \rho) - \xi_1\rho - \xi_2\sigma^*\rho^*\} \\ + P^*X^*\{\rho^* + \xi_2^*(1 - \rho - \rho^*) - \sigma\rho\xi_2^*\}.$$

## 14.3 Variational Dynamics

In benchmark model A, $\Omega$ becomes zero because $\sigma$ and $\rho^*$ are both zero and $\rho$ equals one. In model B, $\sigma^*$ and $\rho$ are both zero and $\rho^*$ equals one; hence

$$\Omega = -PX/E + P^*X^* = i^*F,$$

where (9) has been used, i.e., at the equilibrium $-B_T$ equals $i^*F$. The effects of the term $\delta B_T/Z$ in (14) will be initially ignored. We reintroduce this term later in Section 14.6. The effects of nonzero $\Omega$ on stability and policy effectiveness are evaluated there. [The nonzero elasticity $\Omega$ modifies the parameters $\tau_1$ and $\tau_2$ in the dynamic matrix $\Phi$ defined in (25).]

### 14.3.3 State Equations

With the variation in balance of trade thus neglected and substituting $e$ out by (6) and from (20), we can put (14) into

(23)
$$\frac{d}{dt}\begin{bmatrix} h \\ b_g^* \\ z \end{bmatrix} = \mathcal{H}^{-1}\left\{\mathcal{F}_0 + \begin{bmatrix} \omega\rho \\ -\omega^*\rho^* \\ 0 \end{bmatrix}[\mu_h \ s_2\mu_g \ -\mu_z]\right\}\begin{bmatrix} h \\ b_g^* \\ z \end{bmatrix}$$
$$+ s_1 \begin{bmatrix} \omega\rho \\ -\omega^*\rho^* \\ 0 \end{bmatrix}\delta(\varepsilon + \chi)\right].$$

The expectational term in the above is introduced when (6) is substituted for $e$. Once the expression for the expectational term is specified, the above gives the complete dynamic equation of the model. A general regressive expression for $\delta(\varepsilon + \rho)$ is a function of the state variables, i.e.,

(24)
$$\delta(\varepsilon + \chi) = \kappa_1 h + \kappa_2 b_g^* + \kappa_3 z,$$

where $\kappa_1 \sim \kappa_3$ are as yet unspecified coefficients.[7] We discuss one such specification in Section 14.6. Upon substituting (24) into (23), we derive the state-space representation of the complete dynamics of the basic model:

(25)
$$\frac{d}{dt}\begin{bmatrix} h \\ b_g^* \\ z \end{bmatrix} = \Phi \begin{bmatrix} h \\ b_g^* \\ z \end{bmatrix},$$

---

[7] In the literature, $\varepsilon$ is often assumed to be of the form $\delta\varepsilon = -\mu e$. [See, for example, Dornbusch (1976).] This form of the expectation mechanism supposes that the economic agent expects the exchange rate to revert to a (long-run) equilibrium level $\bar{E}$ so that $\varepsilon = -\mu(E - \bar{E})$. Since $e$ is expressible as a linear combination of $h$, $b_g^*$, and $z$, $\delta\varepsilon = -\mu e$ is a special case of (24). Expectations may additionally depend on the deviation in the current account or on the level of the foreign assets held in country $N$. These forms are all covered by (24). See Appendix C at the end of this book.

where

$$\Phi = \Phi_0 + \begin{bmatrix} \omega\rho \\ -\tau_1 \\ -\tau_2 \end{bmatrix} [\phi_1 \quad \phi_2 \quad -\phi_3],$$

$$\Phi_0 = \mathcal{H}^{-1}\mathcal{F}_0 = \begin{bmatrix} 1 & 0 & 0 \\ 0 & & L \\ 0 & & \end{bmatrix}, \quad L = \mathcal{J}^{-1}\mathcal{L},$$

where

$$\tau_1 = n\rho^*\omega^*\chi_z, \quad \tau_2 = \rho^*n\omega^*\chi_g, \quad n^{-1} = \chi_z - \chi_g Z/B_g^*,$$

and where

$$\phi_1 = \mu_h + s_1\kappa_1, \quad \phi_2 = s_2\mu_g + s_1\kappa_2, \quad \phi_3 = \mu_z - s_1\kappa_3.$$

The matrix $L$ is calculated from the defining relations in (14) as

$$L = \begin{bmatrix} l_{11} & -l_{12} \\ l_{21} & -l_{22} \end{bmatrix} = n \begin{bmatrix} \chi_z & Z/B_g^* \\ \chi_g & 1 \end{bmatrix} \begin{bmatrix} \rho_g & -\rho_z \\ \zeta_g\mu_g & \zeta_z \end{bmatrix}.$$

This matrix represents the asset sector dynamics of deviations in the stocks of $B_g$ and $Z$ when the feedbacks from the real sector are ignored. We assume therefore that $L$ is a stable matrix, i.e., $l_{11} - l_{22}$ and $l_{11}l_{22} - l_{21}l_{12}$ are both negative. (Appendix 2 at the end of this chapter examines implications of these sign assumptions.)

The stability of (25) is determined by the eigenvalues of the dynamic matrix $\Phi$. The first term $\Phi_0$ of the dynamic matrix depends only on the asset sector parameters. The parameter $\omega$ depends on the government budget status of country $N$, while $\tau_1$ and $\tau_2$ depend on that of country $K$.

## 14.4 Stability Analysis under Rigid Wage Rates

Equation (25) shows how the parameters $\omega$ and $\omega^*$ modify the dynamics through $\omega\rho$, $\tau_1$, and $\tau_2$. We inquire how the budget imbalances in one or both countries affect stability of the dynamics governing the variational variables in the three benchmark models. We show that the signs of the parameters $\omega$ and $\omega^*$ defined in (20') are crucial determinants of stability conditions.

## 14.4 Stability Analysis under Rigid Wage Rates

### 14.4.1 Benchmark Model A

With zero $\sigma$, $\rho^*$ becomes zero in (20), hence $\tau_1$ and $\tau_2$ both vanish in (25). The dynamic matrix therefore simplifies to

$$\Phi = \Phi_0 + \omega \begin{bmatrix} 1 \\ 0 \\ 0 \end{bmatrix} [\phi_1 \quad \phi_2 \quad -\phi_3], \tag{26}$$

because $\rho$ becomes one. Because $\sigma$ is zero, $\omega$ is the same as $\omega_p$ in (26). A straightforward calculation shows that the characteristic polynomial of $\Phi$ is

$$|\lambda I - \Phi| = (\lambda - \omega \phi_1)\psi(\lambda), \tag{27}$$

where

$$\psi(\lambda) = |\lambda I - L| = \lambda^2 + n(l_{22} - l_{11})\lambda + n^2(l_{12}l_{21} - l_{11}l_{22}),$$

where, as we remarked below (25), we assume that

$$l_{22} - l_{11} = \zeta_z + \rho_z \chi_g > 0 \quad \text{and} \quad n(l_{12}l_{21} - l_{11}l_{22}) = -\rho_g \zeta_z + \rho_z \mu_g \zeta_g > 0.$$

The matrix of (26) is stable if and only if $\omega \phi_1$ is negative. Equivalently, from (20′) and (12) recalling that $\sigma$ is zero in this model, (26) is stable if and only if $(G - T)\phi_1$ is nonpositive. When $\phi_1$ is positive, this becomes $G \leq T$. When $\phi_1$ is negative this becomes $G \geq T$. Later we show that for reasonable expectational behavior $\phi_1$ is positive.[8] We state this as

**Proposition 1.** When $\sigma$ is zero in (17) and $\phi_1$ is positive, the dynamics (26) are stable if and only if the nonkey-currency country's government budget is not in deficit.

### 14.4.2 Benchmark Model B

Now let $\sigma^*$ be zero in (17) causing $\rho$ to become zero, and $\rho^*$ unity. The dynamic matrix of (25) in this case assumes the form

$$\Phi = \Phi_0 - \begin{bmatrix} 0 \\ \tau_1 \\ \tau_2 \end{bmatrix} [\phi_1 \quad \phi_2 \quad \phi_3]; \tag{28}$$

its characteristic equation becomes, after simple calculation,

$$|\lambda I - \Phi| = \lambda\{\psi(\lambda) + \kappa(\lambda - \theta)\}, \tag{29}$$

---

[8] The sign of $\phi_1$ becomes negative if the foreign goods occupy more than half of the consumption bundle of the nonkey-currency country residents, and inflationary expectations adjust much faster than the exchange rate expectation.

where
$$\kappa = \phi_2 \tau_1 - \phi_3 \tau_2 = n(-\omega^*)(\phi_3 \chi_g - \phi_2 \chi_z)$$
and where
$$\theta = n\{-\phi_2(\tau_1 l_{22} - \tau_2 l_{12}) + \phi_3(\tau_1 l_{21} - \tau_2 l_{11})\}/\kappa$$
$$= (\phi_2 \zeta_z - \phi_3 \zeta_g \mu_g)/(\phi_3 \chi_g - \phi_2 \chi_z),$$

since $\tau_1 l_{22} - \tau_2 l_{12} = \rho^* \omega^* \zeta_z$ and $\tau_1 l_{21} - \tau_2 l_{11} = \rho^* \omega^* \zeta_g \mu_g$ (see Appendix 2). Note that $\theta$ is independent of $\omega^*$. Only $\kappa$ depends on $\omega^*$.

We put (29) into a form in which the root-locus method can be applied to examine the loci of the eigenvalues $(\lambda - \theta)/\psi(\lambda) = -1/\kappa$ as a function of $\omega^*$. The signs of $\kappa$ and $\theta$ are crucial in determining stability. If $\theta$ is negative, then the dynamics are stable for all nonnegative $\kappa$ and for some negative $\kappa$ as well. If $\theta$ is positive, then the dynamics are stable for all $\kappa \geq \tilde{\kappa}$ for some $\tilde{\kappa} > 0$. Assuming that $n(\phi_3 \chi_g - \phi_2 \chi_z)$ is positive, $\kappa$ is positive if and only if $\omega^*$ is negative. From the definitions given below (10) and (20) we can state this condition as

$$\kappa > 0 \Leftrightarrow \omega^* \leq 0 \Leftrightarrow \omega_p^* \leq 0$$

(because $\sigma^*$ is zero in this model). The key-currency country's budget is balanced when the right-hand side of (7) is zero; hence

$$\bar{\omega}_p^* = -i^*(1 - B_c^*/B_g^*) < 0,$$

implying that $\bar{\omega}^*$ is negative, hence the dynamics are stable even for a small budget deficit. This is slightly different from the previous case where the nonkey-currency country's government budget *must* not be in deficit.

**Proposition 2.** Assume that $n(\phi_3 \chi_g - \phi_2 \chi_z)$ and $n$ are positive, and that $\phi_3 \zeta_g \mu_g - \phi_2 \zeta_g$ is negative. Then the world model is stable if and only if $G^*$ is not greater than $T^*$ plus some positive constant and not less than $T^*$ minus another positive constant. When $n(\phi_3 \chi_g - \phi_2 \chi_z)$, $n$, and $\phi_3 \zeta_g \mu_g - \phi_2 \zeta_z$ are positive, then there exists yet another positive constant such that the dynamics are stable for $G^*$ less than it plus $T^*$. Note that the condition on $G^*$ is stricter when the parameter $\theta$ is positive. For negative $\theta$ the condition on $G^*$ is less strict than that on $G$ of Proposition 1.

### 14.4.3 Benchmark Model C

In model C, both $\sigma$ and $\sigma^*$ are nonzero. Stability of (25) now depends on both $\omega$ and $\omega^*$. The characteristic equation of $\Phi$ given in (25) determines the stability in this general case. Appendix 2 calculates the characteristic equation to be

(30) $$|\lambda I - \Phi| = (\lambda - \phi_1 \omega \rho)\psi(\lambda) + \kappa\lambda(\lambda - \theta).$$

Define this to be $\Delta(\lambda)$.

Assume, as before, that the roots of $\psi(\lambda)$ are stable and $\theta$ is negative. From the root-loci consideration the dynamics are stable if and only if (i) $\omega$ is negative and (ii) $\kappa$ is positive, i.e., equivalently $\omega^*$ is negative. In terms of the constraints on $G$ and $G^*$, both can be stated as

$$G < T/(1 - \sigma\tau) \quad \text{and} \quad G^* < T^*/(1 - \sigma^*\tau^*).$$

Thus the closer $\sigma\tau$ or $\sigma^*\tau^*$ is to 1, the larger each government's expenditure beyond its tax receipt can be without destabilizing the system. In terms of the budget deficits, country $K$'s deficit can be larger than that of country $N$ since $(G - T) \leq T\sigma\tau/(1 - \sigma\tau)$ in (8), but

$$G^* - T^* + i(1 - B_c^*/B_g^*) \leq T^*\sigma^*\tau^*(1 - \sigma^*\tau^*)^{-1} + i^*(1 - B_c^*/B_g^*)$$

in (7).

## 14.5 Stability: Flexible Wage Rates

This section re-evaluates stability implications of the budget deficits by letting wage rates respond to excess demands and inflationary expectations. Now, government $K$'s budget deficit is shown to be more crucial in benchmark model $C$ than that of government $N$. In models $A$ and $B$ the wage rate dynamics do not alter our conclusions in Section 4.

Suppose now that wage rates in the two countries respond to excess demands and changes in the inflationary expectations so that the wage rate variational equations are specified by

$$\dot{w} = vy + \delta\pi_i, \quad \text{and} \quad \dot{w}^* = v^*y^* + \delta\pi_i^*,$$

where $v$ and $v^*$ are positive adjustment speed coefficients.

### 14.5.1 Price Index

We take the price index to be $P_i = P^{1-b}(EP^*)^b$ in country $N$ and $P_i^* = (P/E)^{b^*}(P^*)^{1-b^*}$ in country $K$. In variational terms, $p_i = (1 - b)p + b(e + p^*)$ and $p_i^* = (1 - b^*)p^* + b^*(p - e)$. The parameters $b$ and $b^*$ are evaluated at the equilibrium. They are functions of various model parameters evaluated at equilibrium. Their variations do not appear because they are second order of smallness. The above implies that country N consumes $b$ of country $K$ goods while country $K$ consumes $b^*$ of country $K$ goods in their respective bundles of consumption goods. We let $b$ and $b^*$ be equal in all the benchmark models.

### 14.5.2 Inflationary Expectations

Denote the expected inflation rates in country $N$ and $K$ by $\pi$ and $\pi^*$, respectively. Denote the expectation of $\dot{P}_i/P_i$ by $\pi_i$ and $\dot{P}_i^*/P_i^*$ by $\pi_i^*$. Residents of each country form expectations adaptively on $\pi_i$, $\pi_i^*$ and on $\varepsilon$ by assumption, i.e., we postulate

(31) $\qquad \delta\pi_i = -vp_i, \qquad \delta\pi_i^* = -v^*p_i^*, \qquad \text{and} \qquad \delta\varepsilon = -\mu e.$

Because of (31), the wage rate equations become

(32) $\qquad \dfrac{d}{dt}\begin{bmatrix} w \\ w^* \end{bmatrix} = \begin{bmatrix} v & 0 \\ 0 & v^* \end{bmatrix}\begin{bmatrix} y \\ y^* \end{bmatrix} - vb\begin{bmatrix} 1 \\ -1 \end{bmatrix}e - v\begin{bmatrix} 1-b & b \\ b & 1-b \end{bmatrix}\begin{bmatrix} p \\ p^* \end{bmatrix}.$

We modify the variational aggregate supply schedules (17) to read

(17′) $\qquad y = -\sigma(w - p), \qquad y^* = -\sigma^*(w^* - p^*).$

We retain (15) and (16) as the variational aggregate demand schedules. Equating these two to each other, the deviational prices now respond to wage rate deviations in addition to the exchange rate deviation

(33) $\qquad \begin{bmatrix} p \\ p^* \end{bmatrix} = \begin{bmatrix} \rho \\ -\rho^* \end{bmatrix}e + \Theta\begin{bmatrix} w \\ w^* \end{bmatrix},$

where

$$\Theta = \begin{bmatrix} \sigma + d & -(d + \sigma^*\eta) \\ -(d^* + \eta^*\sigma) & \sigma^* + d^* \end{bmatrix}^{-1}\begin{bmatrix} \sigma & -\eta\sigma^* \\ -\sigma\eta^* & \sigma^* \end{bmatrix}.$$

### 14.5.3 Benchmark Model A

In benchmark model A, (33) specializes to

(33A) $\qquad \begin{bmatrix} p \\ p^* \end{bmatrix} = \begin{bmatrix} 1 \\ 0 \end{bmatrix}e + \begin{bmatrix} 1 \\ 1 \end{bmatrix}w^*.$

Because $\sigma$ is zero, only $w^*$ affects price deviations in both countries. Note that $p^*$ fully reflects $w^*$. $p$ now reflects both $e$ and $w^*$. Changes in outputs are

## 14.5 Stability: Flexible Wage Rates

both zero; $y$ is zero because $\sigma$ is zero in (17), and $y^*$ becomes zero because $w^* - p^*$ is zero. From (32) and (33A), the wage rate dynamics also simplify:

$$(32A) \qquad \frac{d}{dt}\begin{bmatrix} w \\ w^* \end{bmatrix} = -v\begin{bmatrix} 1 \\ 0 \end{bmatrix}e - v\begin{bmatrix} 0 & 1 \\ 0 & 1 \end{bmatrix}\begin{bmatrix} w \\ w^* \end{bmatrix}.$$

From (17′) and (32A), the right-hand side of (20) now becomes

$$\mathscr{F}_1\begin{bmatrix} p \\ y \end{bmatrix} + \mathscr{F}_2\begin{bmatrix} p^* \\ y^* \end{bmatrix} = \omega_p\begin{bmatrix} 1 \\ 0 \\ 0 \end{bmatrix}e + \begin{bmatrix} \omega_p \\ \omega_p^* \\ 0 \end{bmatrix}w^*.$$

Hence the total dynamics of the system is changed from (25) to

$$(34) \qquad \frac{d}{dt}\zeta = \Phi\zeta,$$

where $\zeta' = (h\ b_g^*\ z\ w\ w^*)$.

Its (1, 1) submatrix equals

$$\Phi_{11} = \mathscr{H}^{-1}\left\{\mathscr{F}_0 + \begin{bmatrix} \omega_p \\ 0 \\ 0 \end{bmatrix}[\phi_1 \quad \phi_2 \quad -\phi_3]\right\}.$$

This is the same as $\Phi$ of (26). Flexible wage rates affect the dynamics through its (1, 2) submatrix:

$$\Phi_{12} = \mathscr{H}^{-1}\begin{bmatrix} 0 & \omega_p \\ 0 & \omega_p^* \\ 0 & 0 \end{bmatrix} = \phi_{12}[0 \quad 1],$$

where

$$\phi_{12} = n\begin{bmatrix} \omega_p \\ \chi_z\omega_p^* \\ \chi_g\omega_p^* \end{bmatrix}.$$

The remaining submatrices are defined by substituting $e$ out:

$$\Phi_{21} = -v\begin{bmatrix} 1 \\ 0 \end{bmatrix}[\phi_1 \quad \phi_2 \quad -\phi_3] \quad \text{and} \quad \Phi_{22} = -v\begin{bmatrix} 0 & 1 \\ 0 & 1 \end{bmatrix}.$$

Because of the special structure of $\Phi_{12}$ and $\Phi_{21}$, we can write

$$(35) \qquad \Phi_{21}(\lambda I - \Phi_{11})^{-1}\Phi_{12} = -\tilde{\psi}\begin{bmatrix} 1 \\ 0 \end{bmatrix}[0 \quad 1],$$

where $\tilde{\psi}$ is some scalar of no importance, as we see next, in the expression for the characteristic polynomial

(36) $\quad |\lambda I - \Phi| = |\lambda I - \Phi_{11}||\lambda I - \Phi_{22} - \Phi_{21}(\lambda I - \Phi_{11})^{-1}\Phi_{12}|.$

Because $\Phi_{22}$ is lower triangular and because (35) affects only the (1, 2) element of $\Phi_{22}$, the second determinant in (36) equals $|\lambda I - \Phi_{22}|$, i.e., (36) simplifies to

$$|\lambda I - \Phi| = |\lambda I - \Phi_{11}|\lambda(\lambda + v) = (\lambda - \omega\phi_1)\psi(\lambda)\lambda(\lambda + v),$$

where (27) has been used.

We thus conclude that

**Proposition 3.** Flexible wages do not alter stability characteristics of benchmark model $A$ provided $v$ is not negative.

### 14.5.4 Benchmark Model B

In benchmark model $B$, (33) specializes to

(33B) $\quad \begin{bmatrix} p \\ p^* \end{bmatrix} = -\begin{bmatrix} 0 \\ 1 \end{bmatrix}e + \begin{bmatrix} 1 \\ 1 \end{bmatrix}w,$

hence $y$ is zero because $w - p$ is zero, and $y^*$ is zero by $\sigma^*$ being zero by assumption. The wage rate dynamics (32) specialize to

(32B) $\quad \dfrac{d}{dt}\begin{bmatrix} w \\ w^* \end{bmatrix} = -v\begin{bmatrix} 0 \\ 1 \end{bmatrix}e - v\begin{bmatrix} 1 & 0 \\ 1 & 0 \end{bmatrix}\begin{bmatrix} w \\ w^* \end{bmatrix}.$

Next, (20) is replaced by

$$\mathscr{F}_1\begin{bmatrix} p \\ y \end{bmatrix} + \mathscr{F}_2\begin{bmatrix} p^* \\ y^* \end{bmatrix} = -\omega_p^*\begin{bmatrix} 0 \\ 1 \\ 0 \end{bmatrix}e + \begin{bmatrix} \omega_p \\ \omega_p^* \\ 0 \end{bmatrix}w.$$

Hence the $\Phi_{11}$ submatrix in (34) is identical to $\Phi$ of (28). The (1, 2) submatrix equals

$$\Phi_{12} = \phi_{12}[1 \ 0],$$

where $\phi_{12}$ is as defined below (34).

The other two submatrices are given by

$$\Phi_{21} = -v\begin{bmatrix} 0 \\ 1 \end{bmatrix}[\phi_1 \ \phi_2 \ -\phi_3] \quad \text{and} \quad \Phi_{22} = -v\begin{bmatrix} 1 & 0 \\ 1 & 0 \end{bmatrix}.$$

## 14.5 Stability: Flexible Wage Rates

Equation (35) now becomes

$$\Phi_{21}(\lambda I - \Phi_{11})^{-1}\Phi_{12} = -\psi' \begin{bmatrix} 0 \\ 1 \end{bmatrix} [1 \quad 0],$$

where $\psi'$ turns out not to affect the characteristic polynomial, because

$$\left| \lambda I - \Phi_{22} + \psi' \begin{bmatrix} 0 & 0 \\ 1 & 0 \end{bmatrix} \right| = |\lambda I - \Phi_{22}| = \lambda(\lambda + \nu).$$

Again, we conclude that the stability conditions are the same as the previous benchmark case B and can state

**Proposition 4.** Flexible wage rates do not alter stability conditions of the benchmark model B.

As soon as we leave these two benchmark models, however, flexible wage rates affect stability behavior of the model. We turn to this case next.

### 14.5.5 Benchmark Model D

Suppose that the real sector characteristics of the two countries are the same, i.e., $d = d^*$, $y = y^*$, and $\sigma = \sigma^*$. Then $\rho$ and $\rho^*$ are equal. Equation (33) specializes to

$$(33D) \quad \begin{bmatrix} p \\ p^* \end{bmatrix} = \rho \begin{bmatrix} 1 \\ -1 \end{bmatrix} e + \begin{bmatrix} \theta_1 & \theta_2 \\ \theta_2 & \theta_1 \end{bmatrix} \begin{bmatrix} w \\ w^* \end{bmatrix}.$$

No longer do $y$ and $y^*$ remain at zero. They are given by

$$(37) \quad \begin{bmatrix} y \\ y^* \end{bmatrix} = \sigma \left\{ \rho \begin{bmatrix} 1 \\ -1 \end{bmatrix} e + \begin{bmatrix} -(1-\theta_1) & \theta_2 \\ \theta_2 & -(1-\theta_1) \end{bmatrix} \begin{bmatrix} w \\ w^* \end{bmatrix} \right\},$$

where

$$\theta_1 = \{d + \sigma(1-\eta)\}/\{2d + \sigma(1+\eta)\} \quad \text{and} \quad \theta_2 = d/\{2d + \sigma(1+\eta)\}.$$

Model D results by setting $\theta_2$ to zero in (33D) and (37). Zero $\theta_2$ results if $\sigma/d$ is larger.[9] In model D, then, there is no immediate or impact cross-over effect of the wage rate deviations on price and output deviations.

---

[9] The opposite assumption that $\sigma/d$ is sufficiently small results in a model with $\theta_1$ and $\theta_2$ both equal to $\frac{1}{2}$ in (33D). Stability analysis of this model is equally simple as that for model D if the inflationary expectation is assumed to be stationary, i.e., if $\nu$ is zero in (31). A simplifying feature of these two cases is that the column sums of the matrix $\Phi_{22}$ are identical, implying that the changes in $w + w^*$ are a function only of $e$ and $w + w^*$, and not of $w$ and $w^*$ separately.

The right-hand side of (20) now becomes

$$\mathscr{F}_1\begin{bmatrix}p\\y\end{bmatrix} + \mathscr{F}_2\begin{bmatrix}p^*\\y^*\end{bmatrix} = \rho\begin{bmatrix}\omega\\-\omega^*\\0\end{bmatrix}e + \tilde{\Phi}_{12}\begin{bmatrix}w\\w^*\end{bmatrix},$$

where

$$\tilde{\Phi}_{12} = \begin{bmatrix}\omega\theta_1 + \sigma\tau\omega_g & 0\\ 0 & \omega^*\theta_1 + \sigma\tau\omega_g^*\\ 0 & 0\end{bmatrix}.$$

The matrix $\Phi_{11}$ is the same as that of model C. With model D, $\Phi_{22}$ in (34) is diagonal. Let $v$ and $v^*$ also be the same. The matrix $\Phi_{12}$ also simplifies to $\Phi_{12} = [\delta_1\ \delta_2]$ where

$$\delta_1 = (\omega\theta_1 + \sigma\tau\omega_g)\begin{bmatrix}1\\0\\0\end{bmatrix} \quad \text{and} \quad \delta_2 = (\omega^*\theta_1 + \sigma^*\tau^*\omega_g^*)\begin{bmatrix}0\\\chi_z\\\chi_g\end{bmatrix}.$$

The matrix $\Phi_{21}$ equals $\phi[{}_{-1}^{\ 1}]$, where $\phi$ is $\sigma\rho v - v\{b + (1-b)\rho\}$. Noting that $\Phi_{21}(\lambda I - \Phi_{11})^{-1}\Phi_{12}$ equals $\phi[{}_{-1}^{\ 1}][\zeta_1\ \zeta_2]$, where $\zeta_i = [\phi_1\ \phi_2\ -\phi_3]\times(\lambda I - \Phi_{11})^{-1}\delta_i$, $i = 1, 2$, the characteristic polynomial of $\Phi$ is obtained by substituting these into (36) as

(36D) $\qquad |\lambda I - \Phi| = \Delta(\lambda)\{L(\lambda) - \phi(\zeta_1 - \zeta_2)(\lambda + \phi_{22})\},$

where $\Delta(\lambda)$ has been defined in (30), i.e.,

$$\Delta(\lambda) = |\lambda I - \Phi_{11}| = (\lambda - \omega\rho\phi_1)\psi(\lambda) + \kappa\lambda(\lambda - \theta),$$
$$L(\lambda) = |\lambda I - \Phi_{22}| = (\lambda + \phi_{22})^2,$$

and

$$\phi_{22} = \sigma(1 - \theta_1)v + \theta_1 v.$$

Further calculation, recorded in Appendix 3 at the end of this chapter, shows

$$\zeta_i = [\phi_1\ \phi_2\ -\phi_3](\lambda I - \Phi_0)^{-1}\delta_i\psi(\lambda)/\Delta(\lambda), \quad i = 1, 2,$$

where $\Phi_0$ is as defined below (25). Substituting these into (36D), we note that

$$(\zeta_1 - \zeta_2)\Delta(\lambda)/\psi(\lambda) = \phi_1(\omega\theta_1 + \sigma\tau\omega_g)\lambda^{-1} + \psi(\lambda)^{-1}[(\phi_2\chi_z - \chi_g)\lambda$$
$$+ n(\phi_2\zeta_z - \phi_3\zeta_g\mu_g)(\chi_z - \chi_g Z/B_g^*)]$$
$$= \phi_1(\omega\theta_1 + \sigma\tau\omega_\delta)\lambda^{-1} - \psi(\lambda)^{-1}(\phi_3\chi_g - \phi_2\chi_z)(\lambda - \hat{\theta}),$$

## 14.6 Elaborations on the Basic Model

where $\tilde{\theta} = \theta n(\chi_z - \chi_g Z/B_g^*)$. We can write (36D) as

$$0 = (\lambda + \phi_{22})[\Delta(\lambda)(\lambda + \phi_{22}) - \phi\{\psi(\lambda)\phi_1(\omega\theta_1 + \sigma\tau\omega_g)/\lambda - (\phi_3\chi_g - \phi_2\chi_z)(\lambda - \theta)\}],$$

or slightly rearranging terms, we express the characteristic polynomial in the root-locus form:

$$\lambda N(\lambda)/D(\lambda) = -1/\kappa,$$

where

$$D(\lambda) = \{\lambda(\lambda + \phi_{22})(\lambda - \omega\rho\phi_1) - \phi\phi_1(\omega\theta_1 + \sigma\tau\omega_g)\}\psi(\lambda),$$

$$N(\lambda) = \lambda(\lambda - \theta)(\lambda + \phi_{22}) + (\phi_3\chi_g - \phi_2\chi_z)(\lambda - \tilde{\theta})/\kappa$$

$$= \lambda(\lambda - \theta)(\lambda + \phi_{22}) - (\lambda - \tilde{\theta})/n\omega^*\rho^*.$$

Now if

(38) $$\omega_p < -\sigma\tau\omega_g\left(\frac{1 - \theta_1}{\theta_1}\right) < \sigma\tau\omega_g,$$

which occurs if and only if $\eta$ is greater than $\frac{1}{3}$, then both $\omega$ and $\omega\theta_1 + \sigma\tau\omega_g$ are negative. Hence the roots of $D(\lambda)$ are stable. Even if one of the roots of $N(\lambda)$ is positive, which happens if $\theta$ is positive, and $\omega^*$ is negative, if the roots of $D(\lambda)$ are all stable, then for $\kappa \leq \tilde{\kappa}$, for some $\tilde{\kappa}$, the dynamics are stable. Putting the previous statement in terms of $\omega^*$, we state

***Proposition 5.*** In model D, if $\omega_p$ satisfies (38), then the system is stable for any negative $\omega^*$ not less than some negative number. Note that because $G < T/(1 - \sigma\tau) < T/[1 - (1 - \theta_1)\sigma\tau/\theta]$ for $\eta > \frac{1}{3}$, the government of country N can run a larger deficit without destabilizing the system, while the stability condition for country K is the same as before.

## 14.6 Elaborations on the Basic Model

In this section we report on stability implications of several modifications of the basic models; they are (i) nonzero $\Omega$, (ii) more explicit incorporation of inflationary expectations, and (iii) interest sensitive aggregate demands.

### 14.6.1 Effects of Nonzero $\Omega$

So far $\Omega$ in (22) has been assumed zero. When $\Omega$ is nonzero, $-\tau_1$ is replaced with $-\tau_1 + n\Omega/B_g^*$ and $-\tau_2$ by $-\tau_2 + n\Omega/Z$ in (25). In our definitional expression for $\kappa$, incorporate these changes. Assuming that $\theta$ is still negative, that $\omega < 0$, and that $\psi(\lambda)$ is stable [recall that $\psi(\lambda)$ is independent of $\Omega$], $\kappa$ becomes positive if and only if

$$(-\omega^*)(\phi_3\chi_g - \phi_2\chi_z)\rho^* + (\Omega/Z)(\phi_3 - \phi_2 Z/B_g^*) > 0$$

or

(39) $\qquad \omega^* < \rho^*(\Omega/Z)(\phi_3 - \phi_2 Z/B_g^*)/(\phi_3\chi_g - \phi_2\chi_z).$

For an adaptive expectation to be discussed next, $\phi_2$ and $\phi_3$ are given by (40). When these $\phi$s are substituted, then $(\Omega/Z)(\phi_3 - \phi_2 Z/B_g^*)$ is positive if and only if

$$D\Omega\{s_5/H^* + s_2(1/M^* - 1/B^*)\} > 0,$$

where the definitions below (6) have been substituted.

If the private sector of country $K$ holds larger stock of the government bond than money, then the right-hand side of (39) is expected to be positive if and only if $D\Omega$ is positive. From (6), $D$ is positive if and only if $s_5/s_4 > F/B^*$, i.e.,

$$B^* \, \partial \ln(B^*/M^*)/\partial i^* > F \, \partial \ln(F/H^*)/\partial i^*.$$

**Proposition 6.** *A positive sign of the right-hand side of (39) implies that country $K$ with a positive $\Omega$ can run a larger deficit without destabilizing the world economy than with $\Omega$ zero.*

### 14.6.2 Effects of Inflationary Expectations

So far, inflationary expectations in the two countries have appeared only through $\chi$, i.e., as the differences of the expected inflation rates in the two countries. We can treat effects of inflationary expectations more explicitly in two stages: in the first, choose specific price indexes and make explicit the expectations on the price indexes and on the expectations on the exchange rate. This allows us to give explicit expressions for $\kappa_1$, $\kappa_2$, and $\kappa_3$ in (24), heretofore left unspecified. In the second stage, we restore a term in real demand for output which responds to the changes in real inflations.

This causes the deviation in prices and outputs to have more complex responses than specified in (19), and consequently the responses of the trade balances become more complex.

After expressing $p_i$ and $p_i^*$ in terms of $p$, $p^*$, and $e$, and recalling that $\delta\chi$ is defined to be $\delta\pi_i$ minus $\delta\pi_i^*$, we deduce from (31) that

$$\delta(\varepsilon + \chi) = -\Gamma e,$$

where

$$\Gamma = \mu + \{v(1-b) - v^*b^*\}\rho + \{vb - v^*(1-b^*)\}\rho^* + vb + v^*b^* > 0.$$

Together with (6), this implies that

$$\delta(\varepsilon + \chi) = -\Gamma/(1 + s_1\Gamma)\{\mu_h h - \mu_z z + s_2(\mu_g b_g^* - \mu_c b_c^*)\}.$$

Compare this with (24). We conclude that the adaptive expectations on the exchange rate and price indices yield the expectations (24) with

(40)
$$\begin{aligned} \kappa_1 &= -\Gamma(1 + s_1\Gamma)^{-1}\mu_h; & \text{hence} & \quad \phi_1 = \mu_h/(1 + s_1\Gamma) > 0, \\ \kappa_2 &= -\Gamma(1 + s_1\Gamma)^{-1}s_2\mu_g; & \text{hence} & \quad \phi_2 = s_2\mu_g/(1 + s_1\Gamma) > 0, \\ \kappa_3 &= \Gamma(1 + s_1\Gamma)^{-1}\mu_z; & \text{hence} & \quad \phi_3 = \mu_z/(1 + s_1\Gamma) > 0.^{[10]} \end{aligned}$$

The expression for $\delta B_T$ remains as given by (22).

### 14.6.3 Interest-Sensitive Real Demand Terms

Next, we respecify variation of aggregate demands by modifying (15) and (16) into

(41)
$$\begin{aligned} y &= d(e + p^* - p) - a\delta(i^* + \varepsilon - \pi) + \eta y^*, \\ y^* &= d^*(p - e - p^*) - a^*\delta(i^* - \pi^*) + \eta^* y. \end{aligned}$$

We retain (17) as the relations for the aggregate supply variations. When the demand includes a component sensitive to the real interest rate prevailing in a country, (18) and (19) are modified as well. We show in Appendix 2 that with (41) replacing (15) and (16), (20) is modified as

$$\mathscr{F}_1 \begin{bmatrix} p \\ y \end{bmatrix} + \mathscr{F}_2 \begin{bmatrix} p^* \\ y^* \end{bmatrix} = \begin{bmatrix} \omega\tilde{\rho} \\ -\omega^*\tilde{\rho}^* \\ 0 \end{bmatrix} e + \begin{bmatrix} \omega\tilde{\rho}_i \\ \omega^*\tilde{\rho}_i^* \\ 0 \end{bmatrix}(\theta_z z - \mu_g b_g^*),$$

where $\tilde{\rho}, \tilde{\rho}^*, \tilde{\rho}_i$, and $\tilde{\rho}_i^*$ are defined in Appendix 2.

The characteristic polynomial is also altered. Equation (30) changes into

$$(\lambda - \omega\tilde{\rho}\phi_1)\psi(\lambda) + \tilde{\kappa}\lambda(\lambda - \tilde{\theta}) + \phi_1\omega\tilde{\rho}_i\tilde{l}(\lambda + \tilde{s}) = 0,$$

where $\tilde{l}$ and $\tilde{s}$ are as defined in Appendix 2 and where

$$\tilde{\kappa} = \phi_2\tilde{\tau}_1 - \phi_1\tilde{\tau}_2 = n(-\omega^*)(\phi_3\chi_g - \phi_2\chi_z)(\tilde{\rho}^*/\rho^*).$$

Although the expression for the characteristic polynomial is more complicated, the root-locus equation is still of the form

$$\psi_n(\lambda)/\tilde{D}(\lambda) = -1/\tilde{\kappa},$$

---

[10] With these $\phi$s, $\phi_3\chi_g - \phi_2\chi_z$ appearing in the definition of $\theta$ is positive if $1 + s_1\Gamma$ and $D\{s_5/H^* + s_2/M^* - s_2/s_4\}$ are positive.

where

$$\psi_n(\lambda) = \lambda(\lambda - \tilde{\theta}) + \phi_1 \omega \tilde{\rho}_i(\tilde{l}/\tilde{\kappa})(\lambda + \tilde{s}) \quad \text{and} \quad \tilde{D}(\lambda) = (\lambda - \omega\phi_1\tilde{\rho})\psi(\lambda).$$

Now $\lambda = 0$ is not a root of $\psi_n(\lambda)$. Thus, provided $\psi(\lambda)$ is stable, the roots of the characteristic polynomial can be stable for some $\tilde{\kappa} < 0$, i.e., for some $\omega^* > 0$. Even if $\omega$ is positive if $\psi_n(\lambda)$ is stable, then a sufficiently positive $\tilde{\kappa}$ leads to overall stability

**Proposition 7.** Inclusion of the aggregate real demand term depending on the real interest rate raises the upper bound on the deficit that country K can run without destabilizing the dynamics. Even when country N runs a budget deficit to cause $\omega > 0$, a sufficiently negative $\omega^*$ can stabilize the total dynamics.

## Appendix 1  Derivation of Variational Reduced Form Equation (6)

Variations of the three expressions in (6) are three equations in three variables $\delta i^*$, $e$, and $f$. In this appendix, we sketch the derivation of Eq. (6).

Taking the variation of (4a)

$$m - e - h^* = -s_1 \delta(\varepsilon + \chi) - s_2 \delta i^*,$$

where

$$s_1 = -l_1/l + q_1/q > 0 \quad \text{and} \quad s_2 = -l_2/l + q_2/q > 0.$$

Variation of (4b) yields

$$f - h^* = s_3 \delta(\varepsilon + \rho) - s_4 \delta i^*,$$

where

$$s_3 = \alpha_1/\alpha - q_1/q \quad \text{and} \quad s_4 = -\alpha_2/\alpha + q_2/q > 0.$$

Here we do not yet assume $s_3$ is zero. From (2), taking its variation, we derive

$$\xi - (F/B^*)f = s_5 \delta i^*,$$

where

$$s_5 = v'/v - \mu'/\mu > 0 \quad \text{and} \quad \xi = (B_g^* b_g^* - B_c^* b_c^*)/B^* - (B_c^* b_c^* - Zz)/M^*.$$

These variational equations can be arranged as a set of simultaneous equations for $e$, $f$, and $\delta i^*$:

$$\begin{bmatrix} 1 & 0 & -s_2 \\ 0 & 1 & s_4 \\ 0 & (F/B^*) & s_5 \end{bmatrix} \begin{bmatrix} e \\ f \\ \delta i^* \end{bmatrix} = \begin{bmatrix} m - h^* \\ h^* \\ \xi \end{bmatrix} + \begin{bmatrix} s_1 \\ s_3 \\ 0 \end{bmatrix} \delta(\varepsilon + \chi).$$

Upon solving it for $e$, $f$, and $\delta i^*$, noting that $H^* = Z - R$ hence $h^* = (Z/H^*)z - (R/M^*)r$, (6) is derived after setting $b_c^*$ and $r$ to zero. We obtain

$$e = m - h^* - s_2 D(F/B^*)h^* + Ds_2\xi + \{s_1 - (F/B^*)Ds_2 s_3\}\delta(\varepsilon + \chi),$$

$$f = D\{s_5 h^* - s_4\xi\} + Ds_3 s_5 \delta(\varepsilon + \chi),$$

$$\delta i^* = D\{-(F/B^*)h^* + \xi\} - D(F/B^*)s_3 \delta(\varepsilon + \chi), \quad D^{-1} = s_5 - (F/B^*)s_4.$$

When we assume that $F/H^*$ depends only on $i^*$, we can set $s_3 = 0$ in the above. Note that $\delta(\varepsilon + \chi)$ affects only $e$ in that case. This simplifies the dynamics considerably.

## Appendix 2  Characteristic Equation of $\Phi$

From (14),

$$\mathcal{H}^{-1}\mathcal{F}_0 = \begin{bmatrix} 0 & 0 & 0 \\ 0 & \mathcal{J}^{-1}\mathcal{L} & \\ 0 & & \end{bmatrix}.$$

Thus by definition, the characteristic polymonial of $\Phi$ defined in (25) is given by

$$|\lambda I - \Phi| = \left| \lambda I - \mathcal{H}^{-1}\mathcal{F}_0 - \begin{bmatrix} \omega\rho \\ -\tau_1 \\ -\tau_2 \end{bmatrix} [\phi_1 \quad \phi_2 \quad -\phi_3] \right|$$

$$= |\lambda I - \mathcal{H}^{-1}\mathcal{F}_0| \left\{ 1 - [\phi_1 \quad \phi_2 \quad -\phi_3](\lambda I - \mathcal{H}^{-1}\mathcal{F}_0)^{-1} \begin{bmatrix} \omega\rho \\ -\tau_1 \\ -\tau_2 \end{bmatrix} \right\}$$

$$= \lambda|\lambda I - \mathcal{J}^{-1}\mathcal{L}| \left\{ 1 - \frac{1}{\lambda}\phi_1 \omega\rho + [\phi_2 \quad -\phi_3](\lambda I - \mathcal{J}^{-1}\mathcal{L})^{-1} \right.$$

$$\left. \times \begin{bmatrix} \tau_1 \\ \tau_2 \end{bmatrix} \right\}$$

$$= (\lambda - \phi_1 \omega\rho)|\lambda I - \mathcal{J}^{-1}\mathcal{L}| + \lambda[\phi_2 \quad -\phi_3] \operatorname{adj}(\lambda I - \mathcal{J}^{-1}\mathcal{L}) \begin{bmatrix} \tau_1 \\ \tau_2 \end{bmatrix}$$

where adj($\cdot$) is the adjoint matrix.

Let

$$\mathcal{J}^{-1}\mathcal{L} = n \begin{bmatrix} l_{11} & -l_{12} \\ l_{21} & -l_{22} \end{bmatrix},$$

where $n^{-1} = \chi_z - \chi_g Z/B_g^*$. Then

$$[\phi_2 \ -\phi_3] \operatorname{adj}(\lambda I - \mathscr{J}^{-1}\mathscr{L}) \begin{bmatrix} \tau_1 \\ \tau_2 \end{bmatrix} = (\phi_2\tau_1 - \phi_3\tau_2)\lambda + n[\phi_2(\tau_1 l_{22} - \tau_2 l_{12})$$
$$- \phi_3(l_{21}\tau_1 - \tau_2 l_{11})],$$

and define

$$\psi(\lambda) = |\lambda I - \mathscr{J}^{-1}\mathscr{L}| = (\lambda + nl_{22})(\lambda - nl_{11}) + n^2 l_{12} l_{21}.$$

The characteristic polymonial is thus expressible as

$$|\lambda I - \Phi| = (\lambda - \phi_1 \omega \rho)\psi(\lambda) + \kappa\lambda(\lambda - \theta),$$

where

$$\kappa = \phi_2\tau_1 - \phi_3\tau_2$$

and

$$\theta = n\{\phi_2(\tau_1 l_{22} - \tau_2 l_{12}) - \phi_3(l_{21}\tau_1 - \tau_2 l_{11})\}/(\phi_3\tau_2 - \phi_2\tau_1).$$

The element $l$s are calculated according to the definition as follows:

$$\begin{bmatrix} l_{11} & -l_{12} \\ l_{21} & -l_{22} \end{bmatrix} = \begin{bmatrix} \chi_z & Z/B_g^* \\ \chi_g & 1 \end{bmatrix} \begin{bmatrix} \rho_g & -\rho_z \\ \zeta_g\mu_g & -\zeta_z \end{bmatrix}.$$

Hence

$$\tau_1 l_{22} - \tau_2 l_{12} = \rho^*\omega^*\zeta_z \quad \text{and} \quad \tau_1 l_{21} - \tau_2 l_{11} = \rho^*\omega^*\zeta_g\mu_g.$$

Therefore,

$$\theta = (\phi_2\zeta_z - \phi_3\zeta_g\mu_g)/(\phi_3\chi_g - \phi_2\chi_z),$$
$$l_{12}l_{21} - l_{11}l_{22} = n^{-1}\{-\rho_g\zeta_z + \rho_z\mu_g\zeta_g\}.$$

**Inequality $l_{22} - l_{11} > 0$.** $n$ is positive if and only if $[s_5(1 + F/H^*) - s_4 F(1/M^* + 2/B^*)]/(s_5 - s_4 F/B^*) > 0$. Substituting the defining expression, the inequality is expressible as $0 < \chi_g\rho_z - \chi_z\rho_g + \zeta_z - \zeta_g\mu_g Z/B_g^*$. From the definition given in (11) and (13), this inequality can be put into

$$i^*\{1 + 2v_z(F/Z) + s_4(F/B_g^*)\mu_g\}$$
$$+ \mu_g\{F/B_g^* + (1 + v_z F/Z)(1 - B_c^*/B_g^*)\} < \theta_z[1 + s_4\mu_g(1 - B_c^*/B_g^*)]$$
$$\times (F/Z).$$

This shows that $\theta_z$ must be positive for the inequality to hold or $F/H^* > B^*/M^*$ must hold.

## Appendix 2 Characteristic Equation of $\Phi$

**Inequality $l_{12}l_{21} - l_{11}l_{22} > 0$.** Substituting the defining relations this inequality becomes $\rho_z \mu_g \zeta_g > \rho_g \zeta_z$ if $\chi_z - \chi_g Z/B_g^*$ is positive. Expressing them by their definitions, given in (11) and (13), the inequality can be put into

$$i^* v_z \{1 + \mu_g(1 - B_c^*/B_g^*)\} > \theta_z \{1 - s_4 \mu_g(1 - B_c^*/B_g^*)\}.$$

Thus, the quadratic polynomial $\psi(\lambda)$ has two eigenvalues with negative real parts if the two inequalities define nonempty regions in the space of $i^*$ and $\theta_z$:

(42) $$A_1 \theta_z > A_2 i^* + A_3$$

and

(43) $$A_4 \theta_z < A_5 i^*,$$

where

$$A_1 = \{1 + s_4 \mu_g(1 - B_c^*/B_g^*)\} F/Z,$$
$$A_2 = 1 + (2v_z + s_4 \mu_g Z/B_g^*) F/Z,$$
$$A_3 = \mu_g \{F/B_g^* + (1 - B_c^*/B_g^*)(1 + v_z F/Z)\},$$
$$A_4 = 1 + (1 - B_c^*/B_g^*)\mu_g,$$
$$A_5 = 1 - s_4 \mu_g(1 - B_c^*/B_g^*).$$

These two inequalities can be satisfied simultaneously if $A_1/A_2 > A_5/A_4$.

**Sign of $\theta$.** The parameter $\theta$ is negative if $\phi_3 \chi_g > \phi_2 \chi_z$ and $\phi_2 \zeta_z < \mu_g \zeta_g \phi_3$. These inequalities can be satisfied simultaneously if $\phi_2$ and $\phi_3$ are positive and if $\zeta_z/(\mu_g \zeta_g) > \chi_z/\chi_g$. This is equivalently expressed as

(44) $$A_1' \theta_z > A_2' i^* + A_3',$$

where

$$A_1' = s_4 F/Z, \qquad A_2' = s_4(1 + 2v_z F/Z) \qquad A_3' = 1 + v_z F/Z.$$

Therefore the region defined by (43) and the maximum of (42) and (44) is nonempty if $A_5/A_4 > \max(A_2/A_1, A_2'/A_1')$. Assuming this, there is a pair $(\theta_z, i^*)$ for which $\theta$ is negative, and the roots of $\psi(\lambda)$ are stable.

**Interest-Sensitive Real Demand.** With (15) and (16) replaced by (41), (18) changes to

$$\begin{bmatrix} p \\ p^* \end{bmatrix} = \begin{bmatrix} \rho \\ -\rho^* \end{bmatrix} e - \begin{bmatrix} \rho_\varepsilon \\ \rho_\varepsilon^* \end{bmatrix} (\delta\varepsilon - \delta\pi) + \begin{bmatrix} \rho_\pi^* \\ \rho_{\pi^*}^* \end{bmatrix} \delta\pi^* - \begin{bmatrix} \rho_i \\ \rho_i^* \end{bmatrix} \delta i^*,$$

where $\rho$ and $\rho^*$ are as defined in (19), where

$$\begin{bmatrix} \rho_\varepsilon \\ \rho_\varepsilon^* \end{bmatrix} = a\Sigma\,\delta \begin{bmatrix} d^* + \sigma^* \\ d^* + \sigma\eta^* \end{bmatrix}, \qquad \begin{bmatrix} \rho_\pi \\ \rho_{\pi*}^* \end{bmatrix} = a^*\Sigma\,\delta \begin{bmatrix} d + \sigma^*\eta \\ d + \sigma \end{bmatrix},$$

$$\begin{bmatrix} \rho_i \\ \rho_i^* \end{bmatrix} = \begin{bmatrix} \rho_\varepsilon + \rho_\pi \\ \rho_\varepsilon^* + \rho_{\pi*}^* \end{bmatrix}, \qquad \Sigma^{-1} = (1 - \eta\eta^*)\sigma\sigma^* + d(\sigma^* - \sigma\eta^*) + d^*(\sigma - \sigma^*\eta).$$

For simplicity we assume $b = b^*$ and $v = v^*$. Then the relation between $\delta\pi$ and $\delta\pi_i$, given by

$$\begin{bmatrix} 1-b & b \\ b & 1-b \end{bmatrix} \begin{bmatrix} \delta\pi \\ \delta\pi^* \end{bmatrix} = \begin{bmatrix} \delta\pi_i \\ \delta\pi_i^* \end{bmatrix} - b\begin{bmatrix} 1 \\ -1 \end{bmatrix}\delta\varepsilon,$$

can be solved for $\delta\pi$ and $\delta\pi_i^*$ as

$$\delta\pi = -vp + b(\mu - v)e/(1 - 2b) \quad \text{and} \quad \delta\pi^* = -vp^* - b(\mu - v)e/(1 - 2b).$$

Substituting these together with $\delta\varepsilon = -\mu e$ and $\delta i^*$, given by (6), into the above, $p$ and $p^*$ can be expressed as

$$p = \tilde{\rho}e - \tilde{\rho}_i(-\theta_z z + \mu_g B_g^*), \qquad p^* = -\tilde{\rho}^*e - \tilde{\rho}_i^*(-\theta_z z + \mu_g b_g^*),$$

where

$$\begin{bmatrix} \tilde{\rho} \\ -\tilde{\rho}^* \end{bmatrix} = \left[ I + v\begin{pmatrix} \rho_\varepsilon \rho_\pi \\ \rho_\varepsilon^* \rho_\pi^* \end{pmatrix} \right]^{-1}$$

$$\times \begin{bmatrix} \rho + \rho_\varepsilon\{\mu + b(\mu-v)/(1-2b)\} - \rho_\pi b(\mu-v)/(1-2b) \\ -\rho^* + \rho_\varepsilon^*\{\mu + b(\mu-v)/(1-2b)\} - \rho_{\pi*}^* b(\mu-v)/(1-2b) \end{bmatrix}$$

and

$$\begin{bmatrix} \tilde{\rho}_i \\ \tilde{\rho}_i^* \end{bmatrix} = \left[ I + v\begin{bmatrix} \rho_\varepsilon & \rho_\pi^* \\ \rho_\varepsilon^* & \rho_\pi^* \end{bmatrix} \right]^{-1} \begin{bmatrix} \rho_i \\ \rho_i^* \end{bmatrix}.$$

Then, assuming $\Omega = 0$,

$$\mathscr{F}_1\begin{bmatrix} p \\ y \end{bmatrix} + \mathscr{F}_2\begin{bmatrix} p^* \\ y^* \end{bmatrix} = \begin{bmatrix} \omega\tilde{\rho} \\ -\omega^*\tilde{\rho}^* \\ 0 \end{bmatrix}e - \begin{bmatrix} \omega\tilde{\rho}_i \\ \omega^*\tilde{\rho}_i^* \\ 0 \end{bmatrix}(-\theta_z z + \mu_g b_g^*).$$

The dynamic matrix is changed into

$$\dot{\phi} = \mathscr{H}^{-1}\mathscr{F}_0 + \begin{bmatrix} \omega\tilde{\rho} \\ -\tilde{\tau}_1 \\ -\tilde{\tau}_2 \end{bmatrix}[\phi_1 \ \phi_2 \ -\phi_3] - \begin{bmatrix} \omega\tilde{\rho}_i \\ -\tilde{\tau}_1\tilde{\rho}_i \\ -\tilde{\tau}_2\tilde{\rho}_i^* \end{bmatrix}[0 \ \mu_g \ -\theta_z].$$

## Appendix 3  Wage Rate Dynamics

The characteristic polynomial becomes

$$(\lambda - \tilde{\omega}\phi_1)\psi(\lambda) + \lambda\tilde{\kappa}(\lambda - \tilde{\theta}) + \phi_1\omega\tilde{\rho}_i\tilde{l}(\lambda - \tilde{s}) = 0,$$

where

$$\tilde{l}(\lambda + \tilde{s}) = [\mu_g \quad -\theta_z]\begin{bmatrix} \lambda + l_{22} & -l_{12} \\ l_{21} & \lambda - l_{11} \end{bmatrix}\begin{bmatrix} \tilde{\tau}_1 \\ \tilde{\tau}_2 \end{bmatrix}$$

and where

$$\tilde{\kappa} = \phi_2\tilde{\tau}_1 - \phi_3\tilde{\tau}_2 = \tau(-\omega^*)(\phi_3\chi_g - \phi_2\chi_3)(\tilde{\rho}^*/\rho^*),$$

i.e.,

$$\tilde{l} = \tilde{\tau}_1\mu_g - \tilde{\tau}_2\theta_z,$$
$$\tilde{s} = (\tilde{\tau}_1 l_{22} - \tilde{\tau}_2 l_{12})\mu_g - (\tilde{\tau}_1 l_{21} - \tilde{\tau}_2 l_{11})\theta_z = \tilde{\rho}^*\omega^*\mu_g(\zeta_z - \theta_z\zeta_g).$$

## Appendix 3  Wage Rate Dynamics

In this appendix, the characteristic polynomial of the dynamic matrix is derived when the dynamics incorporate the wage rate changes. The matrix is

$$\Phi = \begin{bmatrix} \Phi_{11} & \Phi_{12} \\ \Phi_{21} & \Phi_{22} \end{bmatrix}.$$

The expressions for the submatrices are given as in the main body of the chapter. We use the identity

$$|\lambda I - \Phi| = |\lambda I - \Phi_{11}||\lambda I - \Phi_{22} - \Phi_{21}(\lambda I - \Phi_{11})^{-1}\Phi_{12}|,$$

where $\Phi_{11}$ are the dynamics examined earlier with fixed wage rate. In Appendix 2 we have shown that

$$|\lambda I - \Phi_{11}| = (\lambda - \omega\rho\phi_1)\psi(\lambda) + \kappa\lambda(\lambda - \theta).$$

Define this as $\Delta(\lambda)$.

We note that

$$[\phi_1 \quad \phi_2 \quad -\phi_3](\lambda I - \Phi_{11})^{-1}\Phi_{12}$$
$$= \{\lambda\psi(\lambda)/\Delta(\lambda)\}[\phi_1 \quad \phi_2 \quad -\phi_3](\lambda I - \mathscr{H}^{-1}\mathscr{F}_0)^{-1}\Phi_{12},$$

where the identity

$$(\lambda I - \Phi_{11})^{-1} = (\lambda I - \mathcal{H}^{-1}\mathcal{F}_0)^{-1}$$

$$+ \frac{(\lambda I - \mathcal{H}^{-1}\mathcal{F}_0)^{-1} \begin{bmatrix} \omega\rho \\ -\tau_1 \\ -\tau_2 \end{bmatrix} [\phi_1 \quad \phi_2 \quad -\phi_3](\lambda I - \mathcal{H}^{-1}\mathcal{F}_0)^{-1}}{1 - (\phi_1 \quad \phi_2 \quad -\phi_3)(\lambda I - \mathcal{H}^{-1}\mathcal{F}_0)^{-1}\begin{bmatrix} \omega\rho \\ -\tau_1 \\ -\tau_2 \end{bmatrix}}$$

is used.

After further calculation, we derive

$$\lambda\psi(\lambda)[\phi_1 \quad \phi_2 \quad -\phi_3](\lambda I - \mathcal{H}^{-1}\mathcal{F}_0)^{-1}\Phi_{12} = [a\psi(\lambda) + b\lambda \quad c\psi(\lambda) + d\lambda].$$

where

$$a = \phi_1(\omega\theta_1 + \sigma\tau\omega_g),$$

$$b = n\omega^*\theta_2\{\chi_z(\phi_2\lambda + \tau\phi_2 l_{22} - n\phi_3 l_{21}) - \chi_g(\phi_3\lambda + n\phi_2 l_{12} - n\phi_3 l_{11})\}$$

$$= n\omega^*\theta_2(\phi_2\chi_z - \phi_3\chi_g)(\lambda - \theta) = \bar{b}(\lambda - \theta),$$

where $\bar{b}$ is defined by the above,

$$c = \omega\phi_1\theta_2,$$

$$d = n(\omega^*\theta_1 + \sigma n^*\omega_g^*)\{\chi_z(\phi_2\lambda + n\phi_2 l_{22} - n\phi_3 l_{21})$$
$$- \chi_g(\phi_3\lambda + n\phi_2 l_{12} - n\phi_3 l_{11})\}$$

$$= n(\omega^*\theta_1 + \sigma n^*\omega_g^*)(\phi_2\zeta_z - \phi_3\zeta_z - \phi_3\chi_g)(\lambda - \theta) = \bar{d}(\lambda - \theta),$$

where $\bar{d}$ is defined by the above.

We assume for simplicity that $v = v^*$, $v = v^*$ in addition to $d = d^*$, $\sigma^* = \sigma$, $\eta^* = \eta$. Then

$$\lambda I - \Phi_{22} - \Phi_{21}(\lambda n - \Phi_{11})^{-1}\Phi_{12}$$

$$= \lambda I + v\Theta + \frac{v\phi}{\Delta(\lambda)}\begin{bmatrix} 1 \\ -1 \end{bmatrix}[a\psi(\lambda) + b\lambda \quad c\psi(\lambda) + d\lambda].$$

## Appendix 3  Wage Rate Dynamics

If we set $v = v^*$ to isolate the wage rate dynamics associated with the inflationary expectations the roots of the characteristic polynomial satisfy

$$0 = \Delta(\lambda) \begin{vmatrix} \lambda + v\theta_1 + v\phi(a\psi(\lambda) + \bar{b}\lambda(\lambda - \theta))/\Delta(\lambda) & \\ & v\theta_2 + v\phi\{c\psi(\lambda) + \bar{d}\lambda(\lambda - \theta)\}/\Delta(\lambda) \\ v\theta_2 - v\phi\{a\psi(\lambda) + \bar{b}\lambda(\lambda - \theta)/\Delta(\lambda)\} & \\ & \lambda + v\theta_1 - v\phi\{c\psi(\lambda) + \bar{d}\lambda(\lambda - \theta)\}/\Delta(\lambda) \end{vmatrix}$$

$$= \Delta(\lambda)\{(\lambda + v\theta_1)^2 - (v\theta_2)^2\}$$
$$+ v\phi\{(a - c)\psi(\lambda) + (\bar{b} - \bar{d})\lambda(\lambda - \theta)\}\{\lambda + v(\theta_1 - \theta_2)\},$$

where

$$a - c = \phi_1 \sigma n \omega_g, \quad \bar{b} - \bar{d} = -\{\omega^*(\theta_2 - \theta_1) - \sigma n^* \omega_g^*\}n(\phi_3 \chi_g - \phi_2 \chi_z).$$

# 15 | Interdependence in a Three-Country Model

## 15.1 Introduction

Any two-country model of the world, although an improvement over a small open economy model, still leaves many questions unanswered because of its built-in symmetry. One country's trade surplus is automatically the other country's trade deficit, for example. To discuss the distributional effects of exogenous shocks or policy changes realistically at least three countries are needed.

We can ask the same questions we have asked about the two-country model in Chapter 13 and many more interesting questions on three-country models of the world. This chapter is a natural follow-up on Chapter 13 and includes more extensive discussions of interplays between national characteristic differences and national monetary instruments.

A simple three-country model is constructed from a country model which is analogous to the one of Chapter 13. We use it to examine how national monetary policies affect nations in the world differentially when those nations are coupled together by trade in goods and financial assets. Thus, we go beyond analyses of multiple country world models, which are carried out solely in the monetary sectors as has been done by De Grauwe (1975) or Aoki (1977) or Cooper in the example cited in Section 5.4.

Our approach will apply the analytical framework developed in Chapter 5. We first describe a short-run dynamic model of a country which is to be the building block of the world model in Section 15.2. Each country provides a different bundle of goods to the world markets. To simplify, we assume a single type of international bonds so that the national interest rates in the model are constrained by the interest rate parity condition. We then consider a benckmark or reference world model, in which three countries appear symmetrically, and derive dynamic equations for the world averages and the

## 15.2 The Model

vectors of differences in the endogeneous variables in Section 3. The dynamics for the averages and the differences of this benchmark model are quite similar to those discussed in Chapter 13: The dynamics governing the differences and the averages decouple, each responding independently to the world average and to the difference of monetary instruments.

This dynamic independence disappears, however, when these key national characteristics and/or parameters in the generation of expectations become different from each other. We can still analyze these cases by applying perturbation theory, introduced in Chapter 5. Three possible interaction patterns emerge: In two of them, the average variables affect the difference variables but not conversely, or the difference variables act on the average variables but not conversely; in the third, mutual interactions exist between averages and difference variables. We illustrate one of them in Section 15.4 where we analyze consequences of wage rates responding to excess demands with different speeds in the three countries. Distributional effects of national policy instruments on the time paths of the national wage rates have also been calculated. An exchange rate union is analyzed in Section 15.5. When there are no mutual interactions among the averages and the differences, stability of difference dynamics implies that national differences eventually disappear with time with constant policy instruments. Policy coordination may, however, speed up the convergence process. Policy coordination is definitely needed with unstable difference dynamics or mutual interaction among averages and differences.

For the policy coordination of the countries to be effective in guiding the national economies along mutually agreed-upon paths, the path controllability condition of the difference dynamics must be satisfied.

Implications of alternate assumptions on the model behavior may be illustrated by relative deviations of the exchange rate between country $A$ and $B$, $e_{AB}$. In the benchmark model, $e_{AB}(t)$ is a function only of past histories of $x^A$ and $x^B$, rates of change of the money stocks in countries $A$ and $B$. When the wage rates respond with different speeds to excess demands, and if variational demands are interest inelastic, then $e_{AB}(t)$ is now a function of past histories of not only $x^A$, $x^B$ but also of $x^C$. The influence of the $x^C(t)$, however, is proportional to the difference of the wage rate adjustment speeds of country $A$ and $B$.

### 15.2 The Model

Consider the model composed of three countries, $A$, $B$, $C$, each producing and exporting (composite bundles of) nonidentical goods. The structure of each modeled country is assumed to be identical; only the values of the parameters in the models and the settings of policy instruments may differ. We abstract from growth. The equilibrium of the model is therefore a steady-state equilibrium. The notations closely follow those of Chapter 13. We write $B_g^A$ for the stock of country $A$'s government bonds which are perfect substitutes for the international bonds.

The structure is specified by the following set of equations for country $A$:

$$P_i^A = (P^A)^{s_A^A}(E_{AB}P^B)^{s_B^A}(E_{AC}P^C)^{s_C^A} \quad \text{(price index),}$$

$$Y_s^A = F(W^A/P^A) \quad \text{(supply),}$$

$$Y_d^A = Y[(P_B E_{AB}/P_A)^{s_B^A}, (P_C E_{CB}/P_A)^{s_C^A},$$
$$i^A - \rho^A, Y^B, Y^C] \quad \text{(demand for goods),}$$

$$M^A/P_i^A = M(Y^A, i^A) \quad \text{(demand for money),}$$

$$\dot{M}^A = P^A(\bar{G}^A - T(Y^A)) + i^A B_g^A \quad \text{(government budget constraint),}$$

$$i^A = i^B + \varepsilon_{AB}, \quad i^A = i^C + \varepsilon_{AC} \quad \text{(interest-rate parity condition),}$$

$$\dot{W}^A/W^A = \phi(Y^A, \rho_i^A) \quad \text{(wage dynamics).}$$

Expectational variables $\rho_i^A$, $\varepsilon_{AB}$, $\varepsilon_{AC}$, etc., are discussed later in (8).

In variational terms, the model for country $A$ is the following:

(1) $\quad p_i^A = s_A^A p^A + s_B^A(p^B + e_{AB}) + s_C^A(p^C + e_{AC}) \quad \text{(price index).}$

The coefficient $s_B^A$ indicates the relative share occupied by the goods of country $B$ in consumption by residents of country $A$. Thus, the coefficients are positive and sum to one, $s_A^A + s_B^A + s_C^A = 1$. The price of a unit of country $B$ currency in terms of country $A$ currency is denoted by $E_{AB}$. Its relative deviation is denoted by $e_{AB}$. The variational supply schedule is given by

(2) $\quad\quad\quad y_s^A = -a^A(w^A - p^A) \quad \text{(supply),}$

where $w^A - p^A$ is the real wage rate (in country $A$'s real output). The supply equation indicates that the real wage rate deviation determines the relative output deviation.

Demand for the output of country $A$ is specified by

(3) $\quad y_d^A = d_B^A(p^B + e_{AB} - p^A) + d_C^A(p^C + e_{AC} - p^A) - \sigma^A(i^A - \rho^A)$
$\quad\quad + \xi_{AB} y^B + \xi_{AC} y^C,$

where

$$d_B^A = d^A s_B^A \quad \text{and} \quad d_C^A = d^A s_C^A,$$

## 15.2 The Model

and where $\rho^A$ is country $A$'s expectation of its own inflation rate. Equation (3) shows that consumption demand depends on the terms-of-trade effects and income effects and that investment demand depends only on the real interest rate of the country by assumption. To simplify our analysis, we follow the practice introduced in Chapter 13 and drop this term in Section 15.3. It is reintroduced in Section 15.4.2.

The variational money demand equation is specified by

(4) $\qquad m^A - p_i^A = m_1^A y^A - m_2^A i^A \qquad$ (demand for money).

Again, following our discussion of Chapter 13, we set $m_1^A$ to zero in our analysis. The wage rate is assumed to adjust according to

(5) $\qquad \dot{w}^A = \kappa^A y^A + \rho_i^A, \qquad \kappa^A > 0 \qquad$ (wage rate dynamics),

where $\rho_i^A$ is country $A$'s expected rate of change in the price index $p_i^A$. As we mentioned in Chapter 13, other specifications are possible for wage rate dynamics. Equations (5) is used as a simple illustration. The expectations $\rho^A$ and $\rho_i^A$ [which are about the domestic output inflation rate (expected value of $\dot{p}^A$) and about the inflation rate of the price index $\dot{p}_i^A$] and the expectations about the exchange rate changes $\varepsilon_{AB}$ and $\varepsilon_{AC}$ should not all be independently specified. We discuss this point later after the model specification is completed.

The government budget is assumed to be in balance at the stationary state. Residents of each country hold two financial assets: domestic money, which is a nontraded asset, and international bonds. From the balance sheet identity, we can eliminate the equation for international bonds.

Strictly speaking, the 100% money financing of the government budget deficit yields a variational differential equation for the domestic component of the money stock. Changes in the holding of international securities are accounted for by the current account equation. This equation is residually determined by the balance-of-payment condition in the truly floating exchange rate regimes.

In order to illustrate our novel analytical procedure on simple models, we do not treat the international bond holdings by the private sectors explicitly in this book. See for example, Fair (1979).

Deviation in the real output $y$ causes the budget to be off balance. The resultant deficit (surplus) is assumed to be financed 100% by money creation (destruction). Thus the domestic money stock changes according to

(6) $\qquad \dot{m}^A = -\mu_1^A y^A + \mu_2^A p^A + \mu_3^A i^A + x^A \qquad$ (money stock dynamics),[1]

---

[1] The governments are assumed not to intervene in the markets for international securities and not to change the stocks of monies to reflect valuation changes as the exchange rates vary from their equilibrium levels.

where $x^A$ is an exogeneous instrument for control of the domestic money stock. The coefficients $\mu_1 \sim \mu_3$ are defined analogously to those of Chapter 13.[2]

Because we assume that the interest rate parity condition holds, we impose a restriction that the interest rates $i^A$, $i^C$, and $i^C$, prevailing in countries A, B, and C, respectively, are related by

(7) $$\begin{aligned} i^A &= i^B + \varepsilon_{AB}, \\ i^A &= i^C + \varepsilon_{AC} \end{aligned} \quad \text{(interest parity condition).}$$

Note that other relations, such as $i^B = i^C + \varepsilon_{BC}$, are implied by (7). For example, $\varepsilon_{BC} = \varepsilon_{AC} - \varepsilon_{AB}$ is assumed to hold.

To close the model, we must specify how the expectational variables $\rho^A$, $\rho_i^A$, $\varepsilon_{AB}$, and $\varepsilon_{AC}$ are related to the other model variables. It is reasonable to assume in this model, where deviational dynamic behavior near a stationary state is to be investigated, that expectations on the exchange rates are regressive to the equilibrium level. This translates into the relationships given by

(8) $$\begin{aligned} \varepsilon_{AB} &= -\theta e_{AB}, \\ \varepsilon_{AC} &= -\theta e_{AC}, \end{aligned} \quad \text{etc.} \quad \text{(expectations on exchange rate changes).}$$

Combining (7) and (8), we relate the exchange rate deviations to the interest rates as

(9) $$\begin{aligned} e_{AB} &= -\theta^{-1}\varepsilon_{AB} = -\theta^{-1}(i^A - i^B), \\ e_{AC} &= -\theta^{-1}(i^A - i^C), \quad \text{etc.} \end{aligned}$$

We use the same coefficient of adjustment $\theta$ for all pairwise exchange rate changes because all residents of the three countries have access to identical information in the asset markets. The same may not be true for conditions in the goods markets, however. We postpone specifications of $\rho^A$ and $\rho_i^A$ to Section 15.3, after we derive dynamic equations of the model. Equations (1)–(6), written for the three countries, and the connection equation (9) constitute the world model we use in this chapter. In many ways, the model of a country specified here is similar to the one used in Chapter 13. This fact becomes more apparent when we derive the dynamic equations for the averages and the differences of the endogenous variables for the benchmark model.

Country A is propelled through time by the dynamics of (5) and (6). The wage rates and the money stock variables of the three countries, $w^A$, $w^B$, $w^C$, $m^A$, $m^B$ and $m^C$, serve as the state variables because they, combined with the exogenous instruments, uniquely determine the time evolution of the model.

---

[2] See footnote 17 of Chapter 13.

## 15.3 Benchmark Model $\mathcal{VM}_0$

Other endogenous variables must be related to the state variables before we can discuss the dynamic behavior of the world. In particular, we need to express $y^A$ and $\rho_i^A$, which appear in (5) and (6), in terms of the state variables.

To treat the three countries together, we introduce vectors that are composed of the like variables of the three countries. For example, define the price, the interest rate, and the instrument vectors by

$$\mathbf{p} = (p^A, p^B, p^C)', \quad \mathbf{i} = (i^A, i^B, i^C)', \quad \mathbf{x} = (x^A, x^B, x^C)',$$

and so on, where the prime denotes a transpose of a vector.

The dynamics (5) and (6) can then be written together as

$$(10) \quad \frac{d}{dt}\begin{bmatrix}\mathbf{w}\\\mathbf{m}\end{bmatrix}\begin{bmatrix}\kappa I\\-\mu_1 I\end{bmatrix}\mathbf{y} + \begin{bmatrix}0\\\mu_2 I\end{bmatrix}\mathbf{p} + \begin{bmatrix}0\\\mu_3 I\end{bmatrix}\mathbf{i} + \begin{bmatrix}\boldsymbol{\rho}_i\\0\end{bmatrix} + \begin{bmatrix}0\\\mathbf{x}\end{bmatrix},$$

where $I$ is the $3 \times 3$ identity matrix. This equation is for $\mathcal{VM}_0$ defined below.

One way to relate $\mathbf{y}$ and $\boldsymbol{\rho}_i$ to $\mathbf{w}$ and $\mathbf{m}$ in (10) is to solve the equilibrium conditions of the goods markets and the money markets of the three countries together for the price vector and the vector of the interest rates in terms of the vectors $\mathbf{m}$ and $\mathbf{w}$, and substitute them into $\mathbf{y}$. As we explained earlier, in Chapter 5 and Chapter 13, we do not follow this seemingly straightforward approach because the reduced form expressions for $\mathbf{p}$ and $\mathbf{i}$ turn out to be algebraically cumbersome to deal with. Instead, we apply the framework discussed in Chapter 5 to separate out the average variables and the difference variables, and write (10) separately for the averages and the differences.

### 15.3 Benchmark Model $\mathcal{VM}_0$

#### 15.3.1 Dynamics of the Averages

First, we examine a world model in which three countries enter symmetrically, i.e., each of the three countries has identical parameter values, and investigate how the endogeneous variables, such as outputs, price levels, and the wage rates of the three countries, behave over time by evaluating their means (averages) and the differences. As in Chapter 13, the dynamic equations for the averages and the differences turn out to be independent of each other (except for possible couplings introduced by the instruments) when the three countries in the model are symmetrical. The nonsymmetric case can then be examined as perturbations to the symmetric case.

Let $\mathbf{u} = [1 \quad 1 \quad 1]'$. The mean of the prices is defined by $p_a = \mathbf{u}'\mathbf{p}/3$, that of the interest rates by $i_a = \mathbf{u}'\mathbf{i}/3$ and so on. The difference vectors are defined by $\mathbf{p}_\delta = \mathbf{p} - p_a\mathbf{u}$ and so on. Note that the inner product of a difference vector with **u** vanishes; e.g., $\mathbf{u}'\mathbf{p}_\delta = 0$. In the benchmark model all the parameters such as $a^i$, $d^i$, and $\xi$ are the same across the countries, $i = A, B, C$.

In terms of the averages and vectors of the differences thus defined, we can write the equilibrium conditions in the real sector of the benchmark model by equating (2) to (3) (recall that we have set $\sigma$ to zero in all the countries):

$$A\mathbf{p} + \hat{y}\theta^{-1}B\mathbf{i} - \Gamma\mathbf{y} = \mathbf{w},$$

where we let $\hat{y}$ be the common value of $d_B^A/a^A$, $d_C^A/a^A$, etc.,

$$A = \begin{bmatrix} 1 + 2\hat{y} & -\hat{y} & -\hat{y} \\ -\hat{y} & 1 + 2\hat{y} & -\hat{y} \\ -\hat{y} & -\hat{y} & 1 + 2\hat{y} \end{bmatrix}, \quad B = \begin{bmatrix} 2 & -1 & -1 \\ -1 & 2 & -1 \\ -1 & -1 & 2 \end{bmatrix},$$

and

$$\Gamma = \frac{\xi}{a}\begin{bmatrix} 0 & 1 & 1 \\ 1 & 0 & 1 \\ 1 & 1 & 0 \end{bmatrix}.$$

In the above, we have used (9) to replace $e_{AB}$ by $-\theta^{-1}(i_A - i_B)$, etc.

Substitute **y** out from the above by (2). Noting that

$$A = (1 + 3\hat{y})I - \hat{y}\mathbf{u}\mathbf{u}', \quad B = 3I - \mathbf{u}\mathbf{u}', \quad \text{and} \quad \Gamma = (\xi/a)(\mathbf{u}\mathbf{u}' - I),$$

we can write the equilibrium condition in the real sector

(11) $\{(1 + 3\hat{y} + \xi)I - (\hat{y} + \xi)\mathbf{u}\mathbf{u}'\}\mathbf{p} + \hat{y}\theta^{-1}(3I - \mathbf{u}\mathbf{u}')\mathbf{i}$
$= \{(1 + \xi)I - \xi\mathbf{u}\mathbf{u}'\}\mathbf{w}.$

To write the demands for real balances together for three countries, note first that the consumer price index vector can be written as

$$\mathbf{p}_i = \pi_1\mathbf{p} - (\chi/2)\theta^{-1}B\mathbf{i},$$

(12) $\pi_1 = \begin{bmatrix} 1 - \chi & \chi/2 & \chi/2 \\ \chi/2 & 1 - \chi & \chi/2 \\ \chi/2 & \chi/2 & 1 - \chi \end{bmatrix} = \left(1 - 3\frac{\chi}{2}\right)I + \frac{\chi}{2}\mathbf{u}\mathbf{u}',$

where

$$1 - \chi = s_i^i, \quad i = A, B, C,$$

and

$$\chi/2 = s_j^i, \quad i = j, \quad j = A, B, C.$$

Thus, we assume that two foreign countries are at equal "economic" distances from home in the terminology of Cooper (1973).

From (4) the asset market equilibrium condition is expressible as

(13) $\mathbf{m} = \pi_1\mathbf{p} - \{m_2I + (\chi/2)\theta^{-1}B\}\mathbf{i}.$

## 15.3 Benchmark Model

Now separate (11) out for the averages and the differences:

(14)
$$p_a = w_a,$$
$$(1 + 3\gamma)\mathbf{p}_\delta + 3\gamma\theta^{-1}\mathbf{i}_\delta = \mathbf{w}_\delta,$$

where

$$\gamma = \hat{\gamma}/(1 + \xi) = d/a \quad \text{and} \quad d = \hat{d}(1 + \xi)^{-1}.$$

Equation (13) can be written as

(15)
$$-m_2 i_a + p_a = m_a,$$
$$-[m_2 + \tfrac{3}{2}\chi\theta^{-1}]\mathbf{i}_\delta + (1 - \tfrac{3}{2}\chi)\mathbf{p}_\delta = \mathbf{m}_\delta.$$

If $3\gamma$ is replaced with $2\gamma$ and $\tfrac{3}{2}\chi$ by $2\chi$, then these equations are the same as the corresponding ones of (31a) and (31b) in Chapter 13.

We call the solution of (14) and (15), which express $i_a$, $p_a$, $\mathbf{i}_\delta$, and $\mathbf{p}_\delta$ in terms of $w_a$, $m_a$, $\mathbf{w}_\delta$, and $\mathbf{m}_\delta$, the reduced form. They are

(16)
$$p_a = w_a, \qquad i_a = D_a(w_a - m_a),$$

where

$$D_a = 1/m_2,$$

(17)
$$\mathbf{i}_\delta = D_\delta\{(1 - \tfrac{3}{2}\chi)\mathbf{w}_\delta - \beta\mathbf{m}_\delta\},$$
$$\mathbf{p}_\delta = D_\delta\{(m_2 + \tfrac{3}{2}\chi\theta^{-1})\mathbf{w}_\delta + \alpha\mathbf{m}_\delta\},$$

where

$$\alpha = 3\gamma\theta^{-1}, \qquad \beta = 1 + 3\gamma, \qquad D_\delta^{-1} = 3\gamma(m_2 + \theta^{-1}) + m_2 + \tfrac{3}{2}\chi\theta^{-1}.$$

Rewrite (2) for the three countries as

$$y_a = -a(w_a - p_a), \qquad \mathbf{y}_\delta = -a(\mathbf{w}_\delta - \mathbf{p}_\delta).$$

Using (16) and (17), they are rewritten as

(18)
$$y_a = 0, \qquad \mathbf{y}_\delta = -\eta_1 \mathbf{w}_\delta + \eta_2 \mathbf{m}_\delta,$$

where we now define the coefficients (analogous to those in Chapter 13) as

$$\eta_1 = D_\delta 3d(m_2 + \theta^{-1}), \qquad \eta_2 = 2d\theta^{-1}D_\delta.$$

For later use, we calculate the average price index and the difference of the price indices from (12):

(19)
$$p_{ia} = p_a \quad \text{and} \quad \mathbf{p}_{i\delta} = (1 - \tfrac{3}{2}\chi)\mathbf{p}_\delta - \tfrac{3}{2}\chi\theta^{-1}\mathbf{i}_\delta.$$

From (10) the dynamics for the average become

(20)
$$\frac{d}{dt}\begin{bmatrix} w_a \\ m_a \end{bmatrix} = \mu_2 \begin{bmatrix} 0 \\ 1 \end{bmatrix} p_a + \mu_s \begin{bmatrix} 0 \\ 1 \end{bmatrix} i_a + \begin{bmatrix} 1 \\ 0 \end{bmatrix} p_{ia} + \begin{bmatrix} 0 \\ 1 \end{bmatrix} x_a.$$

To put the dynamic equation into state-space form, $\rho_{ia}$ must be expressed in "reduced" form. We posit a regressive expectation mechanism for $\rho_i^A$ as

$$\rho_i^A = -v_A p_i^A.$$

The other two variables $\rho_i^B$ and $\rho_i^C$ are similarly specified. Then

(21) $$\rho_{ia} = -vp_{ia}$$

in the benchmark model where we set $v_A = v_B = v_C = v$.

When the reduced form expressions for $p_a$, $i_a$ given by (16) and $\rho_{ia}$ of (21) are substituted into (20), the state-space dynamic equation for the world averages results as

(22) $$\frac{d}{dt}\mathbf{z}_a = \phi_a \mathbf{z}_a + \begin{bmatrix} 0 \\ 1 \end{bmatrix} x_a,$$

where $\mathbf{z}_a = [w_a\, m_a]'$ and

$$\phi_a = \begin{bmatrix} -v & 0 \\ \mu_2 + \mu_3/m_2 & -\mu_3/m_2 \end{bmatrix}.$$

The parameter $\mu_1$ is absent from $\phi_a$ because of zero $y_a$. When the $\sigma$ term is reintroduced in (3), $\mu_1$ will appear in $\phi_a$. This dynamic matrix is the same as (39) of Chapter 13.

### 15.3.2 Difference Dynamics

The difference dynamics can be derived from (10) as

(23) $$\frac{d}{dt}\begin{bmatrix} \mathbf{w}_\delta \\ \mathbf{m}_\delta \end{bmatrix} = \begin{bmatrix} \kappa I \\ -\mu_1 I \end{bmatrix}\mathbf{y}_\delta + \begin{bmatrix} 0 \\ \mu_2 I \end{bmatrix}\mathbf{p}_\delta + \begin{bmatrix} 0 \\ \mu_3 I \end{bmatrix}\mathbf{i}_\delta + \begin{bmatrix} \boldsymbol{\rho}_{i\delta} \\ 0 \end{bmatrix} + \begin{bmatrix} 0 \\ \mathbf{x}_\delta \end{bmatrix}.$$

When the reduced form expressions are substituted for $\mathbf{y}_\delta$, etc., (23) can be expressed as

(24) $$\frac{d}{dt}\begin{bmatrix} \mathbf{w}_\delta \\ \mathbf{m}_\delta \end{bmatrix} = \phi_\delta \begin{bmatrix} \mathbf{w}_\delta \\ \mathbf{m}_\delta \end{bmatrix} + \begin{bmatrix} 0 \\ \mathbf{x}_\delta \end{bmatrix},$$

where

$$\phi_\delta = \begin{bmatrix} \kappa I \\ -\mu_1 I \end{bmatrix}[-\eta_1 I \quad \eta_2 I] + \begin{bmatrix} -v\omega_1 I & -v\omega_2 I \\ \omega_3 I & \omega_4 I \end{bmatrix},$$

where

$$\omega_1 = D_\delta(1 - \tfrac{3}{2}\chi)m_2, \qquad \omega_2 = D_\delta 3\{\gamma + \tfrac{1}{2}\chi\theta^{-1}\},$$
$$\omega_3 = \{\mu_2(m_2 + \tfrac{3}{2}\chi\theta^{-1}) + \mu_3(1 - \tfrac{3}{2}\chi)\}D_\delta, \qquad \omega_4 = (\mu_2\alpha - \mu_3\beta)D_\delta.$$

Note the close similarities of these parameters with those in (39) of Chapter 13.

Thus, the benchmark three-country model of the world is remarkably similar to the benchmark model of the two-country world discussed in Chapter 13. In fact, the average dynamics are identical. The policy analysis of Chapter 13 thus applies to the present model with minimal modifications.

## 15.4 Nonsymmetrical Model: Distributional Effects of Instruments

When we leave the benchmark model, we lose the independence of the dynamics for the averages and the differences. We have already illustrated this fact in a two-country setting in Chapter 13. Here, we examine one of the simpler cases of interdependence by assuming that wage rates adjust with different speeds; that is, we assume that the coefficients $\kappa^i$, $i = A, B, C$ in the wage rate adjustment function (5) are not the same in the three countries.[3] To discover the dynamic interactions introduced by this nonsymmetry, we must first rederive the differential equations for the averages and the differences without the symmetry assumption.

Let $N = \text{diag}(\kappa^A, \kappa^B, \kappa^C)$ where $\kappa_a = (\kappa^A + \kappa^B + \kappa^C)/3$ is the average speed of adjustment. We define the difference matrix $N_\delta$ by $N - \kappa_a I$. Equation (5) then separates into the differential equations of the average and the difference vector:

(25) $$\dot{w}_a = \kappa_a y_a + \tfrac{1}{3}\mathbf{n}'_\delta \mathbf{y}_\delta + \rho_{ia},$$

where $\mathbf{n}_\delta = N_\delta \mathbf{u}$ and

(26) $$\dot{\mathbf{w}}_\delta = \kappa_a \mathbf{y}_\delta + (I - \tfrac{1}{3}\mathbf{u}\mathbf{u}')N_\delta \mathbf{y}_\delta + y_a \mathbf{n}_\delta + \boldsymbol{\rho}_{i\delta}.$$

The dynamic equations for $m_a$ and $\mathbf{m}_\delta$ remain the same as in the benchmark model.

The expressions for $y_a$, $\mathbf{y}_\delta$, $\rho_{ia}$ and $\boldsymbol{\rho}_{i\delta}$, which are derived in Section 15.3, remain valid.

---

[3] Implications of other nonidentical system parameters, such as $\sigma^A \neq \sigma^B, m_2^A \neq m_2^B, d_B^A \neq d_C^B$, etc., can be evaluated by following the procedure of this section.

Collecting (25) and (26) together with (22) and (24), the total dynamics become

$$(27) \quad \frac{d}{dt}\begin{bmatrix} \mathbf{z}_a \\ \mathbf{z}_\delta \end{bmatrix} = \begin{bmatrix} \phi_a & \phi_{a\delta} \\ 0 & \phi_\delta + \phi_{\delta\delta} \end{bmatrix}\begin{bmatrix} \mathbf{z}_a \\ \mathbf{z}_\delta \end{bmatrix} + \begin{bmatrix} 0 \\ 1 \\ 0 \\ 0 \end{bmatrix} x_a + \begin{bmatrix} 0 \\ 0 \\ 0 \\ 1 \end{bmatrix} \mathbf{x}_\delta,$$

where $\mathbf{z}'_a = (w_a, m_a)$ and $\mathbf{z}'_\delta = (\mathbf{w}'_\delta, \mathbf{m}'_\delta)$.

The submatric $\phi_a$ is the same as in (22); the submatrix expressing the "strength" of the influences exerted by the difference vector on the averages is

$$(28) \quad \phi_{a\delta} = \frac{1}{3}\begin{bmatrix} \mathbf{n}'_\delta \\ 0 \end{bmatrix}[-\eta_1 I \quad \eta_2 I] \quad (2 \times 6 \text{ matrix}),$$

and the difference vector dynamics are determined by $\phi_\delta + \phi_{\delta\delta}$, where

$$(28') \quad \phi_{\delta\delta} = \begin{bmatrix} I - \frac{1}{3}\mathbf{uu}' \\ 0 \end{bmatrix}[-\eta_1 N_\delta \quad \eta_2 N_\delta] \quad (6 \times 6 \text{ matrix}),$$

where $\phi_\delta$ is as given in (24). We note that with nonidentical $\kappa$s, the submatrix $\phi_{\delta a}$ in (27) is zero. (For other perturbations, averages could affect the difference variables, or mutual interactions could exist.)

To focus on the distributional effects of the instruments, we let $\mathbf{z}_a(0) = 0$ and $\mathbf{z}_\delta(0) = 0$.

The solution of (22) is, in our notation,

$$\mathbf{z}_a = \left(\Phi_a, \begin{bmatrix} 0 \\ 1 \end{bmatrix} x_a\right),$$

where $\Phi_a$ is the transition matrix of (22).

Equation (24) is solved as

$$\mathbf{z}_\delta = \left(\Phi_\delta, \begin{bmatrix} 0 \\ I \end{bmatrix} \mathbf{x}_\delta\right),$$

where $\Phi_\delta$ is the transition matrix of (24). As before, define the variational vectors

$$\delta \mathbf{z}_a = \mathbf{z}_a - \mathbf{z}_a^0 \quad \text{and} \quad \delta \mathbf{z}_\delta = \mathbf{z}_\delta - \mathbf{z}_\delta^0,$$

where superscript zero denotes vectors of the reference model.

## 15.4 Nonsymmetrical Model: Distributional Effects of Instruments

Because the dynamic matrix governing $z_\delta$ changes from $\phi_\delta$ to $\phi_\delta + \phi_{\delta\delta}$, the dynamic equation for $\delta z_\delta$ is slightly different from the one encountered in Chapter 13:

$$\delta \dot z_\delta = \phi_\delta \, \delta z_\delta + \phi_{\delta\delta} z_\delta^0,$$

treating $\phi_{\delta\delta}$ as small.

Solving this equation, we obtain

(29) $\quad \delta z_\delta = (\Phi_\delta, \phi_{\delta\delta} z_\delta^0) = (\Phi_\delta, \phi_{\delta\delta}(\Phi_\delta, \psi_\delta x_\delta)) = ((\phi_{\delta\delta}\Phi_\delta) * \Phi_\delta, \psi_\delta x_\delta),$

where

$$\psi_\delta = \begin{bmatrix} 0 \\ I \end{bmatrix}.$$

The variational vector $\delta z_a$ can be written as

(30) $\quad \delta z_a = (\Phi_a, \phi_{a\delta} z_\delta^0) = (\Phi_a, \phi_{a\delta}(\Phi_\delta, \psi_\delta x_\delta)) = ((\phi_{a\delta}\Phi_\delta) * \Phi_a, \psi_\delta x_\delta).$

With $\sigma$ being zero, $[1 \ 0]\Phi_a \begin{bmatrix}0\\1\end{bmatrix}$ is zero as in Chapter 13. Noting that

$$w_a^0 = [1 \ 0] z_a^0$$
$$= \int_0^t [1 \ 0] \Phi_a(t - s) \begin{bmatrix} 0 \\ 1 \end{bmatrix} x_a(s) \, ds = 0,$$

the average wage rate of the reference model remains zero. Thus the equality

$$w_a = w_a^0 + \delta w_a = \delta w_a = [1 \ 0] \delta z_a,$$

and (30) shows that $w_a$ depends only on $x_\delta$.

Because the off-diagonal submatric $\phi_{a\delta}$ in (27) is sufficiently simple, we can analytically evaluate the effects of the policy instruments. In particular, we next evaluate the distributional effects of constant national instruments on the wage rates and show that $w_a$ is proportional to $\mathbf{n}_\delta' x_\delta$ and that $\mathbf{w}_\delta$ is approximately proportional to $x_\delta$. We consider three types of instrument changes:

(i) The effects when only one nation's instruments change,
(ii) two countries' instruments change while keeping $x_a$ at zero,
(iii) two countries' instruments are the same.

In case (i), there are three possibilities; $x^A = \bar{x}, x^B = x^C = 0; x^A = 0, x^B = \bar{x}, x^C = 0$; and $x^A = x^B = 0$ and $x^C = \bar{x}$. In each of these three cases, $x_a = \bar{x}/3$, $\mathbf{x}_\delta$ can be one of the following:

(31) (ia) $\mathbf{x}_\delta = \dfrac{\bar{x}}{3}\begin{bmatrix} 2 \\ -1 \\ -1 \end{bmatrix},$ (ib) $\mathbf{x}_\delta = \dfrac{\bar{x}}{3}\begin{bmatrix} -1 \\ 2 \\ -1 \end{bmatrix},$ (ic) $\mathbf{x}_\delta = \dfrac{\bar{x}}{3}\begin{bmatrix} -1 \\ -1 \\ 2 \end{bmatrix}.$

In case (ii), there are six possibilities, all leaving $x_a = 0$, but $\mathbf{x}_\delta$ can be one of the following:

(32) (iia) $\bar{x}\begin{bmatrix} 1 \\ -1 \\ 0 \end{bmatrix}$, (iib) $\bar{x}\begin{bmatrix} -1 \\ 1 \\ 0 \end{bmatrix}$, (iic) $\bar{x}\begin{bmatrix} 0 \\ 1 \\ -1 \end{bmatrix}$,

(iid) $\bar{x}\begin{bmatrix} 0 \\ -1 \\ 1 \end{bmatrix}$, (iie) $\bar{x}\begin{bmatrix} 1 \\ 0 \\ -1 \end{bmatrix}$, (iif) $\bar{x}\begin{bmatrix} -1 \\ 0 \\ 1 \end{bmatrix}$.

We consider three cases in (iii): (iiia) $x^A = x^B = \bar{x}$, $x^C = -\bar{x}$, (iiib) $x^A = x^C = \bar{x}$, $x^B = -\bar{x}$, (iiic) $x^A = -\bar{x}$, $x^B = x^C = \bar{x}$. Here $x_a = \bar{x}/3$, and the difference vector is given by one of the following vectors:

(iiia) $\mathbf{x}_\delta = \dfrac{2\bar{x}}{3}\begin{bmatrix} 1 \\ 1 \\ -2 \end{bmatrix}$, (iiib) $\mathbf{x}_\delta = \dfrac{2\bar{x}}{3}\begin{bmatrix} 1 \\ -2 \\ 1 \end{bmatrix}$, (iiic) $\mathbf{x}_\delta = \dfrac{2\bar{x}}{3}\begin{bmatrix} -2 \\ 1 \\ 1 \end{bmatrix}$.

Case (iii) is similar to case (i); $x_a$ is the same and the pattern of $\mathbf{x}_\delta$ is the same. [The magnitude of $\mathbf{x}_\delta$ is twice that of minus (31).] Thus we consider only cases (i) and (ii).

To be specific, we assume that

$$\kappa^A = \kappa_a + \zeta, \qquad \kappa^B = \kappa_a \qquad \text{and} \qquad \kappa^C = \kappa_a - \zeta,$$

i.e., of the three countries, wage rates adjust faster than the world average in country $A$, slower than the world average in country $C$, while country $B$ is the average in wage rate adjustment speed. The vector $\mathbf{n}_\delta$ then equals $\zeta[1 \; 0 \; -1]'$.

The expression we identify as the determinant of the distributional effects $\mathbf{n}'_\delta \mathbf{x}$, then takes on the values $\bar{x}\zeta$, $0$, and $-\bar{x}\zeta$ in case (i) and $\pm\bar{x}\zeta$ and $\pm 2\bar{x}\zeta$ in case (ii).

We now proceed with the demonstration of the distributional effects of the monetary instruments. Note first that

$$[1 \; 0]\delta \mathbf{z}_a = ([1 \; 0](\phi_{a\delta}\Phi_\delta)*\Phi_a, \psi_\delta \mathbf{x}_\delta) = (h, \mathbf{x}_\delta),$$

where

$$h(t-s) = \int_s^t [1 \; 0]\Phi_a(t-\tau)\phi_{a\delta}\Phi_\delta(\tau - s)\begin{bmatrix} 0 \\ 1 \end{bmatrix} d\tau.$$

Since

$$[-\eta_1 I \;\; \eta_2 I)\Phi_\delta(t)\begin{bmatrix} 0 \\ 1 \end{bmatrix} = \{\eta_2 \phi_{22}(t) - \eta_1 \phi_{12}(t)\}I,$$

## 15.4 Nonsymmetrical Model: Distributional Effects of Instruments

where we take advantage of the special structure of $\Phi$, i.e.,

$$e^{\Phi t} = \begin{bmatrix} \phi_{11}(t)I & \phi_{12}(t)I \\ \phi_{21}(t)I & \phi_{22}(t)I \end{bmatrix},$$

and since $[1 \ \ 0]\Phi_a(t)$ equals $[e^{-vt} \ \ 0]$, we can write $h(t-s)$ as $l(t-s)\mathbf{n}'_\delta/3$, where

$$l(t-s) = \int_s^t e^{-v(t-\tau)}\{-\eta_1\phi_{12}(\tau-s) + \eta_2\phi_{22}(\tau-s)\} \, ds, \text{ i.e.,}$$

(33) $$\delta w_a = \frac{1}{3}\int_0^t l(t-s)\mathbf{n}'_\delta \mathbf{x}_\delta(s) \, ds.$$

Thus

$$\mathbf{w} = w_a\mathbf{u} + \mathbf{w}_\delta = \delta w_a\mathbf{u} + \mathbf{w}_\delta^0 + \delta\mathbf{w}_\delta,$$

where

$$\mathbf{w}_\delta^0 = [I \ \ 0]\mathbf{z}_\delta^0 = [I \ \ 0](\Phi_\delta, \psi_\delta \mathbf{x}_\delta)$$

and

$$\delta\mathbf{w}_\delta = [I \ \ 0]\, \delta\mathbf{z}_\delta = [I \ \ 0]((\phi_{\delta\delta}\Phi_\delta)*\Phi_\delta, \psi_\delta\mathbf{x}_\delta).$$

Substituting these into the above, and noting that

$$[I \ \ 0]\Phi_\delta \begin{bmatrix} 0 \\ 1 \end{bmatrix} = \phi_{12}I$$

and

$$[I \ \ 0](\phi_{\delta\delta}\Phi_\delta)*\Phi_\delta\psi_\delta = (I - \tfrac{1}{3}\mathbf{u}\mathbf{u}')N_\delta D(t-s),$$

where

$$D(t-s) = \int_s^t \phi_{11}(t-\tau)\{-\eta_1\phi_{12}(\tau-s) + \eta_2\phi_{22}(\tau-s)\} \, d\tau,$$

we can express the effects of $\mathbf{x}_\delta$ on $\mathbf{w}$ as follows. Let $H(t)$ stand for $\phi_{12} + D(I - \tfrac{1}{3}\mathbf{u}\mathbf{u}')N_\delta$. Then

(34) $$\mathbf{w}(t) = \frac{1}{3}(l\mathbf{u}, \mathbf{n}'_\delta\mathbf{x}_\delta) + (H, \mathbf{x}_\delta) = \mathbf{u}\int_0^t \frac{1}{3}l(t-s)\mathbf{n}'_\delta\mathbf{x}_\delta(s) \, ds$$

$$+ \int_0^t H(t-s)\mathbf{x}_\delta(s) \, ds$$

$$= \mathbf{u}\int_0^t \frac{1}{3}\{l(t-s) - D(t-s)\}\mathbf{n}'_\delta\mathbf{x}_\delta(s) \, ds + \int_0^t D(t-s)N_\delta\mathbf{x}_\delta \, ds.$$

This equation shows that $\mathbf{x}_\delta$ has two effects on $\mathbf{w}$; one effect is directly proportional to $\mathbf{n}'_\delta \mathbf{x}_\delta$ and is common to all countries. The other effect is proportional to $N_\delta \mathbf{x}_\delta$.

Equation (34) completely specifies the distributional effects of the national instruments on the national wage rates. The first term could be zero, for example, case (ib) of (31). The second term is generally nonzero.

To illustrate, consider a hypothetical model (which is similar to the one with parameter set 2 of Chapter 13) with

$$\kappa^A = 0.85, \qquad \kappa^B = 0.80, \qquad \kappa^C = 0.75,$$
$$\eta_1 = 1.837, \qquad \eta_2 = 0.204.$$

Then

$$\Phi = \begin{bmatrix} -1.48I & -0.082I \\ 0.2651 & -2.061I \end{bmatrix},$$

and hence

$$\phi_{12}(t) = 0.164(e^{-1.52t} - e^{-2.02t})$$

and

$$\phi_{22}(t) = 1.08e^{-2.02t} - 0.08e^{-1.52t}$$
$$l(t) = 0.441 - 0.066e^{-0.5t} - 0.205e^{-1.52t} + 0.170e^{-2.02t}.$$

When the off-diagonal elements of $H(t)$, which are less than 10% of the diagonal elements, are ignored, we obtain

$$H(t) = \text{diag}(h_1(t), h_2(t), h_2(t)),$$

where

$$h_1(t) = 0.03 - 0.098e^{-1.46t} + 0.068e^{-2.101t}$$

and

$$h_2(t) = 0.027 - 0.087e^{-1.445t} + 0.060e^{-2.096t}.$$

From (31) and (34), when only one country changes its instrument, the possible patterns are one of the following three:

$$\mathbf{w} = \frac{\bar{x}}{3} \begin{bmatrix} 2h_1 \\ -h_2 \\ h_2 \end{bmatrix} + \bar{x}\zeta l \begin{bmatrix} 1 \\ 1 \\ 1 \end{bmatrix},$$

$$\mathbf{w} = \frac{\bar{x}}{3} \begin{bmatrix} -h_1 \\ 2h_2 \\ -h_2 \end{bmatrix},$$

or

$$\mathbf{w} = \frac{\bar{x}}{3}\begin{bmatrix}-h_1\\-h_2\\2h_2\end{bmatrix} - \bar{x}\zeta l\begin{bmatrix}1\\1\\1\end{bmatrix}.$$

When two countries change their instruments in the opposite direction, the time paths of the wage rates are governed by one of the following six:

$$\mathbf{w} = \bar{x}\begin{bmatrix}h_1\\-h_2\\0\end{bmatrix} + \frac{\bar{x}\zeta}{3}l\begin{bmatrix}1\\1\\1\end{bmatrix},$$

$$\mathbf{w} = \bar{x}\begin{bmatrix}-h_1\\h_2\\0\end{bmatrix} - \frac{\bar{x}\zeta}{3}l\begin{bmatrix}1\\1\\1\end{bmatrix},$$

$$\mathbf{w} = \bar{x}\begin{bmatrix}0\\h_2\\-h_2\end{bmatrix} + \frac{\bar{x}\zeta}{3}l\begin{bmatrix}1\\1\\1\end{bmatrix},$$

$$\mathbf{w} = \bar{x}\begin{bmatrix}0\\-h_2\\h_2\end{bmatrix} - \frac{\bar{x}\zeta}{3}l\begin{bmatrix}1\\1\\1\end{bmatrix},$$

$$\mathbf{w} = \bar{x}\begin{bmatrix}h_1\\0\\-h_2\end{bmatrix} + \frac{2\bar{x}\zeta}{3}l\begin{bmatrix}1\\1\\1\end{bmatrix},$$

or

$$\mathbf{w} = \bar{x}\begin{bmatrix}-h_1\\0\\h_2\end{bmatrix} - \frac{2\bar{x}\zeta}{3}l\begin{bmatrix}1\\1\\1\end{bmatrix}.$$

Another way to characterize the patterns is to examine $w^A(t)$. Depending on $\mathbf{x}_\delta$, it can range between $\{h_1 + (2\zeta/3)l\}\bar{x}$ and its negative. As $t$ approaches infinity $l(\infty)/h_1(\infty)$ is approximately 14.7, hence about 33% of the changes in $w^A$ can be brought about eventually by the interaction patterns $\mathbf{n}'_\delta \mathbf{x}_\delta$.

### 15.4.1 Effects on Exchange Rates

Equation (27) states that $z_\delta^0(t)$ is determined by $\mathbf{x}_\delta(s)$, $0 \le s \le t$ alone. Exchange rates between two countries are determined by the differences of the interest rates of the same two countries. For example, (9) shows that

(35) $\quad e_{AB}^0(t) = -\theta^{-1}\{i^A(t) - i^B(t)\} = -\theta^{-1}[1 \ -1 \ 0]i_\delta^0(t),$

hence $e_{AB}^0(t)$ is determined by $\mathbf{x}_\delta(s)$, $0 \le s \le t$.

From (17) and (35)

$$e_{AB}^0 = -\theta^{-1}D_\delta[1 \ -1 \ 0]\{(1 - \tfrac{3}{2}\chi)I, \ -\beta I\}\mathbf{z}_\delta^0(t).$$

Substitute $(\Phi_\delta, \psi_\delta \mathbf{x}_\delta)$ for $\mathbf{z}_\delta^0$ to see that $e_{AB}^0$ depends only on the time history of $[1 \ -1 \ 0]\mathbf{x}_\delta = x^A - x^B$.[4] When some of the countries are different, $\delta e_{AB}$ is added:

$$e_{AB} = e_{AB}^0 + \delta e_{AB},$$

where

(36) $\quad \delta e_{AB} = -\theta^{-1}[1 \ -1 \ 0]\,\delta \mathbf{i}_\delta$
$\quad\quad\quad\quad = \theta^{-1}D_\delta[1 \ -1 \ 0]\{(1 - \tfrac{3}{2}\chi)I, \ -\beta I\}\,\delta \mathbf{z}_\delta,$

and $\delta \mathbf{z}_\delta$ is given by (29).

Now because

$$\{(1 - \tfrac{3}{2}\chi)I, \ -\beta I\}((\phi_{\delta\delta}\Phi_\delta)*\Phi_\delta, \psi_\delta \mathbf{x}_\delta) = (f(I - \tfrac{1}{3}\mathbf{uu}')N_\delta, \mathbf{x}_\delta),$$

where

$$f(t-s) = \int_s^t [(1 - \tfrac{3}{2}\chi)\phi_{11}(t-\tau) - \beta\phi_{21}(t-\tau)]\{-\eta_1\phi_{12}(\tau-s) + \eta_2\phi_{22}(\tau-s)\}\,d\tau,$$

we can write (36) as

$$\delta e_{AB} = -\theta^{-1}D_\delta \int_0^t f(t-s)[1 \ -1 \ 0](I - \tfrac{1}{3}\mathbf{uu}')N_\delta\mathbf{x}_\delta(s)\,ds.$$

Note that the integrand now depends on $x^A$, $x^B$, and $x_a$:

$$[1 \ -1 \ 0](I - \tfrac{1}{3}\mathbf{uu}')N_\delta\mathbf{x}_\delta = (\kappa^A - \kappa_a)(x^A - x_a) - (\kappa^B - \kappa_a)(x^B - x_a)$$
$$= \tfrac{1}{3}\{(\kappa^A - \kappa^C)x^A + (\kappa^C - \kappa^B)x^B + (\kappa^B - \kappa^A)x^C\}.$$

---

[4] The exact expression is
$$e_{AB}^0(t) = -\theta^{-1}D_\delta \int_0^t [(1 - \tfrac{3}{2}\chi)\phi^{12}(t-s) - \beta\phi^{22}(t-s)][x^A(s) - x^B(s)]\,ds.$$

We state this as

**Proposition.** Unless the coefficients $\kappa$ in the wage rate adjustment equations are the same in the three countries $e_{AB}$ is influenced by the history of the monetary instruments of all three countries. When the coefficients are the same, $e_{AB}$ is determined by the time history of $x^A$ and $x^B$ only.

### 15.4.2 Nonzero $\sigma$

Some additional interaction terms are introduced by the nonzero $\sigma$ term in (3). Let $\sigma = \sigma^i$, $i = A, B, C$. Redefine $\alpha$ and $\beta$ in (17) by

$$\alpha = 3\{\gamma - \tfrac{1}{2}\chi\sigma_2 v(1 - \tfrac{3}{2}\chi)^{-1}\}\theta^{-1}, \qquad \beta = 1 + 3\gamma + v\sigma_2,$$

where

$$\sigma_2 = \sigma/\{a(1 + \xi)\}^{-1}.$$

Then $D_\delta$ is also redefined by

$$D_\delta^{-1} = (1 - \tfrac{3}{2}\chi)\alpha + (m_2 + \tfrac{3}{2}\chi\theta^{-1})\beta.$$

Equation (17) is still valid with these redefinitions. Instead of (16), $i_a$ and $p_a$ are given as the solutions of

$$\begin{bmatrix} \sigma_1 & 1 - \sigma_1 v \\ -m_2 & 1 \end{bmatrix} \begin{bmatrix} i_a \\ p_a \end{bmatrix} = \begin{bmatrix} w_a \\ m_a \end{bmatrix},$$

where

$$\sigma_1 = \sigma/\{a(1 - 2\xi)\}^{-1}.$$

Redefine $D_a$ by

$$D_a^{-1} = m_2 + \sigma_1(1 - m_2 v).$$

Then

$$i_a = D_a\{w_a - (1 + \sigma_1 v)m_a\}, \qquad p_a = D_a(m_2 w_a + \sigma_1 m_a)$$

replaces (16).

Nonzero $\sigma$ causes $y_a$ to be no longer zero. It is now given by

$$y_a = -a(w_a - p_a) = -a(1 - m_2 D_a)w_a + a\sigma_1 D_a m_a$$
$$= -aD_a\sigma_1\{(1 - m_2 v)w_a - m_a\}.$$

The expression for $y_\delta$ in (18) remains valid. To the dynamic matrix $\phi_a$ of (22), we must add a term

$$-aD_\delta\sigma_1 \begin{bmatrix} \eta \\ -\mu_1 \end{bmatrix}[1 - m_2 v \ -1].$$

Then (25) is modified accordingly. With $\phi_a$ replaced with the new dynamic matrix described above, the differential equation for $z_a$ is as given in (27).

The differential equation for $z_\delta$ is modified by nonzero $y_a$ in (26) and there is now a submatrix

$$\phi_{\delta a} = -aD_a\sigma_1 \begin{bmatrix} n_\delta \\ 0 \end{bmatrix} [1 - m_2 v \quad -1].$$

Equation (27) now reads

(37) $$\frac{d}{dt}\begin{bmatrix} z_a \\ z_\delta \end{bmatrix} = \begin{bmatrix} \phi_a & \phi_{a\delta} \\ \phi_{\delta a} & \Phi_{\delta\delta} \end{bmatrix}\begin{bmatrix} z_a \\ z_\delta \end{bmatrix} + \begin{bmatrix} 0 \\ 1 \\ 0 \\ 0 \end{bmatrix} x_a \begin{bmatrix} 0 \\ 0 \\ 0 \\ I \end{bmatrix} x_\delta,$$

where $\Phi_{\delta\delta} = \phi_\delta + \phi_{\delta\delta}$, and $\phi_\delta$ and $\phi_{\delta\delta}$ are as defined in (24) and (28').

The nonzero submatrix $\phi_{\delta a}$ causes $\delta z_\delta$ to depend on $x_a$ additionally, i.e., because the dynamics are

$$\delta \dot{z}_\delta = \phi_\delta \delta z_\delta + \phi_{\delta\delta} z_\delta^0 + \phi_{\delta a} z_a^0,$$

its solution is

$$\delta z_\delta = (\Phi_\delta, \phi_{\delta\delta} z_\delta^0) + (\Phi_\delta, \phi_{\delta a} z_a^0)$$
$$= ((\phi_{\delta\delta}\Phi_\delta)*\Phi_\delta, \psi_\delta x_\delta) + ((\phi_{\delta a}\Phi_a)*\Phi_\delta, \psi_a x_a).$$

To the right-hand side of (36), we add

$$-\theta^{-1}[1 \quad -1 \quad 0]\{(1 - \tfrac{3}{2}\chi)I, -\beta I\}((\phi_{\delta a}\Phi_a)*\Phi_\delta, \psi_a x_a),$$

which can be written as

$$-\theta^{-1}(\kappa^A - \kappa^B)\int_0^t q(t-s)x_a(s)\,ds$$

for some $q(\cdot)$.[5]

Thus, the average affects $e_{AB}$ unless $\kappa^A$ equal $\kappa^B$.

## 15.5 Nonsymmetrical Model: Monetary Union

How would interactions among countries in our three-country model change if two of the countries, $A$ and $B$ say, maintain a fixed exchange rate? Deviation of the exchange rate $e_{AB}(t)$ is zero for all $t$ and people expect it

---

[5] $q(t-s) = -aD_a\sigma_1\int_s^t [1 - 3\chi/2)\phi_\delta^{11}(t-\tau) - \beta\phi_\delta^{21}(t-\tau)][(1 - m_2 v)\phi_a^{12}(\tau - s)]\,d\tau.$

## 15.5 Nonsymmetrical Model: Monetary Union

to be zero, i.e., $\varepsilon_{AB}$ is also identically zero. Equivalently from (9), we can state that $i^A$ is identically equal to $i^B$. To evaluate consequences of such an exchange rate union by two of the three countries on real variables and effectiveness of fiscal instruments, we allow government expenditures of the three countries to vary. Deviations in fiscal expenditures from the reference path, $g^A$, $g^B$, and $g^C$, are the instruments in this section. Otherwise the model of this section is the same as in previous sections.

Initially we assume the parameters of national models are the same. Under this simplifying assumption, differences of endogenous variables of country $A$ and $B$ are determined only by the difference in the wage rate deviations $w^A - w^B$. We denote it by $w_{AB}$ for short. The instruments $g^A$ and $g^B$ must maintain a certain relation to keep $m^A - m^B$ in such a way that $e_{AB}$ is kept at zero. The differences $w_{AC}(\equiv w^A - w^C)$ and $m_{AC}(\equiv m^A - m^C)$ are governed by a second-order differential equation with $g_{AC}(\equiv g^A - g^C)$ as a forcing term. Later, we show that national characteristic differences introduce channels for other interdependence among these variables.

The exchange rate deviation between countries $A$ and $C$ is given by (9). From (17), this can be rewritten in a more revealing way as

$$(38) \qquad e_{AC} = -\theta^{-1} D_\delta \{(1 - \tfrac{3}{2}\chi) w_{AC} - \beta m_{AC}\}.$$

This states that the behavior of $e_{AC}$ is determined by the time paths of $w_{AC}$ and $m_{AC}$. What influences them? To answer this question, we must derive differential equations which generate these time paths. Rather than rederive the variational dynamics for this case, we can impose a constraint that $[1 \ -1 \ 0]\mathbf{i}$ be identically zero on the reduced form expression of (17) and deduce the variational dynamics for the model with monetary union. First, we recall that $\mathbf{i}$ equals $i_a \mathbf{u}$ plus $\mathbf{i}_\delta$. Noting that $[1 \ -1 \ 0]\mathbf{u}$ is zero, the constraint is expressed as a relation between $m^A$ and $m^B$ by solving the constraint relation for $m^B$

$$(39) \qquad m^B = m^A - \lambda w_{AB},$$

where

$\lambda = (1 - \tfrac{3}{2}\chi)/\beta$, and we write $w_{AB}$ for $w_A - w_B$.

To provide a simple illustration of our procedure, we set $v$ to zero, i.e., we assume that expectations on the price index inflations are stationary in the three countries. This allows us to drop $\rho_i$ from the wage rate equations.

Because the government expenditure $G$ is no longer kept constant, the variational expression for the money stock deviation changes from (6) to

$$(40) \qquad \dot{m}^j = -\mu_1^j y^j + \mu_2^j p^j + \mu_3^j i^j + \mu_4^j g^j - \mu_5^j m^j, \qquad j = A, B, C,$$

where

$$\mu_4^j = P^j G^j / M^j \quad \text{and} \quad \mu_5^j = \dot{M}_j / M_j.$$

One of the equations is, however, dependent because the relation (39) must be maintained at each time. Differentiate it and substituting $\dot{w}^A$ and $\dot{w}^B$ out by the appropriate component of $\dot{\mathbf{w}} = \kappa \mathbf{y}$ and substituting out $\dot{m}^A$ and $\dot{m}^B$ by (40), we can write the relation as

(41) $\quad \mu_4 g^B = \mu_4 g^A - \lambda(\kappa^A y^A - \kappa^B y^B) - \mu_1(y^A - y^B) + \mu_2 p_{AB} - \lambda \mu_5 w_{AB}.$

We choose $w_{AB}, w_A, w_C, m_A,$ and $m_C$ as the basic state variables, because this choice simplifies the state-space representation of the model dynamics. We collect here some relations needed in relating the endogenous variables to the state variables. From the definitional relation

$$\mathbf{w} = \begin{bmatrix} 0 & 1 & 0 \\ -1 & 1 & 0 \\ 0 & 1 & 1 \end{bmatrix} \begin{bmatrix} w_{AB} \\ w^A \\ w^C \end{bmatrix},$$

we can express the average and the difference of the wage rates as

(42) $\quad w_a = \tfrac{1}{3} \mathbf{u}' \mathbf{w} = -\tfrac{1}{3} w_{AB} + \tfrac{1}{3}[2 \ 1] \mathbf{w}.$

where

$$\mathbf{w} = \begin{bmatrix} w^A \\ w^C \end{bmatrix}$$

and

(43) $\quad \mathbf{w}_\delta = \dfrac{1}{3} \begin{bmatrix} 1 \\ -2 \\ 1 \end{bmatrix} w_{AB} + \dfrac{1}{3} \begin{bmatrix} 1 \\ 1 \\ -2 \end{bmatrix} w_{AC}.$

Similarly,

(44) $\quad m_a = \tfrac{1}{3}[2 \ 1]\mathbf{m} - \tfrac{1}{3}\lambda w_{AB},$

where

$$\mathbf{m} = \begin{bmatrix} m^A \\ m^C \end{bmatrix},$$

and

(45) $\quad \mathbf{m}_\delta = \dfrac{1}{3} \begin{bmatrix} 1 \\ 1 \\ -2 \end{bmatrix} m_{AC} + \dfrac{\lambda}{3} \begin{bmatrix} 1 \\ -2 \\ 1 \end{bmatrix} w_{AB}.$

From (17),

$$\mathbf{p} = p_a \mathbf{u} + \mathbf{p}_\delta = w_a \mathbf{u} + D_\delta\{(m_2 + \tfrac{3}{2}\chi\theta^{-1})\mathbf{w}_\delta + \alpha \mathbf{m}_\delta\}.$$

## 15.5 Nonsymmetrical Model: Monetary Union

On substituting (42), (43), and (45), **p** becomes

$$(46) \quad \mathbf{p} = -\frac{1}{3}\left\{\mathbf{u} - D_\delta(m_2 + \tfrac{3}{2}\chi\theta^{-1} + \alpha\lambda)\begin{bmatrix}1\\-2\\1\end{bmatrix}\right\}w_{AB} + \frac{\alpha D_\delta}{3}\begin{bmatrix}1\\1\\-2\end{bmatrix}m_{AC}$$

$$+ \frac{1}{3}\left\{\mathbf{u}[2\ \ 1] + D_\delta(m_2 + \tfrac{3}{2}\chi\theta^{-1})\begin{bmatrix}1\\1\\-2\end{bmatrix}[1\ -1]\right\}\mathbf{w}.$$

Then the reduced form expression for **y** becomes, from (2) and (46),

$$(47) \quad \frac{\mathbf{y}}{a} = \frac{\alpha D_\delta}{3}\begin{bmatrix}1\\1\\-2\end{bmatrix}m_{AC} - \frac{1}{3}\{1 - D_\delta(m_2 + \tfrac{3}{2}\chi\theta^{-1} + \alpha\lambda)\}\begin{bmatrix}1\\-2\\1\end{bmatrix}w_{AB}$$

$$- \frac{1}{3}\{1 - D_\delta(m_2 + \tfrac{3}{2}\chi\theta^{-1})\}\begin{bmatrix}1\\1\\-2\end{bmatrix}w_{AC}.$$

Also from (17)

$$(48) \quad \mathbf{i} = \begin{bmatrix}i^A\\i^C\end{bmatrix} = D_a(\mathbf{w}_a - \mathbf{m}_a)\begin{bmatrix}1\\1\end{bmatrix} + D_\delta\begin{bmatrix}1 & 0 & 0\\0 & 0 & 1\end{bmatrix}\{(1 - \tfrac{3}{2}\chi)\mathbf{w}_\delta - \beta\mathbf{m}_\delta\}$$

$$= -\frac{1}{3}\{(1 - \lambda)D_a - D_\delta(m_2 + \tfrac{3}{2}\chi\theta^{-1} + \alpha\lambda)\}\begin{bmatrix}1\\1\end{bmatrix}w_{AB}$$

$$+ \frac{1}{3}\left\{D_a\begin{bmatrix}1\\1\end{bmatrix}[2\ \ 1] + D_\delta(m_2 + \tfrac{3}{2}\chi\theta^{-1})\begin{bmatrix}1\\-2\end{bmatrix}[1\ -1]\right\}\mathbf{w}$$

$$- \frac{1}{3}\left\{D_a\begin{bmatrix}1\\1\end{bmatrix}[2\ \ 1] - \alpha D_\delta\begin{bmatrix}1\\-2\end{bmatrix}[1\ -1]\right\}\mathbf{m}.$$

Differences between countries $A$ and $C$ are similarly expressed using (46)–(48):

$$p_{AC} = [1\ \ 0\ -1]\mathbf{p} = \alpha D_\delta m_{AC} - D_\delta(m_2 + \tfrac{3}{2}\chi\theta^{-1})w_{AC},$$
$$y_{AC}/a = \alpha D_\delta m_{AC} - (\phi_w + \alpha\lambda D_\delta)w_{AC}, \qquad i_{AC} = p_{AC},$$

where

$$\phi_w = 1 - D_\delta(m_2 + \tfrac{3}{2}\chi\theta^{-1} + \alpha\lambda) > 0.$$

We are now ready to show that the dynamics for $w_{AB}$ separate from the rest of the dynamics when $\kappa^A$ and $\kappa^B$ are equal. From (5) and (47),

$$(49) \quad \frac{d}{dt}w_{AB} = \kappa^A y_{AB} = \kappa^A[1\ -1\ \ 0]\mathbf{y} = -a\kappa^A\phi_w w_{AB}.$$

We note that $p_{AB}$ and $y_{AB}$ depend only on $w_{AB}$ as we can see from (46),

$$p_{AB} = [1 \ -1 \ 0]\mathbf{p} = (1 - \phi_w)w_{AB},$$

and from (47), $y_{AB} = -\phi_w w_{AB}$.

The countries $A$ and $B$ behave independently of country $C$. From (41) the fiscal instruments $g^A$ and $g^B$ are tied by a relation

$$\mu_4 g^B = \mu_4 g^A + \gamma w_{AB},$$

where

$$\gamma = -\lambda\mu_5 + \mu_2(1 - \phi_w) + (\mu_1 + \lambda\kappa^A)\phi_w$$

to maintain $e_{AB}$ at zero.

When $\kappa^A$ and $\kappa^B$ are unequal, the dynamics for $w_{AB}$ also depend on $\mathbf{m}$ and $\mathbf{w}$. We return to this point later. If $\kappa^A$ and $\kappa^C$ are equal, the dynamics for $\mathbf{w}$ also simplify. By calculating

$$\mathbf{y} = \begin{bmatrix} 1 & 0 & 0 \\ 0 & 0 & 1 \end{bmatrix}\mathbf{y}$$

from (47),

$$\dot{\mathbf{w}} = \frac{a\kappa^A}{3}\left\{\alpha D_\delta \begin{bmatrix} 1 \\ -2 \end{bmatrix}m_{AC} - \phi_w \begin{bmatrix} 1 \\ 1 \end{bmatrix}w_{AB}\right\}$$

$$- \frac{1}{3}\left\{1 - D_\delta\left(m_2 + \frac{3\chi\theta^{-1}}{2}\right)\right\}\begin{bmatrix} 1 \\ -2 \end{bmatrix}w_{AC}.$$

Calculating $[1 \ -1]\dot{\mathbf{w}}$ from above, the dynamics of $w_{AC}$ depend only on $m^A - m^C$ and $w^A - w^C$:

(50) $\qquad \dot{w}_{AC} = a\kappa^A[\alpha D_\delta m_{AC} - \{1 - D_\delta(m_2 + \tfrac{3}{2}\chi\theta^{-1})\}w_{AC}].$

From (4) and (40),

$$\dot{m}^A - \dot{m}^C = [1 \ -1]\dot{\mathbf{m}} = [1 \ -1](-\mu_1 \mathbf{y} + \mu_2 \mathbf{p} + \mu_3 \mathbf{i} + \mu_4 \mathbf{g} - \mu_5 \mathbf{m}),$$

where from (47),

$$[1 \ -1]\mathbf{y} = [1 \ 0 \ -1]\mathbf{y} = \alpha a D_\delta m_{AC} - a\{1 - D_\delta(m_2 + \tfrac{3}{2}\chi\theta^{-1})\}w_{AC},$$

from (46),

$$[1 \ -1]\mathbf{p} = D_\delta\{\alpha m_{AC} + (m_2 + \tfrac{3}{2}\chi\theta^{-1})w_{AC}\},$$

## 15.5 Nonsymmetrical Model: Monetary Union

and from (48), $[1\ -1]\mathbf{i}$ is seen to be the same as $[1\ -1]\mathbf{p}$. Thus, the dynamics for $m^A - m^C$ are seen to depend only on $m_{AC}$ and $w_{AC}$ as

(51) $$\dot{m}_{AC} = -\mu_m m_{AC} + \mu_w w_{AC} + \mu_5 g_{AC},$$

where

$$\mu_m = \mu_5 + \alpha D_\delta(\mu_1 a + \mu_2 + \mu_3) \quad \text{and} \quad \mu_w = \mu_1 a - D_\delta(m_2 + \tfrac{3}{2}\chi\theta^{-1}) \times (\mu_1 a - \mu_2 - \mu_3).$$

The exchange rate deviation $e_{AC}$ is thus governed jointly by the dynamics (50) and (51).

The wage rate difference between the two countries in the monetary union gradually disappear according to (49). The differences of the other endogenous variables $y_{AC}$ and $p_{AC}$ also depend only on $m_{AC}$, $w_{AC}$, and $g_{AC}$. The difference $y_{AC}$, for example, can be made positive or negative depending on a particular time path taken by $g_{AC}$.

When $\kappa$s differ among countries, $w_{AB}$ does not separate from the rest of the dynamics, and differences of national endogenous variables in the monetary union are influenced by country $C$ as well. From (5) and (47),

$$\frac{\dot{w}_{AB}}{a} = [\kappa^A\ -\kappa^B\ 0]\mathbf{y}$$

$$= -\frac{\phi_w}{3}(\kappa^A + 2\kappa^B)w_{AB} + \frac{(\kappa^A - \kappa^B)}{3}\{(\alpha D_\delta m_{AC} - (\phi_w + D_\delta\alpha\lambda)w_{AC}\}.$$

Note that both $m_{AC}$ and $w_{AC}$ affects $\dot{w}_{AB}$ through the coefficient $(\kappa^A - \kappa^B)$. Similarly $\dot{w}_{AC}$ and $\dot{m}_{AC}$ now depend on $w_{AB}$. Also from (5) and (47),

$$\dot{w}_{AC} = [\kappa^A\ 0\ -\kappa^C]\mathbf{y}$$

$$= -a(\phi_w + D_\delta\alpha\lambda)\tfrac{1}{2}(\kappa^A + 2\kappa^C)w_{AC} + \alpha D_\delta\tfrac{1}{3}(\kappa^A + 2\kappa^C)m_{AC} - \tfrac{1}{3}(\kappa^A - \kappa^C)\phi_w w_{AB}.$$

A similar expression can be obtained for $m_{AC}$. We leave the deviation and examination of the effects of $g_{AC}$ on real variables to the interested reader.

# Appendixes

# A | Dynamic Multipliers of ARMA Model

We calculate dynamic multipliers of an autoregressive moving average (ARMA) model by first putting it into state-space representation and applying the formula for the dynamic multipliers we derived in Chapter 4. This procedure is to be compared with calculations as described by Brissimis (1976), for example. The comparison will convince the reader of the simplicity of our procedure. The reader will note that multipliers are much easier to calculate when the model is in the state-space form.

The system is as in Brissimis (1976)

(1) $$\mathbf{y}_t = A_1 \mathbf{y}_{t-1} + \cdots + A_p \mathbf{y}_{t-p} + B_0 \mathbf{x}_t + \cdots + B_q \mathbf{x}_{t-q},$$

where

$$A_i: G \times G, \quad i = 1, \ldots, p,$$
$$B_i: G \times k, \quad i = 1, \ldots, q,$$
$$q \leq p.$$

Define $G$-dimensional vectors $\mathbf{z}_1(t), \ldots, \mathbf{z}_p(t)$ by

$$\mathbf{z}_1(t) = \mathbf{y}_t - B_0 \mathbf{x}_t,$$
$$\mathbf{z}_{k+1}(t-1) = \mathbf{z}_k(t) - A_k \mathbf{z}_1(t-1) - D_k \mathbf{x}_{t-1},$$

where

$$D_k = A_k B_0 + B_k, \quad k = 1, \ldots, p-2,$$

and

$$\mathbf{z}_p(t) = A_p \mathbf{z}_1(t-1) + D_p \mathbf{x}_{t-1}, \quad D_p = A_p B_0 + B_p.$$

When $q < p$, $B_{q+1}, \ldots, B_p$ will be set to zero in the above.

Define
$$\mathbf{z}_t^* = \begin{bmatrix} \mathbf{z}_1(t) \\ \vdots \\ \mathbf{z}_p(t) \end{bmatrix}.$$

By construction (and it is easy to verify) we obtain an alternate representation

(2) $$\begin{aligned} \mathbf{z}_t^* &= A^*\mathbf{z}_{t-1}^* + B^*\mathbf{x}_{t-1} \\ \mathbf{y}_t &= (I \ 0 \ \cdots \ 0)\mathbf{z}_t^* + B_0\mathbf{x}_t, \end{aligned}$$

where

$$A^* = \begin{bmatrix} A_1 & I & & 0 \\ & 0 & \ddots & \\ \vdots & & & I \\ A_p & 0 & \cdots & 0 \end{bmatrix}, \quad B^* = \begin{bmatrix} D_1 \\ \vdots \\ D_p \end{bmatrix}.$$

Note that unlike in Brissimis, we can use $\mathbf{x}_{t-1}$ alone in (2). We need not use the stacked vector $\mathbf{x}_t^*$.

Solve (2) to obtain the final form,

(3) $$\mathbf{z}_t^* = (A^*)^t \mathbf{z}_0^* + \sum_{\tau=1}^t W_\tau \mathbf{x}_{t-\tau},$$

where

$$W_\tau = (A^*)^{\tau-1} B^*, \quad \tau = 1, \ldots, t.$$

Thus the dynamic multipliers associated with $\mathbf{x}_{t-\tau}$ are

$$\partial \mathbf{y}_t / \partial \mathbf{x}_t = B_0$$

and

$$\begin{aligned} \partial \mathbf{y}_t / \partial \mathbf{x}_{t-\tau} &= [I \ 0 \ \cdots \ 0] W_\tau \\ &= \text{1st row of } W_\tau, \quad \tau = 1, \ldots, t. \end{aligned}$$

Let
$$[I \ 0 \ \cdots \ 0](A^*)^{\tau-1} = [E_{\tau-1} \ E_{\tau-2} \ \cdots \ I \ 0 \ \cdots \ 0]$$

where
$$E_0 = I.$$

Then $E$s are generated recursively by

(4) $$E_\tau = E_{\tau-1} A_1 + E_{\tau-2} A_2 + \cdots + A_\tau.$$

This is valid for all $\tau$ provided we adopt a convention of $E_\tau = 0$ with $\tau$ negative and $A_\tau = 0$ for $\tau > p$.

Thus substituting $E$s and collecting terms and noting (4), we have

$$\partial \mathbf{y}_t/\partial \mathbf{x}_{t-\tau} = [E_{\tau-1} \quad \cdots \quad I \quad 0 \quad \cdots \quad 0]B^*$$
$$= E_\tau B_0 + E_{\tau-1}B_1 + \cdots + B_\tau, \qquad \tau = 0, 1, \ldots.$$

# B | Disposable Income Calculation

The nominal wealth of the private sector consists of stocks of money, of domestic government bonds, of equities, and of foreign (international) bonds,[1]

(1) $$W = M + B/i + EF/i^* + qPK,$$

where the money is assumed to be a nontraded asset.

Suppose a country produces a single output good at price $P$ and imposes the purchasing power parity relation $P = EP^*$ with $P^*$ exogenously fixed. The real wealth, in terms of the domestic output good, is then $W/P$. Its rate of change is

$$d(W/P)/dt = \dot{W}/P - (WP)(\dot{P}/P),$$

where the first term is the increase in the real wealth at constant output price and the second term represents a decrease in real wealth due to a price rise. From (1),

$$\dot{W} = \dot{M} + \dot{B}/i + E\dot{F}/i^* + qP\dot{K} + qK\dot{P} + T_c,$$

where $T_c$ stands for terms of capital gains and losses due to changing rates of yields $i$ and $i^*$ and the market valuation term $q$.[2] Note that the $qK\dot{P}/P$ term cancels out from $\dot{W}/P$ and $(W/P)\dot{P}/P$.

The domestic government budget constraint equation is

$$\dot{M} + \dot{B}/i - E\dot{R}/i^* = P(G - T) + B - ER,$$

where $R$ is the stock of international reserve that the government (the central bank) holds. Thus

$$(\dot{M} + \dot{B}/i)/P = G - T + (B - ER)/P + E\dot{R}/i^*P.$$

---

[1] See Chapter 11 for explanation of symbols.
[2] $T_c = -(B/i)\dot{i}/i + (EF/i^*)(\dot{E}/E - \dot{i^*}/i^*) + qPK(\dot{q}/q)$.

## Disposable Income Calculation

Hence

$$d(W/P)/dt = (X - I_m) + E(F + R)/P + G - T + (B - ER)/P \\ + q\dot{K} + T_c - (M/P + B/iP + EF/i^*P)\dot{P}/P.$$

In the above, we use the current account relation

$$E(\dot{F} + \dot{R})/i^* = P(X - I_m) + E(F + R),$$

in domestic currency, to replace $E(\dot{F} + \dot{R})/i^*$ by the right-hand side.

From the GNP identity by the purchases $Y = C + I + G + (X - I_m)$, we note that

$$X - I_m + G - T = Y - T - C - I.$$

Therefore,

$$C + d(W/P)/dt = Y - T + (B + EF)/P + q\dot{K} - I \\ - (M/P + B/iP + EF/i^*P)(\dot{P}/P) + T_c.$$

The disposable income is, by definition, the rate of consumption which leaves the perceived level of real wealth constant. Thus, it is given by

$$Y' = Y - T + (B + EF)/P - (M/P + B/iP + EF/i^*P)\pi + T_c + (q\dot{K} - I),$$

where $\pi$ is the expected rate of inflation.

If $q = 1$, then $\dot{K} = I - \lambda K$. Except for the capital gains and loss terms, the real disposable income is equal to

$$Y' = Y - T + (B + EF)/P - \lambda K - (M/P + B/iP + EF/i^*P)\pi.$$

When the assumption of the purchasing power parity is dropped, we must distinguish the domestic output price $P$ from the consumer price index which we take as $P_I = P^\chi(EP^*)^{(1-\chi)}$. By using $W/P_I$ instead of $W/P$, we can recalculate the disposable income as above, after redefining $C$ by $(PC_d + EP^*I_m)/P_I$, where $C_d$ is the domestic residents' consumption of domestic output.

Because the expected rate of inflation of the consumer index equals $\chi\pi + (1 - \chi)\varepsilon$, where $\varepsilon$ is the expected rate of depreciation of the exchange rate, the real wealth loses at the rate $\chi\pi + (1 - \chi)\varepsilon$. Foreign bonds, on the other hand, will gain at the rate $\varepsilon$ due to the valuation effect. The domestic equities also gain at the rate $\pi$ due to inflation.

The net effects, then, depend on the composition of the asset portfolio. Let $\gamma$ be the proportion of wealth held in equities and $\xi$ be the proportion of wealth held as foreign bonds. Then the disposable income is given by $P_I Y' = P(Y - T) +$ (interest receipt from domestic and foreign bonds expressed in domestic currency) $-$ (capital stock depreciation expressed in domestic currency) $- W\{\chi\pi + (1 - \chi)\varepsilon\} + \gamma\pi W + \xi W\varepsilon$.

# C | Regressive Expectations and Perfect Foresight Assumption

In this book most expectations are generated regressively. We clarify the relation between regressive expectations and perfect foresight or self-fulfilling expectations in this appendix.

Models with perfect foresight in which all prices can discontinuously adjust usually are only conditionally stable, i.e., some eigenvalues of the variational dynamics are unstable.[1] In the two-dimensional dynamics, this is the well-known property associated with a long-run equilibrium. See Kouri (1976), for example. In models incorporating perfect foresight assumption we must impose the stability requirement to confine model time paths to conditionally stable subspace, i.e., subspace spanned by eigenvectors with stable eigenvalues, if stability is not ensured on some institutional or economic grounds. [See Bellman (1953) or Coddington and Levinson (1955) for the notion of conditional stability.] Kouri has suggested that

---

[1] Gertler (1979a, b) considered imperfect price adjustment and its implication on stability under perfect foresight (rational) inflationary expectations for a simple closed macroeconomic model. In particular, he showed that the assumption of perfect foresight does not lead to instability with imperfect price flexibility. Here, we show that his specifications of imperfectly flexible prices with perfect foresight are quite similar to some of our specifications on expectations by regressive mechanisms. To illustrate we treat inflationary expectations.

In variational terms Gertler's equations [Gertler, 1979a, (3)–(5)] $\delta \pi^d = \lambda(y - \hat{y}) + \delta \pi^e$, $\delta \pi = \phi \, \delta \pi^d + (1 - \phi) \, \delta \tilde{\pi}$, $\delta \dot{\tilde{\pi}} = \beta \, \delta(\pi^d - \tilde{\pi})$, and $\delta \pi^e = \delta \pi$, where $\pi^d$ is the desired rate of price adjustment, $\tilde{\pi}$ is the actual (built-in) rate of price adjustment due to rigidities, $\pi$ is the actual rate of inflation, and $\pi^e$ is the anticipated rate of inflation. The variable $\hat{y}$ is the variational full employment real output which we shall set to zero without loss of generality. We drop the distinction of $\pi$ and $\pi^e$ because of perfect foresight assumption. Then, these equations are seen to be reducible to $\delta \pi = [\phi \lambda/(1 - \phi)]y + \delta \tilde{\pi}$ and $\delta \dot{\tilde{\pi}} = [\beta \lambda/(1 - \phi)] y$.

This is a special case of $\delta \pi = [\phi \lambda/(1 - \phi)]y + \delta \tilde{\pi}$, where $\delta \tilde{\pi}$ is now interpreted as the expected rate of inflation which is generated by a regressive mechanism $\delta \tilde{\pi} = \rho_1 p + \rho_2 y + $ (other variables such as $e$ in open economies).

This ends our illustration of the similarities of these two seemingly different specifications of expectations.

"long-run rationality" will lead market participants to choose a stable path.[2] In his model, there is only one stable solution; the exchange rate has to "jump" instantaneously to the saddle path in response to, say, an increase in the supply of money. However, it is not clear how market participants calculate the correct jump or what market forces would lead them to it.

This type of problem should be more properly posed in a stochastic framework by replacing the perfect foresight assumption by that of rational expectations. In stochastic models the role of incomplete or imperfect information and nonidentical information sets of economic agents can be discussed more precisely. [See Futia (1979) for one such approach to rational expectation calculations by means of $z$-transforms.]

Because this books deals exclusively with deterministic models, we restrict our attention to deterministic models with perfect foresight expectations and impose stability conditions, i.e., self-fulfilling expectations with stability. Dornbusch (1976) postulated an autoregressive expectations mechanism, then he showed that these expectations can be made "consistent" or self-fulfilling in his "small country" model by a proper choice of parameters in the autoregressive expectations mechanism. Unfortunately, autoregressive expectations cannot generally be made consistent for models with more than one dynamic equation. Both the models of Dornbusch and Kouri had only one essential dynamic equation.

Thus, the Dornbusch procedure does not generalize to higher-dimensional dynamic systems directly to generate consistent expectations. We show in this appendix that more inclusive regressive expectations can be made consistent under certain conditions. This is done as an existence proof. Actual construction of consistent expectations cum stability involves solutions of nonlinear algebraic equations. We illustrate choices of coefficients of regressive expectations to be consistent by extending Dornbuch's small country model to a two-country world model. We model the two countries symmetrically except that we assume that the goods market in one country adjusts more slowly than the goods market in the other country.[3] In addition, we show that monetary policy is not symmetric in this two-country model.

## C.1 Consistency of Regressive Expectations

Suppose a variational model, i.e., a model specified in log-linear form of the economy, is put into the following form (which is half-way between the

---

[2] In this he is essentially following Sargent and Wallace (1973); this stability problem has a long history in the monetary growth literature.

[3] Frankel (1979) examines a two-country model with the same set of parameters in both countries.

structural and state-space form) as

(1) $$\dot{z} = Az + b\,\delta\varepsilon,$$
(2) $$e = c'z + d\,\delta\varepsilon,$$
(3) $$\delta\varepsilon = -ve - \omega'q,$$
(4) $$q = Dz,$$

where $\delta\varepsilon$ is a scalar variational expectation variable, $z$ is state vector, and $q$ is some endogenous variable. In (1), $\delta\varepsilon$ is not yet separately shown, i.e., is not solved out by some regressive expectation assumption. When $\omega$ is zero, (3) reduces to an autoregressive scheme. With $\omega \neq 0$, (3) states that the expectations on the exchange rate changes are also influenced by a vector of some endogenous variables $q$. In (1)–(4), $A$ and $D$ are matrices; $b$, $c$, and $\omega$ are vectors.

Equations (2) and (3) can be solved together to express $e$ and $\delta\varepsilon$ in reduced forms:

(5) $\quad e = f'z, \quad$ where $\quad f' = (c' - d\omega'D)/(1 + dv),$

(6) $\quad \delta\varepsilon = -h'z, \quad$ where $\quad h' = vf' + \omega'D.$

When (6) is substituted into (1), we obtain a state-space representation of the dynamics

(7) $$\dot{z} = Fz,$$

where

$$F = A - bh'.$$

To be perfect foresight, the derivative of $e$ must equal $\delta\varepsilon$ of (6), i.e.,

$$\dot{e} = f'\dot{z} = f'Fz = -h'z \quad \text{for all } z,$$

or

(8) $$f'F = -h'$$

must hold.

First suppose $\omega$ is zero, i.e., the expectation is autoregressive. Then (8) becomes

(8') $$c'F = -vc',$$

or in terms of the original matrix $A$

$$-c'A = v[1 - c'b/(1 + dv)]c'.$$

This reduces to $-c'A = vc'$ if $b$ is zero.

With $A$ scalar dynamics any $c$ satisfies this condition. When $F$ is second- or higher-order dynamics, **c** must be chosen to be a row eigenvector of $A$ to be consistent. Because $A$ and **c** are given by model specifications, it is only by chance that this condition is satisfied in higher-order dynamics.

With nonzero $\omega$, the consistency condition becomes

$$\mathbf{f}'F = -v\mathbf{f}' + \omega'D \quad \text{or} \quad \mathbf{c}'(vI + F) = \sigma'(dF - I),$$

where $\sigma' = \omega'D$.

This is equivalent to a nonlinear relation:

(9)
$$\sigma'\left\{dA - I + \frac{dv}{1+dv}(\mathbf{cb}' - \mathbf{bc}') - \frac{d}{1+dv}\mathbf{b}\sigma'\right\} = \mathbf{c}'\left\{A + vI - \frac{v\mathbf{bc}'}{1+dv}\right\}.$$

This states that provided regressive expectations are constructed using $\omega$ and $D$, such that (9) is satisfied, then the regressive expectation (3) can be made consistent.

For example if **b** is zero in (1), (9) reduces to

(9')
$$\sigma'(dA - I) = \mathbf{c}'(A + vI).$$

When $dA - I$ is not singular, we can choose $\sigma$ by

$$\sigma' = \mathbf{c}'(A + vI)(dA - I)^{-1},$$

then (3) is consistent. When **b** is not zero, (9) cannot be explicitly solved for $\sigma$ but a solution of $\sigma$ is likely to exist at least for small **b**. We state:

**Proposition.** Autoregressive expectations are generally inconsistent for nonscalar dynamics. Regressive expectations can be made consistent even for higher-dimensional dynamics [for example when **b** is zero and $(dA - I)$ is nonsingular].

Although the existence is thus established, the actual calculation requires solving nonlinear equations. We illustrate this on a simplified two-country model.

## C.2 Example: Two-Country Model[4]

In this section, Dornbusch's model is extended to include a second country. Here to preserve Dornbusch's notation we deviate from our usual notation. As in the single-country version, financial markets will be assumed to clear instantaneously, while goods markets adjust slowly over time.

---
[4] This example is based in part on an unpublished work by Aoki and Canzoneri.

The two-country model can be represented by five equations:

(10) $\dot{p} = \pi[\ln D - \bar{y}] = \pi(\bar{g} + \mu(e + p^* - p) + (\gamma - 1)\bar{y} - \sigma r]$,[5]

(11) $\bar{m} - p = \phi\bar{y} - \lambda^{-1}r$,

(12) $r - r^* = x$,

(13) $\bar{m}^* - p^* = \phi\bar{y}^* - \lambda^{-1}r^*$,

(14) $\dot{p}^* = \pi^*[\ln D^* - \bar{y}^*] = \pi^*[\bar{g}^* - \mu(e + p^* - p) + (\gamma - 1)\bar{y} - \sigma r^*]$,

where $x$ is the expectation variable.

Output in each country is assumed to be fixed at its full employment level. Equations (10) and (14) explain the adjustment of the goods market in each country. Without loss of generality, we can assume that the home country adjusts more slowly than the foreign country; that is, $\alpha = \pi^*/\pi > 1$. Equations (11)–(13) are the equilibrium conditions for the asset sector. The two countries' bonds are perfect substitutes, so incipient capital movements hold the interest rate differential equal to the expected rate of depreciation of the domestic currency, $x$. Equations (11) and (13) imply equilibrium in the money markets; if they are in equilibrium, the bond market must also be in equilibrium.

Dornbusch's expectations hypothesis is also extended to a more inclusive regressive mechanisms:

(15) $x = -\theta(e - \bar{e}) - \omega(p - \bar{p}) + \omega^*(p^* - \bar{p}^*)$.

If $\omega$ and $\omega^*$ are set equal to zero, then (15) reduces to Dornbusch's autoregressive hypothesis. Consistency requires that $(\theta, \omega, \omega^*)$ be chosen so that $\delta x = \delta \dot{e}$.

The dynamics of the two-country model reduce to a system of differential equations in $\delta p$ and $\delta p^*$ [Eq. (20)]; so $\delta p$ and $\delta p^*$ are the "state" variables that propel the system through time (as explained by Eq. (21) below). It seems reasonable to assume that "rational" market participants will be able to discern this and that they will incorporate this information into their expectation formation. This results in Eq. (15).

We shall show that an autoregressive mechanism cannot be consistent, while the more inclusive mechanism (15) can.

---

[5] Perhaps $\bar{y}^*$ should appear in ln $D$ and in the demand for domestic money, and similarly $y$ should appear in ln $D^*$ and the demand for foreign money. These extensions would not change the results below.

The long-run equilibrium can be found by setting $\dot{p}$, $\dot{p}^*$, and $x$ equal to zero in Eqs. (10)–(14). It turns out that

(16) $\quad \bar{e} + \bar{p}^* - \bar{p} = (1/2\mu)[\bar{g}^* - \bar{g} + (1 - \gamma)(\bar{y} - \bar{y}^*)]$,

(17) $\quad \bar{r} = \sigma^{-1}(\bar{g} + (\gamma - 1)\bar{y} + \mu(\bar{e} + \bar{p}^* - \bar{p}))$,

$\quad \bar{r}^* = \sigma^{-1}[\bar{g}^* + (\gamma - 1)\bar{y}^* - \mu(\bar{e} + \bar{p}^* - \bar{p})]$,

$\quad \bar{r} = \bar{r}^*$,

(18) $\quad \bar{p} = \bar{m} - \phi\bar{y} + (1/\lambda)\bar{r}$,

$\quad \bar{p}^* = \bar{m}^* - \phi\bar{y}^* + (1/\lambda)\bar{r}^*$,

(19) $\quad \bar{e} = (\bar{m} - \bar{m}^*) + \phi(\bar{y}^* - \bar{y}) + (\bar{e} + \bar{p}^* - \bar{p})$.

The terms of trade depend upon the autonomous demands for the two goods, $\bar{g}$ and $\bar{g}^*$, and upon the fixed supplies of the two goods, $\bar{y}$ and $\bar{y}^*$, in the long run. Interest rates equalize and are independent of the two currencies. The exchange rate and the price levels do depend upon the supplies of the two currencies.

In deviation form, the model reduces to

(20) $\quad \begin{bmatrix} \delta\dot{p} \\ \delta\dot{p}^* \end{bmatrix} = \pi\mu \begin{bmatrix} -(c + 1 + \gamma) & c^* + 1 \\ \alpha(c + 1) & -\alpha(c^* + 1 + \gamma) \end{bmatrix} \begin{bmatrix} \delta p \\ \delta p^* \end{bmatrix}$,

(21) $\quad \begin{bmatrix} \delta e \\ \delta r \\ \delta r^* \\ \delta x \end{bmatrix} = \begin{bmatrix} -c & c^* \\ \lambda & 0 \\ 0 & \lambda \\ \lambda & -\lambda \end{bmatrix} \begin{bmatrix} \delta p \\ \delta p^* \end{bmatrix}$,

where $c = (\lambda + \omega)/\theta$ and $c^* = (\lambda + \omega^*)/\theta$ and where $\gamma = \sigma\lambda/\mu$.[6] Equation

---

[6] Under the perfect foresight, the dynamic equations for $\delta e$, $\delta p$, and $\delta p^*$ are

$$\frac{d}{dt}\begin{bmatrix} \delta e \\ \delta p \\ \delta p^* \end{bmatrix} = F \begin{bmatrix} \delta e \\ \delta p \\ \delta p^* \end{bmatrix}, \quad \text{where} \quad F = \begin{bmatrix} 0 & \lambda & -\lambda \\ \pi\mu & -\pi\mu(1 + \gamma) & \pi\mu \\ -\pi^*\mu & \pi^*\mu & -\pi^*\mu(1 + \gamma) \end{bmatrix}.$$

With a regressive mechanism (15), $\delta x = -\theta \delta e - \omega \delta p + \omega^* \delta p^*$. From (12) and (13), $\delta x = \lambda(\delta p - \delta p^*)$. From these equations the expression for $\delta e$ in (21) follows. From (10), (11), and (12), $\delta\dot{p} = \pi\mu[\delta e - (1 + \gamma) \delta p + \delta p^*]$. From (12), (13), and (14), a similar equation for $\delta\dot{p}^*$ is derived. Upon substituting the expression for $\delta e$ in these equations, (20) results.

The three-dimensional dynamic matrix $F$ can be shown to have one unstable eigenvalue for positive $\alpha$, $\lambda$, and $\gamma$, for example, by using the root-locus plots. Note that the two eigenvectors and the corresponding two stable eigenvalues are *nonlinear* functions of these system parameters. An alternate way to regard the consistency conditions is to think of them as defining the conditionally stable two-dimensional subspace for the three-dimensional dynamics, i.e., the space spanned by the two eigenvectors with stable eigenvalues. This conditionally stable subspace depends on system parameters nonlinearly.

(21) gives the values of $e - \bar{e}$, $r - \bar{r}$, $r^* - \bar{r}^*$, and $x$ that clear the money markets at each instant in time. Equation (20) reflects the adjustment processes in the two goods markets, and serves to propel the instantaneous equilibrium through time.

One immediate implication of Eqs. (20) and (21) is that many combinations of $\omega$, $\omega^*$ and $\theta$ yield identical results. Only $c$ and $c^*$ appear in (20) and (21), so changes in $\omega$, $\omega^*$, and $\theta$ that do not alter the values of $c$ and $c^*$ will have no effect upon the outcome. This means, among other things, that consistency can be discussed in terms of $c$ and $c^*$ rather than $\omega$, $\omega^*$, and $\theta$. If $c$ and $c^*$ are chosen to make $x = \dot{e}$, then any combination of $\omega$, $\omega^*$, and $\theta$ that yields these values of $c$ and $c^*$ will make the regressive expectations (15) consistent. In this sense the combinations of $\theta$, $\omega$, and $\omega^*$ are not unique. Moreover, we show later that $c$ and $c^*$ themselves need not be unique.

### The Effects of Monetary Policy

Suppose the home monetary authority purchases bonds, thereby increasing the domestic money supply by $\Delta \bar{m}$. The long-run effects may be calculated from Eqs. (16)–(19):

$$\Delta \bar{e} = \Delta \bar{p} = \Delta \bar{m}, \qquad \Delta \bar{p}^* = \Delta \bar{r} = \Delta \bar{r}^* = \Delta(\bar{e} + \bar{p}^* - \bar{p}) = 0.$$

Money is neutral in the long run, but not during the period of adjustment. The immediate impact of an increase in the domestic money supply can be calculated from Eq. (21)[7]:

$$\Delta e = (1 + c)\,\Delta \bar{m}, \qquad \Delta r = -\lambda\,\Delta \bar{m}, \qquad \Delta r^* = 0,$$
$$\Delta x = \Delta(r - r^*) = -\lambda\,\Delta \bar{m}.$$

An increase in the supply of domestic money forces the domestic interest rate down and creates the expectation of an appreciation of the exchange rate; this raises the demand for home currency and equilibrates that market. If $c$ is positive, then the exchange rate initially overshoots its (new) long-run value and slowly appreciates back over time.

Note the short-run appreciation. This must occur if $c$ and $c^*$ are chosen to make the regressive expectations consistent; the predicted appreciation, which equilibrates the domestic money market, must be realized.

If $c$ is negative but greater than minus one, then the exchange rate initially undershoots its long-run value and must eventually depreciate further.

Undershooting was not possible in Dornbusch's "small country" version of the model; the dynamics were one dimensional.

---

[7] For example, the first row of (21) can be written $e - \bar{e} = -c(p - \bar{p}) + c^*(p^* - \bar{p}^*)$, so $\Delta e - \Delta \bar{e} = -c(\Delta p - \Delta \bar{p}) + c^*(\Delta p^* - \Delta \bar{p}^*)$ or $\Delta e - \Delta \bar{m} = -c(0 - \Delta \bar{m}) + c^*(0 - 0)$, which implies $\Delta e = (1 + c)\,\Delta \bar{m}$. The other relationships are derived in a similar manner.

With the simple autoregressive mechanism, the only way to create an expectation of an appreciation (which is needed to clear the domestic money market) is to have the exchange rate shoot past its long-run value so that $e > \bar{e}$. The two-dimensional dynamics, together with the more inclusive expectations hypothesis, admit a wider range of responses.

The effects of an increase in the foreign money supply are analogous, but they are not necessarily symmetric. The long-run effect is again neutral: a proportionate increase in the foreign price, a proportionate appreciation in the exchange rate, and no change in anything else. However, the immediate effect on the exchange rate is

$$\Delta e = -(1 + c^*) \Delta \bar{m}^*,$$

and $c^*$ need not equal $c$. Put another way, a 1% increase in the domestic money supply has the same effect as a 1% decrease in the foreign money supply in the long run, but in the short run the two policies will have different effects if $c^*$ does not equal $c$.

Clearly, much depends upon the size of $c$ and $c^*$, or equivalently $\theta$, $\omega$, and $\omega^*$. For some values of $c$ and $c^*$, the model will not be stable, and for most values of $c$ and $c^*$ the expectations generated by (15) will not be consistent. Following Dornbusch (1976), Kouri (1976), and Sargent and Wallace (1973), we consider only the values of $c$ and $c^*$ that result in consistent expectations and a stable exchange rate. We shall show that these desirable values of $c$ and $c^*$ are nonlinear functions of the model parameters. They depend in particular on $\alpha = \pi^*/\pi$, $\beta = \lambda\pi/\mu$, and $\gamma = \sigma\lambda/u$. We assume these are all positive to avoid degenerate cases. For example with $\alpha = 0$, the dimension of the dynamics drops by one.

## Stability and Consistency

Stability depends upon the 2 × 2 matrix in Eq. (20). The system is stable if and only if its trace is negative and its determinant is positive. So the stability requirements for $c$ and $c^*$ are

(22) $\quad c + \alpha c^* > -(\alpha + 1)(1 + \gamma) \quad$ (trace condition),

(23) $\quad c + c^* > -2 - \gamma \quad$ (determinant condition).

The consistency requirements are more complicated. Letting $z = [\delta p \;\; \delta p^*]'$, (20) is expressible as $\dot{z} = Az$ and $\delta e = Cz$ where $A$ is the 2 × 2 matrix in (20) and $C$ is the first row of the 4 × 2 matrix in (21). Now differentiate the expression for $\delta e$, and use (20) and (21) to note that

$$\delta \dot{e} = C\dot{z} = CAz.$$

On the other hand, from (15) and (21),
$$\delta x = [\lambda \quad -\lambda]\mathbf{z}.$$
So consistency ($\delta x = \delta \dot{e}$) requires that these two expressions are the same for all $\mathbf{z}$, i.e., consistency requires that $c$ and $c^*$ be chosen to satisfy $CA = [\lambda \quad -\lambda]$, or

(24) $\quad\quad\begin{aligned} c(c + 1 + \gamma) + \alpha c^*(c + 1) &= \beta \\ c(c^* + 1) + \alpha c^*(c^* + 1 + \gamma) &= \beta, \end{aligned}\quad$ (consistency),

where $\alpha = \pi^*/\pi$, $\beta = \lambda/\mu$, and $\gamma = \sigma\lambda/\mu$.

Note that these are nonlinear relations in $c$ and $c^*$. From (24) we see that when $\alpha = 1$, i.e., with $\pi = \pi^*$, all the solutions are of the form $c = c^*$. With $\beta > 0$, there is a unique value which determines the stable dynamics, $c = [-(2 + \gamma) + \{(2 + \gamma)^2 + 8\beta\}^{1/2}]/4$ [conditions (22) and (23) degenerate into $c = c^* > -1 - \gamma/2$ when $\alpha = 1$].

When $\alpha \neq 1$, use the first equation in (24) to eliminate $\alpha c^*$ in the second to obtain a cubic equation for $c$

(25) $\quad\quad\quad\quad\quad\quad D(c) - \alpha N(c) = 0,$

where
$$D(c) = (\gamma c - \beta)\{c^2 + (1 + \gamma)c - \beta\},$$
$$N(c) = (c + 1)[\gamma c^2 + \{(2 + \gamma)\gamma + \beta\}c - \gamma\beta].$$

Knowing a solution for $c$, the corresponding solution for $c^*$ can be determined from the first equation in (24),

(26) $\quad\quad\quad\quad \alpha c^* = -(c + \gamma) + (\beta + \gamma)/(c + 1).$

The stability conditions (22) and (23) can be expressed in terms of $c$ alone. Solving the first equation of (24) for $\alpha c^*$, the trace condition can be expressed in terms of $c$ as
$$c + \alpha c^* = -\gamma + (\beta + \gamma)(c + 1)^{-1} > -1(1 + \gamma)(1 + \alpha)$$
or

(22′) $\quad\quad\quad\quad (\beta + \gamma)/(c + 1) > -1 - (1 + \gamma)\alpha.$

The determinant condition becomes

(23′) $\quad\quad\quad\quad (\beta + \gamma)/(c + 1) > -(\alpha - 1)c - 2\alpha - (\alpha - 1)\gamma.$

A solution of (25) yields a stable dynamic equation (20) if and only if it is also satisfies (22′) and (23′).

We show by an example that there are two solutions of (25) which generate stable dynamics for a particular choice of the system parameters; $\alpha = 11$,

$\beta = 0.1$, and $\gamma = 12$. They are $c = 0.007$, $c^* = 0.001$; $c = -1.092$, $c^* = 12.91$.

We can examine the sensitivity of the solutions with respect to the system parameters by examining how the three solutions of (25) move on the $c$ axis with other choices of the system parameters. However, it suffices to note that it is quite possible that only one or two stable solutions exist. For example with $0 < \alpha < 1$, $\beta = 1$, and $\gamma = 1$, there is a single solution with stable dynamics.

When there are two or more solutions with stable dynamics, dynamic paths of the variables $\delta e$, $\delta p$, and $\delta p^*$ are generally different, although they are all stable.

The reason for nonunique solutions $(c, c^*)$ is easy to see. Although the subspace is unique, the parameters $c$ and $c^*$ which specify the subspace are not unique because $c$ and $c^*$ appear in the expression for the subspace nonlinearly. In other words, the direction perpendicular to the subspace is a nonlinear function of $c$ and $c^*$. Two different sets of $c$ and $c^*$ specify the same direction. (Such nonuniqueness of system properties with respect to system parameters are well known in the literature on "system parameter estimation.")

## *The Inconsistency of Autoregressive Expectations*

Autoregressive expectations cannot be consistent in the two-country model unless $\alpha = 1$. The regressive expectations mechanism (15) is autoregressive if $\omega$ and $\omega^*$ are set equal to zero. But in this case $c = \lambda/\theta = c^*$, and there is no value of $\theta$ that can make these expectations consistent unless $\alpha = 1$.

Autoregressive expectations work in the special case $\alpha = 1$ for the same reason that they work in Dornbusch's "small country" version of the model. If $\alpha = 1$, the dynamics of the model may be represented by a single differential equation instead of the system of differential equations (20).[8] The solution to this differential equation is an exponential function in time, and the "state" variable associated with this equation propels the rest of the endogenous variables through time. So all of the endogenous variables must grow at the same exponential rate. If $\theta$ is set equal to this common rate of growth, then $\dot{e} = -\theta(e - \bar{e})$, and the autoregressive version of (15) will give accurate predictions of exchange rate movements.

---

[8] For example, letting $\omega = \omega^*$ (so that $c = c^*$) we might replace (20) with an equation in $z \equiv \delta p - \delta p^*$; (20) implies $\dot{z} = \pi\mu[\alpha(c + 1 + \gamma) + c + 1]\delta p^* - \pi\mu[\alpha(c + 1) + c + 1 + \gamma]\delta p$ and if $\alpha = 1$, $\dot{z} = \pi\mu(2c + 2 + \gamma)(\delta p^* - \delta p) = -\pi\mu(2c + 2 + \gamma)z$ which is stable for $c > 1 - \gamma/2$. Equation (21) could then be used to express $\delta e$, $\delta r$, $\delta r^*$, and $\delta x$ in terms of $z$, completing the description of the system.

However, we are interested in the case $\alpha \neq 1$. In this case, the model must be represented by a system of equations like (20). The solution for the exchange rate (or any other endogenous variable) will be a linear combination of exponential functions (instead of a single exponential function); it cannot, in general, be represented by an autoregressive process. One might guess that it could be represented by a more general regressive process, one that accounted for both "state" variables. This speculation led the present author to the hypothesis (15), which, as we have seen, can be made consistent through a proper choice of $c$ and $c^*$.

# D | Short-Run Stability of Variational Equations

Dynamic adjustment paths of open economies under alternate macroeconomic policy settings have been examined by a number of writers. [See, for example, Kouri (1976), Turnovsky (1977), or Viotti (1978).] Stability analysis, which occupies a prominent place in many such studies, is mostly confined to analyzing dynamics of the economy in a neighborhood of a long-run (equilibrium or steady-state) state. Analysis of variational dynamics of the economy about a reference path that is not a long-run equilibrium state is rarely carried out. We call the latter type of stability as short-run stability analysis and distinguish it from the more traditional and well-established long-run stability analysis. This chapter presents a tool for short-run stability analysis of varational dynamics. It has a wide applicability to analysis of model in which rates of changes of stocks along reference paths are not necessarily constant along the paths.

Variational variables are governed by linear differential equations. The homogeneous part of a variational equation is of the form

$$d\mathbf{z}/dt = \Phi(t)\mathbf{z}(t),$$

where $\mathbf{z}(t)$ is a state vector of variational variables. We have noted earlier in Section 2.3 that the dynamic matrix $\Phi(t)$ is the matrix of partial derivatives of the nonlinear differential equation, evaluated on the reference time path. For some choices of the reference paths, the dynamic matrix becomes a constant matrix. For other choices, it will be varying with time. For example, if the reference path leads into a long-run equilibrium state in which every endogenous variable remains constant, or only ratios of some endogenous variables growing at the same rate appear in $\Phi$, then $\Phi$ will be constant. When $\Phi(t)$ approaches a constant matrix $\bar{\Phi}$ as time approaches infinity we can decompose $\Phi$ into

(1) $$\Phi(t) = \bar{\Phi} + \Psi(t),$$

where $\Psi(t)$ will vanish as time approaches infinity.

With a constant matrix $\bar{\Phi}$, stability of the solution of the differential equation $\dot{\mathbf{z}} = \bar{\Phi}\mathbf{z}$ is determined by the eigenvalues of $\bar{\Phi}$. Unfortunately, with general time-varying matrix $\Phi(t)$, the real part of all eigenvalues being negative for all $t$ is not sufficient to guarantee asymptotic stability for all solutions. [See, for example, Bellman (1952, p. 43).] For time-varying matrices that approach constant matrices as time approaches infinity, we have a variety of results ensuring boundedness of solutions. One of the most useful is the following: If all eigenvalues of $\bar{\Phi}$ have negative real parts, and if $\Psi(t) \to 0$ as $t \to \infty$, then the solutions of the dynamics with the matrix $\Phi(t)$ of (1) are asymptotically stable. [See Brauer and Nohel (1969, Theorem 4.2).] Furthermore, if the eigenvalues of $\bar{\Phi}$ are distinct, so are the eigenvalues of $\Phi(t)$. [See Bellman (1953, p. 26).]

These theorems ensure stability of variational variables about reference paths which are not necessarily long-run equilibrium states. Beyond these qualitative results, we can bound the effects of $\Psi(t)$ [i.e., deviation of $\Phi(t)$ from its long-run limit $\bar{\Phi}$] on variational variables. Such bounds are often important in assessing the effects of temporary deviations of the government budget from the balanced budget condition or temporary imbalance in the current account, because both the government budget and the current account must be zero in the long-run (stationary, i.e., not growing steady-state) equilibrium state but need not be zero off the long-run equilibrium states. There are several bounds. We describe one that involves cumulative budget deficits or cumulative current account imbalance.

Choose a short-run time interval $\omega$ over which we wish to impose some bounds on the endogenous variable $\mathbf{z}(t)$. We write the solution of the differential equation

$$\dot{\mathbf{z}}(t) = \{\bar{\Phi} + \Psi(t)\}\mathbf{z}(t),$$

where $\bar{\Phi}$ is constant as

$$(2) \qquad \mathbf{z}(t + \omega) = e^{\bar{\Phi}\omega}\mathbf{z}(t) + \int_t^{t+\omega} e^{\bar{\Phi}(t+\omega-s)}\Psi(s)\mathbf{z}(s)\,ds.$$

We use $|\cdot|$ to denote a vector norm and the induced or subordinate matrix norm.[1]

We obtain from (2) the inequality

$$(3) \qquad |\mathbf{z}(t+\omega)| \leq |e^{\bar{\Phi}\omega}\mathbf{z}(t)| + \int_t^{t+\omega} |e^{\bar{\Phi}(t+\omega-s)}|\|\Psi(s)\||\mathbf{z}(s)|\,ds.$$

---

[1] For example, if we take $|\cdot|$ to be the Euclidean norm then the matrix norm is the maximum eigenvalue of $(\bar{\Phi}' + \bar{\Phi})/2$. There are several other such pairs.

## Short-Run Stability of Variational Equations

Now because we assume that all eigenvalues of $\bar{\Phi}$ have negative real parts, we can choose two constants $\sigma$ and $\phi$ such that

$$|e^{\bar{\Phi}t}| \leq \phi e^{-\sigma t}.$$

Using this and defining $u_t = e^{\sigma t}|\mathbf{z}(t)|$, rewrite (3) as

(4) $$u_{t+\omega} \leq \phi \left\{ u_t + \int_t^{t+\omega} |\Psi(s)| u_s\, ds \right\}.$$

Since $u_s$ is nonnegative and so is $|\Psi(s)|$, we preserve the inequality when we write (4) as

$$u_{t+\omega} |\Psi(t+\omega)| \Big/ \left( u_t + \int_t^{t+\omega} |\Psi(s)| u_s\, ds \right).$$

In this form, we can integrate the inequality to produce

$$\ln\left\{ \left( u_t + \int |\Psi(s)| u_s\, ds \right) \Big/ u_t \right\} \leq \phi \int |\Psi(s)|\, ds$$

or

(5) $$u_t + \int_t^{t+\omega} |\Psi(\tau)|\, d\tau \leq u_t \exp \phi \left( \int_t^{t+\omega} |\Psi(s)|\, ds \right).$$

Since the integral is nonnegative, we can combine (4) and (5) as

(5') $$u_{t+\omega} \leq \phi u_t \exp\left( \phi \int_t^{t+\omega} |\Psi(s)|\, ds \right).$$

Therefore, the condition that $\Phi(t)$ does not cumulatively deviate from $\bar{\Phi}$ by more than $\sigma\omega/\phi$,

(6) $$\phi \int_t^{t+\omega} |\Psi(s)|\, ds \leq \sigma\omega,$$

implies that $u_{t+\omega} \leq \phi u_t \exp \sigma\omega$. In the original variable, the inequality can be stated as

(7) $$|\mathbf{z}(t+\omega)| \leq \phi |\mathbf{z}(t)|.$$

If (6) is replaced with

(7') $$\phi \int_t^{t+\omega} |\Psi(s)|\, ds \leq \sigma\omega + \ln(\kappa/\phi),$$

for some $\kappa > 0$, then (7) becomes

(7') $$|\mathbf{z}(t+\omega)| \leq \kappa |\mathbf{z}(t)|.$$

Inequality (7) states that over a prescribed period of duration $\omega$, if $\Phi(t)$ does not deviate from its long-run limit $\bar{\Phi}$ by more than (6), then the norm of the vector $\mathbf{z}(t + \omega)$ does not differ from $|\mathbf{z}(t)|$ by more than $\phi$. Equation (7) or (7′) is a boundedness result that we can use in short-run stability analysis since we can relate the bound we want to the cumulative deviation (6) or (6′).

Incidentally, the fact that a function governed by (4) can be bounded as (5′) is known as Bellman–Gronwall inequality (Brauer and Nohel, 1969).[2]

---

[2] For discrete-time version of the inequality, see Miller (1968).

# E | Calculation of the Transition Matrix

Of several ways to calculate the matrix exponential $e^{At}$, perhaps the most straightforward is to take the inverse Laplace transform of $(sI - A)^{-1}$. We illustrate this procedure for

$$A = \begin{bmatrix} a_{11} & a_{12} \\ a_{21} & a_{22} \end{bmatrix}.$$

Then

$$(sI - A)^{-1} = \begin{bmatrix} s - a_{11} & -a_{12} \\ -a_{21} & s - a_{22} \end{bmatrix}^{-1} = \frac{1}{q(s)} \begin{bmatrix} s - a_{22} & a_{12} \\ a_{21} & s - a_{11} \end{bmatrix},$$

where

$$q(s) = |sI - A|.$$

Suppose $q(s)$ has two distinct roots, i.e.,

$$q(s) = (s + s_1)(s + s_2).$$

Then

$$(e^{At})_{11} = \mathcal{L}^{-1}\left(\frac{s - a_{22}}{q(s)}\right) = \frac{1}{s_2 - s_1}\{-(s_1 + a_{22})e^{-s_1 t} + (s_2 + a_{22})e^{-s_2 t}\},$$

$$(e^{At})_{12} = \frac{a_{12}}{s_2 - s_1}(e^{-s_1 t} - e^{-s_2 t}),$$

$$(e^{At})_{21} = \frac{a_{21}}{s_2 - s_1}(e^{-s_1 t} - e^{-s_2 t}),$$

$$(e^{At})_{22} = \frac{1}{s_2 - s_1}\{-(s_1 + a_{11})e^{-s_1 t} + (s_2 + a_{11})e^{-s_2 t}\}.$$

These formulas are valid even when $s_1$ and $s_2$ are complex conjugate.

# F | Perturbation Analysis of Matrix Exponential Functions

We calculate the matrix exponential function $e^{At}$ for a constant matrix $A$ in terms of its eigenvalues and eigenvectors. This is known as a modal representation. See Takahashi, Rabins, and Auslander (1970), for example. We then examine the modal representation of a perturbed matrix.

The modal representation is based on the following:

### F.1 Fact

If $A$ has $n$ distinct eigenvalues, with right and left eigenvectors $\mathbf{u}_i$ and $\mathbf{v}'_i$ for the eigenvalue $\lambda_i$, then we can express the matrix exponential function as

$$e^{At} = \sum_{i=1}^{n} e^{\lambda_i t} \mathbf{u}_i \mathbf{v}'_i,$$

where we have

$$\mathbf{v}'_i \mathbf{u}_j = 0, \qquad i \neq j.$$

This representation works well only if none of the eigenvalues are too close to each other. Given $\dot{\mathbf{z}} = A\mathbf{z} + B\mathbf{x}$, we can write its time responses due to a nonzero initial condition and instrument variations as

(1) $\qquad \mathbf{z}(t) = \sum_{i=1}^{n} e^{\lambda_i t}(\mathbf{v}'_i \mathbf{z}(0))\mathbf{u}_i \qquad \text{with} \quad \mathbf{x} \equiv 0,$

and

(2) $\qquad \mathbf{z}(t) = \sum_{i=1}^{N} e^{\lambda_i t} \chi_i(t)(\mathbf{v}'_i B)\mathbf{u}_i \qquad \text{for} \quad \mathbf{z}(0) = 0,$

# Perturbation Analysis of Matrix Exponential Functions

where

$$\chi_i(t) = \int_0^t e^{-\lambda_i s} \mathbf{v}'_i B \mathbf{x}(s) \, ds.$$

Equation (1) shows that if $\mathbf{z}(0)$ is orthogonal to $\mathbf{v}_i$ then $e^{\lambda_i t}$ does not appear in $\mathbf{z}(t)$. From (2) we note that if $B$ is orthogonal to $\mathbf{v}_i$, i.e., if $\mathbf{v}_i B$ is zero, then the dynamic response due to $\lambda_i$ does not contribute to $\mathbf{z}(t)$.

We next derive the expressions for these same two effects when the matrix $A$ is slightly perturbed to become $A + \zeta C$. The eigenvalues of the perturbed matrix, $A + \zeta C$, change from $\lambda_i$ to $\lambda_i + \zeta \mu_i$, and the eigenvectors change from $\mathbf{u}_i$ to $\mathbf{u}_i + \zeta \xi_i$, and $\mathbf{v}'_i$ to $\mathbf{v}'_i + \zeta \eta'_i$, where $\xi_i$ is some linear combination of $\mathbf{u}_j$, and $\eta_i$ is of $\mathbf{v}'_j$, $j \neq i$. To derive these changes, multiply the definitional equation of the $i$th eigenvalue from the left by $\mathbf{v}'_i$

$$\mathbf{v}'_i (A + \zeta C)(\mathbf{u}_i + \zeta \xi_i) = (\lambda_i + \zeta \mu_i) \mathbf{v}'_i (\mathbf{u}_i + \zeta \xi_i).$$

The resulting equation is solved for the perturbed eigenvalue as

$$\mu_i = \mathbf{v}'_i C \mathbf{u}_i / (\mathbf{v}'_i \mathbf{u}_i) + O(\zeta),$$

where we use the fact that $\mathbf{v}'_i \mathbf{u}_j = 0$, $i \neq j$.

Now solve the eigenvalue relation for the perturbed eigenvector from

$$(A + \zeta C)(\mathbf{u}_i + \zeta \xi_i) = (\lambda_i + \zeta \mu_i)(\mathbf{u}_i + \zeta \xi_i)$$

by expanding $\xi_i$ as $\sum_{j \neq i} t_{ji} \mathbf{u}_j$ and multiplying it from the left by $\mathbf{v}'_i$ to obtain the coefficient $t_{ji}$. The result is the expression

$$\xi_i = \sum_{j \neq i} \frac{\beta_{ji} \mathbf{u}_j}{\{(\lambda_i - \lambda_j) \mathbf{v}'_j \mathbf{u}_j\}},$$

where

$$\beta_{ji} = \mathbf{v}'_j C \mathbf{u}_i.$$

Similarly, we obtain the expression for the perturbation of the left eigenvector as

$$\eta'_i = \sum_{j \neq i} \frac{\beta_{ij} \mathbf{v}'_j}{(\lambda_i - \lambda_j) \mathbf{v}'_j \mathbf{u}_j}.$$

See Wilkinson (1968, Chapter 2) for additional details.

With these perturbed eigenvalues and eigenvectors, (1) now becomes

(1') $$\mathbf{z}(t) = \sum_i e^{(\lambda_i + \zeta \mu_i)t} [\mathbf{v}'_i \mathbf{z}(0) \mathbf{u}_i + \zeta \{\eta'_i \mathbf{z}(0) \mathbf{u}_i + \mathbf{v}'_i \mathbf{z}(0) \xi_i\}],$$

and (2) is changed into

(2') $$\mathbf{z}(t) = \sum_i e^{(\lambda_i + \zeta\mu_i)t}[\chi_i(t)\mathbf{u}_i + \{\kappa_i \mathbf{u}_i + \chi_i(t)\boldsymbol{\xi}_i\}],$$

where

$$\kappa_i = \int_0^t e^{-(\lambda_i + \zeta\mu_i)s}(\boldsymbol{\eta}_i' B + \mathbf{v}_i' D)\mathbf{x}(s)\,ds.$$

Comparing (1') with (1), the perturbed system adds

(3) $$\sum_i e^{\lambda_i t}[\{(e^{\zeta\mu_i t} - 1)\mathbf{v}_i' + \zeta\boldsymbol{\eta}_i'\}\mathbf{z}(0)\mathbf{u}_i + \zeta\mathbf{v}_i'\mathbf{z}(0)\boldsymbol{\xi}_i]$$

to the response of the basic system (1) due to $\mathbf{z}(0)$. Similarly from (2') and (2), the term

(4) $$\sum_i e^{\lambda_i t}[\{(e^{\zeta\mu_i t} - 1)\chi_i(t) + \kappa_i\}\mathbf{u}_i + \chi_i(t)\boldsymbol{\xi}_i]$$

is added to the response due to the instrument.

Next, we consider the modal representation of the matrix $\Phi$

$$\begin{bmatrix} A & 0 \\ 0 & A^* \end{bmatrix}$$

and its perturbed version

$$\begin{bmatrix} A & \zeta A_1 \\ \zeta A_2 & A^* \end{bmatrix},$$

where $\zeta$ is a small perturbation parameter.

Assume that $\Phi$ is a stable constant matrix. Let $\lambda_i$, $i = 1, \ldots, n$, be distinct eigenvalues of the dynamic matrix $A$ with right and left eigenvectors $\mathbf{u}_i$ and $\mathbf{v}_i'$. Similarly, let $\lambda_j^*$, $j = 1, \ldots, n^*$, be distinct eigenvalues of $A^*$ with right and left eigenvectors of $\mathbf{u}_i^*$ and $\mathbf{v}_i^{*\prime}$. We assume that the eigenvalues of $A$ and $A^*$ are also distinct.[1] Then the dynamic matrix $\Phi$ with the zero perturbation parameter has eigenvalues $\lambda_i$, $i = 1, \ldots, n$, $\lambda_j^*$, $j = 1, \ldots, n^*$, with the right and left eigenvectors $\begin{bmatrix}\mathbf{u}_i\\0\end{bmatrix}$ and $[\mathbf{v}_i', 0]$, $i = 1, \ldots, n$, and $\begin{bmatrix}0\\\mathbf{u}_j^*\end{bmatrix}$, $[0, \mathbf{v}_j^{*\prime}]$, $j = 1, \ldots, n^*$. The matrix $C$ is now

$$\begin{bmatrix} 0 & A_1 \\ A_2 & 0 \end{bmatrix}.$$

---

[1] Our applications satisfy this condition. We show that the dynamics for the averages and the differences have distinct eigenvalues of their own.

Then the eigenvalue $\lambda_i$ and $\lambda_j^*$ remain the same, ignoring terms of the order $\zeta^2$ and higher, because

$$[\mathbf{v}_i' \;\; 0]\begin{bmatrix} 0 & A_1 \\ A_2 & 0 \end{bmatrix}\begin{bmatrix} \mathbf{u}_i \\ 0 \end{bmatrix} \quad \text{and} \quad [0 \;\; \mathbf{v}_i^{*\prime}]\begin{bmatrix} 0 & A_1 \\ A_2 & 0 \end{bmatrix}\begin{bmatrix} 0 \\ \mathbf{u}_i^* \end{bmatrix}$$

are both zero.

The perturbed eigenvectors are different, however. To the first order in $\zeta$, they are given by

$$\begin{bmatrix} \mathbf{u}_i \\ \boldsymbol{\xi}_i \end{bmatrix}, [\mathbf{v}_i', \boldsymbol{\eta}_i'], i = 1, \ldots, n \quad \text{and} \quad \begin{bmatrix} \boldsymbol{\xi}_i^* \\ \mathbf{u}_i^* \end{bmatrix}, [\boldsymbol{\eta}_j^{*\prime} \;\; \mathbf{v}_j^{*\prime}],$$

$j = 1, \ldots, n^*$, where from the definitional relations

$$\Phi\begin{pmatrix} \mathbf{u}_i \\ \boldsymbol{\xi}_i \end{pmatrix} = \lambda_i \begin{pmatrix} \mathbf{u}_i \\ \boldsymbol{\xi}_i \end{pmatrix} \quad \text{and} \quad \Phi\begin{bmatrix} \boldsymbol{\xi}_i^* \\ \mathbf{u}_i^* \end{bmatrix} = \lambda_j^* \begin{bmatrix} \boldsymbol{\xi}_j^* \\ \mathbf{u}_j^* \end{bmatrix},$$

we can express $\boldsymbol{\xi}_i$ and $\boldsymbol{\xi}_j^*$ as

(5) $$\boldsymbol{\xi}_i = \zeta(\lambda_i I - A^*)^{-1} A_2 \mathbf{u}_i, \quad i = 1, \ldots, n,$$

and

$$\boldsymbol{\xi}_j^* = \zeta(\lambda_j^* I - A)^{-1} A_1 \mathbf{u}_j^*, \quad j = 1, \ldots, n^*.$$

This indicated inverse exists because $\lambda_i \neq \lambda_j^*$ for all $i$ and $j$ by assumption. Similarly, from the definitional relation for the left eigenvectors we deduce

(6) $$\begin{aligned} \boldsymbol{\eta}_i' &= \zeta \mathbf{v}_i' A_1 (\lambda_i I - A^*)^{-1}, & i &= 1, \ldots, n, \\ \boldsymbol{\eta}_j^{*\prime} &= \zeta \mathbf{v}_j^{*\prime} A_2 (\lambda_j^* I - A)^{-1}, & j &= 1, \ldots, n^*. \end{aligned}$$

From these relations, the spectral representation of the perturbed dynamic system can be given as

(7) $$\begin{aligned} e^{\Phi t} &= \sum_{i=1}^{n} e^{\lambda_i t} \begin{bmatrix} \mathbf{u}_i \\ \boldsymbol{\xi}_i \end{bmatrix} [\mathbf{v}_i' \;\; \boldsymbol{\eta}_i'] + \sum_{j=1}^{n^*} e^{\lambda_j^* t} \begin{bmatrix} \boldsymbol{\xi}_j^* \\ \mathbf{u}_j^* \end{bmatrix} [\boldsymbol{\eta}_j^{*\prime} \;\; \mathbf{v}_j^{*\prime}] \\ &\simeq \sum_{i=1}^{n} e^{\lambda_i t} \begin{bmatrix} \mathbf{u}_i \\ 0 \end{bmatrix} [\mathbf{v}_i' \;\; 0] + \sum_{j=1}^{n^*} e^{\lambda_j^* t} \begin{bmatrix} 0 \\ \mathbf{u}_j^* \end{bmatrix} [0 \;\; \mathbf{v}_j^{*\prime}] \\ &+ \sum_{i=1}^{n} e^{\lambda_i t} \left\{ \begin{bmatrix} \mathbf{u}_i \\ 0 \end{bmatrix} [0 \;\; \boldsymbol{\eta}_i'] + \begin{bmatrix} 0 \\ \boldsymbol{\xi}_i \end{bmatrix} [\mathbf{v}_i' \;\; 0] \right\} \\ &+ \sum_{j=1}^{n^*} e^{\lambda_j^* t} \left\{ \begin{bmatrix} 0 \\ \mathbf{u}_j^* \end{bmatrix} [\boldsymbol{\eta}_j^{*\prime} \;\; 0] + \begin{bmatrix} \boldsymbol{\xi}_j^* \\ 0 \end{bmatrix} [0 \;\; \mathbf{v}_j^{*\prime}] \right\} + o(\zeta). \end{aligned}$$

## F.2 Effects of Initial Displacements

When the domestic and foreign economic states are shifted off the reference time path at time 0, the subsequent behavior of the economies is given by

$$(8) \quad \mathbf{z}(t) = \sum_{i=1}^{n} e^{\lambda_i t}\{\mathbf{v}'_i\mathbf{z}(0) + \boldsymbol{\eta}'_i\mathbf{z}^*(0)\}\mathbf{u}_i + \sum_{j=1}^{n^*} e^{\lambda_j^* t}(\mathbf{v}_j^{*\prime}\mathbf{z}^*(0))\boldsymbol{\xi}_j^*$$

and

$$(9) \quad \mathbf{z}^*(t) = \sum_{j=1}^{n^*} e^{\lambda_j^* t}\{\mathbf{v}_j^{*\prime}\mathbf{z}^*(0) + \boldsymbol{\eta}_j^{*\prime}\mathbf{z}(0)\}\mathbf{u}_j^* + \sum_{i=1}^{n} e^{\lambda_i t}(\mathbf{v}'_i\mathbf{z}(0))\boldsymbol{\xi}_i.$$

Comparing (8) with (1), we see that the first term in the braces represents its own effect, while in (8) the second term in the braces expresses the effects of $\mathbf{z}^*(0)$ on $\mathbf{z}(t)$. In (9) the second term in the braces represents the effects of $\mathbf{z}(0)$ on $\mathbf{z}^*(t)$.

Equations (8) and (9) can be put into a form which reveals dynamic interactions between the two countries more clearly. For this, define coefficients $\kappa_{ij}$ and $\kappa_{ji}^*$ by $\kappa_{ij} = \mathbf{v}'_i A_1 \mathbf{u}_j^*$ and $\kappa_{ji}^* = \mathbf{v}_j^{*\prime} A_2 \mathbf{u}_i$, $i = 1, \ldots, n, j = 1, \ldots, n^*$. Because $A^*$ can be written as $\sum \lambda_j^* \mathbf{u}_j^* \mathbf{v}_j^{*\prime}$ and the identity matrix as $I = \sum_j \mathbf{u}_j^* \mathbf{v}_j^{*\prime}$, the expression $(\lambda_i I - A^*)^{-1}$ is equal to $\sum_j (\lambda_i - \lambda_j^*)^{-1}\mathbf{u}_j^*\mathbf{v}_j^{*\prime}$ because none of the eigenvalues of $A$ and $A^*$ overlap by our assumption. Substituting these relations into the definition, we can write $\boldsymbol{\xi}_i$ as

$$\boldsymbol{\xi}_i = \zeta \sum_j (\lambda_i - \lambda_j^*)^{-1}\kappa_{ji}^*\mathbf{u}_j^*.$$

Similarly, we can write

$$\boldsymbol{\xi}_j^* = \zeta \sum_j (\lambda_j^* - \lambda_i)^{-1}\kappa_{ij}\mathbf{u}_i.$$

Express $\boldsymbol{\eta}'_i$ and $\boldsymbol{\eta}_j^{*\prime}$ in an analogous manner. Then (8) and (9) become

(8)

$$\mathbf{z}(t) = \sum_{i=1}^{n} e^{\lambda_i t}(\mathbf{v}'_i\mathbf{z}(0))\mathbf{u}_i + \zeta \sum_j \left\{ \sum_j (\lambda_i - \lambda_j^*)^{-1}(e^{\lambda_i t} - e^{\lambda_j^* t})\kappa_{ij}(\mathbf{v}_j^{*\prime}\mathbf{z}^*(0)) \right\}\mathbf{u}_i + o(\zeta),$$

and

(9')

$$\mathbf{z}^*(t) = \sum_{j=1}^{n^*} e^{\lambda_j^* t}(\mathbf{v}_j^{*\prime}\mathbf{z}^*(0))\mathbf{u}_j^* + \zeta \sum_j \left\{ \sum_i (\lambda_j^* - \lambda_i)^{-1}(e^{\lambda_j^* t} - e^{\lambda_i t})\kappa_{ji}^*(\mathbf{v}'_i\mathbf{z}(0)) \right\}\mathbf{u}_j^* + o(\zeta).$$

# Perturbation Analysis of Matrix Exponential Functions

The coefficients $\kappa_{ij}$ and $\kappa_{ji}^*$ represents the "strength" of interdependence or dynamic couplings between the two countries. For example, if only the foreign economy experiences a sudden shift, then $z(0) = 0$, $z^*(0) \neq 0$. The nonzero foreign initial condition's effect on $z(t)$ is captured by the second term in (8′). For small $t$, it is approximately equal to $t\zeta \sum_i \{v_1' A_1 z^*(0)\} u_i$.

## F.3  Instrument Spill-Over Effects

More important than the initial displacement effects are the instrument spill-over effects for policy makers. Suppose that $x$ is scalar. Using Fact in Section F.1, we can write (2) as

$$(10) \quad z(t) = \sum_i e^{\lambda_i t}(v_i' B)\chi_i(t) u_i + \zeta \sum_i \sum_j (\lambda_i - \lambda_j^*)^{-1} \kappa_{ij}(v_j^{*\prime} B^*)$$
$$\times \{e^{\lambda_i t}\chi_i(t) - e^{\lambda_j^* t}\chi_j^*(t)\} u_i,$$

and

$$(11) \quad z^*(t) = \sum_j e^{\lambda_j^* t}(v_j^{*\prime} B^*)\chi_j^*(t) u_j^* + \zeta \sum_j \sum_i (\lambda_j^* - \lambda_i)^{-1} \kappa_{ji}^*(v_i' B)$$
$$\times \{e^{\lambda_j^* t}\chi_j^*(t) - e^{\lambda_i t}\chi_i(t)\} u_j^*,$$

where

$$\chi_i(t) = \int_0^t e^{-\lambda_i \tau} x(\tau)\, d\tau \quad \text{and} \quad \chi_j^*(t) = \int_0^t e^{-\lambda_j^* \tau} x(\tau)\, d\tau,$$

where we use the relation

$$\eta_i' B^* = \zeta \sum_j (\lambda_i - \lambda_j^*)^{-1} \kappa_{ij}(v_j^{*\prime} B^*).$$

If there are no impact effects of $x$ on the foreign economy, then $B^*$ is zero. Comparing (10) with (2), we see then the instrument $x$ affects $z(t)$ by the first term in (10) which is the same as the case of the closed economy if $B^*$ is zero. The foreign economy is affected by $x$ also even if $B^*$ is zero. This spill over of the effects of the instrument $x$ to the foreign economy is shown by the second term in (11).

# References

Aliber, R. Z. (1976). Equilibrium and Disequilibrium in the Internal Money Market, *Weltwirtschaftliches Arch.* **112**, 78–89.
Allen, P. R. (1973). A Portfolio Approach to International Capital Flows. *JIE* **3**, 135–160.
Aoki, M. (1976). "Optimal Control and System Theory in Dynamic Economic Analysis." Amer. Elsevier, New York.
Aoki, M. (1977). A Note on the Stability of the Interaction of Monetary Policies, *J. Intl. Econ.* **6**, 81–94.
Aoki, M. (1978). Conditions for Short-Run Stability of a Small Open Economy under Flexible Exchange Rates, *Economics Letters* **1**, 157–162 (1978).
Aoki, M. (1980). Short-Run Asset and the Real Sector Dynamics of a Small Open Economy under Flexible Exchange Rates. Presented at the Vienna Conf. on Flexible Exchange Rates, Vienna, March 1978, in H. Frisch and G. Schwödiauer, (eds.), "The Economics of Flexible Exchange Rates." Supplement to *Kredit und Kapital* **6**, 50–80, Duncker and Humbolt, Berlin.
Aoki, M. (1979). Perturbation and Robustness Analysis of a Closed Macroeconomic Model. *J. Econ. Dyn. & Control* **1**, 3–37.
Aoki, M. (1980a). Note on Comparative Dynamic Analysis, *Econometrica* **48**, 1319–1325.
Aoki, M. (1980b). The Role of Fiscal Policy in a Financially Disaggregated Macroeconomic Model: A Comment. *J. Mon. Credit and Banking* **12**, 552–556.
Aoki, M. (1980c). "Stability of a Two-Country Model of the World with Flexible Exchange Rates under a Key Currency Regime." Presented at 4th World Congress of the Econometric Society, Aix-en-Provence, France.
Aoki, M. (1980d). "How Much Do Structural Differences Matter?: A Method for Comparative Dynamic Analysis." National Bureau of Economic Research Summer Institute Paper, No. 80-2.
Aoki, M. (unpublished). "Distributional Effects of Fiscal Policies in a Three-Country Model of the World under Flexible Exchange Rates."
Aoki, M., and M. B. Canzoneri (1978a). Macroeconomic Policy in a Dynamic Two-Country Model. *Ann. Econ. and Social Measurem.* **6/5**, 631–650.
Aoki, M., and M. Canzoneri (1978b). Sufficient Conditions for Control of Target Variables and Assignment of Instruments in Dynamic Macroeconomic Models. *Intl. Econ. Rev.* **20**, 605–616.
Aoki, M., and M. Canzoneri (1979a). "The Short-Run Response of a Small Open Economy to an Oil Price Increase." Presented at Control and Decision Conference, *IEEE*, Ft. Lauderdale, Florida.

Aoki, M., and M. B. Canzoneri (unpublished, 1979b). "Exchange Rate Dynamics and the Consistency of Regressive Expectations Mechanisms."
Argy, V., and J. Salop (1979). "Price and Output Effects of Monetary and Fiscal Expansion in a Two-Country World under Flexible Exchange Rates." IMF DM/79/33, May.
Bellman, R. (1953). "Stability Theory of Differential Equations." McGraw-Hill, New York.
Bender, M., and S. A. Orszag (1978). "Advanced Mathematical Methods for Scientists and Engineers." McGraw-Hill, New York.
Bigman, D., and T. Taya, (eds.). (1980). "The Functioning of Floating Exchange Rates: Theory, Evidence, and Policy Implications." Ballinger Publishing Company, Cambridge, Massachusetts.
Bilson, F. O. (1978). A Dynamic Model of Devaluation, *Can. J. Econ.*, **11**, (May), 194–209.
Black, S. W. (1977). "Floating Exchange Rates and National Economic Policy." Yale Univ. Press, New Haven, Connecticut.
Black, S. W. (1978). Policy Responses to Major Disturbances of the 1970s and Their Transmission through International Goods and Capital Markets. *Weltwirtschaftliches Archiv* **114**, 614–641.
Boyer, R. S. (1978). Financial Policies in an Open Economy, *Economica* **45**, (February), 39–57.
Branson, W. H. (1975). Monetarist and Keynesian Model of the Transmission of Inflation. *Amer. Econ. Rev.* **65**, (May), 115–119.
Branson, W. H. (1976a). "Asset Markets and Relative Prices in Exchange Rate Determination," Seminar Paper No. 66, Inst. for International Econ. Stud., Univ., Stockholm, December.
Branson, W. H. (1976b). Portfolio Equilibrium and Monetary Policy with Foreign and Nontraded Assets, pp. 421–250, in E. Claassen and P. Salin (eds.), "Recent Issues in International Monetary Economics, North-Holland Publ., Amsterdam.
Branson, W. H. (1980). Lecture note. Economics 503, Princeton Univ., December.
Branson, W. H., and J. Myhrman (1976). Inflation in Open Economies—Supply-Determined Versus Demand-Determined Models, *European Economic Review* **7** 15–34.
Branson, W. H., and J. J. Rotenberg (1980). International Adjustment with Wage Rigidity, *European Econ. Rev.*, **13**, pp. 309–332.
Brauer, F., and J. A. Nohel (1969). "Qualitative Theory of Ordinary Differential Equations." Benjamin, New York.
Brissimis, S. (1976). Multiplier Effects for Higher Than First Order Linear Dynamic Econometric Models, *Econometrica* **44**, 593–595.
Brock, W. A. (1975). A Simple Perfect Foresight Monetary Model, *J. Monetary Econ.* **1**, 133–150.
Brockett, R. W. (1970). "Finite Dimensional Linear Systems." Wiley, New York.
Brunner, K., and A. H. Meltzer (eds.), (1977). "Stabilization of the Domestic and International Economy." **5**, Carnegie-Rochester Conference Series, North-Holland Publ., Amsterdam.
Bruno, M., and J. Sachs (1979). "Macroeconomic Adjustment with Import Price Shocks: Real and Monetary Aspects," Seminar Paper No. 118, Inst. Int'l. Econ. Studies, February, Stockholm, Sweden.
Buiter, W. H., and M. Gersovits (1979). "Issues in Controllability and the Theory of Economic Policy," forthcoming in *J. Public Econ.*
Calmfors, L., and S. Viotti (1979). "Wage Indexation and Macroeconomic Stability in the Open Economy," IIES Seminar Paper No. 127.
Calvo, G. A., and C. A. Rodriguez (1977). A Model of Exchange Rate Determination Under Currency Substitution and Rational Expectations, *JPE* **85**, No. 3, 617–625.
Casas, F. R. (1975). Efficient Macroeconomic Stabilization Policies Under Floating Exchange Rates, *IER* **16**, No. 3, (October), 682–698.
Clark, P., and S. Kwack (1976). "Asset Markets and Interest Rate Determination in the Multi-

County Model," International Finance Discussion Papers, No. 94, Board of Governors Federal Reserve System, December.
Coddington, E. A., and N. Levinson (1955). "Theory of Ordinary Differential Equations." McGraw-Hill, New York.
Cohen, D., and J. S. McMenamin (1978). The Role of Fiscal Policy in a Financially Disaggregated Macroeconomic Model, *JMCB* **10**, August, 322–336.
Cooper, R. N. (1968), "The Economics of Interdependence Economic Policy in the Atlantic Countries." McGraw-Hill, New York.
Cooper, R. N. (1969). Macroeconomic Policy Adjustment in Interdependent Economies, *QJE* **83**, No. 1, February, 1–24.
Cooper, R. N. (1974). "Economic Mobility and National Economic Policy," Wicksell Lecture 1973, Almquist & Wicksell, Stockholm, Sweden.
Cruz, J. B., Jr. (ed.), (1973). "System Sensitivity Analysis." Dowden, Hutchinson & Ross, Inc., Stroudsburg, Pennsylvannia.
Deardorf, A. V., and R. M. Stern (1978). What Have We Learned from Linked Econometric Models? A Comparison of Fiscal-Policy Simulations, *Banca Nazionale del Lavoro Quarterly Review*, 415–432.
Dornbush, R. (1971). Notes on Growth and the Balance of Payments, *Can. J. Econ.* **4**, 389–395.
Dornbush, R. (1975). A Portfolio Balance Model of the Open Economy *JME* **1**, 3–20.
Dornbusch, R. (1976). The Theory of Flexible Exchange Rate Regimes and Macroeconomic Policy, *Scan. J. Econ.*, **78**, 255–275.
Dornbush, R. (1976a). Capital Mobility, Flexible Exchange Rates and Macroeconomic Equilibrium, Chapter 9 in E. Claassen and P. Salin (eds.), "Recent Issues in International Monetary Economics, No. **17**, 261–278. North-Holland Publ., Amsterdam.
Dornbusch, R. (1976b). "Expectations and Exchange Rate Dynamics," *J.P.E.* **84**, (December), No. 6, 1161–1176.
Dornbusch, R., and P. Krugman (1976). Flexible Exchange Rates in the Short-Run, *Brookings Papers on Econ. Act.* **3**, 537–575.
Eaton, J. (1976). "Four Essays in the Theory of Uncertainty and Portfolio Choice," Ph.D. Dissertation, Yale.
Eichengreen, B. J. (1979). "Protection, Real Wage Resistance and Employment: An Analysis of Some Proposals of the Cambridge Economic Policy Group," No. 150, Intl. Finance Discussion Paper, Board of Governors.
Evans, W. R. (1953). "Control System Dynamics." McGraw-Hill, New York.
Fair, R. C. (1979). A Model of the Balance of Payments, *J. Intl. Economics* **9**, 25–46.
Fair, R. C. (1980). Estimating the Uncertainty of Policy Effects in Nonlinear Models, *Econometrica* **48**, 1381–1391.
Falb, P. L., and W. A. Wolovich (1967). Decoupling in the Designed Synthesis of Multivariable Control Systems, *IEEE Trans. Ant. Cont.* **AC-12**, 651–659.
Fischer, S. (1977). Wage Indexation and Macroeconomic Stability, in K. Brunner and A. Meltzer (eds.), "Stabilization of the Domestic and International Economy." North-Holland Publ., Amsterdam.
Fleming, J. M. (1962). Domestic Financial Policies Under Fixed and Under Floating Exchange Rates, *IMF Staff Papers*, **2**, 369–379.
Flood, R. (1976). Asset Trading, Exchange Rate Determination and Exchange Rate Dynamics," presented at SSRC-Ford Foundation Conference on "Macroeconomic Policy and Adjustment in Open Economies," Ware, England.
Flood, R. P. (1977). Growth, Prices in the Balance of Payments, *Can. J. Econ.*, **10**, 193–207.
Frankel, J. A. (1979). On the Mark: A Theory of Floating Exchange Rates Based on Real Interest Rate Differential, *AER* **69**, 610–622.

Frankel, J. A. (1980). "A Synthesis of the Monetary and Portfolio-Balance Approaches to Exchange Rate Determination." Presented at the World Congress of the Econometric Society, Aix-en-Provence, France, September.

Frenkel, J. A., and H. G. Johnson (1978). "The Economics of Exchange Rates." Addison-Wesley, Reading, Massachusetts.

Futia, C. A. (1981). "Rational Expectations in Linear Stationary Models," *Econometrica* **49**, 171–192.

Gertler, M. (1979a). Imperfect Price Adjustment and the Optimal Assignment of Monetary and Fiscal Policies, *J. Econ. Dynamics and Control*, **1**, 305–320.

Gertler, M. (1979b). Money, Prices and Inflation in Macroeconomic Models with Rational Inflationary Expectations, *JET*, **21**, 222–234.

Girton, C., and D. Henderson (1977). Central Bank Operations in Foreign and Domestic Assets under Fixed and Flexible Exchange Rates, in Peter B. Clark, Dennis E. Logue, Richard James Sweeney (eds.), "The Effects of Exchange Rate Adjustments." U.S. Govt. Printing Press, Washington, D.C.

Girton, L., and D. Henderson (1973). "A Two-Country Model of Financial Capital Movements as Stock Adjustments with Emphasis on the Effects of Central Bank Policy," Intl. Finance Discussion Papers No. 24.

Golub, G. H., and J. H. Wilkinson (1976). Ill-conditioned Eigensystems and the Computation of Jordan Canonical Form, *SIAM Review* **18**, 578–618.

Gordon, R. J. (1972). Wage-price Controls and the Shifting Phillips Curve, *Brookings Papers on Econ. Act.* **3**, No. 2, 385–421.

Gordon, R. J. (1976). Recent Developments in the Theory of Inflation and Unemployment, *J. Mon. Econ.* **2**, (April), 185–219.

Gordon, R. J., and J. Pelkmans (1979). "Challenges to Interdependent Economies: The Industrial West in the Coming Decade," McGraw-Hill, New York.

Grassman, S. (1973). A Fundamental Symmetry in International Payment Patterns, *J. Inst. Econ.*, **3**, 105–116.

De Grauwe, P. (1975). The Interaction of Monetary Policies in a Group of European Countries, *J. Intl. Economics* **5**, 207–228.

Gray, J. A. (1976). Wage Indexation: A Macroeconomic Approach, *J. Monetary Econ.* **2**, No. 2, 221–235.

Hamada, K., and M. Sakurai (1978). International Transmission of Stagflation Under Fixed and Flexible Exchange Rates, *JPE* **86**, (October), 877–895.

Hanson, J. A. (1971). "Growth in Open Economies." Lecture Notes in Operations Research and Mathematical Systems, Springer-Verlag, Berlin and New York.

Helliwell, J. (1979). "Policy Modeling of Foreign Exchange Rates," Seminar Paper No. 123, IIE, July, Univ. Stockholm, Sweden.

Henderson, D. W. (1977). Macroeconomic Theory: Modelling the Interdependence of National Money and Capital Markets, *AER* **67**, No. 1, (February), 190–199.

Henderson, D. W. (1978a). Fiscal Policy in Closed and Open Economies: A Comment, in K. Brunner and A. H. Meltzer (eds.), "Public Policies in Open Economy." No. 9, North-Holland Publ., Amsterdam.

Henderson, D. W. (1978b). "The Dynamic Effects of Exchange Market Intervention Policy: Two Extreme Views and a Synthesis," presented at the conference on the economics of flexible exchange rates, Inst. Advanced Stud., Vienna, Austria, March.

Henderson, D. W., and T. J. Sargent (1973). Monetary and Fiscal Policy in a Two Sector Aggregative Models, *AER* **63**, (June), 345–365.

Hernandez-Cata, E., Howe, H., Kwack, Y., Stevens, G., Berner, R., and Clark, P. P. "Monetary Policy Under Alternative Exchange Rate Regimes: Simulations with a Multiple Country Model," No. 130, International Finance Discussion Paper, February.

Hickman, B. G., and S. Schleifer (1978). Interdependence of National Economies and the Synchronization of Economic Fluctuations: Evidence from the Link Project, *Welt. Archiv*, **114**: 4, 642–708.

Hirsch, M. W., and S. Smale (1974). "Differential Equations, Dynamical Systems and Linear Algebras." Academic Press, New York.

Hodgeman, D. R. (1976). Coordination of European Macroeconomic Policies, Chapter 13 in R. I. McKinnon (ed.), "Money and Finance in Economic Growth and Development," Dekker, New York.

Householder, A. S. (1964). *The Theory of Matrices in Numerical Analysis*, (Blaisdell), Boston, Massachusetts.

Howe, H. *et al.* (1979). "Assessing International Interdependence With a Multi-Country Model," International Finance Discussion Paper, No. 138, April.

Ingram, J. C. (1973). Expectations and Floating Exchange Rates, *Welt. Archiv.*, **114**: 3, 422–447.

Isard, P. (1978). "Exchange-Rate Determination: A Survey of Popular Views and Recent Models," Princeton Studies in Intl. Finance No. 42, Intl. Finance Section, Princeton Univ.

Johnson, H. (1972). "Further Essays in Monetary Economics." Allen and Unwin, London.

Johnson, O., and J. Salop (1980). Distributional Aspects of Stabilization Programs in Developing Countries, *IMF Staff Papers* **27**, 1–23.

Katseli-Papaefstratiou, L., and N. P. Marion (1980). "Adjustment to Variations in Imported Input Prices: The Role of Economic Structure," Nat. Bureau of Econ. Research Working Paper No. 501, July.

Knight, M. D., and C. R. Wymer (1978). A Macroeconomic Model of the United Kingdom, *IMF Staff Papers* **25**, No. 4, December, 742–778.

Kouri, P. J. K. (1976a). The Exchange Rate and the Balance of Payments in the Short Run and in the Long Run: A Monetary Approach, *Scan. J. Econ.* **78**, No. 2, 280–304.

Kouri, P. J. K. (1976b). "International Investment and Interest Rate Linkages Under Flexible Exchange Rates," Memorandum No. 201, Center for Research in Economic Growth, Standord Univ., June.

Kouri, P. J. K., and J. B. de Macedo (1978). Exchange Rates and the International Adjustment Process, *Brookings Papers on Econ. Act.* **1**, 111–150.

Krugman, P. (1979). A Model of Balance-of-Payments Crisis, *J.M.C.B.* **11**, 311–325.

Krugman, P. (1980). "Oil and the Dollar," National Bureau of the Econ. Research Working Paper, June.

Kudo, K. (1978). International Capital Transfer, Supply of Money and Exchange Rate Regime, (in Japanese) *Keizaigaku Ronshu* **44**, July, 45–62.

Lindbeck, A. (1977). "Economic Dependence and Interdependence in the Industrialized World," Seminar Paper No. 83, IIE, June.

Lindbeck, A. (1978). "Imported and Structural Inflation and Aggregate Demand: The Scandinavian Model Reconstructed," Seminar Paper No. 95, IIE, February.

Lindbeck, A. (ed.), (1979). "Inflation and Employment in Open Economies." North Holland, Publ., Amsterdam.

Livesey, D. A. (1980). "Stabilization Policy: A View from the Complex Plane," CARESS Working Paper, No. 80–09, University of Pennsylvania.

McGrath, B. (1977). Implications of the Government Budget Constraint, *J.M.C.B.* **9**, 304–315.

Marston, R. C. (1980). "Exchange-Rate Unions and the Volatility of the Dollar," Nat. Bureau of Econ. Research Working Paper No. 492, June.

Metzler, L. A. (1942). The Transfer Problem Reconsidered, *J.P.E.* **50**, (June), 397–414.

Metzler, L. A. (1950). A Multiple-Region Theory of Income and Trade, *Econometrica* **18**, 329–354.

Metzler, L. A. (1950). A Multiple-Country Theory of Income Transfers, *JPE* **59**, 14–28.

Miller, K. S. (1968). "Linear Difference Equation," Benjamin, New York.

Modigliani, F., and T. Padova-Schioppa (1978). "The Management of an Open Economy with '100% plus' Wage Indexation," Essay in International Finance, No. 130, December, Princeton Univ.

Moore, B. C. (1978). "Singular Value Analysis of Linear Systems, Part I and II," Systems Control Report 7801, 7802, Univ. of Toronto, April and July.

Mundell, R. (1963). Capital Mobility and Stabilization Policy under Flexible Exchange Rates, *Can. J. Econ. and Political Sci.* **29**, 475–485.

Mundell, R. (1964). A Reply: Capital Mobility and Size, *Can. J. Econ. & Pol. Sci.* **30**, 421–31.

Mundell, R. A. (1968). "International Economics." Macmillan, New York.

Mussa, M. (1979). Macroeconomic Interdependence and the Exchange Rate Regime in R. Dornbusch, J. A. Frenkel (eds.), "International Economic Policy," Johns Hopkins Univ. Press.

Myhrman, J. (1976). Balance of Payments Adjustments and Portfolio Theory: A Survey, in E. M. Claassen and P. Salin (eds.), "Recent Issues in International Monetary Economics," North-Holland Publ., Amsterdam.

Myhrman, J. (1978). A Macroeconomic Model with Asset Equilibrium for An Open Economy, *J. Monetary Econ.* **4**, (April), 249–262.

Nordhaus, W. D. (1971). Recent Developments in Price Dynamics, in O. Eckstein (ed.), "The Econometrics of Price Determination, "Board of Governors of the Federal Reserve System.

Nyberg, Lars (1978). "Imported and Homemade Inflation Under Fixed and Floating Exchange Rates," Seminar Paper No. 97, (April), IIE, University of Stockholm, Sweden.

Nyberg, L., and S. Viotti (1976). "Controllability and the Theory of Economic Policy: A Critical Note," Seminar Paper No. 61, IIE, University of Stockholm, Sweden.

Oniki, H. (1973). Comparative Dynamics (Sensitivity Analysis) in Optimal Control Theory, *J.E.T.* **6**, 265–283.

Oppenheimer, P. M. (1974). Non-traded Goods and the Balance of Payments, A Historical Note, *J. Econ. Literature* **12**, No. 3, (September) 882–888.

Phelps, E. S. (1978). Trans-national Effects of Fiscal Shocks in a Two-Country Model of Dynamic Equilibrium, *in* Brunner and Meltzer (eds.), *Public Policies in Open Economies* **9**, Carnegie-Rochester Conf., Series on Public Policy, North-Holland Pub., Amsterdam.

Porter, M. G. (1976). International Financial Integration: Long-Run Policy Implications, Chapter 12 in R. I. McKinnon (ed.), "Money and Finance in Economic Growth and Development." Dekker, New York.

Purvis, D. (1979). "Wage Responsiveness and the Insulation Properties of a Flexible Exchange Rate," Chapter 9 in A. Lindbeck (ed.), "Inflation and Employment in Open Economies," North Holland Publ., Amsterdam.

Richard, D. M. (1980). "International Adjustment, Exchange Rates and Growth," presented at World Congress of the Econometric Society, Aix-en-Provence, France.

Rodriguez, C. A. (1976). The Terms of Trade and the Balance of Payments in the Short-Run, *AER* **66**, No. 4, (September), 710–716.

Rodriguez, C. A. (1979). Short- and Long-Run Effects of Monetary and Fiscal Policies Under Flexible Exchange Rates and Perfect Capital Mobility, *AER* **69**, No. 1, (March), 176–182.

Roper, D. E. (1971). Macroeconomic Policies and the Distribution of the World Money Supply, *QJE* **85**, 119–146.

Rutledge, J. (1977). Irving Fisher and Autoregressive Expectations, *AER* **67**, No. 1, (February), 200–205.

Sachs, J. (1980). Wage Indexation, Flexible Exchange Rates, and Macroeconomic Policy, *QJE* **94**, 731–747.

Salant, W. S. (1977). International Transmission of Inflation, 167–227, in L. B. Krause and W. S. Salant (eds.), "Worldwide Inflation." The Brookings Institute, Washington, DC.

Sargent, T., and N. Wallace (1973). The Stability of Models of Money and Growth with Perfect Foresight, *Econometrica* **41**, 1043–1048.
*The Scandinavian J. of Economics* (1976). **78**, No. 2.
Schadler, S. (1977). Sources of Exchange Rate Variability: Theory and Empirical Evidence, *IMF Staff Papers* **24**, (July), 253–296.
Segel, Lee A. (1972). Simplification and Scaling, *SIAM Review*, **14**, (October), 547–571.
Shafer, J. R. (1976). The Macroeconomic Behavior of a Large Open Economy with a Floating Exchange Rate, Ph.D. Dissertation, Yale, May.
Stein, G. (1979). Generalized Quadratic Weights for Asymptotic Regulator Properties, *IEEE Trans. Ant. Control*, **AC-24**, 559–566.
Stern, C., J. Makin, and D. Logue (eds.), (1975). "Eurocurrencies and the International Monetary System," Am. Enterprise Institute.
Stewart, G. W. (1973). Error and Perturbation Bounds of Subspace Associated with Certain Eigenvalue Problems, *SIAM Review* **15**, 727–764.
Takahashi, Y., M. J. Rabins, and D. M. Auslander (1970). "Control and Dynamic Systems," Addison-Wesley, Reading, Massachusetts.
Takayama, A. (1978). The Wealth Effect, the Capital Account and Alternative Policies Under Fixed Exchange Rates, *QJE* **92**, 117–147.
Takayama, A., and Y. N. Shieh (1980). "Flexible Exchange Rate Under Currency Substitution and Rational Expectations—Two Approaches to the Balance of Payments," Mimeo, January.
Taylor, J. B. (1979). "An Econometric Business Cycle Models With Rational Expectations: Some Estimation Results." Discussion Paper, Columbia University.
Tinbergen, J. (1955). "On the Theory of Economic Policy," 2nd ed., North-Holland Publ., Amsterdam.
Tobin, J. (1969). "A General Equilibrium Approach to Monetary Theory," *JMCB* **1**, 15–29.
Tobin, J., and J. B. de Macedo (1979). "The Short-Run Macroeconomics of Floating Exchange Rates: An Exposition," Cowles Foundation Discussion Paper No. 522, Cowles Foundation, April, New Haven, Connecticutt.
Turnovsky, S. J. (1977). "Macroeconomic Analysis and Stabilization Policy," Cambridge Univ. Press, London and New York.
Turnovsky, S. J., and A. Kaspura (1974). An Analysis of Imported Inflation in a Short-Run Macroeconomic Model, *C. J. Econ.* **7**, 355–380.
Viotti, S. (1980). "Inflation, the Terms of Trade and Flexible Exchange Rates," Vienna Conf., March 1978, in Frisch, H., and G. Schwodiauer (eds.), *The Economics of Flexible Exchange Rates*, Supplement to *Kredit und Kapital*, **6**, 1980.
Wan, H. Y., Jr., and M. Majumdar (1980). Trade under Temporary Equilibrium, *J. Intl. Economics*, **10**, 37–62.
Wilkinson, J. H. (1968). "The Algebraic Eigenvalue Problem," Oxford Univ. Press (Clarendon), London and New York.

# Index

## A

Absorption, 11
Accounting identity, 6
Adjustment
   coefficient, 28, 76, 200, 203, 255
   instantaneous, 4
   of output prices, 27
   partial, 70
   of wage rates, 27, 141, 284
Aggregate demand, 46
   interest elastic components of, 222
Aggregate supply (schedule), 46, 249
Analysis
   impact, 4, 38
   long-run, 33, 122, 141
   partial equilibrium, 4
   sensitivity, *see* Sensitivity
   short-run, 4, 244
   static, 174
   variational dynamic, *see* Variational equation
Analytical models, 3
Arbitrage, uncovered, 104
ARMA model, 7
Assignment problem, 65, 69
Average dynamics, *see* Dynamics, for averages
Averages, 58, 60, 69, 190, 205, 208

## B

Balance
   external, 126, 163
   internal, 126, 163
Balanced budget, 21, 46, 79n
   condition, 179
   constraint, 11
Balanced growth path, 9, 67, 110, 124, 125
Balance-of-payments, 81n
Balance sheet constraint, 32n, 47, 86, 108, 243
Balance of trade, *see* Trade balance
Bellman–Gronwall inequality, 318
Benchmark model, 242, 249, 250, 251, 253, 254, 258, 259, 272, 277
Budget constraint
   government, 33, 72, 78, 79, 109, 274
Budget deficit, 80n, 140, 242
   bond financed, 39, 80, 97
   money financed, 99
Budget imbalance, 103, 105, 246, 252

## C

Capital gain, 46
Capital growth, 119
Capital mobility, 30, 173
   perfect, 74n
Capital stock
   per capita, 25
   valuation ratio, 32
Characteristic equation, *see* Characteristic polynomial
Characteristic polynomial, 27, 101, 156, 157, 253, 254, 255, 258, 260, 261, 263, 265, 269
Comparative dynamic analysis, *see* Dynamics, comparative
Comparative static analysis, 20, 241n

Consistency (assumption, equation, or
   relation), 9, 44, 121, 122, 203
  cum stability, 93
Constraint
  flow, see Flow constraint
  joint, 129
  government, see Government constraint
Consumption, 140, 179n
  wealth elasticity of, 166
Continuing-flow effect, 17
Control experiment, 14
Controllability, 65, 66, 67, 69
  characterization of, 67
  implication of, 70
  path, 67, 68, 69, 215, 273
  point, 67
  sufficient condition for, 68, 215
Control solution, see Reference (time) path
Control (time) path, see Reference (time) path
Coordinated expansion, 196, 217
Coordination
  of national policies, 58, 59, 172, 188, 191, 215, 273
Current account, 78, 79, 81, 87, 98, 103, 105, 109, 134, 137, 140, 141, 180, 275, 303

## D

Debt service term, 79, 79n, 80, 99n
Decoupled, 209
Decoupling, 69
  sufficient condition for, 69
Deficit
  bond-financed, 39, 100
  money-financed, 37, 202
Demand (function)
  for assets, 9, 30, 32n, 78, 97, 107, 121, 124
  for domestic goods, 140
  for equity, 31
  for foreign goods, 121
  for money, 8, 17, 18n, 180, 200, 275
  for real balances, 8, 31, 178, 211
Detrended
  log-linear form or model, 1, 18, 20, 21
  variables, 20
Detrending, 15
Devaluation, 153

Difference dynamics, see Dynamics, for differences
Differences, 58, 60, 69, 190, 205, 208
  of impact effects, 63
  of national characteristics, 64, 172
Direct effects, 73
Disaggregation, 3
Disposable income, 11, 32, 46, 77, 87, 88, 98, 108, 121, 132, 140, 145, 146n, 169, 178, 302
Distributional effects or questions, 58, 61, 64, 172, 173, 174, 174n, 185, 210, 272
  of exogenous shocks, 59
  of instruments, 58, 210, 281, 284, 286
  of national policies, 56, 172, 273, 283
Domestic credit, see Money stock, domestic component of
Dynamic model, 5
Dynamic (policy) multipliers, 22, 23, 41, 48, 91, 91n, 99n, 105, 195, 300
  fiscal, 39
  incremental, 42n
  monetary, 187
  oscillatory, 119
  variational, 31, 42
Dynamics
  adjustment, 75n
  comparative, 1, 13, 14, 19, 24, 52, 135, 175, 189
  due to current account, 79, 81, 98
  due to government budget constraint, 79, 200
  due to wage rate change, 200
  for averages, 273, 276, 279, 322n
  for differences, 273, 276, 280, 322n
  short-run, 128, 136
  sources of, 2, 78, 126, 134, 141, 241, 249
  wage rate, see Wage rate, dynamics

## E

Econometric model, 3
Economic distance, 61, 63, 278
Effects
  of budget deficits, 242
  distributional, see Distributional effects or questions
  feedback, see Feedback

*Index* 337

impact, 12, 241n
income, 146n
long-run, 12
policy, 251
real wealth, 181
spill-over, *see* Spill-over effects
steady-state, 12
Equilibrium, 7
  balance-of-payments, 75n, 98, 109
  condition in asset sector, 80n, 277
  condition in real sectors, 185, 277, 278
  economic notion of, 8
  long-run, 8, 33, 87, 174, 180, 247n
  mathematical notion of, 8
  momentary, 33, 35, 111, 126, 140, 142, 147, 174, 203
  state, 7
Equity, 31
Exchange rate
  depreciation, 48
  dynamics, 79
  expectations, 203
Exchange-rate union, 273
Expectations, 83
  adaptive, 86, 121, 126, 256, 263
  autoregressive, 83, 89, 305
  consistency of, 84, 87, 89n, 93, 305
  dynamics, 103
  inflationary, 28, 75, 136, 253n, 255
  myopic perfect foresight, *see* Expectations, perfect foresight
  perfect foresight, 2, 17n, 77, 83, 84, 92, 93, 96, 126, 167, 245, 304
  regressive, 2, 83, 84, 86, 89n, 92, 93, 158, 159, 166, 200, 203, 245, 251, 276, 280, 304
  self-fulfilling, 84
  stabilizing, 158
  stable, 84
  static, 10, 46, 90, 92, 129, 134n, 147, 154, 
  stationary, 92, 159, 160, 185
Exponential growth path, 8
External balance, *see* Balance, external

**F**

Feedback, 78, 112, 126, 142, 144n, 148, 150, 157, 163, 171, 244, 248
  effects, 73

path, *see* Feedback
rule, 70
Fiscal expenditure
  balanced-budget, 4
Fiscal multipliers, 115
  dynamic, 39
  impact, 35, 187
Fleming–Mundell model, 30
Flow constraint, 134
Full employment (assumption), 84, 87, 99, 173, 174, 202, 304n
Fundamental matrix of solution, *see* State transition matrix

**G**

Goods
  intermediate, 75
  nontraded, 74n, 75n, 121, 134n
  traded, 74n, 121, 134n
Government budget
  constraint, 33, 124, 134, 140, 173
  imbalance, 126, 128
  variational, 71, 151
Growth
  balanced, 9
  exponential, 8
  path, 107
  trend, 14

**H**

Home goods, *see* Nontraded goods

**I**

Image space, *see* Range space
Impact multipliers, 37, 38, 41, 45, 48, 59
  effects of, 55, 59, 194
  fiscal, 35, 37, 39, 49, 50, 57, 60, 187n
  monetary, 37, 38, 186
Imperfect substitutability, *see* Substitutes
Implicit function theorem, 33, 245
Impulse response (function), 41, 43, 136
Income effects, 275
Indexation, *see* Wage rate, indexation of

Indirect effects, 73
Inflation
  convergence of national, 74n, 191, 191n, 192
  effects of wage rate changes on,
Innovation processes, 83
Instrument
  design of, 65
  effectiveness of, 65
  to stabilize, 65
Interactions, 55, 90, 191
  of monetary policies, 173
  of national policies, 69
Interdependence, 55, 171, 173
  degree of, 59
  econometric study of, 73n
  of economies, 58, 59
  of monetary policies, 188
  mutual, 52
  of national incomes, 60, 173
  of national policies, 69, 176
Interest elasticity, 36, 221
Interest-rate parity (condition), 105, 107, 121, 179, 202, 272, 276
  covered, 74
  uncovered, 17n, 74
Interest receipt, 98, 140, 180
Internal balance, *see* Balance, internal
Intertemporal optimization, 120, 203
Investment, 32, 103, 180, 202n

## J

Jacobian, 33, 139, 245

## K

Kalman filter, 83, 84
Key currency, 172, 241

## L

Labor market, 136, 137, 138, 174, 178
Laplace transform, 199, 220, 221, 319
Linkage
  dynamic, 177
  exchange rate, 74
  expectations, 114
  interest rate, 74
  of national economies, 1, 73
  price, 74
  terms-of-trade, 74, 76
Log-linear form, 15, 17, 185
  detrended, 1, 18, 20, 53, 175
Log-linear model, *see* Log-Linear form
Long-run equilibrium
  properties, 87
Loss
  inflation, 120
  unemployment, 120

## M

Marginal propensities, 87
  to import, 59
  to save, 25
Market clearing conditions, 179
  asset, 179
  goods, 179, 204
Market valuation term, 302
Market value, 137
Markov process, 5n
Markovian property, 5n
Mark-up pricing, 72, 84
Marshall–Lerner condition, 153, 169
Matrix exponential function, 53n, 55
Measure of openness, 75, 76
Model, 5
  autoregressive moving average (ARMA), 7
  of a growing economy, 107
  of small open economies, 103
  static, 59
  three-country, 59, 272
  two-country, 59, 178, 185, 200, 241
  with nontraded goods, 75n
Model representation, 320
Monetary policy
  effects, 185
Money financing of deficits, 10, 37, 124, 127, 150, 152
Money illusion, 174
Money stock
  domestic component of, 121, 123, 275
  expansion, 207
Mundellian result, 30, 51, 208
Myopic perfect foresight, *see* Expectations

# Index

## N

Nontraded goods, 74, 75
Normality, wealth, 139
Null space, 67

## O

Observation equation, 6
Open market operation, 49, 81n
Optimization problem, 190
   intertemporal, 70, 203
Output–capital ratio, 10

## P

Partial equilibrium analysis, 4, 146
Path
   controllability, *see* Controllability
   growth, 8
   reference, 13, 14
   trend, 8, 13, 14
Pattern
   of excess demands, 173n
   of expansion, 62, 63
   of trade, *see* Trading pattern(s)
   root-locus, 131
Perfect foresight, *see* Expectations
Perpetuities, 140, 178, 277
Perturbation, 18, 52, 53, 159, 273, 282
   analysis, 53, 53n, 105, 320
   singular, 6
   structural, 55, 175, 176, 181
   theory, 58
Phillips curve, 126
Policy
   for demand management, 137
   long-run, 13
   with no spill-over effects, 65, 67, 69
   short-run, 13
Policy coordination, 190
Policy effects, 215, 245n
   on growth, 107
   long-run, 79
   monetary, *see* Monetary policy, effects
   sensitivity study of, 189
Policy multipliers, 5, 12, 135, 136
   of ARMA models, 299
   continuous-time, 43
   cross-country, 188
   discrete-time, 45, 299
   dynamic, 1, 22, 41, 45, 65
   finite-time, 13
   fiscal, 155, 166
   impact, 12, 13, 38, 41, 45
   inter-run, 13
   long-run, 12, 13, 41
   monetary, 116, 186
Policy with no spill-over effects, 69
Policy objective, 120
Policy reaction functions, 52, 70, 72, 81n, 105, 120, 124, 130, 150, 202n
   optimal, 71
   stabilizing, *see* Stabilization policy
Policy response, 73n
Portfolio balance (approach), 103, 126, 142
Price
   flexibility, 173
   imperfectly flexible, 304n
   variable output, 174
Price index, 255, 274, 278
   consumer, 75, 136, 200n
Purchasing power
   parity, 10, 18n, 74, 85, 87, 98, 104, 105, 121, 134n, 173, 303
   generalized, 174

## R

Range space, 66, 67
Rank
   conditions, 68
   of matrix, 67, 68
Rationality assumption, *see* Consistency (assumption, equation, or relation)
   long run, 305
Real balances, 10, 17, 30, 50, 51, 185
Reduced forms, 36, 72, 100, 111, 154, 206, 279
   partially, 202
Reference model, 175, 177, 193n, 194, 211
Reference (time) path, 1, 13, 14, 18n, 20, 53, 120, 124, 141, 193n
Regressive expectations, *see* Expectations
Relative prices, 75n, 146n, 248
Repercussion, 104
Riccati equation, 71

Risk
  averseness, 178n
  characteristics, 104
Robust results
  non- , 30, 51
Root-locus form, see Root-locus method
Root-locus method, 27, 52, 101, 102, 102n, 105, 115, 119, 120, 156, 254, 261, 309n
Routh's test, 27n

## S

Saving, 180
  real, 181
Scale variables, 108, 121n, 244
Sensitivity, 27
  analysis, 1, 5n, 23, 23n, 25, 28, 29
  function, 24, 25
  of growth path, 25
  parameter, 148
  policy, 189
  structural, 105, 135, 172, 176, 177
Sensitivity of a growth path, 25
Service Term, see Debt service term
Singular perturbation method, 6
Small open economy, 53, 55n, 56n, 85, 136
Specification
  asset sector, 166
  model, 30
  real sector, 6
  structural form, 41
Spill-over effects, 83, 148, 149, 188, 226, 325
  no, 65
Stability analysis
  long-run, 126
  short-run, 85, 97, 102, 120, 126, 128, 130
Stability, conditional, 304
Stabilization policy, 70, 105, 120
Stable manifold
  conditionally, 245
State-space form, see State-space representation
State-space representation, 1, 3, 5, 39, 42, 48, 89, 100, 111, 114, 128, 181, 209, 251, 280, 299, 306
State transition matrix, 20, 53, 54n, 66, 67, 319
State variable, 136, 203, 276, 292
State vector, 5
  average, see Averages
  difference, see Differences

Steady state, 8
Steady-state growth path, 8
Stock-flow relation, 6
Stock-shift effect, 17
Structural changes, 29, 30
Structural characteristics, 52
Structural difference, 52
Structural equation, 6, 182
Substitutability
  degree of, 30
Substitutes
  close, 36, 51
  imperfect, 46, 49, 74, 85n, 108, 134
  gross, 137, 139
  perfect, 10, 51, 74, 74n, 85, 97, 98, 104, 121, 134n, 137, 144, 178, 178n, 274
Successive approximation scheme, 54n
Superposition principle, 21, 191
Supply
  function, 140
  response or responsiveness, 135, 151, 242
  schedule, 135, 201

## T

Target variables or vectors, 1, 7, 41
Tax receipt, 72, 140, 178
  changes in, 74, 75n, 76, 109, 112, 114, 119
Terms-of-trade, 74, 75n, 76, 109, 112, 114, 119, 121, 127, 146n, 153, 202, 207, 248, 275
Three-country model of the world, 53, 56n, 59, 61, 172, 272
Time path
  neighboring, 175
  perturbed, 18
  reference, 13, 14, 18, 175
Trade balance, 11, 98, 123, 141, 153, 179, 180, 182, 184, 248n, 250
Trading pattern(s), 61
Transfer, 13, 14
  income, 173
  real, 121
Transition matrix, 20, 26, 193
Transmission linkage, see Transmission path
Transmission path, 53, 74, 75, 104, 108, 126, 139n, 145, 169, 172, 177, 192, 223
  of inflation, 74n
Trend rate, 8
  of change, 19

Trend (time) path, 1, 13
Two-country model of the world, 53, 55n, 56, 56n, 59, 73, 172, 173, 200, 241

## U

Unit cost, 75

## V

Valuation, 144, 275n
Valuation effects, 139, 145, 303
Variational dynamic analysis, *see* Variational equation
Variational Dynamic Equation, *see* Variational equation
Variational equation, 1, 15, 19, 25, 26, 31, 37, 52, 53, 60
Variational model, 15

Variational variables, *see* Variations
Variations, 18, 193
  structural, 1

## W

Wage rate
  dynamics, 84, 103, 108n, 135, 147, 185, 187, 200, 269, 274
  effects on distribution, 185
  indexation of, 76, 84, 174, 178
  real, 71, 201
  variable, 105, 135, 174
Wealth
  constraint, 139
  desired, 173
  effects, 13, 166
  elasticity, 166
  real, 178, 181